THE REACH OF POETRY

THE REACH OF POETRY

Albert Cook

Purdue University Press
West Lafayette, Indiana

The paper used in this book meets the minimum requirements of
American National Standard for Information Sciences—
Permanence of Paper for Printed Library Materials,
ANSI Z39.48-1984.

Printed in the United States of America
Design by Chiquita Babb

Library of Congress Cataloging-in-Publication Data

Cook, Albert Spaulding.
   The reach of poetry / Albert Cook.
   p. cm.
   Includes bibliographical references and index.
   ISBN 1-55753-068-8 (alk. paper). — ISBN 1-55753-069-6 (pbk. :
alk. paper)
   1. Oral interpretation of poetry. 2. Poetry—History and criticism.
3. Narration (Rhetoric) 4. Oral communication. I. Title.
PN 4151.C67 1995
809.1—dc20   94-44602
                                                        CIP

To Saul Touster
and Irene Tayler

The beautiful is to be defined in relation to knowledge, the good in relation to desire.

(The beautiful disposes itself to being-good as a supplementary ordering.)

—*Thomas Aquinas,*
cited and interpreted by Hans-Georg Gadamer

Contents

Acknowledgments

I should like to thank those who have commented on parts of the manuscript, including Peter Baker, Michel-André Bossy, James Bunn, Irving Feldman, Irving Massey, Robert Mueller, Aaron Rosen, Max Wickert, and others who heard presentations from it at Brown, SUNY Buffalo, Michigan State, and the University of Urbino, as well as the meetings where I have given papers from parts of individual chapters: the International Association for Philosophy and Literature, the American Comparative Literature Association, the Thirteenth International Congress of Anthropological and Ethnological Sciences in Mexico City, and the Intercongress of the same organization in Lisbon. I am much indebted, as well, to an anonymous reader for this press, whose detailed commentary gave me a basis for what I hope were improvements in my presentation. I should also like to thank Margaret Hunt of the Purdue University Press for an unusually perceptive and attentive job of editing. My thanks go also to the editors of the journals where some of these chapters have appeared in earlier form, the *Centennial Review* (introduction), *American Poetry* (chapter 2), *Studies in Romanticism* (chapter 3), *Exemplaria* (chapter 6), *Arethusa* (chapter 8), and *Hellas* (chapter 10). I remain grateful to my ever-resourceful research assistant, Blossom S. Kirschenbaum, and as always to my wife, Carol.

THE REACH OF POETRY

Introduction

IN THIS BOOK I address a number of questions about the reach of which poetic utterance is capable by taking a long look at some imposing poets in various traditions. I offer not a definition of poetry, but a characterization of it by testing its "reach" through the pressure that some poets have been able to put on the condition of their utterance and thus to attain a further range of expression. In this sense, I come at the nature of poetry obliquely. To do so directly would be a vast philosophical enterprise, unless it confined itself to a characterization of effects, as Jacques Derrida does in his *Qu'est-ce que la poésie?* And to offer a census of functions for poetry would be tautologous in that it would necessitate a number of theoretical deductions about language and the world prior to the definition of poetry, which would then simply be equal to the sum of those deductions.

We hear much about oral and written conditions for poetry; and we can learn much about the circumstances of poetry by attending both to the distinction between oral and written and to various combinations that exhibit and conflate or modify the distinction.[1]

But there is another distinction, which the difference between epigram or an epigrammatic style and hymn or prophecy may exemplify: the distinction between a low pitch and a high, as these may interact with the distinction between a compressed utterance such as an epigram or couplets that offer sequenced compressions and, on the other hand, an expansive utterance such as those of William Wordsworth or Vladimir Mayakovsky. Both Archilochus and Pindar are poets who prepare their work for oral delivery, but their pitch is at different extremes, the former often close to the conversational, the latter to the oracular. These poles may be seen as a version—comprehensive because not comparably contrastive—of the ancient division of styles into low or Attic, middle, and high or Asian.[2]

While the topic of the oracular might seem very specialized, it is in fact comprehensive for poetry in that it touches on the concerns of many theoreticians about poetry and about literature generally. Insofar as the term suggests a heightened discourse, the oracular raises questions about the nature of all literary discourse; it emphasizes some access to the channeling of religious utterances and covers not only such "secularized" writings as those of Walt Whitman and St. John Perse, or even Mayakovsky, but those of Pindar, which were performed at religious festivals, and those of the Hebrew Prophets, which were brought to bear on a religious interpretation of political struggles. Oracularity, indeed, could be connected to most Greek poetry, and to much of Romantic poetry in English and German. It would also include conventions such as those of Orphic poetry, which may express the doctrines of a mystery religion, and the use of verse to convey oracles from the gods. It covers a large share of Sanskrit poetry. And it has engaged modern theoreticians because of its very contrast with the convention that verse be conversational and nonoracular.

The oracular and the conversational, however, are not opposites in a single dimension, any more than oral and written are. In fact, oracular and conversational are characterizing points of emphasis that play across all the many dimensions of social connection evoked by, and coded into, poetic utterance. They are a special version of the dimensions of reference coded into any utterance whatever. The oracular is set to speak from a high or privileged position to the implied multitudes, as with Isaiah. But the privilege can be a privilege of suffering, as with Jeremiah. And the multitudes may include those even more privileged, as in Pindar's address to the tyrant-patron of the athletic contest and in his evocation of the differently, but sublimely privileged, subjects of the moment, the winners of the contests. The oracularity of Whitman contains as part of its rhetoric an abandonment of any privileged position in favor of an equalizing embrace that the poetry itself is conceived of as empowering for a future society it claims to help bring into being. "To be great poets there must be great audiences too," as the magazine *Poetry* had for decades quoted Whitman, perhaps somewhat wistfully.

Correspondingly, the conversational may imply an equality between speaker and hearer, an abandonment of privilege in favor of equality. But the conversational flow of Alexander Pope's poetry, for example, implies a privilege prior to the equality; it envisages a conversation among the well-born and intellectually capable or "witty." The very presence of wit in the poetry attests to this social compact, as does its absence in "dunces" such as the Thomas Shadwell of Pope's *Dunciad.* The virtuosity of the utterance celebrates as well as employs its access to the compact. Something like that compact, poetry as a test of membership through reference to attitudes and subjects that are "in," still obtains in various circles. Under the aegis of the compact to be witty, the poetry can coil into significant compression as it can eschew lofty flights. Its sequences of compression can result in a considerable expansiveness, as in his *Epistle to Arbuthnot* or, earlier, in John Dryden's *Religio Laici* or *Absalom and Achitophel,* where the cleverness of some identifications between biblical originals and contemporary political figures invites the production of others: successful compression leads to expansion. So, too, Pindar is compressed in the small but is expansive in the large. And Whitman, again, oracular in the expansiveness of his long line, allows himself such looseness of expansion that he begins to sound conversational, as the oracular Mayakovsky programmatically does, abandoning less comradely, mannered utterance "to set my heel / on the throat / of my own song" in "Vo Vyes' Golos" ("With Full Voice"). At the same time, like most poets he is attentive to the carefully formed rhythmic and verbal detail of his poems.

Moreover, the oracular and the conversational are limits, rather than defined postures, and limits with an extreme that cannot be attained. The wholly oracular would be so distant or so lofty as to be unintelligible, as oracular poetry anyway risks seeming to be. The wholly conversational would simply dissolve into conversational exchange, without any poetic character. Even if a segment of actual conversation were transcribed and printed as "poetry," it would not have reached that limit, because the act of so labeling it would detach it, however slightly, from its initial context and make it something different from simple conversation.

Poetry is "relational," then, across the whole spectrum of social perception and interaction. This is saliently evident when we come to deal with the religious or spiritual element in poetry, which is at once essential to it and evasively ineffable. The problematic and relational character of such (and all poetic) utterance comes into view if we try to define exactly what the religious element is in Homer, who served as something like a scripture for later Greek society, or how that element differs from the comparable element in the Prophets of the Hebrew Bible. One would have to have recourse to a description of the sort offered elaborately by modern scholars from Martin Nilsson to Gregory Nagy and Walter Burkert of just how "religious" or codified ritual gestures function in Greek society, and how they are taken up in or reverberate through or enlist or even somewhat displace the poetic "text"—and all that process runs the risk of mere circular description, leaving us with the ineffable. Not just with Paul Celan and Wallace Stevens, then, but also with Homer, or even, spectacularly, Isaiah, the spiritual content has to be come at indirectly, and it may enlist play as well as solemnity.[3] The ineffability of the spiritual element in poetry drives it toward "occlusions," to use the key term of my last chapter. The necessary angel is the invisible angel.

Poetry is marked as set off from ordinary language while it draws upon it. Hence in Roman Jakobson's terms it foregrounds, as the "poetic," the message among the six constituents of linguistic utterance (sender, receiver, message, context, contact, and code). Put differently, as Jakobson himself did when he spoke of the projection of the axis of selection on the axis of combination, poetry subjects its utterances to a "modeling" that results in an implicitly binary reordering (implying both selection and combination) of what it names, according to Yuri Lotman.[4] He further stresses what he calls the "Bakhtinian" side of a poetic statement, its inevitable tendency toward combining codes: "Either we may speak of continuous encoding by means of a double code—in which case readers perceive one or the other organization depending on their viewpoints—or we may note the combination of general codifications, beginning with a dominant code and continuing with local coding at the second, the third, and further degrees." In this view, literary expression tends toward the super-dialogic.[5]

We move toward greater complication in the poetic act—which can

4

lead, the way it does with Dante, to greater simplicity of utterance. As we do so, we move toward the ineffability of the overtone in its message. Come at another way, through Erving Goffman's fine-tuned discriminations of the social constraints on normal oral interchange, these constraints provide not just a single framework but dimensions of frameworks—"a framework of frameworks," in Goffman's phrase (70)— which is another way of looking at Lotman's interesting codes. An attention to these social constraints on discourse throws into relief not only the rich complexity of the poetic act but—surprisingly—its strategic exclusion, whether in oral delivery or written transmission, of the cues that reveal and enlist those constraints.[6] Suspended in poetry is Goffman's "footing," which does not have to be established in poetry between poet and auditor, since it exists as a precondition. "Set alignment" is not shaken in poetry while the poetry lasts, though it may be shaken in ordinary discourse. "Projection" for poetry is always either much longer than in ordinary conversation, or with a sharper marking. And the poem, though dialogic, cues not to retort but to meditative silence. The "continuity" does not shift, as it does constantly in conversation, but remains immobile. In poetry there is no "bracketing of liminal roles," and no two-person arrangement is improvised. Both of these can be set up in a poem, however, when the addressee is pulled rhetorically into the poem as his or her role is in the process of being complexly defined by it.

In the expansion of the poet's voice—as an implied justification for the important move from private to public utterance—there is a reach toward an extremity of definition at once summary, purgative, and exposed. This is apparent in Isaiah, in the beleaguered troubadour, in François Villon, in John Keats, in William Butler Yeats, in Hart Crane, and through our blurrings of social siting in Sappho, Alcman, and Archilochus. It is manifest in the sonnets of William Shakespeare. Catullus, too, is summary, purgative, and exposed. These traits single him out, finally, from the more decorous Alexandrians; since decorum, *pace* the Aristotelian tradition, is only one face of the achieved poetic expression, even for such a master of decorum as Horace. The extremity involves in itself reaches of perception, and in the case of Emily Dickinson, for example, only recently has commentary risen to understanding the extreme power of her theological thought; nor has there been previously noticed her surprising and deep reliance on what would seem remote from her, a set toward the body's subjection to power that enlists an iconology and a subliminal psychology formulated by the Marquis de Sade.[7]

Prophecy does tend toward the extreme. The prophetic element surfaces again and again in unusual mutations. Dickinson and Whitman both have a prophetic function, the utterance of a truth that operates a religious definition. Bob Dylan, and others in his tradition, sing out an oracular message also, one that asserts its ethical content and therewith its prophetic impetus and onus. Allen Ginsberg's use of himself as an example blazing through the world out of his troubled early life resembles Jeremiah's presentation of himself as an example. The Jeremiah example, the jeremiad, is the element that distinguishes his confessional poetry from Robert Lowell's, not the degree of formal finish. Indeed, in his rhetorical fusions, Ginsberg equals Lowell formally, and in his elaborate rhythms he surpasses him. Ezra Pound and T. S. Eliot also take on the mantle of the prophet, and it would be hard to find a viable poet in our tradition who does not have a tinge of the prophetic in his or her work. But we should hesitate to assert as much of all poetry, even of all religious poetry. There would seem to be little or nothing prophetic in the Chinese *Book of Odes* or in the *Fasti* of Ovid.

As the prophetic voice gets expansive, it may press the boundaries of prose and create the sort of form that some commentators have taken Hebrew verse generally to be: not verse exactly, but a heightened expression that merely pushes lightly the features of recursion that are already present in the "prose" parts of Scripture. We need not go far to see such proselike pressures in Whitman and in the expansive verse derived from him, of Paul Claudel and others, which differs markedly from the more sculptured free verse of H. D. and William Carlos Williams. The relation of the poetry parts to the prose parts in Jeremiah is close enough that it is possible to assert a rhythmic continuum between them. The same is true for the prophet-echoing "Thanksgivings" of Thomas Traherne, which stand midway between the rhymed "Poems" and the prose "Centuries," establishing a graded continuum among all three. Yet the "Centuries" do not have the tight closure of prose poems from Baudelaire to the present.

The attention of linguists to binarity in poetry, through rhyme and other formal features, and the concentration of a generation of critics on the sort of equivocation between paradox and antithesis to be found in Andrew Marvell, John Donne, and other metaphysical poets, point up the propositional complexity of the statements composed into such poems. All these features have the not incidental function of also raising the pitch of the utterance, of broadening it by complication.

The same can be said of the intrication of images, which often work so fully within the poem that they cannot be understood without reference to the poet's whole cultural context and system of ideas.[8] Image crops up as metaphor in the speech of children and in such ordinary-language conventions of surrealized bravura wit as Cockney rhyming slang, where "fried eggs" stands for "legs," "frog in the throat" for "foot," "bird lime" for "time," "Duke of Kent" for "rent," "bees and honey" for "money." It would be supercilious to deny a startling "poetic" inventiveness to this common currency, as to the ballad. But it would be sentimental to give their inventive extravagances the ineffability to which the ballad does attain, even though in the use of this Cockney rhyming slang, a protopoetry is put at the service of keeping a secret argot going and celebrating its very complexities.

In the matter of metaphor, not only modern "absolute metaphor" in poetry but also the uses in Chinese poetry, in early Greek poetry down to Pindar, in biblical prophecy, in Dante—and no doubt in other traditions, too—are so transcendent, comprehensive, and rooted to a social worldview that the post-Aristotelian analysis that sees metaphor linked to propositions of comparisons, even the deep-rooted ones of George Lakoff and Mark Johnson, and of Mark Turner, is deeply inadequate to address them.[9] The propositions cannot take over; they do not lay out or yield the full sense of a poem, and the poetry will not yield its wisdom to their strictures. Nor will the opening on myth do so of itself. To speak of metaphor as "literature's access to myth," as I have done, merely names the domain of power and does not delineate the power.[10] If we are left with a mystery, the use of language itself is inherently mysterious, or at least poses unresolvable problems, in Wittgenstein's view—and poetry does all the more: "A poet's words can run through and through us. And that is of course *causally* connected with the use that they have in our life. And it is also connected with the way in which, conformably to this use, we let our thoughts roam hither and thither into the well-known surroundings of the words."[11]

Whether image, itself often irreducible to being spelled out in the propositions of thought, is a form of thought, is very much open to question. Images, too, are presented in words and could tentatively but not firmly be included in "a poet's words." Moreover, to speak of image, as I have done elsewhere, changes the discussion but does not of itself exhaust the question because to posit a sort of thinking in images still leaves unanswered the different kinds of utterance, in different cultures, that employ images. Other traditions, the Greek, the Hebrew, and perhaps the Chinese, do not enlist the same norms for employing images that are found variously in Marvell, the surrealists and postsurrealists, and others whom I have discussed in *Figural Choice*.

There is surely a social orientation and focus, assertable but not recuperable, as well as a sharp image, in this fragment of Archilochus:

> ἡ δὲ οἱ κόμη
> ὤμους κατεσκίαζε καὶ μετάφρενα

> her hair
> shadowed her shoulders and forehead.

Is a metaphor also present? "An element takes on its symbolic value to the extent that it departs from a norm, a norm which may, itself, be symbolic." So Dan Sperber, who is discussing butter used for ritual purposes as against butter as a source of food. The originality of this picture of the girl's shadowing hair, unprecedented in earlier poetry, suggests that a norm is being pressed. Sperber further qualifies: "Symbols are not signs. They are not paired with their interpretations in a code structure. Their interpretations are not meanings."[12] This means that the image can stand in its force. We do not have to rise to its irrecoverable contextual meanings; we can feel its force as poetry, even in this fragment of Archilochus. The shadowy hair is erotic, but we cannot confidently confine it just to the erotic, nor just to the visual. Is a realization of the other at work here? What led Archilochus to this startling invention? The lines press these questions.

In *The Critique of Judgment* (para. 59), Immanuel Kant speaks of "practical" and "theoretical" sides of the symbol, which through analogy is therefore equated to understanding.[13] Such philosophical coordinates, along with anthropological ones, would ultimately be necessary to map the shadowed hair of Archilochus as well as the rose of Dante or of Blake, and even then we would be returning to the poem. Its reach would exceed even that grasp. The logic of images in Eliot, Perse, Arthur Rimbaud, and René Char has an oracular profundity. But on the other hand, there is the deliberately casual metaphor, like Yeats's "struggle of the fly in marmelade," which describes the literary efforts of politicians. "Hell" and "thicket" in Charles Olson's "In Cold Hell, in Thicket" are meant to be allegorical, but only casually so, pulling away from the Dante whom they at the same time evoke. If they were systematized, they would subvert the conversational progress of the poem. On the other hand, Leonard Barkan connects allegory with the dialogic progression of the poem, as Mikhail Bakhtin differently does.[14]

Heinz Werner sees metaphor as derived from taboo, an explanation that will serve both to emphasize these anthropological connections and account for their sensitivity.[15] But in this light, the poem, when it uses metaphor, also domesticates taboo and overcomes it, redirecting its force away from dire silence. With or without metaphor, the poem faces down the possible direness in the silence it masters.

The fictive is only the beginning; it is the licensing silence, the implied initial declaration that the poetry is made up, a pretense of unreality, that empowers its access to the real, the attainment of finalities of utterance through modalities of expression.[16] In the paradox of this expression, poetry gives up the power of efficient reference to assume the power of ultimate reference; it comes at performatives indirectly and in some mediated modality. The performative dimensions of language themselves, elaborately sketched by J. L. Austin, may be extended to the power relations, and to the relations of complementarity and equality, underlying language and triggered by it. As Pierre Bourdieu has delineated them, these power relations are constantly present, and through many dimensions, in any act of utterance.[17] As he says about the social siting and power dynamics of all speech, "through the medium of the structure of the linguistic field, conceived as a system of specifically linguistic relations to power based on the unequal distribution of linguistic capital (or, to put it another way, of the chances of assimilating the objectified linguistic resources), the structure of the space of expressive styles reproduces in its own terms the structure of the differences which objectively separate conditions of existence" (57). The poet can be measured by such a sociolinguistic calculus, if not totally confined by it. Poetry, subject to these conditions, also manipulates them. The *Divina commedia* is a whole long dramatization of a power that is coextensive with love and so provides an induction to complementarity and equality.

Poetry's constant "exposure" through an utterance gratuitous in some ways, and its resourceful adaptiveness, are well characterized by Bourdieu's further formulation:

9

The legitimate language no more contains within itself the power to ensure its own perpetuation in time than it has the power to define its extensions in space. Only the process of continuous creation which occurs through the unceasing struggles between the different authorities who compete within the field of specialized production for the monopolistic power to impose the legitimate mode of expression can ensure the permanence of the legitimate language and of its value.

In elaborate and multiplex subjection to its own conditions, at its best poetry at the same time rises above them by playing them back against themselves in a freedom whose ineffability is the sign of its ultimate lucidity. Even in ordinary conversation, clarity can come through less than the dialogists may wish. In the dialogic gambit of a poetic utterance, initial obscurity can burn through to a final clarity, and initial clarity can itself carry auras of suggestiveness, empowering the silence of the auditor with the ring of achieved perception.

After my initial chapter, I shall begin with modern poetry and go progressively backward in time, aiming at the effect of echoes as much as of cumulations. I intend to show how in each movement forward the intensities are gathered by Dante or the troubadours or Catullus or Alcman. But it is also a reach backward: Alcman's fusions are in a certain sense permanent within the Western tradition and are accessible in the stream of discourse to modern poets who may never have heard of him. In my first chapter, I try to show how, in the short compass of epigram, ballad, and similar poems, the markings that seem to have carved out the kinds of poetic statement are themselves characterized by blendings and fusions, codes not only complicating one another but paradoxically simplifying one another too. In my next chapter, I try to show how modern poetry's reach toward inclusiveness and its indirect spirituality inform each other. Chapter 3, on the transformations of "point," examines the social constraints that have been redefined and transformed by Wordsworth, Rimbaud, and Whitman. Turning round through "point" to Pope and Donne, I then analyze the elaborate gestures underlying the ambivalent expressions about women in late versions of the Petrarchan tradition, in Donne and Shakespeare chiefly but also in others, including Edmund Spenser and Geoffrey Chaucer. Dante, of course, is the great, overarching figure who fuses all such attitudes into a simply expressed and tremendous hierarchy. After discussing him in chapter 5, I turn back to the condensations and resolutions of desire in the troubadour poetry that preceded him. Catullus, on different ground, reaches comparable complexity, while Lucretius combined poetry and philosophy in ways that need to be discriminated for his very achievement. Pindar, too, brought his utterance into a peerless integration that harnesses and resolves contradictions, as does Alcman, the subject of chapter 10. The modern poets of my last chapter carry out prophecies through subtly managed occlusions and, in their own very different circumstances, achieve comparable sets of fusion.

Of course, there are reaches I have left out: the constructions of epic and drama; of proverbial saw and riddle and charm; of hybrid narratives and quasi-philosophical verse systems. My earlier books discuss some of these: the epic in *The Classic Line;* the verse drama chiefly in *Enactment: Greek Tragedy, Shakespeare's Enactment,* and *French Tragedy: The Power of Enactment* (conceived as one book, though published as three); for "simple forms" and others, *Myth and Language;* for Blake and other philosophical extrapolations, *Thresholds: Studies in the Romantic Experience.*

I have drawn on these books, but I hope I have here been able to add to them and show their conclusions in something of a different light.

1

Blendings in Short Compass
The Reach of Poetry

CRITICAL DISCOURSE in our time is remarkable for uncovering in literary works not only an underlying propositional calculus but even the evasion of a propositional calculus. It is no less remarkable for connecting these oppositionally related gestures to imbrications of social givens—to densities, nested contradictions, and overriding social matrices in the *mentalités* exhibited by literary works. Such admirable depth probes carry with them the danger that they will affect, overshadow, or obscure the still deeper integrations effectuated by the poet, whose singular and unified utterances challenge us to assess their special quality. We must try to account for their transcendence of the codes, and of the very combinatory statements utilizing the codes, without remaining content merely to praise their ineffability, and still less without resolving them back into the propositions and gestures of which, paradoxically, they seem to be wholly composed. To speak of the disappearing subject, of the creative reader, of shifters in utterance, and of various constituent psychological mechanisms, while enlightening, would evade this paradox by the oversimplification of overemphasis. We can empathetically ask for more from our accounts of poems, and we should do so, engaging ourselves thereby in the intimate subtlety of an account of the poem that approaches adequacy by refusing to settle for the relativisms of situational description.

I have elsewhere argued for the wisdom in poetry, though this argument at its best (in both positive and negative senses of the word "best") is a circular argument.[1] Here I shall assume it and shall move through the high points of that wisdom as it is cumulatively derived, often mysteriously, sometimes not so mysteriously. Moving backward in time from modernity to early classical antiquity, and then turning back around to the high moderns, this book will touch on those cumulations and reverberate with them, I trust somewhat mysteriously. Among the poets who come to expression at various points through the whole Western tradition, both Alcman and Isaiah, for example, can be heard in Rainer Maria Rilke, though neither in the other, except where they rise to plumb this common, deep function of human utterance.

The forms of poetry do blend into one another, and they can often be perceived as doing so in poems of short compass. Consider what we have of Alcaeus's poem on the death of a tyrant at the end of the seventh century B.C.:

νῦν χρὴ μεθύσθην καί τινα πὲρ βίαν
πώνην, ἐπειδὴ κάτθανε Μύρσιλος.

Now a man must get drunk and is forced
to drink, for Myrsilos is dead.[2]

Though we have only these two lines, the sound of something like a popular ballad can be heard here, and that simplicity is carried out in other poems of the early poet. Friedrich Schlegel's assertion—implicitly followed by Martin Heidegger—that the fragment shines with the feeling of the whole poem is here splendidly exemplified.[3] Even here the impromptu character of the celebration—the specific reference to the death of a tyrant—makes it a variant on either celebration or satire. Both celebration and satire can be matched to other poems of Alcaeus. The inclusion of wine in the celebration keys it deeply into folk festivals and to the complex ritual use of the beverage in antiquity throughout the Mediterranean.[4] Horace, adopting Alcaeus's meter, adds (or finds in the rest of Alcaeus's poem) a dance element that goes with such celebrations: "Nunc est bibendum, nunc pede libero / Pulsanda tellus" ("Now we must drink, now earth / must be beat with the free foot")

(*Odes,* 1.37). Already this is an art song, moving to a self-consciousness of its folk assimilations. This poem blends further complications when it turns out to be celebrating a military victory at the Battle of Actium as well as the death of an overbearing ruler. The ruler is a foreigner, and she is also a woman; she is a queen, hated because the Roman professed to hate the trappings of royalty; but also the poet sympathizes with her, and Cleopatra's fortitude as well as her death is also ambivalently celebrated by the poem.[5]

Poetry, if it is launched, will be poetry even in a single line. There is some ineffability clinging to the single line of Alcaeus's vocative to Sappho, which, as a fragment, has an epigrammatic mystery it might retain if we were to find the whole poem of the original:

ἰόπλοκ' ἄγνα μελλιχόμειδε Σάπφοι

Violet-tressed, pure, honey-smiling Sappho.

Epithets are a usual feature of the epic style just preceding Alcaeus, but this line is not in the epic meter, and epithets are not usually addressed to live contemporaries in that poetry. Legendary figures and gods and goddesses get epithets, and the effect is to give Sappho the air of a goddess, like her own "Daedal-throned immortal Aphrodite." In Alcaeus's vocative, the rapture of something like courtship is turned toward something like professional praise. And there are one too many epithets for any analogue in the epic style. Hair and mouth (or eyes) are traditional loci of beauty, but these physical attributes are broken by something invisible (unless "pure" or "chaste" refers to her skin, which is doubtful). She is "pure," and the effect of this middle epithet is to cast its brightness upon the ones before and after it; the effect of the surrounding epithets on "pure" is to anchor it in an (imagined) actual presence.

Even when the ballad, which tends to remain brief, is heavily formalized, it still has a wide range. Not infrequently it draws on the convention of a courtship between a high-born lover and a low-born maid; it blends into *pastourelle.* The *pastourelle,* from Marcabru in the early twelfth century to *The Nut-Brown Maid* at the turn of the sixteenth, has the ring of ballad. Indeed, the latter is included in *The Oxford Book of Ballads.* Add poetic activity plus shepherding to the male lover, in a blend of artificial and natural or urban and rural, and the form of pastoral itself has already been brought into view.[6]

Speaking of genres in this way has the advantage of labeling constituents in poems and demarcating types of poems, but the disadvantage of drawing attention away not only from blendings but from the deep wisdom of an utterance. One could hardly dissociate this short poem from some echo of the ballad form:

> Foweles in the frith
> The fisses in the flod,
> And I mon wax wod.
> Mulch sorw I walke with
> For beste of bon and blod.

> Birds in the wood
> The fishes in the flood
> And I must grow mad.
> Much sorrow I walk with
> For the best of bone and blood.

That this is a lover's lament attunes it to medieval love poetry, and its attention to every single syllable makes it *durchkomponiert* like the work of the troubadours and the Minnesänger, with which its date of about 1270 would make it roughly contemporaneous. Ballads are full of lovers' laments, and even of the mad lovers of the troubadour tradition. This poem has a religious tinge, too; the last line has a possible eschatological ring. And the cosmic census of the first two lines would blend it, if briefly, into still another poetic register, that of Hesiod and some of Homer, and in fact of Near Eastern cosmologies generally. It is useful to recall Denys Thompson's summary in his own survey of the verse and song indigenous to various societies: "In archaic cultures poetry was at one and the same time ritual, entertainment, artistry, riddle-making, persuasion, sorcery, soothsaying, prophecy."[7] If we match this list to the small poem before us, we cannot exclude any of these (somewhat incommensurate) functions.

At the same time, something is happening in the wrought music of this poem, in its stern monosyllables, its laconic parataxis, its dominant rhyme conjunction of "flod," "wod," and "blod," its revelatory pattern variation of capping "flod" immediately with "wod" while strengthening the last word in an initial as well as a terminal echo of the first rhyme word ("flod"/"blod"). Like much poetry, it seems to rise to the oracular while remaining conversational, and the process involves a riddlelike but not riddle-formed utterance. It involves type-images but no metaphors

—or nothing that could be called metaphor without highlighting the cosmologizing feature of the poem, a feature that works as overtone rather than as designation.

What is that overtone? We would want to know, but perhaps we can do no more than notice the power of its presence. In ballads there is a swell of overtone not through metrical forcefulness, as here, but through slight metrical variation. Such variations give the haunting ring to English ballads as Sidney characterized them—"I never heard the old song of Percy and Douglas that I found not my heart moved more than with a trumpet"—and to Spanish ballads, the *romances*. The variations add the quick of verse instances, the *parole* of an imagined, privately responding speaker, to the *langue* of the verse design, a staple that amplifies the recursions into patterns immemorially associated with public speech, here at a pitch that retains some adaptiveness of the conversational while verging on the formal elevation of the oracular:

> Las campanicas del cielo
> sones hacen de alegría.
> Las campanas de la tierra
> ellas solas se tañían;
> el alma del penitente
> para los cielos subía
>
> The little bells of heaven
> made sounds of joy.
> The bells of earth
> rang out by themselves.
> The soul of the penitent
> went up to the heavens.
> ("El romance de la penitencia del rey Rodrigo")

Here, in the last lines of the poem, is a response to the confessions of a penitent, defeated, and wandering king to a charitable hermit he had met in a hilly wilderness. Corresponding to the syllabic variation and the mutings but persistences of echoes that are less than either rhyme or full assonance, this narrative runs its feeling through the slippages of simple opposition ("earth" versus "heaven") compounded by small qualifications ("little bells" versus "bells," "heaven" versus "heavens") with the mystery clinging to the details as an analogue to the access of the suppliant king. Why are the bells of heaven little? Do they ring of themselves, as those of earth are here strangely said to do, and mysteriously (one usually infers that earthly bells have been rung by someone)? And does the final plural "heavens" open into some rudimentary version of Dante's hierarchies? To ask is to press too far; not to ask is to lose sight of the precisions of this poetic language.

The overtone, as is somewhat the case in these delicate changes, can be one of awe, within the orbit of the nearly oracular, brought about when the story of the ballad recounts a glorious battle against odds or some conjunction of the amorous and the occult-sinister side of mortality, a conjunction shared by Wordsworth's balladlike "Lucy" poems and Keats's "La Belle Dame Sans Merci." Keats's art ballad evokes the obsessive love of an earthly knight for an unearthly woman in a setting of correspondent withering in nature:

> O what can ail thee, knight-at-arms,
> Alone and palely loitering?
> The sedge has withered from the lake,
> And no birds sing.

This poem has much in common with a traditional ballad, "The Unquiet Grave," though that ballad deals not with an unearthly woman but with a mortal beloved. "The Unquiet Grave" draws its occult power from the ability of the dead beloved to speak once the lover has been loitering at her grave for a whole year. The grave has been unquiet because he sits there:

> "Oh who sits weeping on my grave,
> And will not let me sleep?"
> "'Tis I, my love, sits on your grave,
> And will not let you sleep;
>
> For I crave one kiss of your clay-cold lips,
> And that is all I seek."

A strange love, one that transcends the bounds of mourning—as love is felt in any case to contain an element that moves to transcendence. The lover is obsessed but clear in his awareness of the physical senses. He knows her lips are "clay-cold," and she picks that up in a monitory reply:

> You crave one kiss of my clay-cold lips;
> But my breath smells earthy strong;

If you have one kiss of my clay-cold lips,
Your time will not be long.

'Tis down in yonder garden green,
Love, where we used to walk,
The finest flower that ere was seen
Is wither'd to a stalk.

The stalk is wither'd dry, my love,
So will our hearts decay;
So make yourself content, my love,
Till God calls you away.[8]

The repetitions in this reply are like an incantation, fueled by the traditional tetrameter/trimeter quatrains of the ballad measure; the incantation swells as the repetitions come in the longer lines. The dead girl has somehow made the tenderness of her devotion-in-death serve not for any assertion of the eternal quality in the love that the story implies but rather for a religious memento mori. It shares something of the tone of the last lines of Wordsworth's "A Slumber Did My Spirit Seal":

No motion has she now, no force;
She neither hears nor sees;
Rolled round in earth's diurnal course
With rocks, and stones, and trees.

The girl's words in the ballad have an effect like that of the speaker's realization in Wordsworth's poem. Awe is brought forward to press a limit. And when we are presented with the figure of a dead woman urging a devoted man to transform eros into deep piety, we have been brought onto a typological ground that this ballad shares with the Beatrice of Dante and beyond her to the general conception of the wise beloved.

Elusive as the reverberations in all these poems are, bringing them into the presence of another body of work, that of Dickinson, would accentuate the peculiar depth and breadth of an utterance that shares, like hers, elements of the oracular, the prophetic, the riddling, the diversionary, and the sibylline, all sounding together. Plutarch, writing on oracles ("On the Pythian Oracle," 6, 397A), slides from the effect of Sappho's poetry to the utterances of the Sibyl: "Don't you see . . . how much grace the songs of Sappho have, enchanting and charming the hearers; 'the Sibyl with maddened mouth' as Heraclitus says [92], 'uttering words that are laughless, unornamented, and unsalved, reaches with her voice across a thousand years through the god.'" Even if Plutarch intends a contrast, the association sets Sappho and the Sibyl in the same sphere.

Dickinson is also epigrammatic, carrying an extra sense of finality from the shortness of the utterance, and a mysteriousness in the finality, as though the question of how the statement could be over lingers to reinforce the mystery. This sense of finality hangs over those epigrams, including a fair share of the ones in the *Greek Anthology*, which are epitaphs, carrying an air of mortality, since they sum up a person's life after his/her death, and also an air of completeness, since this is a last summation. The whole life is encapsulated, as it were, in the vision of the whole life offered by the summary. Forms do blend, and one cannot divorce from this epigram-template the numerous succinct summaries of a life that are given in the *Divina commedia* by Dante and by the souls themselves—of Paolo and Francesca, Brunetto Latini, Pier delle Vigne, Arnaut Daniel, Manfred, Pia dei Donati, St. Bonaventure, and many others. Another form blends into these, that of the age-old praise for a hero, which the Chadwicks signal as one of the earliest of poetic kinds.[9] This praise blends into lament when it comes in the form of a lament for the dead, the elegy or *planh,* and Dante's summaries blend into that rhetoric as well. The epitaph makes a poised statement of the blend of praise with lament.

Lament tends to go on, as though grief were endless, and early laments such as that over the death of En-kidu in the Gilgamesh epic or that over the death of Beowulf swell into amplification. Typically expansive in this way is Whitman's lament for the death of Lincoln, "When Lilacs Last in the Dooryard Bloomed." The Book of Lamentations goes on at great length over the losses of a personified city rather than of a person, though at the same time it structures the amplifications into the strict containment of each strophe to a letter of the Hebrew alphabet, the whole finishing with that indicated by the last letter.

The shortness of epigram, by contrast, sets finality as an initial rhetorical control on the sense of expressive impulse, and the *Tombeaux* of Stéphane Mallarmé, sonnets on the deaths of notable literary contemporaries, are curtailed in comparison with long laments but amplified in comparison with epigrams. Part of the rhetoric of epitaph-epigram consists in the felt suppression of lament-outpourings by poised, succinct statement. Take this elegy of Walter Savage Landor:

Ah what avails the sceptred race,
Ah what the form divine!
What every virtue, every grace!
Rose Aylmer, all were thine.

Rose Aylmer, whom these wakeful eyes
May weep but never see,
A night of memories and of sighs
I consecrate to thee.

The general theme of the vanity of human wishes is broached by the first line, which seems in an assimilated Horatian way to point to the transitoriness of even royalty, and Rose Aylmer is assimilated to their number by metaphorical hyperbole. The strength of the speaker's grief is indicated by the refrainlike repetition of her name in this short compass, and yet he stays short of the psychological frontiers broached by Wordsworth in "A Slumber Did My Spirit Seal" or the stirrings and intensities of "The Unquiet Grave." Nearly his whole work of assimilation and definition is carried through by having his final verb the longest word in the poem, "consecrate," with "memories" its only close competitor. The first three lines, indeed, begin to rise into the Ecclesiastes theme, but they blend over into eulogy, and that rounds out the first stanza, linked to the second by the naming of the defunct. This poem admits of an expression a shade larger than an epigram, but it is determined to make a point of its self-containment. Epigrams for their very brevity do this, though in doing so they can be turned to a large spectrum of poetic functions, not only for witty satire but, therewith, for the succinct depiction of complex structures in a society, as in the epigrams of Martial.[10]

Having the length of an epigram, "Foweles in the frith," quoted above, has also the force of one. Epigram sharpens the presence of the ineffable in a poem, beyond the constituent features that many analysts offer—such as Jakobson or Lotman. We could subject "Foweles in the frith" to systematic analysis through many approaches, and still the perceptible ineffability would be left over, the "tone" of the poem, just as it is in Charles Baudelaire's "Les Chats."[11] The first two of the poem's five lines are devoted to the large cosmic opposition between birds and fish, and between land and sea, all four named. Against that pattern in the middle line the possible madness of the speaker concenters the poem, especially since the word "wod" provides not only the strongest rhyme link but also the first rhyme we have had this far (now more than halfway) in the poem. Further, four of these five words in this line are arguably accented, "Í món wáx wód," whereas in the first two lines those in the corresponding position find only one firm accent, the last word; "-es in the" stands unaccented in the middle of each line. The centering emphasis of this middle line provides a stable definition of growing instability, "grow mad."

Only the last line brings the beloved into the picture, and then by an expression that is indifferently either anatomical or theological, seeing her either as a fleshly creature or as an imaginably saved soul, the "beste of bon and blood." In the whole poem, there are only two words of more than one syllable, "foweles," and "fisses." These words are matched in syntactic function and in line position, matched, but with rhythmic variation between them. They are given no verb, but they cannot be imagined as stationary, these proverbially nimble and mobile creatures, both with an undercurrent of religious symbolism (archetypically, bird = soul, and fish = Christ). There are two whole lines in which the speaker speaks of himself, and he appropriates the sole adjective in the poem, "mulch." "Mulch" modifies "sorw," the tonic mood that the whole poem would both express and transcend by expressing—a key gesture that sweeps up all these semantic and rhythmic structures into itself. The two verbs, "wax" and "walke," match a psychological change with a change in space. The "walke" of the speaker exceeds the unmentioned motion of the birds and the fish; he is anchored in a dominant feeling, "mulch sorw." But his motion also is slower than theirs: walking is slower than either flying or swimming. The beasts are secure in their locations; "frith" matches "flod," and neither is threatened with losing that native element, whereas the speaker is threatened with being out of himself, "wod." "Wax" and "walke" also nearly rhyme, though of course they would then be internal rhymes, both alliterating with "wod." "With," an unusual terminal rhyme, also enters into the alliteration of the third and fourth lines, and it is the only alliteration in them. But the first two lines alliterate four times on the letter f, the more markedly in that each of the four times it is on an accented word, and these are the only accented words in the two lines, as though to give rhythmic emphasis but also semantic closure to the security of the birds and the fish.

As Stephen Owen says, glossing Chinese critical commentary on Chinese poetry, "Literature is a gate for the latent and inarticulate to become manifest. The poem is not simply the manifest state of the world's inherent order; its movement is the process of that order *becoming* manifest." And again "Wang Wei writes not 'poems' in the Western sense but *shih* (etymologically explained as 'to articulate what is intensely on the mind'), verbal manifestations of inner states." But Western poems, too, answer to this description.[12] The common ground of poetry and the mystery in mythology comes into view if it is noted that *muthos* is from *muo* ("enclose"), a word that also produces "mystery" and indicates a special language as opposed to ordinary language.[13] An attention to the ineffability even of epigram will broaden that aura of poetry beyond the "Lyrik" of Emil Staiger, which is characterized by the (re)memoration, the hypostatized transience of an "Erinnerung."[14] Intertextuality is only the tip of this iceberg.

Consider both the echoes and the differentiations in these two epigrams, the second in response to the first, which it quotes as an epigraph:

Thanks for a Wedding Present

[It was a compass on a necklace, with the poem:

> *Magnetic Powers cannot harm your House*
> *Since Beauty, Wit and Love its walls de-Gauss.*
> *And if, when nights are dark, your feet should stray*
> *By chance or instinct to the* Load of Hay
> *With me drink deep and on th'uncharted track*
> *Let my Magnetic Power guide you back.*]

She bears your gift as one safe to return
From longer journeys asking braver fuel
Than a poor needle losing itself an hour

Within a *Load of Hay* needs heart to learn.
She wears the birth of physics as a jewel
And of the maritime empires as a flower.

William Empson's own six lines take the couplets accompanying the gift compass and level their pointed wit by expanding beyond it in the suggestive range of his comparatives, "longer" and "braver." The bridegroom here, or at least the admirer of the bride, responds to the track from house to sociable tavern by seeing the woman on that homely track in a cosmic dominance, a playfully metaphysical one, in which the compass on the necklace puts intellect and power, the birth of physics and

22

of the maritime empires, at her service as an adornment. The nameless member of this little group begins to take on, faintly to be sure, the attributes of Lady Philosophy; and if the maritime empires and a compass are in view, some hint of an analogy to a ship's figurehead cannot be wholly absent. At the same time, she has a capacity of being "safe to return" from more demanding journeys than can be guided by this "poor needle." She is at once alone in that mastery and able to wear the concentrated emblem of her dominance. But the very form of the response is controlled by the politeness of the gesture: six lines to answer for six lines, and the homage of a rhyme scheme to vary the couplets of the initial epigram. The pastoral touch is carried by the name of the tavern, the Load of Hay, with its formalized reference to the agricultural cycle that its patrons are at least pretending to honor. The name occasions the connection between the homely wisdom of the proverbial expression "a needle in a haystack" and the uses, both literal and metaphorical, of this more sophisticated and more ornamental compass needle.

The context of this polite exchange has an oriental flavor, and it takes place among the literate members of a close expatriate society. At the point of writing, Empson had been teaching in China for years. Poetry need not lose its ineffability for its serviceability as compliment, and epigram furthers this end when it adds the politeness of "point," of confining its discourse so as not to engage in overassertion. Consider the succinctness of Mallarmé's little occasional poems, such as the epigram that accompanies a gift of fruits at the new year.[15]

Polite exchange can take on many dimensions, as in the tradition of the *surimono,* the poem sent with an artwork to friends by Japanese poets of past centuries as a gift for the new year. Referring to the artwork they accompany as well as to the year, these poems bear, and modify, the gestures of ekphrasis. In one such surimono, for example, from the mid-1820s by the poet Hananari, a block print by the artist Keisai, the portrait of a geisha seated on a porch by a plum tree, shows her reading a letter with poems by Hananari beside a scroll bearing another poem of Hananari.[16] The verse reads: "Through the mediation of the wind, the snow melts on the eaves; the crimson of both lips and plums break into a smile." The puns characteristic of the genre, the oblique topical references, and the rhythms, as well as much else, are lost to one who knows no Japanese. But the social intricacy of an epigram attached to an artwork that joins it in the service of polite exchange still can be heard to carry through the ineffability of a poetic act, highlighting the moment of crimson for lips and for plums. The heightened transience of Staiger's "Lyrik" can still be felt. So, too, in another surimono, a print by Hokkei in which a woman watches children who carry a melting sheet of ice horizontally on a bamboo pole at the entrance of a bath house. The poems, four of them, hang vertically from the bamboo pole in the print. In one poem, "Spring mist is drawn like a sacred rope across the entrance gate; ice melts and children play": that which is lightly visible, the spring mist, is paired with the transparent ice melting into invisibility. In another, the woman herself is drawn into the comparison: "Even the sash, loosely fastened for the trip home from the bath, gradually comes untied like slowly melting ice in Spring." The play of nature and culture through homely goings-and-comings is itself turned into an epigrammatic compliment to the sensibility of the recipient; he will not miss the ineffability.

There is an epigrammatic cast to Williams's "The Red Wheelbarrow":

> so much depends
> upon
>
> a red wheel
> barrow
>
> glazed with rain
> water
>
> beside the
> white chickens.

A vast amount of interpretation has been brought to bear on this poem, usually along the lines of its implied assertions about poetic theory. But the very obliquity of its directness opens it into a larger field. It runs the beginning of a Möbius strip between the one capitalized "Wheelbarrow" of its title and the two-word repeat across a line break of the same word uncapitalized, "wheel / barrow." It schematizes color. It opens into silence, the ineffability of the epigram, as does the slightly longer "This Is Just to Say" (also much discussed), about eating plums that had been left in the icebox.

A further bareness in this "gnomic" verse of Robert Creeley enlists the elision of punctuation to keep a large, mobile rhythmic expression on top of a space-time expansion into the ineffable:

Here

You have to reach
Out more it's
Farther away from
You it's here[17]

This poem achieves its effect by forcing enjambments up against line breaks in all four lines. The language gives the impression of speeding up so fast it slides off into an ineffable silence before a reader takes notice—or almost before. The poem makes all its references to space, but the pressured forward movement enlists the voice to harness itself to a sense of vanishing, to time. Of these twelve words, there are only two that are not monosyllables, and they come together, "Farther away." "Farther" is strategically placed as the initial word of the third line, and as a trochee it pushes forward in its semantic antithesis to the title ("here"/"farther"). "Away" stands close in sense to "farther," but as an iamb, the sound of the word inverts the trochee of "farther." Together they form a choriamb, while the whole line, "Farther away from," comprises the dochmiac phrase that Pound's *Cantos,* in its vaster compass, revivified for modern use. The last line, "You it's here," a blunt cretic, clips the whole to a close, compressing trochee and iamb into a single foot, /-/.

This pressured, laconic conversational epigram achieves its own blending in a very short compass. Its brevity, as always in such poems when they succeed, is itself an important part of the message. The careful music of this "gnomic verse," where every syllable is weighed, enlightens and vivifies the reader's perceptions as these weights are harmoniously shifted through the integers of sense in the simple words.

2

The Stance of
the Modern Poet

MODERN POETRY establishes, like all poetry, an intimate communication that depends on the suspension of some conversational and logical rules, though it can reinvoke these rules on its own chosen ground of merely virtual utterance. Or the utterance would be merely virtual if it did not succeed in carrying through the sense of something urgent in it to justify its being set off from the conversational flow, and also of something expansive enough to be a covering case. To call such utterance "religious" would emphasize what it has in common with the utterances of Isaiah and Homer while eliding the vast difference, which is the difference of the context of the speaker more than of the overtone in the message. What is meant by "religious" with relation to Homer is itself a very obscure question, but certainly it is different from what might be meant by the term with respect to Isaiah. Yet on the other hand, to call modern poets "secular" is either a nearly tautological characterization of their social situations as not connected to doctrinal emphases or an unwarranted exclusion or limitation on the reach of their messages, their expansiveness, and with it a limitation on the intimate quick of what they communicate.

Bracketing various philosophical objections, one could confidently call this reach of poetry's utterance a corollary of its immediacy. Poetry gets across directly; the words sink in. This immediacy, an access to a statement privileged enough to be arresting in certain ways, lies, to take Heidegger's examples, more in the bells-ringing-through-snow quality of Georg Trakl's verse or, for that matter, Rilke's, than in the extrapolable aptness of the aphorisms that can be mined from their poetry, though certainly that extrapolable wisdom contributes to, and in fact derives from, the initial metalinguistic sense of their communicative acts.

The recursive questioning of language that leads to an ultimate affirmation centers into poetry after the Industrial Revolution. In various intense manifestations, the poet's act of self-questioning, a testimony of self-awareness, evokes an activation of the poet's role in address that to some degree represses, or, to speak more accurately, sublates, that awareness. These processes get an intensification from Baudelaire on, in the mutual qualification set up between a flower, which is desirable, and evil, which is not: *Les Fleurs du mal.* When Baudelaire says: "O Mort, vieux capitaine, il est temps, levons l'ancre," he does not wish to die; and yet his statement is not ironic in an ordinary sense. No more do his poems about his central subject, the dominance of evil, either oppose evil or accord with it. The poems sharpen a vision of a recursive questioning that leads to a counteraffirmation; and in this Baudelaire, conceptually as well as formally, begins the line that goes from Paul Valéry to Char via Mallarmé, and to all the surrealists as well. The disrupted surrealist surface that amounts to a recursive questioning allows their notorious link between politics and dream. The line, in this fundamental modernist reinvention, includes Jules Laforgue as well, and of course Eliot right through the *Quartets,* till long after he has given up the superficial Laforguean persona.

Eliot's children in the rose garden, and even the fire and the rose that are one, levitate their devotional affirmation by an absolutizing, and by a built-in, elusive, but not deconstructive, absoluteness of metaphor,[1] by a contradiction that contains an affirmation, under the seal of that old contester of the law of contradiction, Heraclitus, who supplies not one but two epigraphs to the *Quartets.* If we remember that Stevens converted to Roman Catholicism on his deathbed, we will have a measure of affirmation that will bring his poems closer to Eliot's. Stevens's early "sister and mother of diviner love" is not so far from Eliot's "Lady of silences," whose "torn and most whole" is in the same register as Stevens's "the clashing of two words that kill." I am here not indicating the affiliations of the poet, however, nor am I trying to erase the distinction between the doctrinal affirmations of Eliot and the denials of Stevens. Rather, I am indicating a fundament of intentional or proprioceptive focusing in their work that is characteristic of, and characteristically questioning in the domain of, spirit, the old traditional area of poetry that the modern poet, like the modern theologian after Nietzsche, has radically altered but not abandoned. Even in Eliot, the watershed before and after belief is incidental to the common note of identification and montage in the St. Augustine of *The Waste Land* before his conversion and the Dante of the *Quartets* afterwards. Many of the most attentive students of Stevens have taken the wrong turn of trying to precipitate a doctrine from the philosophical complications and tentatives of his poems. Certainly, to be sure, his most famous poem, "Sunday Morning," is set in the key of negation; but its subject is spirit. The reference of the title is to a time, a bright and beginning open time set aside for worship. It speaks of "not as a god but as a god might be"; and the pigeons of the conclusion—which was originally a beginning—though surely they constitute a Flaubertian parody of the Holy Ghost, "make / ambiguous undulations as they sink / Downward to darkness on extended wings." As Stevens said decades after he had written this poem, "Now, if the style of a poem and the poem itself are one; if the style of the gods and the gods themselves are one; and if the style of men and men themselves are one; and if there is any true relation between these propositions, it might well be the case that the parts of these propositions are interchangeable."[2] Of course, Stevens is no more defining style here than I am defining spirit.

We could characterize the stance of the modern poet in various ways. First, as I have been saying, the poet exhibits a self-consciousness of the act, often of the spiritual component in the act, to such a degree that modern poetry from Mallarmé on has often been called poetry about poetry. It is never exactly that, but it includes an awareness of, and therefore it is a presentation of, the virtual character of the utterance, beyond the mere Jakobsonian concentration on the message above code, referent, contact, speaker, and auditor—though in fact it can be shown that a poetic utterance generally includes a special concentration on all of these, a situation about which, again, the modern poem manifests its awareness.

This self-consciousness is not just a reflexivity. It includes a metastatement about its own nature built into the relation of the statements it includes. We can see that already Baudelaire presents himself in a way beyond seventeenth-century criteria of self-fashioning, which are caught in what are effectually Aristotelian categories. The Romantics struggle in their various ways toward such vision, while Baudelaire, Mallarmé, Rimbaud, and Laforgue in their various ways have got through to the implications of an easily incorporated metastatement. Surrealism seen in this light only consolidates the self-reflexive posture. Rilke's severe control in the *Sichtwerk* of the *Neue Gedichte* is passed on through the poem as reflexive, and more. It already posits the self-transcendence of the *Duino Elegies,* which sets up a register of free-flowing wisdom that in fact shows some similarity to the register of still more obviously meta-stated poems such as John Ashbery's "A Wave" and *Flow Chart*.[3]

To explain this modern poetic procedure, it would not suffice to relate it to various systems with which it would in fact exhibit congruence. For the unconscious of Sigmund Freud, it does often show awareness, sometimes deep awareness, of the unconscious. For the symbolic of Jacques Lacan, it sets up its own armature to locate an understanding of the symbolic. For the episteme of Michel Foucault, it constitutes, often, a kind of preemptive episteme or overall conceptual superstructure that includes and governs other codes, a code of codes.[4] For the rhizoma formation of Gilles Deleuze and Félix Guattari, each poem sets up a tiny rhizoma, a spreading and fertilely connected root system.[5]

In a further characterization, modern poetry in its self-consciousness shows a second characteristic, an awareness of a multiplicity of data that it can bring together, sometimes in the suspension of explicitness in metaphoric reference that I have elsewhere called "generality."[6] Alfred Lord Tennyson's "Flower in the Crannied Wall" names this impulse but stands at a distance from it that Gerard Manley Hopkins manages to close when he moves in, for poem after poem, on "All things counter, original, spare, strange." In the work of such as Giuseppe Ungaretti, Charles Reznikoff, Trakl, and many others from E. A. Robinson to Carl Dennis, for example, the poet manages to close the gap between the anecdotal and the archetypal. The particular rhythms of such poems posit an awareness that such ranges are being compassed, and a communication of that awareness. Confessional poetry, without the control of the full metacoded self-consciousness in the best such work, dissolves into display. The best of confessional poetry, however, does make comparable connections, as does postconfessional poetry, too. In the title poem of

Willingly, Tess Gallagher manages to get into the same frame a sense of daily recurrence, a sense of bodily perception, and a sense of rooted establishment, all derived from having the house painted. "Like the shark it contains a shoe," Louis Simpson declares in his self-consciously condensed and ranging poem about American poetry. I use these recent examples to stress the point that it is not just the "epic" poets such as Pound, Williams, Perse, Louis Zukofsky, and Olson who have built into their work an awareness, and an established communicative structure to cue the awareness, of the reach to compass multiplicity. Frank O'Hara does it through the gestures well summarized, as well as instantiated, in "Picasso made me tough, and quick, and the world," which begins "Memorial Day 1950," a poem whose immediate occasion is looking out the window as trees are being cut down on a neighboring square. Marianne Moore makes a series of comments about a glacier open out into a survey of mountains, of their flora and fauna, and of crystallized attitudes and reactions to them ("An Octopus of Ice"). The tension between high-focus and wide-lens approaches may be said to characterize her work, and she has this is common with Stevens, for all their differences. Such awareness of the impulse to carry through a sense of perceived range in experience can be seen even in this short poem by Salvatore Quasimodo:

Ed è subito sera

Ognuno sta solo sul cuor dellá terra
trafitto da un raggio di sole:
ed è subito sera.[7]

And It's Suddenly Evening

Everyone stands alone on the heart of the earth
pierced by a ray of sunlight:
and it's suddenly evening.

Here the classicist Quasimodo has managed to apply the epigram form to a subject like that of William Collins's "Ode to Evening," a standard romantic, and indeed preromantic, posture that is attributed by literary history as a name to the very poets who preceded Quasimodo, the "Crepuscolari," the "Twilight Poets." But the foreshortening advertises a distancing from such gestures, as well as a self-conscious acquiescence in them and an inspection of such a momentary coming-to-awareness, "hey look, it's night already." The quick turn allows it easy generalizable access to a day-as-life metaphor, without closing the poem around it. Such play of self-consciousness leads to multiplicity of applicability for this simple sense that begins by attributing it to common humanity, "ognuno." It would be easy to move toward a Heideggerian approach to this poem and dwell on what is meant by "sul cuor della terra," and what sort of predicative equivalence is set up by the colon at the end of line 2. In so doing, the well-elided push toward multiplicity of meanings here is also a push toward convergence and toward the associability of a long, if not of an infinite, regress that would be affirmative and so the opposite of its cousin, the relegation to the infinite regress of an abyss, a *mise en abîme.*

With respect to this opening for poetic language, the infinite regress in itself hovers near poetic expression but enters at its peril. It may further orient us to recall that Francis Ponge, who comes close to using the phrase, does not exactly do so. "Le Soleil *placé* en abîme" is the title of a poem on which he worked for thirty-six years. And so in this instance the sponge, the "éponge" of his poem and his persona, does not quite wipe the slate clean, nor does it reduce to a puzzle, however complex, about self-referring signs, a "signéponge."[8]

Or take a poem of Eugenio Montale's, long enough not to be an epigram but short enough to be a sort of note:

Motet XVI

Il fiore che ripete
dall'orlo del burrato
non scordarti di me,
non ha tinte piú liete né piú chiare
dello spazio gettato tra me e te.

Un cigolío si sferra, ci discosta,
l'azzurro pervicace non ricompare.
Nell'afa quasi visibile mi riporta all'opposta
tappa, già buia, la funicolare.[9]

The flower that repeats
from the edge of the crevasse
forget me not,
has no tints fairer or more blithe
than the space tossed here between you and me.

A clank of metal gears puts us apart.
The stubborn azure fades. In a pall of air
grown almost visible, the funicular
carries me to the opposite stage. The dark is there.

[I.B.] (Irma Brandeis)

This is a sort of love poem (translated by the woman to whom it was perhaps addressed), but it says nothing about love, leaving an unstated riddle behind the riddle that is presented by the perceptions registered, which turn out to add up to the solution "funicular ride." A flower is compared to space, and then the space disappears, and then the flower is replaced, in repeated sentence and strophe pattern, by a clank of gears, and then there is a motion, here remembered and so obedient to the injunction of the flower, a small movement that love's vividness may have heightened. But the moment begins to be overtaken by a darkness, even before the vehicle of transportation is named in the last word of the poem, "tappa, già buia, la funicolare" ("platform, already dark, the funicular").[10]

Jean Follain begins in the register of nostalgic genre depiction but has his particulars levitate the poem into a communicated self-consciousness of contributory extensibilities in his data, so that his last word, "l'oubli," is at once a simple hortatory notation, a participatory conclusion, and a metacommentary on the range in what has been offered:

Rue Verte

Rue verte, beaucoup qui te longeaient
se payaient de mots et d'espoirs:
jeunes ménages entrant dans la vie
la dame en chapeau à plumes
et l'homme en chapeau de soie
et moustaches de campagne
rentraient dans tes boyaux, rue verte
aux pissenlits touffus
aux chats massifs;
d'immenses tartines d'enfants
sur qui le beurre fraîchissait
sur qui la confiture glaçait
étaient parfois pendant le jeu
posées sur une borne grise
jusqu'à l'oubli.[11]

Green Street

Green street, many that coursed you
were content with words and hopes,
young couples entering life
the lady in a feathered hat
the man in a silk hat
and country mustaches
came back to your tunnels, green street,
to the tufted dandelions
to the massive cats;
huge slices of bread for children
on which the butter cooled
on which the jam iced
were sometimes during play
set on a gray boundary stone
until forgotten.

The context here is a rich one, with elements skewed in it. Going backwards, we can certainly locate the speaker as a member of a class only faintly indicated in the poem, the cultivated bourgeoisie, which in one professional dimension sponsors the ordered functioning of society through the magistracy that Follain the lawyer exercised. Such a profession touches in no direct way on any of the simple, presented activities of a villagelike existence not so remote from that of Canisy in Normandy, where Follain grew up, and about which he wrote a memoir that shares the tonality of this poem. This simple village life is fleshed out in his other poems, though here the only touch cuing to such simplicity is the "moustaches de campagne," which at least potentially could work as a fashionable pastoralizing reminiscence in, let us say, a magistrate. These country mustaches, of course, do not have to be worn just in the country. The plumed hat of the lady and the silk hat of the man, indeed, set the existence at the intersection of village and suburb, with the plentiful dandelions and the massive cats, as well as the boundary stone referred to later. They tilt the representation, always faintly, toward village rather than suburb-imitating-village or village-become-suburb.

The backward glance of the poem takes us from the new households, again shown as confined in perceptions the way we think of the magistrate not to be, and it shifts abruptly to an earlier stage, to the children who in the deliberately vague time frame of the poem could be either the children of the new households or the husbands and wives of the new households in the time of their own childhood. The blurring of time lines fosters the pastoralizing tone of the poem, always with the proviso that the blurring of social lines keeps the anonymous persons from being locked into the systems that are almost always mounted for the pastoral poems of antiquity, where poet equals lover equals shepherd. Nor does "Rue Verte" conform to the various mutations of the pastoral in the Renaissance, where sets of moral valuations are sometimes more explicit, nor even to the eighteenth-century pastoral lying behind *The Beggar's Opera* as represented in the discussions of Empson. Here there are no coordinates set where one segment of society measures another. An existence is idealized that within the world of the poem includes everybody, and the criticisms we can mount of such an attitude would have to be mounted outside the poem and in contradiction of its tone, rather than in supposed definition of it. The poem posits, within itself, a quiet absoluteness of its experience, and this absoluteness turns out to be not only self-conscious and comprehensive; it also finds an outlet in the absoluteness of its metaphors, to use an expression of Beda Alemann. There is a contrast between green and gray built into the poem, between the green of a street that can be literally so from late spring through early autumn (and by extension from childhood through maturity) and the gray of a boundary stone that is always literally so and would also lend itself faintly to a suggestion of something the opposite of green. This gray-green contrast could be expanded on, but not structurally analyzed, because the poem allows no such purchase. Even if we take the contrast between the green and the gray to echo the old Indo-European catchphrase "the oak and the rock," found in Homer, it still cannot be resolved into any kind of system of the Aristotelian analysis dear to the theoreticians of metaphor. Arguably the only out-and-out metaphor in the poem is the "boyaux," the tunnels, or perhaps the tubes, formed by the green street. This overstresses a visual appearance, and it is at the very least a catachresis, the quasi-invention of a term for which there is no word in the language, as we speak of the leg of a table. Certainly the usage here is unique enough to isolate it in the normal-seeming ongoing series of narrative statements, and that is enough to allow us to conceive of at least two spaces in the poem: that of the one-dimensional "tunnel vision" along the street, which is easily transposed from space to time for a hint of the course of human life, and the other more open space where a boundary stone not only sets off miles or kilometers but just sits as a receptacle for the *tartines* of the children, whose attention is called so fully outward that a forgetfulness takes over.

To ask about the figural structure here, in its curious elisions, is to remind ourselves that Follain is operative within another system available to the high-bourgeois culture of the twentieth century, the surrealism of his contemporaries Char, Georges Guillevic, Paul Éluard, and others. As in their work, there is also a contrast in this poem that wants to suggest a mystery. The initial opposition between green and street retains a Breton-like contradiction, since a street would not usually get such a name (though it is possible that there was a street so named in Canisy[12]), nor can the adjective really be returned to the simple descriptive "street lined with trees in leaf," even if the metaphoric associations are added. Follain, however, is careful to keep obtrusive surrealizing out of the poem. The only other such touches are the perspectival puzzles of "immenses" and "massifs," which are initially just colloquial hyperboles. Then there is the abrupt shift to the children, who are approached at the extreme metonymic angle of the big slices of buttered bread with jam that are given them, presumably to fortify them for the play so absorbing they can forget this food.

Again, to introduce what might obtrude on our consciousness—that in the world of widespread hunger it is a kind of fantasy to posit such casual abundance as a normative question—is immediately to reclassify the poem as a document. This would be all right if we did not first realize that it should be experienced, as an art song is experienced, in all the subdued tonality of its short lines, for the assimilating values it is positing. Whether as actuality or possibility, the poem offers, and self-consciously offers, a vision that anchors the sequence of life in an easy continuity with the natural and cultural world, complete with boundary stones that could have been set down at any time between Roman times and the twentieth century. Another contrast built into the poem, intersecting with that between green and gray, is that between the rememoration that is implied either in the "return," which is the sole main verb given to the "young couples," or in the rememoration implied by the very act of presenting the poem. The rememoration is keyed into the poem by setting all its verbs into the lingering pastness of the imperfect, rather than in such other possibilities as the historical present, the *passé composé,* or the *passé simple.* The speaker remains in the mode of recall, as though faithful to Staiger's dictum that classifies all lyric poetry (oversimply) as a kind of memory, "Erinnerung." And certainly the force of the imperfects here is powerful enough for us to apply Marcel Proust's observation that Gustave Flaubert's use of the tenses functions philosophically in as full a way as Kant's use of categories. Here, on the other hand, in opposition to memory is the "oubli," the forgetfulness, which is the last word of the poem, and a sort of limit, "jusqu'à l'oubli." The poem closes by announcing a closure, a shutting off that is also an openness, because while the "tartine" is left behind in the narrative about the children's play, the children move out inevitably, so far as the poem is concerned, into the life that the green street holds ready for them, a life that will include a final "oubli." And the rememoration of the poem gathers that up as well. It remembers forgetfulness as happening typically in the proximate imagined past.

Forgetfulness is a Baudelairean category, and the memory of childhood is a modern as well as a romantic topos, giving onto Proust and the Perse of *Éloges* as well as onto many others, and perhaps leading back to the Muses as the daughters of memory. Yet such a literary notion about the poem itself is buried in the poem; it may imply, but it does not offer, such theories, and one cannot line it up with the more precise, related psychologizing of Baudelaire's "Le Voyage": "Ah que le monde est grande à la clarté des lampes, / Aux yeux de souvenir que le monde est petit" ("Ah how large is the world in the clarity of lamps! / In the eyes of memory how small is the world!"). Baudelaire's statement, in a sense, is counter-Wordsworthian, because the child trails no special clouds of glory. Yet if we measure the "words and hopes" of the second line with the heedlessness of the children, we have a sort of Wordsworthian contrast, though one not explicitly drawn, between child and adult. And if we measure Follain against both Baudelaire and Wordsworth, it can be seen that there is no way we can accord superiority, or even essential difference, between child and adult. All are at the appropriate point of the "Rue Verte," all points merge, and forgetfulness as a general category must be seen as benign, as is a joy so intense that it momentarily leads the children to forget their nourishment—which, in this world, easily merges all the contrast in favor of a communicated contentment.

Another contrast is present besides those between green and gray, child and adult, memory and forgetfulness. In the modeling system of the poem, to adopt Lotman's term, there is a more subdued contrast between the outdoors, where all is said to take place, and the indoors, from which the slices of bread and jam, and so the children, and so the parents, must have issued. Indeed, the term "ménage" overlaps these categories, because the exemplum of the couple, the "jeune ménage," bears a name that means "household" and merges the man and the woman into a unanimity that makes the sexual differentiation of their hats merely decorative and celebratory. They are spoken of as walking on the street, to which they "returned" or "kept returning" ("rentraient"). This word choice is a sort of reversal, since more normally one returns to the house from the street, not the other way around. An unnamed twilight will overtake the children, who at the imagined but unnamed end of day will return to the house. In another sense, they will remain on the green street, moving from one stage to another, leaving the *tartines* behind, to an oblivion that is surely felt as partaking of the benignity, and of the perceptions of the benign.

In this poem, the self-consciousness, the range and comprehensiveness of the poem, come through indirectly, or "surrealistically," though the indirectness comes clear only if we ask ourselves whether such a poem would be conceivable at another time. Indeed if we compare the poem to the mature work of Eliot and Stevens, roughly contemporaneous with it, "Rue Verte" is more surrealistic, though in tune with "The Blue Guitar" or the three white leopards under a juniper tree of "Ash Wednesday," just because it has not effectually marked its images by such disjunctions. To put it differently, "Rue Verte" can be seen not to accommodate in its register such statements as Eliot's "Midwinter spring is its own season" or even Stevens's "We are not / At the center of a diamond." Follain's statements are more indirect than these, and the seemingly ordinary rhetoric of "se payaient de mots et d'espoirs" evades the possibility of our affirming or denying that the figure of zeugma, the linkage of disparities to a single verb, is operative here. Do words express hopes? Or do words exist on one plane and hopes on another? "Rue Verte" shifts itself past such questions by staying on its pattern of quasi-frequentative narrative. The self-conscious closure of the poem pretends to describe, and effectually praises, the forgetfulness by taking the onrush of childhood as a sort of blest state, and by confidently including the reader in the indirect perception of that implicit judgment by not indulging in the sort of explicit conclusion that the similarly postured but more classical early Robert Frost was fond of.

The free verse of Follain's poem is of the low-keyed sort, rather than the Whitmanian or Persean or Claudellian afflatus; it is conversational rather than oracular. While getting a lift from the romantic symbology, it leaves the romantic amplitude behind for the self-confidence and the urbanity of what could be called a normal tone of voice. It is assured enough to approximate at points the classical meters, though in free verse the syllable count is less certain because no rules are given for handling the normally mute syllables. However, the second and third lines, and possibly the first, set a tonic note of the eight-syllable line, the iambic tetrameter, which is in fact possibly the oldest of Indo-European meters, found first in the Vedic *tristubh*. The pattern is repeated in lines 7, 11, and 12, making for six in all. Lines 4, 5, 6, and 8, and possibly lines 10 and 14, match this common meter with a constituent of high-toned French verse. These other four or six lines are half an alexandrine, and that echo is the stronger because the alexandrine, of course, has a caesura that calls for a comparable pause at the end of six syllables. The last line is shorter than any of these possibilities, "jusqu'à l'oubli." The poem is cut off in its closure metrically as well as semantically. Moreover, there is only one other line in the poem to match its four syllables, as though to guarantee the assimilation of the last line into the system of the poem, to keep it wholly from changing register. It is matched by "aux chats massifs" ("with massive cats"), the phrase descriptively appended to the green street at the point where the children enter the poem, themselves at first appended to their *tartines.*

I am asserting that the free verse here is shadowed by ordinary meters in a way that makes its freedom lightly bound. The sound tells us that it can accommodate to being bound without losing its freedom.[13] I am not, however, asserting that sound here is an exact echo of sense (nor am I asserting the contrary). I am trying to account for the transmission of a clear but undefined vision in this poem that carries through not only a communication of wisdom but a sort of voiced confidence that the wisdom need not be underscored to be communicated. A more programmatic surrealism than Follain's, especially in Éluard and André Breton, makes a virtue of erotic affirmation, and their poems attain to a richness and a value for which we may be grateful. But it would be fair to say that Follain also here contains the erotic, though once again not explicitly, and to say so is to move beyond the particular experience of this poem, which part of its assurance can be said to invite us to do.

There is a word, and also a symbol, nowhere mentioned in this poem but everywhere drawn on, the "village," a shadowy, paradisal, intimate, and deep conception that Frost shares with Follain and many others, beyond the confines of the modern or of a given national tradition, the evocative village of William Blake's "village green" as well as of

Wordsworth, of Thomas Gray's "Elegy in a Country Churchyard," of George Crabbe and Eduard Mörike along with Rimbaud's "Larme." It is a village that Follain reevokes in his densely textured prose memoir, *Canisy*. The force of the symbol, its overshadowing community among such poets, the evocative depth of the topos, can be measured by setting Follain's use of it beside that of a contemporary with very different origins and purview (but comparable poetic means), Jules Supervielle. Supervielle was an orphan who traversed the Atlantic from Uruguay, circumstances he mixes into his work, as he does in the poem "Le Village sur les flots," which sets the word "village" as well as the topos squarely through the center of his poem—along with the visual attributes (through negation) and the children (through personal identification) on which Follain also calls. The poem need not be drawn on in its entirety for its tonalities to be brought forward:

> Je frôlai un jour un village
> Naufragé au fil de vos eaux
> Qui venaient humer d'âge en âge
> Les maisons de face et de dos,
>
> Village sans rues ni clocher,
> Sans drapeau, ni linge à sécher,
> Et tout entier si plein de songe
> Que l'on eût dit le front d'une ombre
> . . . .
>
> Un écolier taché d'embruns
> Portant sous le bras un cartable
> Jetait un regard outrebrun
> Sur les hautes vagues de fable,
> . . . .
>
> Dans ce village sans tombeaux,
> Sans ramages ni pâturages,
> Donnant de tous côtés sur l'eau,
> Village où l'âme faisait rage,
>
> Et qui, ramassé sur la mer,
> Attendait une grande voile
> Pour voguer enfin vers la terre
> Où fument de calmes villages.[14]

Village on the Flood

I grazed one day a village
Shipwrecked on the thread of your waters
Which came to drink from age to age
The houses, before and behind,

Village without streets or belltower,
Without flag or washing to dry,
And entirely so full of dream
One would have called it the face of a shadow
. . . .

A schoolboy freckled with mists
Carrying under his arm a schoolbag
Cast a super-brown look
On the high waves of fable
. . . .

In this village without tombs,
Without bird song or pasture-land
Giving at all sides on the water,
Village where the soul worked its rage,

And which, gathered on the sea,
Was awaiting a large sail
To ride at last toward the land
Where smoke calm villages.

This fantasy village in the floods draws on the same common life and
large horizons as Follain's slightly surrealized one, as the declared har-
monization of the last line implies. The symbol is one where the roman-
tic and the modern are indistinguishable, and Supervielle has brought
his vision to expression not only by combining the flood with his vil-
lage but by tilting somewhat a topos that traditionally conceives not a
village but a kingdom or a city or a castle or a cathedral under the water:
Atlantis; Ille, the legendary island off Brittany; the "submerged cathe-
dral" that inspired Claude Debussy's "La Cathédral engloutie." Moreover,
in his last lines, the submerged habitations are endowed with motion
like a ship and surrealistically spoken of as capable of merging with their
originals on land—a land evoked solely by the smoke that could only
subsist on the sea in the form of mist.

Like Rilke, Richard Wilbur sets a focus that metaphysically expands in a range beyond his objects:

Wyeth's Milk Cans

Beyond them, hill and field
Harden, and summer's easy
Wheel-ruts are congealed.

What if these two bells tolled?
They'd make the bark-splintering
Music of pure cold.[15]

Here Wilbur offers a minimalist ekphrasis replete with muted philosophical meditations; it is a poem that could only have been written after Stevens. The roughening of meter, possibly the most extreme in all of Wilbur's poetry, is the more striking for its use in the epigrammatic form to which he often has recourse, and for its retention, nonetheless, of a firm regularity. Its indirectness accords it the same reflexive register as the maximalist and expansive ekphrasis of Irving Feldman's *All of Us Here,* a nearly book-length exposition of the sculptures of George Segal, though of course there are crucial differences in much of the technique, in the actual direction of the philosophical inductions, and in the style and social orientation of the artist attended to. A comparable self-consciousness is at work to focus the statements ranging over a set of objects in a way freer than such standard ekphrases as in the first six stanzas of Wilbur's "A Baroque Wall-Fountain in the Villa Sciara" (271–73), though it, too, goes on to reflections that, like Feldman's later poems, lean heavily on a moral vision. On the other hand, Robert Creeley's "Nationalgalerie Berlin" is a sort of anti-ekphrasis:

Nationalgalerie's
minute spasm's
self-reflective—
art's meager agony?

Two hundred years
zap past
in moment's
echoing blast!

No one apparently left
To say "hello"—

> but for the genial
> late Romanticists.
>
> God, what a life!
> All you see is *pain*.
> I can't go through *that* again
> —gotta go![16]

These adaptive quatrains begin with the rhythmic buildup of an enjambed compound substantive title in another language, "National-galerie," and ends with a quick cretic, "Gotta go." This climb down from the stiffness—and alleged pain—of high culture also serves antiphrastically as a climb up to the self-possession of the self-preserving man on the move, a persona who retains, because he guards it against incursions, his capacity for the traits of the modern poet that I have been stressing—for self-consciousness, for compassing multiplicities, and for ranging outward: here he is in Berlin, the tourist refusing to be a tourist. The bravura of tonal leaps here serves a livening of communicated consciousness.

A comparably condensed transmutation of ekphrasis is found in the work of Aaron Rosen, as in this poem from *Traces:*

> Embarrassed
> Flowers to quote
> From all sides invite
> Forgetfulness.
>
> They are terraces of error
> Like rain inscribed beside
> Raindrops or spent petals written
> Into a primal setting.
>
> Losing ground we propose
> Journals thick with the room's
> Inconsequence. What other news
> Stays on as if for nothing?[17]

This poem is twenty-seventh in a sequence of sixty "Traces" prevailingly given over to fruits or flowers, and all to still lifes. They are as proportionate, as structured, as solidly present, and as abstractly sensed as the Cézannes they do not describe either individually or collectively but "imitate" in a way that raises and also answers questions about the nature of perception, the nature of poetic language, the relation of poetic language to art and to depth psychology, and the upshot of the very integrations they are brilliantly effectuating by ringing these changes on conventionally beautiful perceptual objects conventionally enlisted by painters. As the title of the sequence, and the book, implies, this poetry has ingested and replayed the "postmodern" conception of sequentially vanishing language offered by Derrida, but it has also returned that conception robustly to an act of attention that owes something to Ponge while handling his method at once more normatively and more flexibly.

Federico García Lorca, in comparison with the above poems, frames his images in an art song that is simple in its classicism:

Gacela de la raíz amarga

Hay una raíz amarga
y un mundo de mil terrazas.

Ni la mano más pequeña
quiebra la puerta del agua.

¿Dónde vas, adónde, dónde?
Hay un cielo de mil ventanas
—batalla de abejas lívidas—
y hay una raíz amarga.

Amarga.

Duele en la planta del pie,
el interior de la cara,
y duele en el tronco fresco
de noche recién cortada.

¡Amor, enemigo mío,
muerde tu raíz amarga!

Gacela of the Bitter Root

There is a bitter root
and the world has a thousand terraces.

Nor can the smallest hand
shatter the door of water.

Where are you going, where, oh where?

The sky has a thousand windows
—battle of livid bees—
and there is a bitter root.

Bitter.

The ache in the sole of the foot
is the ache inside the face,
and it aches in the fresh trunk
of night only just lopped off.

Love, my enemy,
bite your bitter root!
(Edwin Honig, tr.)[18]

Here the initial contrast between the bitter root and the thousand ter-
races advertises the poem's expatiating range while eliding it into the
artful folk vocabulary, leading then into the typical Lorcan turn of sur-
realizing a folklike apothegm. The self-awareness of a hinting speaker,
not getting the name "Amor" till the apostrophe of the final couplet,
dominates as it conceals itself.

In this late poem, Lorca has left behind the more complex self-pre-
sentation of his amplified and long surrealist poems such as the "Llanto
por Ignacio Sanchez Mejías" and the "Ode to Walt Whitman." Aimed
toward an utterance that condenses to the simplicity of art song, the
poems in the sequence from which this one comes have given several
twists even to art song. *El Diván del Tamarit,* the title of the collection,
poses as a resurrection of a whole early Arab civilization not only strange
in the world of Spanish tradition but traditionally antithetical to it. The
predecessor, once an enemy, is elevated to a privileged source, a courtly,
and also a historicized, pastoral ideal society where high developments
of civilization are still consonant with well-pitched attention to defining
the essentials of love and song in a way not less direct than the *duende*
("spirit") Lorca had borrowed as a term and goal from the gypsies. So
the "directness" of this "Gacela" (lit., "gazelle") draws on many indirec-
tions, beginning with the technical exoticism of its title.

Anna Akhmatova handles such inclusions with masterly condensation
and indirectness:

He loved three things in the world:
Singing at vespers, white peacocks,

And blurred maps of America.
He did not love it when children cried,
Did not love tea with raspberry jam
And feminine hysterics.
But I was his wife.[19]

The last line reverts to metrical reinforcement of its metacommentary, concluding the conversational randomness of the rhythms in the first five lines with the exactness of a classical Russian iambic tetrameter: "A ya bhila yevo zhenoi." The regularity of this line sweeps into another, suggested range of experience hinging on the oppositions in gender-differentiation and conditioning.

In a very different mode, Marianne Moore comes onstage as a poet, so to speak, offering recuperation from infinite regress by performing the act of subjecting an object to the most unlikely associations, inferences, and figural turns, ending arbitrarily and definitively in such a way that her closures make the point of their own arbitrariness. Ponge, to whom she has sometimes been superficially compared, does likewise. The metacommentary implied by the severity of his high focus allows him to generate what sounds like more and more recuperation from an inexhaustible store, and the end is arbitrary as well.

Celan turns a comparable process inward, setting up a situation where the resourceful inferences are cut back to disjunct, self-deprecatory jottings. Here is a poem that begins with a characterization truncated from a full quotation by Baudelaire, itself quoted by Hugo von Hofmannsthal:[20]

À la pointe acérée

Es liegen die Erze bloss, die Kristalle,
die Drusen.
Ungeschriebenes, zu
Sprache verhärtet, legt
einen Himmel frei.

(Nach oben verworfen, zutage,
überquer, so
liegen auch wir.

Tür du davor einst, Tafel
mit dem getöteten
Kreidestern drauf:

ihn
hat nun ein—lesendes?—Aug.)

Wege dorthin.
Waldstunde an
der blubbernden Radspur entlang.
Auf-
gelesene
kleine, klaffende
Buchecker: schwärzliches
Offen, von
Fingergedanken befragt
nach—
wonach?

Nach
dem Unwiederholbaren, nach
ihm, nach
allem.

Blubbernde Wege dorthin.

Etwas, das gehn kann, grusslos
wie Herzgewordenes,
kommt.[21]

With Point of Steel

The ores lie bare, the crystals,
the geodes.
What is not written, into
speech hardened, lays
a heaven free.

(Thrown up, by day,
crosswise, so
lie we also.

Door you before once, table
With the killed
chalk star on it:
That
held now by one—reading?—eye.)

Ways there.
Wood hour at
the bubbling wheel track, along.
Picked
out
little gaping
beechnuts: blackish
open, of
fingerthoughts asked
after—
after where?

After
the unrepeatable, after
it, after
all.

Bubbling ways thereto.

Something that can go, greetingless,
like what's heart-become,
comes.

The first strophe here gives a collocation reminiscent of Stevens but with a tone very different from Stevens, of ores, crystal, geodes. Aspects in the same domain in the second sentence then open into, and set relations to, very different domains, writing and speech on the one hand, heaven on the other. This collocation is almost classically tonic, and the rest of the poem could be derived from it, down to the access of the steadfastly general and mysterious "Herzgewordenes" ("heart-become"). The first syllable here closes the sound as well, because it is the only word in the poem that rhymes with the first noun in the poem, "Erze." Celan's customary reflexive invocations, built on blunt inferences, recycle elements in nature that are intensified through syncopations to become disturbing evocations, "blubbernde Radspur"—something obsessing enough to be repeated with clearer variation, "Blubbernde Wege." This is a greeting that characterizes its inferences, finally, as beyond greeting, "grusslos." It does not know where the fingerthoughts are pointing. The unwritten hardens into speech, but this is a modality that also involves "the unrepeatable," and in a way in which the poetic assertions de facto stubbornly transcend their self-canceling predications:

by moving on. But the sharp point of the poem begins with irrepressible recrudescences of a Holocaust contemplation, the dead star, including the one the Jew was forced to wear; and perhaps even "Buchecker" carries reminiscences of Buchenwald.[22]

Derrida remarks generally of Celan's poetry that the very dates attached to it or cited in it are both exact and suspended into a virtual exemplariness. The dates are, in his terms, both empirical and essential, contemplating and offering to the auditor a sort of shibboleth. He includes this poem specifically in his discussion—and we can gather these and other poetic gestures under the definitions he accords:

> With this distinction between the empirical and the essential a limit gets confused, the limit of philosophy as such, the philosophical distinction. Philosophy finds itself, and finds itself once again then in the trappings of the poetic, that is, of literature. It finds itself there again because indecision about this limit is perhaps that which provokes it the most to think. It finds itself there again, but it is not necessarily lost there, as those believe, in their tranquil credulity, who think they know where this limit crosses and hold to it fearfully, ingenuously, though without innocence, denuded of that which one could call *philosophical experience:* a certain questioning traversal of the limit, insecurity with regard to the boundary of the philosophic field—and above all *the experience of the language,* always as poetic, or literary, as it is philosophic.[23]

One can take these fine discriminations still further, without directing ad hominem arguments, as this passage does, to those who might take an opposing or qualifying stance. And in doing so, we can assert that the experience of language may indeed be as poetic as it is philosophic, and always so, but only prior to an act of utterance. Once an act of utterance has been made—a supposition on which this passage itself rightly rests —one can always ascertain the primary thrust, except in the rare cases (there are no modern ones) where the philosophic act and the poetic act wholly converge. On the ground of philosophic utterance, we can without confusion recognize the discourse as such to be aiming at decidability even when it makes the case for radical undecidability, whether it enchains arguments in the mode of Hume or Kant or Husserl, on the one hand, or presents hermeneutic extrapolations, on the other hand, in the mode of Hegel or Heidegger or Deleuze or Foucault—or Derrida. The two modes, argument and interpretation, can be combined as they are in Plato.

There is, for this reason, no "undecidedness" about the limit between poetry and philosophy once an actual utterance has been brought before us, though in a still different mode—which Plato begins to use, following Heraclitus—it is possible to combine their procedures. No one would make the mistake, and not just because of meter, of confusing Nietzsche's poems or, for that matter, his musical compositions with his philosophical statements, though they may contain assertions of their own limits and extrapolations into historical discourse at greater length or lesser. No one would remove Lacan's discourse—however it be classified—from a psychoanalysis that amounts to a hermeneutic and linguistic epistemology, though it borrows both from poets like Sophocles and from philosophers like Kant in ways so allusive as not easily to rise either to argument or to interpretation. Therefore it might seem ornamental; but that question—Is it argument or interpretation or ornament?—can itself be left undecided, or even undecidable, and still we could decide on the nature and thrust of Lacan's discourse. We could decide, indeed, on its clear intention of decidability, and even without having to define it.

So much of Celan's language, in its modernity, jibes with the philosophical presuppositions of Stevens, for example, and the title of the collection from which this poem comes, *Die Niemandsrose,* is quite reconcilable with such statements of Stevens as "Nothing that is not here and the nothing that is," though in terms of temperamental affiliation Celan is the more Heideggerian, Stevens the more Husserlian. Both start for their discourse with the presupposition that a strength is gained and a door to wisdom opened wide when, to reverse Derrida's keen and commutable proposition, poetry finds itself once again in the trappings of philosophy. Moreover, what Philippe Lacoue-Labarthe calls the "vertigo of the vertigo" in Celan puts his philosophical concerns at the center of theological ones, the questioning in which the "nothing" of Heidegger converges with the "Niemandsrose" to address God in his absence.[24] Such questionings, as Hans-Georg Gadamer had earlier pointed out, converge with the self-questioning of the poet: "Where shadows fall and darken there is always also a light present, and light generally. . . . The I is a fisher who throws out his net. Throwing out the net is a procedure of pure awaiting. Who has thrown out his net has done all he can and must wait till something gets caught."[25]

The radicality of this initial supposition puts either Celan or Stevens, for all their own differences from each other, into a different mode from Blake (whom Derrida happens to quote here), since Blake is one of the rare poets after antiquity, perhaps the only one, who enunciates philosophical propositions and interpretations in poetic form. And all modern poets incorporate ideas very differently from, say, the Pope of the *Essay on Man,* who adopts and versifies the opinions of Shaftesbury, contextualizing them complexly by addressing the whole to Bolingbroke, but without either rethinking them or sublating them into the Celanesque and Stevensesque reworkings of philosophical questions.

On the side of philosophy, it is one thing for Heidegger to assert that the encoding of wisdom into poetry is what makes it abide; as Friedrich Hölderlin said, "Was bleibet aber stiften die Dichter" ("What poets establish abides"). And it is a different practice for Heidegger's own discourse to play hermeneutically and ratiocinatively with combining terms —such as *Welt, Erde, Ding, Er-eignis*—that he treats as though they were condensed or thickened (another meaning of "dichten," as he reminds us) into the language. In his terms, the "thing" of an artistic perception opens up for the "unconcealedness" (*Unverborgenheit*) of the many relations to the perceptual world—these relations (*Bezüge*) distinct from but ultimately including other kinds of relations (*Beziehungen*). This thing, as it is embedded in a word, posits through the artistic act an awareness that it is a unity of the multiplicity, the manifoldness, in the perceptions that it encodes. And in modern poetry, the handling of the poem compasses and sets forth not only such an act of intensive "saying" (*Sagen*) but also an awareness that the act has been carried through.

Extending this point, we could quote Derrida again: "Second parenthesis: I have several times abstained from evoking a strong addressing of Heidegger or to Heidegger. His necessity can escape no one. For the same reason I shall say nothing here of what there would be to say about other thinkers—Buber, Levinas, Blanchot, and others."[26] Here Derrida calls thinkers a quartet of writers who base themselves on philosophical discourse in modes that shade into religious thought or theoretical criticism. In abstaining from evoking their notions, he does a silent homage to the principle I am here asserting not only of the primacy of the wisdom in the utterances of achieved modern poetry but of the poet's awareness of that primacy and of its access to spirit.

Open forms are especially congenial to such modes of poetic reflexivity; they allow the poem to look associative and conversational. Such is the case even with the poems in blank verse that Stevens characteristically leaves open-ended. Regularity of form, when it is invoked to handle the reflexive, may tend toward irony, and this is the case not only with the rhymed poems of Eliot and Pound but with much of the rhymed work of later formal poets such as James Merrill and Wilbur, when they get beyond versified opinion or tourist watercolors. Merrill's shorter poems are arch, and they organize their perceptions so as successfully to countenance multiplicity, advertising their tightness, as do Empson's short poems. Wilbur's shorter poems achieve a fusion of nostalgia and archness, as do his sub-Stevensesque blank-verse meditations in the vein of "Walking to Sleep" and "Lying." Such poems do succeed in dramatizing a self-questioning that the form keeps short of final reverberations. The reverberations of image-thinking become just a play on top of the essaylike conclusions. They operate at the border between the traditional and the modern, where self-consciousness, multiplicity, and the dramatized impulse to range are still discernible, even when some evenness of the expected threatens to subvert them. That, of course, is the threat against any poetic expression; it may not get out into the clear of perception, a fact that facility in this or that technique can disguise but not conceal.

When it does get into the clear of perception, an actual experience—that of the poem—has been hieraticized into value, the value of the poem and of its experience. The self is two selves, that of before the poem and that of after. But these two selves are, as it were, split and rejoined in a time sequence. The same self is split and rejoined through the epiphany that spreads "evenly" through the poem. The reader has become a sort of initiate through the epiphany of the poem.[27] As I said at the beginning of this chapter, the term "secular" is too exclusive, the term "religious" too assertive and oversimplifying, to be applied to such utterances and the experience of them. We could call them "spiritual"—and this seems the most appropriate term, in spite of all the attendant and elusive difficulties in using it—as we can see a spiritual element, taking the term in its broadest sense, in the poems I have quoted.

If we ask what the spiritual element in Ponge, for example, might be, it would be connected to the characteristics I have been tracing in modern poetry—his as well as others'—to a self-consciousness, a containment of multiplicity, and an address of range. His poems are spiritual in that they produce a refreshment of the world activated between an "estrangement" ("ostranyenie") of the object and extrapolations from familiarization. Ponge speaks in "L'Assiette" of "l'humble interposition de porcelaine entre l'esprit pur et l'appétit" ("the humble interposition of porcelain between pure spirit and appetite").[28] "N'est-ce trop pour l'esprit pur?" ("Is this not too much for pure spirit?") he says, returning the rhetoric of the rhetorical question to a verbalizing ease of withdrawal from the Valéryesque assertion in the very estranging act of asserting it.[29]

Modern poetry's very uncertainties move it into a sort of questing, as well as questioning, of the spirit, whereas even the theological poets of earlier traditions, such as Dante, John Milton, or even Blake, rest on the givens of their situation. They do not need such initiation, while the modern reader, like the modern poet, does. This poetry, again to adapt Heidegger, comes in a time of need, "in dürftiger Zeit." Self-awareness, multiplicity, and range—when the poet brings them to perception— allow the spirit a purchase on the world, even if it be accomplished at the cost of occasional triviality—as in Ashbery, Breton, or, rarely, Stevens —or even at the cost of an integral doctrine with an evil component— as in Pound. The act of bringing the self-awareness to its encompassing utterance, brief or lengthy, transcends such limiting attributes.

3

Point, Closure, Amplitude, and the
Conditions of Utterance

Wordsworth, Whitman, and Rimbaud

1

THE RHETORICAL STRUCTURES to which recent critics have given attention are usually internal to the work and do not directly involve the social conditions in which a poetic utterance is brought forward, conditions that operate as *pragmatic* in the sense that linguists have borrowed from Rudolph Carnap, that is, those conditions which cannot be accounted for by the analysis of diction and syntax. As Goffman and others have shown us, these social circumstances, as their *pragmatics* surround an utterance of any sort, can go fairly deep. Setting forth an utterance will characteristically involve all kinds of prior constraints.[1] And this will be all the more the case for so full and so special an utterance as a poem. Just in terms of its rhetoric, a poem's communicative act involves more than just its technical turns, what for Aristotle is its art or *techné*. Rhetoric, in these ancient terms, is an art of persuasion, and poems do more than just persuade, as the ancient distinction between rhetoric and poetics implies. Without looking at more modern formulations, we may note that poetry, to begin with, can be seen to comprise and conflate the three Aristotelian types of rhetoric: it is epideictic in that it praises and/or censures a present state of affairs; it is deliberative in that it goes through the process of working out what amounts to an assessment for the future; and it is even forensic in that it carries implications for what amounts to a conclusion about the past—for Wordsworth a personal past, for Milton a generic one. And in Wordsworth the procedure of inference moves ahead in a constant access to foreshortened logical-philosophical enchainments very similar to the kind that Aristotle sets at the base of an informed rhetorical practice.

The pragmatic situation of a poem is deep and complicated, respond-ing to conditions that reach through the whole society. These conditions are, of course, dialogic in ways Bakhtin has elaborated.[2] The dialogic itself is a recoverable echo of the conditions that define its mode of pre-sentation, and this is the case even if in particular instances we do not (or cannot) perform the complex acts of historical recovery. Moreover, as has often been observed, poetry is a sort of seismograph for changing assumptions, and these will tie in with both the extrapolable doctrines and the special compositional practices of such poets as Wordsworth, Rimbaud, and Whitman, whose practices and techniques have often been discussed but whose conditions have less often been assessed. Without at all attempting a full account, I should like to make some observations about their own redefinitions of the poetic situations in which they found themselves.[3] One can begin by observing that each of these poets in his own way subverts the literary goal of "point." The denial of point is the needle's eye that each poet had to get through in order to find a voice for measuring his expansive universe.

Point was a predominant goal of eighteenth-century poetic style, whether in the satiric or the sublime mode. This "quality in speech or writing which arrests attention," this "pungency" or "witty and inge-nious turn of thought"—I take and meld these definitions from the NED—"arrests" the expression into what we can imagine as the silence that invites assent and the feeling of completion or closure. It is an eco-nomical, even a parsimonious, stylistic goal, and as such it is well suited to epigram; James Hutton has traced it in the persistence of the *Greek Anthology* tradition into the Renaissance.[4] Pope refers to it, and Dr. Johnson is praised for it. When Samuel Taylor Coleridge describes his own poetic formation in the first chapter of the *Biographia Literaria,* he already puts himself at one remove from "those with whom I con-versed," from the admirers of Pope, whose verse he praises as having "condensed and invigorated" the poetry of the previous century. In commenting on their "logic of wit," he goes on to state as a limiting defect—using "point" in the sense of a period at the end of a sentence, though the other point is also at issue—that "a point was looked for at the end of each second line, and the whole was, as it were, a *sorites,* or, if I may exchange a logical for a grammatical metaphor, a conjunction disjunctive, of epigrams." Here, in Aristotelian fashion, he connects too concise a style with too closely enchained an argument, with the syllogistic figure in which the conclusion of one in a series is the premise of another. And this is what the expatiations that Wordsworth was to engage in would never reduce themselves to.

Point is perpetually bringing expression to a head. It at once displays and completes wit, and in its social manifestations it could be described as an antithetical counterpart to Renaissance *sprezzatura,* since it does not just extravagantly take the stage but, in its concision, also implies that it will carry out all its utterance within the confines of the polite reciprocity of social interchange, going silent within its circle so that others may speak. Such a literary convention is congruent with such conversational conventions as gossip, and it would put us on the trail of such congruences to note that gossip is quite close to the poetry of Pope and Dryden, and even somewhat to that of Ben Jonson, Donne, and even Marvell, for all their differences. But gossip is quite far from the work of the three poets I am addressing.[5]

Wordsworth curiously describes the goal of the *Lyrical Ballads* in the first preface almost exclusively in terms of his aiming for a normal and conversational language of "a man speaking to men," to use the language of the second preface. In the first preface, he defines it more specifically, and with less oracular sweep, as "the language of conversation in the middle and lower classes of society," which he "adapted to the purposes of poetic pleasure." As A. C. Goodson says of the deep currents running here for the theory of language, "The change of air had everything to do with a changing sense of the possibilities of public discourse."[6] Wordsworth locates the possibility of a new approach, oddly, in the area of diction rather than in the area of the rules of linguistic interchange. Diction remains his explicit focus in the longer second preface, where he provides a much broader theoretical grounding for his consistent claim and speaks of the "expectation" that a reader brings to a poem and the "promise" made implicitly by the poet—an expectation and a promise he says he is revising, again in terms of diction. He also discusses the appropriately humble subject matter for reflecting "feeling." He seems here not to see that the ultimate locus of feeling is his own intimate response, and in the arrangement of the first *Lyrical Ballads,* his contributions of "natural" poems (against Coleridge's "supernatural" ones) give narratives of humble sorrow the pride of place, from "The Foster Mother's Tale" and "The Female Vagrant," "The Thorn" and "The Idiot Boy," to "The Mad Mother" and "The Convict." "Lines Written a Few Miles above Tintern Abbey" is placed symptomatically last, as though his sense of his audience led him to want to place them in a grave frame of mind through contemplation of sorrow to soften them up for his own introspective gravity. Both *The Prelude* and *The Excursion* draw intermittently on such sorrowing tales as well, in ways that revise the posture of the poet toward his readers.

This double pull, toward introspection and toward empathy with man-in-nature, continues throughout Wordsworth's work, tending to set both himself and his reader off, but problematically. Resolving the problem of his double pull would be impossible on the ground of the poetry because its effort to compass its own shifts obliges it to endless amplification, which characterizes his poetic practice in both the general sense and in the sense of technical rhetoric (Aristotle's *to auxein, ta auxetika*). The large, comprehensive poem he never achieved has the paradoxical title *The Recluse,* but no recluse, no shut-in, could ever accomplish the act of merging with the sights and persons out in the wide world. Vis-à-vis such experiences, a recluse would resemble the Blind Beggar, whose story is pinned to his chest in *The Prelude.* Wordsworth calls him a "type / Or emblem, of the utmost that we know / Both of ourselves and of the universe" (7, 617–19). And in this light, the deferral even of *The Prelude* itself through the decades of its revisions almost founders on the paradox, escaping miraculously through the amplitude to which the poet continues his access. Indeed, for Wordsworth this is a lifelong process if one takes the viewpoint that the unfinished *Recluse* was a project allowing for perpetual fragmentation on the one hand and endless amplification on the other. And this persists, as Alan Bewell argues, in the face of Wordsworth's deeply ingrained intention to continue the humanistic projects of the Enlightenment.[7]

This amplitude, however, reaches not only out of the Enlightenment but beyond it. As a means of escape, it has as its signature not only the imitation of Milton's high style, rising above both Pope and Dryden, but also the deeper subversion of Milton's verse paragraph. What Milton

shares with Dryden is an orbicularity of style in which the verse para-
graph comes to a stop, distributes its members in an elaborate ordon-
nance, and constitutes a controlled and internally closed unit, suggesting
a link that is not at all tentative between poet and reader. Wordsworth's
verse paragraphs are very different. Without being exactly paratactic,
they are additive and can be amplified endlessly. Lines can be added to
them on and on—as he himself added them in the revised *Prelude*. And
so the whole poem itself is an amplification of the two-book, and then
the five-book *Prelude,* just as the *Excursion* is a further amplification; and
all are conceived as giant fragments to be fitted into *The Recluse* at some
time so remote that it could never have been carried through—the first
verses of *The Prelude* were written in 1798 at Goslar, and Wordsworth
died more than fifty years later, in 1850. All these efforts carry traces of
the reach toward a vast comprehensiveness, and at the same time they
are fragmentary, connecting as they keep producing large glimpses of the
transcendental signifier, Man.

The first part Wordsworth wrote for the poem, "Was it for this,"
retains its character as an associative break in the middle of the line,
through its entire fifty-year progress from fragment to final version:

> Then feels immediately some hollow thought
> Hang like an interdict upon her hopes.
> This is my lot; for either still I find
> Some imperfection in the chosen theme,
> Or see of absolute accomplishment
> Much wanting, so much wanting, in myself,
> That I recoil and droop, and seek repose
> In listlessness from vain perplexity,
> Unprofitably travelling towards the grave,
> Like a false steward who hath much received
> And renders nothing back.
>   Was it for this
> That one, the fairest of all rivers, loved
> To blend his murmurs with my nurse's song,
> And, from his alder shades and rocky falls,
> And from his fords and shallows, sent a voice
> That flowed along my dreams? For this, didst thou,
> O Derwent! travelling over the green plains
> Near my "sweet birthplace," didst thou, beauteous stream,

Make ceaseless music through the night and day,
Which with its steady cadence, tempering
Our human waywardness, composed my thoughts
To more than infant softness, giving me
Among the fretful dwellings of mankind
A knowledge, a dim earnest, of the calm
That Nature breathes among the hills and groves?

(1805 *Prelude*, 1, 261–79)[8]

The midline subject-changing break is characteristic of Wordsworth. There are, for example, before this early occurrence in the first book, at least fifteen instances of sentences that come to a full stop in the middle of a line, where a new sentence more than a line in length is then begun.[9] In the passage quoted, a general lack is superseded by the question of specific memories of what has an air of plenitude, though a lack is still being queried. This query he posits as participatory rather than just summary, the way Milton saw *Paradise Lost* ("to justify"), however processively Milton's poem be read. Here "Was it for this" is one of a series of rhetorical questions, roughly to be paraphrased: "Did nature shower me with treasures so that I would be incapable of settling on a theme?" or, more emphatically: "Did my early bliss come to nothing?" The answer to these questions is no insofar as he has indeed got the poem under way. But it is yes insofar as by this point in the poem, he has not been able to bridge the gap between the search he has amplified in description and the treasures he has not yet quite got to explanatory fullness. Consequently there is a sort of double gap: first, between the present verbal attempt and the actual past experiences; second, between the declaration of incapacity and the questions that fail to bridge it. Rhetorical questions, in ordinary language, tend to be aimed squarely at a prior declaration when there is one. The gapping allows Wordsworth, I would assert, not to document incapacity further but to use these indirections as a spur to the amplifications that will exactly get him over the gap by an overfullness of language; the gap is there for him to make such leaps.

Such dialogic self-presentation implies a profound transposition of terms in the contract between poet and reader in their social setting. The poet may participate to some degree in the nexus of patronage, but even a poet such as Crabbe, who was so dependent on the patronage he received, aims the presentation of his narratives at a version of point, thereby keeping them within the set bounds of converse. Wordsworth, on the other hand, casts himself as a ruminating solitary and also as a sort of sage. The world is to sit up and listen; and he behaved this way in social conversation, according to Keats's testimony. Insofar as Wordsworth's poems are an unbridled conversation, they imply the dialogic contract of an open-ended democratic society, a world that borrows the attributes of private sociability rather than those just of public self-presentation. But to the degree that he presents himself as an oracle, he acts as a prophet, the aristocrat of nature, who behaves in profoundly different ways, and by profoundly different rules, from Pope, who was an aristocrat of society.

Such subject-breaks as the one that Wordsworth built into his poem when he mounted the "Was it for this" passage into his sequence also organize larger sections of the poem within a given book. Such breaks are endemic to *The Prelude,* and to the whole enormous project of which it is itself a disjunct part. The breaks often occur between largish sections. To show this, I should like to revert to the familiar nest-robbing passage, a characteristically long run. It is also characteristically so digressive that the poet's very amplitude obliges us to look carefully to see how the topics meld and disjoin:

> Low breathings coming after me, and sounds
> Of undistinguishable motion, steps
> Almost as silent as the turf they trod.
>
> . . . .
> . . . Oh! when I have hung
> Above the raven's nest, by knots of grass
> And half-inch fissures in the slippery rock
> But ill sustained, and almost, as it seemed,
> Suspended by the blast which blew amain,
> Shouldering the naked crag, oh, at that time
> While on the perilous ridge I hung alone,
> With what strange utterance did the loud dry wind
> Blow through my ears; the sky seemed not a sky
> Of earth—and with what motion moved the clouds!
>
>   The mind of man is framed even like the breath
> And harmony of music. There is a dark
> Invisible workmanship that reconciles
> Discordant elements, and makes them move

In one society. . . .
. . . .
    One evening—surely I was led by her—
I went alone into a shepherd's boat,
A skiff that to a willow tree was tied
Within a rocky cave, its usual home.
. . . .
She was an elfin pinnace; lustily
I dipped my oars into the silent lake,
And, as I rose upon the stroke, my boat
Went heaving through the water like a swan—
When, from behind that craggy steep, till then
The bound of the horizon, a huge cliff,
As if with voluntary power instinct
Upreared its head. I struck and struck again,
And, growing still in stature, the huge cliff
Rose up between me and the stars, and still
With measured motion, like a living thing
Strode after me. . . .

                    (1805 *Prelude*, 1, 330–412.)

Here the full blocks of verse (I quote about half of the fifty-eight lines
in the run) have the double character of terms in an argument and points
in an association-pattern, keeping open the inferential structure for the
reader. The jump from nest robbing to hearing the music of the spheres
and then to solitary rowing assimilates the two country-boy activities to
a full-scale participation in what the speaker's younger self both fears
and defers. The deep harmony of mind and nature, the concrete experi-
ences and the epistemology can be joined, of course, in the well-known
Wordsworthian psychology, to which commentators have justifiably
given much attention over recent years. But the abstract speculations and
the narratives of actual experience can be joined only by acts of recol-
lection and by a resolute confrontation of not self-consciousness but its
very lack. All of this has dialogic implications and, beyond them, social
ones as well. In the terms of Aristotelian rhetoric, the speaker attempts to
arouse the auditor not by a self-concealing and polished presentation of
ordered utterances but by a self-revelation in which the arousal of emo-
tion will come about by a sort of sympathy with the released expression
of like emotion in the poetry. The philosophical disquisitions subserve

this probing of the mind and heart; they are not the separate marshaled arguments of Pope's *Essay on Man*.

What all this does to the language and to the consequent posture of the poet is to pull in two directions: toward definition insofar as the episodes and their relation to argument are distinct, and at the same time toward endless deferral insofar as all statements enter the free association. Is, for example, the muffled music of "steps / Almost as silent as the turf they trod" thus to be accounted part of "The mind of man . . . framed even like the breath / And harmony of music?" Yes, as a participation; no, as an evasion. But finally yes, under the injunction "Praise to the end," which itself has the double character of a momentary influx of joy and a permanent philosophical principle.

I am not deconstructing Wordsworth here, as I might be if I were arguing that just one of these moves operated, or that the two aspects of the double approach were radically out of synchronization. I am in fact arguing the contrary: that they are radically in synchronization, and that the paradox which they defer also demonstrably finds expression in the force, and in what we can continue to call the sublimity of the poem. This sublimity is a central feature of the poem's evocative stance to the reader. So "workmanship" as well as "harmony"—and also "elements," "society," plus (which I have not quoted) "terrors," "thoughts," "feelings," "infused," "mind," "existence," "means," "Nature," "end," "ministry" (all in the "mind of man" segment)—cannot be said to evade the philosophical definitions from Aristotle or even Plato through Leibniz, not omitting Locke, that hover over the passage. But they cannot be said to reticulate into an argument, either. They do not cheat the argument but rather defer it to a moment—or a verbal situation—beyond rapture, which at the same time turns out to be the developing subject of this poem ("The Growth of a Poet's Mind"). They offer the materials of ongoing definition rather than a fully consistent definition. Instead of further definition, indeed, the speaker shifts to another moment of rapture; and it is not till another twenty lines or so that he verges once again—under both excitement and emotion-recollected-in-tranquillity—on the philosophical abstractions "voluntary power instinct" (389), "dim and undetermined sense / Of unknown modes of being" (392–93), "thoughts," "shapes," "objects," "images" (394–96). The revisions in the 1850 version do not here move to further sharpness of definition, as they sometimes try to do, but rather to the suppression of some narrative detail, except at the hinge on "Nature." Thus instead of "ministry / More palpable, and so she dealt with me. / . . . / One evening (surely I was led by her)," the 1850 version has "ministry / More palpable, as best might suit her aim. / . . . / One summer evening (led by her) I found." It adds the sub-Aristotelian "aim" and the specificity of season ("summer"), while it subtracts the effusive "surely."

To dwell on the poet's assumptions, it may be seen that Pope's style, or for that matter Collins's, employs a diction that Coleridge has shown to contain elements that are partially retained by Wordsworth, whose verse is not so conversational as he fancies.[10] But insofar as the eighteenth-century poet attains to point, he/she has constantly in view, through the poem's organization, the constriction of polite society and of its codes, which do not give the floor for long to anyone. Walter Jackson Bate shows well that Coleridge's conversation poems, one of which is so labeled in the first *Lyrical Ballads,* have their roots in the play of voice in Pope and Dryden.[11] But their sense of newness is linked to a sense of superseding that particular code of polite and witty conversation. The range of diction does not change very much, but the assumptions of the ruminative speaker do change radically, and when Coleridge and Wordsworth stress diction, they are unwittingly confining themselves to eighteenth-century postulates. The critic's mantle thus retained a cut that the poet's did not, in ways they could not see. In both Wordsworth and Coleridge, point, with its goal of concision, is being superseded by a profoundly different approach to closure, an access to an amplitude that redefines the relation between the poetic speaker and the presumed audience.

The speaking subject in such a poetry carries a tremendous communicative weight because it has programmatically ceased to rely on the polite society in which the coded literary utterance had a recognized place. It divides itself, evanesces, and in *The Prelude* calls on an idealized addressee, the "Friend," whose intimacy and lack of need for instruction place him on a par with the speaker—a heavy revision of the classical addressee in Ptah-Hotep, Theognis, or Lucretius, who is a generalized recipient of instruction. The Romantic poet also revises the biblical addressee of the prophet, a collective nation urgently in need of reformation. Hence the prophetic element in Wordsworth, too, well noted by Hartman, gets reabsorbed into the expanding and self-criticizing self. Conversations, with the Leech Gatherer or the Wanderer, are themselves framed and reabsorbed as lessons for the speaker, verging on near-identification in such third-person narratives as the Boy of Winander (1805 *Prelude*, 389–449); the self-division, into perceptive youth and ruminative poet, helps to license this very identification.[12]

The onward thrust of the poet's rumination keeps the subject, and the lines of communication, characteristically open and undefined, a direction that is hinted at even in *Poetical Sketches* and *An Evening Walk*, where Wordsworth keeps spilling ahead out of his couplets, slurring the goal of point, which had seemed an inescapable attribute of the well-formed "pointed" couplet. And once he has got into the open with his voice, the ruminative character folds his language over into an elusive fusion of ongoing approximation on the one hand—Donald Davie's "fiduciary symbols"[13]—and on the other hand a use of abstractions that will allow the interpreter to place pressure on them and derive something approaching a consistent doctrine. Such a fusion of indeterminacy with achieved expression is found in short poems, and the use of "thing" in "A Slumber Did My Spirit Seal" is a notable example. It also comes about in "The stationary blasts of waterfalls," in a physical characterization where the disjunctive paradox pointed out by Paul de Man is only part of what is going on in such lines.[14] In its further capabilities, Wordsworth has managed to designate referentially an apprehension that the eye takes when it looks at a waterfall, much as a painter might vividly designate the mane of a horse by leaving certain lines and connections out that the eye would actually record. All such perceptions are put at the service of an amplifying rumination that at once comprises and falls short of the goal of comprehensive understanding. And the fixing of such a particular goes beyond the (itself complex) nature description of James Thomson in two directions: it is at once more particularized and more philosophized. Both these advances, again, are posited on a new sense of freedom in utterance, giving the amplitude a depth that redefines, as it engages, the dialogic. One intimation of how this works can be derived from the fact that these waterfalls are modalized as contingent examples at this moment of enraptured speaking, many sights rather than just a single sight, caught up in the ongoing self-presentation and large deduction:

> The immeasurable height
> Of woods decaying, never to be decayed,
> The stationary blasts of waterfalls,
> And everywhere along the hollow seat

Winds thwarting winds, bewildered and forlorn,
The torrents shooting from the clear blue sky,
The rocks that muttered close upon our ears—
Black drizzling crags that spake by the wayside
As if a voice were in them—the sick sight
And giddy prospect of the raving stream,
The unfettered clouds and region of the heavens,
Tumult and peace, the darkness and the light,
Were all like workings of one mind, the features
Of the same face, blossoms upon one tree,
Characters of the great apocalypse,
The types and symbols of eternity,
Of first, and last, and midst, and without end.

(1805 *Prelude*, 6, 556–73)

The vividness of individual descriptive traces passes rapidly, gathered up in the almost breathless recounting of the emotional attributes in all their large range, for which the initial paradox of the "stationary blasts" may be taken to stand. It broaches a unity among all these extremities that the staggeringly large attributions of theological and philosophical inference in the crescendo of the passage both gather up and master. Thomson, by contrast, keeps his eye steadily on the object:

Thus up the mount, in airy vision wrapt,
I stray, regardless whither; till the sound
Of a near Fall of water every sense
Wakes from the charm of thought: swift-shrinking back
I check my steps, and view the broken scene.
    Smooth to the shelving brink a copious Flood
Rolls fair, and placid: where collected all,
In one impetuous torrent, down the steep
In thundering shoots, and shakes the country round.
At first, an azure sheet, it rushes broad;
Then whitening by degrees, as prone it falls,
And from the loud-resounding rocks below
Dash'd in a cloud of foam, it sends aloft
A hoary mist, and forms a ceaseless shower.[15]

The description as such is totally subsumed to the accuracy of picturing a single scene, as though Thomson were fulfilling a contract for a landscape that could be hung. He is present, and his mood of "airy vision"

64

could be accommodated to Wordsworth's—except that Wordsworth insists on putting himself at the center of the picture, and of letting his feeling engulf the many scenes, so that they become instantiations of what he felt, as he may go on to imply, while Thomson subserves an ideal of point in the careful coherence and finish of his phrases, even though the wittier versions of point are totally absent. The jags of philosophical summary in Wordsworth, in fact, have the succinctness and the ratiocinative quickness of point; but they entirely lack not only the measured rhythms of that ideal but also its direction toward social converse. Not banter but testimony is the mode, a testimony that quietly declares it can go on as long as it has to, without Thomson's Horatian obligation of being useful and pleasing.

2

IN WHITMAN, the famous unstable "you," which at times could be either the poet or the single "intimate" reader, converges with the idealized collective audience of a future in which the proper place of the poet's text will itself converge to the center of the society it has helped to bring about:[16]

> Diverge, fine spokes of light, from the shape of my head, or any one's head, in the sunlit water!
> Come on, ships from the lower bay! pass up or down, white-sail'd schooners, sloops, lighters!
> Flaunt away, flags of all nations! be duly lower'd at sunset!
> Burn high your fires, foundry chimneys! cast black shadows at nightfall! cast red and yellow light over the tops of the houses!
> Appearances, now or henceforth, indicate what you are,
> You necessary film, continue to envelop the soul,
> About my body for me, and your body for you, be hung our divinest aromas,
> Thrive, cities—bring your freight, bring your shows, ample and sufficient rivers,
> Expand, being than which none else is perhaps more spiritual,
> Keep your places, objects than which none else is more lasting.
>
> You have waited, you always wait, you dumb, beautiful ministers,
> We receive you with free sense at last, and are insatiate henceforward,
> Not you any more shall be able to foil us, or withhold yourselves from us,

We use you, and do not cast you aside—we plant you permanently within us,
We fathom you not—we love you—there is perfection in you also,
You furnish your parts toward eternity,
Great or small, you furnish your parts toward the soul.[17]

This conclusion to "Crossing Brooklyn Ferry" subsumes transience and permanence into one another; Wordsworth's "spot of time" has become a universe and includes all those in it, the "you" in the flow of the river ebbing and flooding to embrace future generations as well: "I am with you, you men and women of a generation, or ever so many generations hence" (21). The afflatus of such long lines pulls up for closure the two blank-verse lines at the end of the poem. But before he gets to them in his final section, the poet lets out the stops with a long series of imperatives, which do not soften to mere declaratives till "You have waited, you always wait." "[Y]ou dumb, beautiful ministers" cannot be anything less than everything named. More particularly, "you" here refers to cities; but since cities comprise the crowds of persons invoked, past and future, the one merges into the other. The very audience is being defined and in a sense created as its members are being collectively addressed. They may find articulation, turning their beauty away from dumbness in the voice of the poet, and so may carry out the function of "ministers" by being called so by him.

I am emphasizing that the expansion of the connecting link between poet and presumed auditors, and the ad hoc, ongoing definition of who those auditors might be, licenses not only Whitman's amplitude in general, here and throughout his life, but also the posited continuity in which the speaker can be at once suspended on a boat moving across a narrow channel and in touch with his own past and prospective lives on both sides of that channel, as well as beyond it to nation, to sea and sky, and to all the participatory realizations that he invokes. "What is it then between us?" he asks (54), where "it" is as general as possible, and the "us" has already been made to include cities and people, past and future, as well as his presumed immediate auditors. And his very specification amplifies, "What is the count of the scores or hundreds of years between us?" (55). "It avails not," he goes on to say (56), and this asseveration is itself anaphorically swept up in the amplification of the poem, because he had already said it: "It avails not, time nor place—distance avails not" (20).

Here one of Whitman's many statements about his poetic aims is particularly apposite, and so vivid in its description that he actually incorporated some of its phrasing into the poems of Leaves of Grass:

I want that tenor, large and fresh as the creation, the orbed parting of
whose mouth shall lift over my head the sluices of all the delight yet dis-
covered for our race.—I want the soprano that lithely overleaps the stars,
and convulses me like the love-grips of her in whose arms I lay last
night.—I want an infinite chorus and orchestrium, wide as the orbit of
Uranus, true as the hours of the day, and filling my capacities to receive,
as thoroughly as the sea fills its scooped out sands.—I want the chanted
Hymn whose tremendous sentiment shall uncage in my breast a thousand
wide-winged strengths and unknown ardors and terrible ecstacies—
putting me through the flights of all the passions—dilating me beyond
time and air—startling me with the overture of some unnameable hor-
ror—calmly sailing me all day on a bright river with lazy slapping
waves—stabbing my heart with myriads of forked distractions more furi-
ous than hail or lightning—lulling me drowsily with honeyed mor-
phine—tightening the fakes of death about my throat, and awakening me
again to know by that comparison, the most positive wonder in the
world, and that's what we call life.[18]

Here Whitman expresses aims in which point would never have a place.
Point is a literary ideal with social correlatives of the polite laconic state-
ment, the verbal exhibition of modesty by self-containment and of skill
by condensation. The ideal of the newspaper writer is one that leads at
least to an impression of amplitude, an impression that much has been
communicated, although in a little space. But though such a newspaper
as the *Brooklyn Eagle* would inevitably take as some of its grist the *faits
divers* that are so close to gossip, the poet Whitman himself eschews the
very gossip that Pope embraced. His conception of the poet did not
allow for it, and it would take such further mutations as Pound's revi-
sion of Browning to bring such small change back into the poetic cash
register.

Not only Whitman's newspaper apprenticeship opened him to what
ultimately became the long line of a rhythm that, looking back now over
more than a hundred years, is an atypical free verse, since free verse very
soon left behind the Whitmanian amplitude for a modernist version of
point. Opera, too, that other tradition to which Whitman was deeply
devoted,[19] is a tradition of amplitude, one that in the passage quoted he
expands into a set of desiderata for his poetry that, if realized, would
constitute a transcendent version of the Wagnerian *Gesamtkunstwerk*.

3

RIMBAUD so to speak assumes the "hypocrite lecteur, mon semblable, mon frère" of Baudelaire, another kind of equal addressee.[20] The sooth-saying in *Une Saison en enfer* need not even pause to insist that there might be a resistance to these uncomfortable home truths; and the instabilities of Wordsworth's self or Whitman's "you" get involved in the apocalyptic schematization of a visionary letter, "Je est un autre."[21] Later critics have got caught up in the possible intricacies of this proposition, but in the communicative context of this poem, it functions flatly, at the pitch of an ongoing utterance that absorbs the well-formed Baudelairean poems such as "Larme" into a flow as just momentary eddies in an onrush of a prose poetry that also lacks the formedness and closure, the classical stance, of Baudelaire's prose poems:[22]

> Ce fut d'abord une étude. J'écrivais des silences, des nuits, je notais l'inexprimable. Je fixais des vertiges.
>
> _____
>
> Loin des oiseaux, des troupeaux, des villagoises,
> Que buvais-je, à genoux dans cette bruyère
> Entourée de tendres bois de noisetiers,
> Dans un brouillard d'après-midi tiède et vert?
>
> Que pouvais-je boire dans cette jeune Oise,
> —Ormeaux sans voix, gazon sans fleurs, ciel couvert!—
> Boire à ces gourdes jaunes, loin de ma case
> Chérie? Quelque liqueur d'or qui fait suer.
>
> Je faisais une louche enseigne d'auberge.
> —Un orage vint chasser le ciel. Au soir
> L'eau des bois se perdait sur les sables vierges,
> Le vent de Dieu jetait des glaçons aux mares;
>
> Pleurant, je voyais de l'or—et ne pus boire.
> . . . .
>
> _____
>
> La vieillerie poétique avait une bonne part dans mon alchimie du verbe.
>
> Je m'habituai à l'hallucination simple: je voyais très franchement une mosquée à la place d'une usine, une école de tambours faite par des anges, des calèches sur les routes du ciel, un salon au fond d'un lac; les monstres, les mystères; un titre de vaudeville dressait des épouvantes devant moi.

Puis j'expliquai mes sophismes magiques avec l'hallucination des mots!

Je finis par trouver sacré le désordre de mon esprit. J'étais oisif, en proie à une lourde fièvre: j'enviais la félicité des bêtes,—les chenilles, qui représentent l'innocence des limbes, les taupes, le sommeil de la virginité![23]

It was at first a study. I wrote out silences and the nights. I recorded the inexpressible. I described frenzies.

———

> Far from birds, flocks and village girls,
> What did I drink, on my knees in that heather
> Surrounded by a graceful copse of hazel trees,
> In an afternoon mist warm and green?

> What could I drink in that young Oise,
> —Voiceless young elms, grass with no flowers, overcast sky!—
> Drinking from those yellow gourds, far from my beloved
> Cabin? Golden drinks that bring out sweat.

> I made a disreputable sign for an inn.
> —A storm came to chase off the sky. At evening
> The water of the woods was lost in the virgin sand,
> And God's wind cast icicles into the ponds;

> Weeping, I saw gold—and could not drink.
> . . . .

———

Poetic old-fashionedness figured largely in my alchemy of the word.

I grew accustomed to simple hallucination: I saw quite frankly a mosque in place of a factory, a school of drummers made up of angels, carriages on roads in the sky, a parlor at the bottom of the lake; monsters, mysteries. The title of a vaudeville conjured up horrors before me.

Then I explained my magic sophisms with the hallucination of words!

At the end I looked on the disorder of my mind as sacred. I was idle, a prey to a heavy fever. I envied the happiness of animals—caterpillars representing the innocence of limbo, moles, the sleep of virginity![24]

"Délires II, Alchimie du verbe" is the only one of the nine sections of *Une Saison en enfer* that presents rhymed poems. The poet breaks suddenly into the poem, as quoted above; and then in a fairly short space, he quotes six poems, a small anthology of his work, an exhibit of the activities he has been describing, as well as a continuation of them in a different key. The key has the character of retrospect, since the poems are brought in and framed as of his own earlier time. In the poem "Larme" itself, which he here inserts, revised, into his ampler poem, the Baudelairean point and closure have been softly imploded into the poem so that it reaches no rounded conclusion but dwells on visionary fragments that have drawn much commentary. "Je est un autre" reaches an extreme in "Je faisais une louche enseigne d'auberge"; or does it, since "Je faisais" could indicate not identification or even pretense but simple artisanal construction, a construction that the imperfect leaves open as to its completion?[25] But in all these cases, the "enseigne d'auberge" resists the closure of relationship to the prevailing memories of the speaker's kneeling in a quiet semipastoral landscape to drink, and then being unable to drink. Here all these marvelous gestures are at once subsumed and amplified into a list of examples. The poem "Larme" becomes an "étude," a "silence," perhaps even a sort of "nuit," if the "soir" of line 10 is taken for a key to the poem. And his final inability to drink is easily associable to both the "inexprimable" and an instance of "vertiges."

In "Alchimie du verbe," the gold of the water takes on another dimension, and the transformations continue in the rapid list of the next prose run, as though the evocation of "Larme" had licensed them. The new list of the second paragraph swiftly encompasses the sort of intense condensations of image—"des calèches sur les routes du ciel, un salon au fond d'un lac," and so on—that suggest Rimbaud's *Illuminations*. The poems there offer a kind of closure not found in *Une Saison en enfer*, but exploding still more richly into image-amplifications so open-ended that the very discontinuities between poems keep the associations moving, and we are not really allowed closure in the same sense that we are in the prose poems of Baudelaire's *Spleen de Paris*. Moreover, many of the poems in *Illuminations* are divided into sections, or spaced out into separable aphoristic-apocalyptic sentences in the fashion later adopted by Char, or cast into metrical lines.

4

WORDSWORTH, in a kind of contradiction, subverted the conversational element toward the oracular, and then advertised it as an ordinary language. Point came to Rimbaud sanctified by the whole French tradition, exemplified in Baudelaire's closeness to Racine. Radical as he was, Baudelaire never questioned what amounted to the goal of point, and his prose poems always opt, more even than Aloysius Bertrand does, for a neat closure after a short span. Point, in the slightly different sense of the continually arresting, remains in the journalistic world as the ideal of the sparkling piece that holds the attention of the reader. It is, of course, as a journalist that Whitman came to his style, writing daily in that prose idiom whose very point he would subvert by abandoning not only adherence to the classics, which he often stated, but what he never mentioned, the space limitations of the newspaper writer. He subverted the time constraint that lies faintly over even books of poems by keeping *Leaves of Grass* open-ended throughout his life.

All three of these poets operated at a strategic distance from their audience, Wordsworth in an initial near-obscurity; Whitman in quasi-disreputability; and Rimbaud in an intermittent notoriety, managed by withdrawals and returns until a very extensive withdrawal deferred return until too late. This strategic distance entailed intimating something that had changed, for which, in a circular fashion, our best evidence is such expressions as are to be found in these poets themselves. One can find an underlying new social assumption, which they at once intuited and provided, not only in their themes, and not just characteristically—as I have been arguing—in the particular license of an amplitude that for each of them kept the poem either open-ended or unfinished. This new assumption can be found in them as a tendency toward a panorama that includes both city and country, nature and a telescopic view of humanity, so that one could in some cases match their sense of time, for example, without reference to sources on which they might have drawn. So, as a concrete instance, Wordsworth can at times sound like Whitman (or vice versa):

> Briefly, we find (if tired of random sights
> And haply to that search our thoughts should turn)
> Among the crowd, conspicuous less or more
> As we proceed, all specimens of man
> Through all the colours which the sun bestows,
> And every character of form and face:
> The Swede, the Russian; from the genial south,
> The Frenchman and the Spaniard; from remote

America, the hunter Indian; Moors,
Malays, Lascars, the Tartar and Chinese,
And Negro Ladies in white muslin gowns.

(1805 *Prelude*, 7, 219–28)

In calling their assumptions "dialogic," one only begins to character-
ize the underlying social situation to which they are responding. In
Bakhtin's discussions, as in Aristotle's and Wordsworth's own, the atten-
tion is also to rhetoric, to the mix of diction and styles. "The word is
born," Bakhtin aptly says, "in a dialogue as a living rejoinder within it;
the word is shaped in dialogic interaction with an alien world that is
already in the object." Yet this "alien" world is also an intimate world of
deep assumption to which these poets keep a certain distance but deeply
intuit. Whitman, to begin with, emerges from nowhere. Rimbaud writes
—when he writes—constantly on the move, and finally in a state of
shocked disreputability withdrawn to the family village. The first lines
of *The Prelude* came to Wordsworth at Goslar, just as Frost wrote his
best-known New England poems in England. To characterize these
poets' deep assumptions that led them to amplitude—and were modified
in such later counterparts as Frost so as to lead him back to a version of
point—would involve attention to historical conditions, and a descrip-
tion of them would be endless. Industrialization, attention to the sub-
lime, and a threshold consciousness, Wordsworth's "something evermore
about to be," would surely figure in such a description. My intention,
however, has been not so much to describe as to indicate where the
characteristics of utterance show us a description might be called for.[26]

4

Image Intensification, the Self's Dialogic Posture, and Petrarchan Mutations

Donne and Shakespeare

POINT CONTAINS THE conversational in an order that implies an ideal of both politeness and concision. It is found not only in Frost, and in the poets against whom Wordsworth is reacting but in the Western tradition all the way back to the shaped epigram or epigrammatic poems of Alcaeus. If the conversational and the oracular represent poles of poetic utterance, through all its conflations of oral and written, then point may be seen as a force holding both the conversational and the oracular to a norm whose controlled middle asserts order. Point sharpens the work not only of Dante but also of his immediate predecessors and of all his various successors, through Chaucer and Shakespeare. The suppleness of Thomas Wyatt, the sobriety of Philip Sidney, the controlled richnesses of Spenser, the archnesses of Jonson, the delicacies of Robert Herrick and Marvell, the clarities of George Herbert, the intricacies of Donne, all exhibit point. And it is Milton's oracular pressures against the conversational "middle flight" he explicitly abjures that made him the model for those like Wordsworth and Blake, who sought a poetry that would reach beyond point.

The couplet, masterfully manipulated at the hands of Dryden and

Pope, is an appropriate, and in retrospect an inevitable, vehicle for point. It advertises its closure, its sharpness, its control and self-control, with every capping rhyme. It returns the poem to order and to a conception of order. In its swooping "middle flight" it does so conversationally, attaining a suppleness that within its conversational purview can imitate the oracular satirically, as in Dryden's *MacFlecknoe* and Pope's *Dunciad*. A norm is assumed, to which the deviations of the satire testify; and the language, as commentators have elaborately explained, remains normative.

So in the *Dunciad,* the firm ironic turn of praising "Dulness" and blaming "Wit" holds constantly to the point of providing a norm by the alert attention to subverting it. The achieved point of each couplet carries the Wit that Dulness, it is steadily implied, cannot attain:

> O! ever gracious to perplex'd mankind,
> Still spread a healing mist before the mind;
> And lest we err by Wit's wild dancing light,
> Secure us kindly in our native night.
> Or, if to Wit a coxcomb make pretense,
> Guard the sure barrier between that and Sense;
> Or quite unravel all the reas'ning thread,
> And hang some curious cobweb in its stead!
> As, forc'd from wind-guns, lead itself can fly,
> And pond'rous slugs cut swiftly thro the sky;
> As clocks to weight their nimble motion owe,
> The wheels above urg'd to the load below:
> Me emptiness, and Dulness could inspire,
> And were my Elasticity and Fire.
>
> (1742 *Dunciad,* book 1, 173–86)

The wit operative here is an instrument used to cut obliquely through the elaborate social process by which a Colley Cibber, the imagined speaker of these lines, can have become Poet Laureate. The darkness of that social process is so ominous that it indeed functions as a "mist," which is somehow misunderstood as salutory, or it would not be operative. Hence it is conceived of as "healing," though in fact it has, the poet is urging, the opposite effect. Consequently he provides the "reas'ning thread": the progress of these lines in his hands. The physics governing ballistics and the mechanics of clocks are enlisted to underscore both the possibility of apparent contradictions in the world of natural law and the consequent, analogous fatality of the lodged contradiction between poetic reception and poetic merit.

Pope's pride in his own poetic instrument, and his assuredness about it, were great enough for him to rewrite Donne, whom he "Versifyed," a procedure implying for Donne not just (in Pope's famously mistaken view) defective meter but also an uncertain handling of point. So Pope offers for the opening of Donne's second satire these lines:

> Yes; thank my stars! as early as I knew
> This Town, I had the sense to hate it too:
> Yet here, as ev'n in Hell, there must be still
> One Giant-Vice, so excellently ill,
> That all beside one pities, not abhors;
> As who knows Sapho, smiles at other whores.

This performs its wrought-iron work on Donne's fewer lines:

> Sir; though (I thank God for it) I do hate
> Perfectly all this town, yet there's one state
> In all things so excellently best,
> That hate, towards them, breeds pity towards the rest.[1]

The modulation of Donne's first line, from the abrupt monosyllabic opening through the parenthesis and on to the simple emphasis of the final "hate," allows itself more play of mind than Pope can accommodate (and, strangely, than he seems to understand). He sets up an antithesis between "know" and "hate," which Donne implies, and which induces the Roman Catholic Pope to mute Donne's "God" into "stars," perhaps so that no devotional perspectives can impede the play of mind that he then easily unleashes, a play that permits him then to invent a "Hell" and a "Giant-Vice," and to introduce the contrast between Sappho and other whores. He varies the word "hate" to "abhors" after a delay of four lines, thus changing Donne's initial rhyme word. Donne, however, following the train of mind he creates, is able to build the firmness of his own stance into the one word "perfectly," and to give it the emphasis of a dactylic inversion.

Pope strikes the posture of boiling Donne down and simplifying him into point. But Donne here is actually more condensed than Pope. Here six lines of Pope cover four of Donne, and Pope's whole version of this satire is sixteen lines longer than Donne's. Pope's point makes him seem to condense, when actually he is amplifying; he calls on his "Wit" to generate an even flow of pointed contrasts. An invariant norm sponsors a flow of varied juxtapositions.

Already in the work of Donne, the norms that Pope will bring to high polish are being stretched, the couplet harnessed to more robust work than the simple antitheses of point. And through all the range of Donne's work, in the pressure of his reach beyond point, a single poem, his Eighth Elegy, may be taken to show what his capabilities entail.

Along with Donne's robustness here, as it happens, goes a sharpness and complexity of image that was deeply exploited by Marvell, Herbert, and Milton, among others, but elided from Dryden through Pope in ways that Dr. Johnson famously misunderstood. Visibility is screened and categorized very simply in the earliest poetries, which are notably all but barren of visualization for intellectual structuring—of simile and metaphor. The *Gilgamesh Epic* has almost no such figures, and the Homeric poems indicate their advanced status within a tradition that has disappeared by their elaborate and visually strong similes. Still, Homer has a scant repertory of no more than three or four color words. The situation changes across the centuries, of course, and by the time of the Renaissance, poetry was ripe for extensions beyond even what Dante, a great visualizer, had added to medieval practice. The Italian poets who followed him were somewhat less sharp-sighted than he. Donne, however, is not only a notable inventor of intricate similes and metaphors. He is also a sharp visualizer, under pressures that may be deduced from the focus and progression of his Eighth Elegy.

Donne was or had recently been a law student when he wrote the *Elegies* and *Satires*. We may conjecture that the constant banter about legal definitions, fortified by long practice at theological speculation, fed the organized conversational discourse of this young, highly accomplished poet to press toward a pseudo-oracularity that upsets its own norms by stretching the language of hyperbole and paradox beyond the mere back-reference to the counterweight of normative perception, aided by the advanced development of the very tradition, simply called "Petrarchan," from which he is departing.

Donne's *Elegies* are early poems that exhibit a certain stiffness, but they are notable for rising to a forceful intensification of illustrative image, and concurrently for an extravagant display of paradox and hyperbole, so much so that he stretches the poise of point into new shapes, as is especially evident in "The Comparison":

As the sweet sweat of roses in a still,
As that which from chafed musk cat's pores doth trill,
As the almighty balm of th' early east,
Such are the sweat drops of my mistress' breast.
And on her neck her skin such lustre sets,
They seem no sweat drops, but pearl carcanets.
Rank sweaty froth thy mistress' brow defiles,
Like spermatic issue of ripe menstruous boils,
Or like that scum, which, by need's lawless law
Enforced, Sanserra's starved men did draw
From parboiled shoes, and boots, and all the rest
Which were with any sovereign fatness blessed,
And like vile lying stones in saffroned tin,
Or warts, or weals, they hang upon her skin.
Round as the world's her head, on every side,
Like to the fatal ball which fell on Ide,
Or that whereof God had such jealousy,
As for the ravishing thereof we die.
Thy head is like a rough-hewn statue of jet,
Where marks for eyes, nose, mouth, are yet scarce set;
Like the first Chaos, or flat seeming face
Of Cynthia, when th'earth's shadows her embrace.
Like Proserpine's white beauty-keeping chest,
Or Jove's best fortune's urn, is her fair breast.
Thine's like worm-eaten trunks, clothed in seal's skin,
Or grave, that's dust without, and stink within.
And like that slender stalk, at whose end stands
The woodbine quivering, are her arms and hands.
Like rough-barked elmboughs, or the russet skin
Of men late scourged for madness, or for sin,
Like sun-parched quarters on the city gate,
Such is thy tanned skin's lamentable state.
And like a bunch of ragged carrots stand
The short swoll'n fingers of thy gouty hand.
Then like the chemic's masculine equal fire,
Which in the limbeck's warm womb doth inspire
Into th'earth's worthless dirt a soul of gold,
Such cherishing heat her best loved part doth hold.
Thine's like the dread mouth of a fired gun,

Or like hot liquid metals newly run
Into clay moulds, or like to that Etna
Where round about the grass is burnt away.
Are not your kisses then as filthy, and more,
As a worm sucking an envenomed sore?
Doth not thy fearful hand in feeling quake,
As one which gathering flowers, still fears a snake?
Is not your last act harsh, and violent,
As when a plough a stony ground doth rent?
So kiss good turtles, so devoutly nice
Are priests in handling reverent sacrifice,
And such in searching wounds the surgeon is
As we, when we embrace, or touch, or kiss.
Leave her, and I will leave comparing thus,
She, and comparisons are odious.

"The Comparison" enlists various classical paradoxes, but it subverts them as it enlists them and so suggests a richness beyond itself that it has succeeded in expressing through the force of its images.[2] In range of detail and force of comparison, this poem is so monstrous that it transmogrifies the topos of the Petrarchan antitype in Donne's own "Anagram" and in Shakespeare's Sonnet 130:"My mistress' eyes are nothing like the sun." The complication and the strength of the illustrations in "The Comparison" exceed the topos of the paradoxical praise of ugliness in "The Anagram," where ugliness is praised because it guarantees fidelity. In the former, an earlier work, the speaker's pretended savage misogyny arrests the reader more because the singular title really involves a plural—first because not one but two women are set up, one of them attractive, setting the love-hate ambivalence into figural sharpness. There are so many comparisons in the poem that the term "comparison" (if the title is Donne's) must refer to the principle rather than to the verbal act, and so by implication to the relation between the making of poetry and the praising or blaming of a desired object. Here one object is recommended and the other rejected, inspiring the speaker to disgust, but he does not begin the comparison (again varying the antitype) till line 7. The movement from easy delight to strained disgust is rhythmically anticipated in the movement from the easy first line—where the echoing pause on "sweet sweat" turns out to be ominous—to the slowly labored monosyllables of the second line. The notion that even sweat (normally displeasing) is beautiful will turn out to mean that anything normally beautiful is in her displeasing. The underlying initial comparison, that pleasing perfumes are made from separate ingredients, themselves disgusting, is never carried through; the poem moves too quickly for this to happen. Its speed, like its sharp focus, both reveals and creates the extremity of perception that its extremity of utterance manages.

The two women are antithetically comparable but distinctly separate, in a multiplication and contrast of persons that has become possible, we may infer, after a long dialectic of persona distinctions in the rhetoric of the generation immediately before him—in Wyatt's shadowy interactions, in the Shakespeare who divides both himself through self-reference in the *Sonnets* and the beloved into two persons of opposite sex—along the lines of the general tendency of the time to construct and test the self.[3] The sweat thrice named changes to an adjective for its fourth appearance, and changes also from the delightful "pearl carcanets" of one woman to the "Rank sweaty froth" of the other. Once the keynote of the rhetoric has been so extravagantly reversed, the act of extravagance is taken rhetorically to open the gates on the most disgusting comparisons: "spermatic issue of ripe menstruous boils," "scum," and on and on. This "scum" combines, perhaps, Donne's fear of poverty with the oppression that his relatives had suffered in the religious struggles, but its function is here reversed, since the besieged, starving citizens of Sancerre, who must eat the scum, are under duress because of their religion. In their case they are Protestants—neither the Catholics nor the Anglicans who were at odds in Donne's time. And like every other turn here, the reversal is eroticized through the central tenor of the comparison.

Here the poet achieves a keenness of visualization that betrays, triumphs over, and modulates what psychoanalytically it would seem to derive from, a hysterical revulsion before the female genitalia. These are already fused with the male ones in "spermatic issue of ripe menstruous boils"—an image that encapsulates a self-confounding proposition, because sperm finds nothing to fertilize during menstruation. The "scum," too, another disgusting liquid, is sterile; it is the useless and repugnant effluvium of the process of improvising a desperate nourishment out of shoes. The besieged impair their walking and denude themselves in order to eat.

The movement is from liquid to solid: to stones, warts, and weals. Then, after the respite of his run of classical comparisons, the poet brings the passage to a climax that begins another sexual conjunction, the alchemist's "masculine fire" in the womb of the alembic compared to the "cherishing heat" in one woman's "best part." Abruptly, once again, this gives way to the other woman's "dread mouth of a fired gun," which casts the feminine organ in a form that suggests the masculine and turns love into war. The vagina dentata has been activated as a phallic mother and enlisted in the hostile activity that assailed the citizens of Sancerre. Then the fairly neutral "hot liquid metals" in "clay moulds" are seen as just an alternate comparison; the capping one is to the gigantic, cataclysmic, and all-destructive archetypal southern volcano, a scorched-earth Etna.

The inverted Petrarchan convention of praising the beloved fuses here with the tradition from Juvenal and others of searingly satirical "blame of women," an early type of classical satire that goes back to the *Psogos Gunaikōn* ("Blame of Women") of Semonides in the seventh century B.C. Such statements are so intense in the Eighth Elegy that they take over the poem. This note is struck from the very first line, and the "medical" empiricism is so sharply cast that we are reminded we are dealing with a contemporary of William Harvey and Francis Bacon, who can be taken to provide a climate for this kind of "observation."

An extreme of imaging is reached here that surpasses for concreteness and force the turns of the normal anti-Petrarchan tradition. Among the *Elegies* generally the range and variety of the hyperbolic comparisons, as especially here, are more emphatic than the acuteness of their wit. We are offered nothing so dialectical as expressions in the *Songs and Sonets* such as "This Ecstasy doth unperplex" ("The Ecstasy") or "Whatever dies was not mixed equally" ("The Good Morrow"). Such lyric poems of Donne as these later ones are more limpid on the surface, investing their profundities in the enchained propositions that have much exercised commentators. Using the same ratiocinative energy differently, this elegy, by contrast to the later poems, bases itself on what are initially simple contradictions of attitude fleshed out in visual perception. Its range and variety of reference are the more impressive for the mixture of positive qualities and negative ones. It is also the more impressive for confining itself to these alternations of image. The sense here is of overload, but the overload is carried by the strong sense of the simple propositions that are held short of Donne's powerful ratiocinative capabilities.

Donne's brother merely died in prison, where he was put for harboring a priest, but line 31 refers to the barbarous practice, still carried out in Donne's youth,[4] of exposing on the city gates the body parts of a drawn and quartered victim of execution. That barbarous execution, though not the exposure, in fact, was undergone by the priest whom Donne's brother had harbored. After the horror of the flogged madmen or sinners, "the russet skin / Of men late scourged for madness, or for sin," and the "sun-parched quarters on the city gate," the series continues at the same pitch with the revolting comparisons of the female genitalia.

As "The Comparison" moves, like "The Anatomy," toward the genitals of its object, it allows itself the tonal variation of a more neutral curiosity after the disgust of the scum from parboiled shoes. One woman's head is compared to the ball that began the judgment of Paris, which places Donne's figure at the edge of Eros's legendary dominance as well as of a legendary conjunction of love and war. And indeed, in the rhetorical tradition of such paradoxes, the Praise of Helen is a classical one, going back to the set piece on that theme by Gorgias, the "first rhetorician." This praise of the blameworthy Helen is an initial inversion, which this poem in its blast may be said to reinvert, as perhaps the grazing reference to the Trojan War hints. The speaker of this poem modulates his tone throughout; the reference to the "rough-hewn statue of jet" introduces variety by mitigating the disgust. The name of Cynthia, a delicate term for the moon, mutes the "flat seeming face" "when th'earth's shadows her embrace," a phrasing that is attractive enough to set up a contrast with the central assertion of ugliness in the other. This contradiction continues in "Proserpine's white beauty-keeping chest," with its oblique suggestion that not a piece of her property but the expanse of her breast is spoken of. The reference to "Jove's best fortune's urn" adds a third to the classical instances of fortune and brings to a close, in its neutrality, the writer's abstention from the merely disgusting.

At the end, the poet prepares the terms that will continue ambivalence in his adduction of kissing turtle doves, priests, and a probing surgeon. "And such in searching wounds the surgeon is / As we, when we embrace, or touch, or kiss." Who can "we" be but the speaker and, at least in one contingency, the woman whom the potential reader has been led to believe so disgusting as to be untouchable? The final couplet, "Leave her, and I will leave comparing thus, / She, and comparisons are odious," would be weak and would violate Donne's principle of the capping ending[5] if we could take it straight. But the very exaggeration in the hyperbole, and the tonal variations, do not allow us to. The effect of the poem is to open a Pandora's box of speculation that the final couplet does not so much close as walk away from. What is left is the rich yield from the poem's communicative assertions, and a sense of its constant insistence on carrying through these extravagances.

The note of extravagance turns on the intensified love-hate ambivalence toward women, which can be traced elaborately in "early modern" European culture, as many recent critics have shown us; and we can imagine this ambivalence as particularly sensitized in the secular all-male aspiring urban enclave of the Inns of Court. The public perception of the sexual pressures at the Inns finds expression in the frequent suspicion of the time that unidentified bastards may well have been secretly fathered by these students.[6] This social fact gives the fantasy-reality setting for the pressures that Donne has here managed to forge into a hyperbole exceeding even the raw conventions of gynophobic misogyny. The force is great enough to spread out into the world of his time in a tour of fantasy whose gratuitousness (there is no reason to connect women with besieged cities) testifies to its mastered compulsions. The tour is thereby incidental and sublated into ongoing metaphor, which thereby partly avoids the miscellany for which Donne denigrated the tour of Thomas Coryat's *Crudities* in a satire, while at the same time gaining the unremitting pressure of his sharp delineations. The rhetorical procedure of point has in fact been stretched throughout. These couplets are at once rounded to point and pressed beyond their self-containments by the ongoing energy they evoke and evince.

Hunger for the boiled shoes in war and death for heresy enter into the comparisons, along with the range of brawling activities in the urban settings of his time; the Continent here is as prominent as London. But the pressure is there from the image of the very first line, "As the sweet sweat of roses in a still." Donne's statements are subjected to the same refining process that the roses undergo, but he provides not beauties like perfume nor merely disgusting odors and sights but a transforming perception that includes both. His conflations allow him to move the poem's assertions at an extreme that presses them without reconciling them, except in the splendid reconciliation of utterance that this poem constitutes.

The dialogic address of desire tends to conform to the deep convention and psychological fact that a love address fixes on a single object. The multiplication of that object from one to two, in a rhetoric analogous to the sonnets of Shakespeare, here complicates the already complicated reversals from praise to blame. The torsion engaged by these reversals of perspective is "baroque" in its evolutions while "classical" in its confinement to the rhythm of neatly pointed couplets and the rhetorical form of elegy. In a way analogous to the torsions of Bernini's St. Teresa, this poem's focus on desire enlists the denial of desire and, like a premonition of Lacanian interaction, links lack to communication, expressive possibility to its transgression, receding as it progresses. In its hyperbolic modulations, it encompasses both desire and disgust, along with disgust-in-desire, without systematizing them or setting them at odds. The small acts of setting-at-odds are drowned in the poem's wide dialogic range of tonal shift and figural reference.

Perhaps it seems that I have presented this odd poem somewhat abruptly. Yet the very fact that I have done so may draw attention to how large a latitude is afforded by the vast tradition that runs from Dante through Donne. That latitude is incorporated as a possibility into even so extravagant a poem as this one. There are many other possibilities that were actualized, of course, from Chaucer onwards. One large domain of actualized possibility is represented by the transmutation of the Petrarchan fictive set at the hands of Spenser, whose *Fowre Hymnes* and *Amoretti* bring it to Platonic heights, while in the *Faerie Queene* he takes the narrative conventions of Ludovico Ariosto and abstracts them into a concentering labyrinth of idealized and abstracted convergences upon images of a queen. This elaborate system, without being oracular, is also very far from such conversational poetry as that exemplified by Jonson's lyrics. Rather, Spenser exemplifies a language that has been so abstracted that it has merged those usual orientations. The oracular and the conversational come to a dead heat in this even style—as they had in Dante, and then in Petrarch, through a refined style already remodified and recomplicated in the conversational brio of *The Canterbury Tales*.

In ordinary language, in actual conversation, people either mean what they say or have some sort of reason for not meaning what they say. The frame is stable, the addressee is conceived of as standing in place, and the message does a definable task whose coordinates will be completely defined by its own cues. In this stability of "meantness," statements very different in character—"Bring me the nails," "I love you," "You know I only like Vivaldi sometimes"—are alike in not raising doubts.

Poetry that exhibits (and poetry of its very nature does exhibit) such a stability of meantness will ring as plain-spoken, as having the conversational accent we hear in Jonson or in Fulke Greville, Landor, Alexander Pushkin, and many others. But stable meantness, the *sermo humilis,* or common style, of stylized conversation, is only a pendulum center for the possibilities open to poetry, which can, and indeed must, use its fictiveness to play with many aspects of the frame.

At one end of the pendulum, poetry can be so labile in its meantness, so fluidly composite in what I call its modalities[7] that the very richness of language seems to empty it of content, or nearly. This tends to happen when the ostensible subject and the real subject of the poem diverge and the poem verges toward the oracular, as in Milton's *Lycidas.* The ostensible subject is mourning for the death of a friend, but the real subject is the bearing of mortality on the literary vision. Hovering in that uncertain frame, directed at an iridescent and vanishing addressee, are injunctions whose very suggestive fullness seems to undermine their force. What meantness can reside in "Weep no more, woful shepherds, weep no more" or in "Look homeward, angel, now, and melt with ruth / And, O ye dolphins, waft the hapless youth"?

This lability cannot be ascribed to the artificiality of the verse, to any analyzable syntactic or stylistic devices; nor is stability just an effect of the plain style: Jonson, Greville, Landor, and Pushkin, among others, are notable masters of artifice. It might be found to correlate with complexity of verse pattern; certainly, so far as we can judge, Pindar swings in the pendulum of his oracularity over to the labile side, meaning what he says less stably than in ordinary language.

At the other end of the pendulum, the statement in verse possesses an urgency of meantness, as though it were trying to forge an entirely new frame, a new addressee. Oracular verse of this nearly biblical sort resounds with a prophetic intention in the work of Blake, Whitman, and Rimbaud. It tends to consume the life of the poet; the words are glowing coals on the tongue. The prophets in Scripture are the great exemplars of urgent meantness. In such verse, the categories of vision and of command break down, and other categories tend to break down, too. The words carry not only the permanence of artifacts, which all verses pretend to do; they are also eschatological and apocalyptic. They announce a judgment that they are calling for, they cleanse and ask to cleanse, they render null the whole question of stability or instability, since their invocation is directed at a sort of fully established Eden where such questions could not be asked.

Dramatic verse in Shakespeare's hands possesses a meantness that draws on the whole range of the pendulum: it advertises its fictiveness, it is notably labile; and at the same time, it holds almost always to the directness of ordinary speech. It means what it says; its meantness has the neutral stability of the morality play. However, it also thrusts forward in a mighty oracular rush that at nearly every moment carries with it the air of urgent meantness, of the prophetic onus. His language and his style set forth not an Eden but a world whose rich possibilities are Edenic in seeming fulfilled, in being charged at every point with both past and future, invented just for the moment, and rationally continuous with anything one might possibly know. This is true of Homer and Dante, too, but in the dramatic form, Shakespeare possesses and uses fully a set of divisions between speaker and speaker, actors and audience, that keeps alive both the provisionality of the utterance and its largeness of inclusive aspiration.

Shakespeare manages a comparable reach even in the short compass of the sonnet:

Sonnet 107

Not mine own fears, nor the prophetic soul
Of the wide world dreaming on things to come,
Can yet the lease of my true love control,
Suppos'd as forfeit to a confin'd doom.
The mortal moon hath her eclipse endur'd,
And the sad augurs mock their own presage;
Incertainties now crown themselves assur'd,
And peace proclaims olives of endless age.
Now with the drops of this most balmy time
My love looks fresh, and Death to me subscribes,
Since, spite of him, I'll live in this poor rhyme,
While he insults o'er dull and speechless tribes.
    And thou in this shalt find thy monument,
    When tyrants' crests and tombs of brass are spent.

The assimilative and expansive power of the troubadour construct of address, lover to beloved—usually given the name of its much later harmonizer, Petrarch—shows remarkably in this poem. It carries out its flights of eulogy from a base of sequentially rhetorical injunctions to a beloved. The *Sonnets,* as a whole, break the mold of arbitrary lability without abandoning it, and at the same time, as the first line of Sonnet

107 declares, it can expand to broach without incoherence the broad apocalyptic note of prophecy. Such a poem as Virgil's Fourth Eclogue licenses such subjects in the context of love exchange. But here they are included in the compass of a single sonnet, concluding on the Horatian topos that poetry endows a statement with permanence. The statement at this relatively late point in the sequence begins to melt into lability through a repetition that verges on the uncommunicative redundancy attendant on overfrequent repetition: "Not marble nor the gilded monuments / Of princes shall outlast this powerful rhyme" (Sonnet 55). So the speaker has kept saying. Such a redundancy haunts the poem: to say that "peace proclaims olives" adds, in one sense, nothing to the notion of peace, all the more since the richness of the symbolic identification of the plant with the condition is rooted in the earliest biblical traditions (Genesis 8.11). What else would peace proclaim but olives? To say so means only, redundantly and nearly tautologically, that peace proclaims peace. That these are "olives of endless age" would add little to "the prophetic soul / Of the wide world dreaming on things to come." There is a mollification in this vision, however, that already enters the state it looks ahead to. "Balmy," too, grazes repetition by connoting much that "olives" and "peace" do.

By objectifying the beloved, "mine own fears" are set to merge concern about the love with concern for the whole universe. Dante had similarly connected the devotion to Beatrice to such apocalyptic concerns, from her very first appearance in the *Divina commedia* at the end of the *Purgatorio*. In Sonnet 107, the speaker's "fears" fuse cosmic concerns about the fate of everyone in time with the ongoing course of his love, which cannot be defined by limits, cannot be "Suppos'd as forfeit to a confin'd doom." It can be controlled neither by the emotions of the speaker ("mine own fears") nor by cosmic long-range actions condensing a super-Platonic perception in its purview, "nor the prophetic soul / Of the wide world dreaming on things to come." The elusiveness of this formulation adds to its comprehensiveness and power, especially as against the next quatrain, where the wise predictors of the state are cast as Roman religious officials, as "augurs," and caught in self-contradiction; they "mock their own presage." The poem at this point makes both evasively and unmistakably a reference to actual political events that cannot be felt as other than a portent. If the death of Queen Elizabeth is indicated by "The mortal moon," then the date that capable commentators favor is 1603, and "this most balmy time" indicates the accession of James I.[8] The poem sets into place something that is at once itself a portent, as eclipses are, and the arresting but transient event. Desperation and peace have become kin: "Incertainties now crown themselves assur'd / And peace proclaims olives of endless age." This note of peace leads forward not to a long future but to a now realized present: "Now with the drops of this most balmy time / My love looks fresh, and Death to me subscribes." Up to this point, this last clause would mean that the freshness of the look of the speaker's love redeems him, in a loose analogy to the Redemption—very much in harmony with the redemptive function of Beatrice that the Tridentine editors took out of the *Vita nuova*. The line, though, revises such notions back to something more conventional but still copious and plenary, since "Death to me subscribes" uses a word, "subscribes," that is active in a wide repertory of senses for Shakespeare.[9] These poems will live on, while whole peoples who have no expression will therefore die: "Since, spite of him, I'll live in this poor rhyme, / While he insults o'er dull and speechless tribes." As the Latin "sub" is active in "subscribes," perhaps faintly reinforcing the subtext of a Roman rather than a British commonwealth with the reference to "augurs," so the Latin is active through the word "insult," used in the sense of "leap exuberantly."

A sonnet sequence in itself both splits and joins its utterances, if it is compared to large, integrative poems expressing and plumbing desire—such as the *Divina commedia* or *The Fairie Queene*. When Dante and Spenser did write sonnets, like Petrarch and many others, they addressed them to a single object. But Shakespeare, by shuffling the identities of his objects, enlists in the addressee the very feature of the sonnet sequence that differentiates it as a form from larger structures. Something unified is said in fourteen lines, and then the poet repeats with variation, beginning another fourteen lines at another angle of the approach—but with repetitions that are all but inevitable, given the rhetorical set of idealizing courtship. A sonnet, then, is continuous with the one preceding it, the one following it, and all the others in the sequence. But it is also discontinuous; it breaks off to conclude and starts anew. Multiplying the objects thematizes the discontinuities and foregrounds the effort of focusing that lies at the heart of each sonnet as the presumptive impetus for its energy. Consequently, the sonnet in a loosely or tightly focused sequence is an astonishingly durable vehicle for the organization of a multiform self in kaleidoscopic confrontation with a flow of experience. Ampler and more various than an epigram, but poised to the certain rounding out of its finish like an epigram, each sonnet draws on the feigned spontaneity of the improvisatory while presenting the tightness of the balanced statement. The silence after one such polished utterance is broken by the presentation of a like-but-different utterance. In its continuous discontinuity, the sequence is both complete and incomplete, and it has so been enlisted in our time by Ted Berrigan, John Clarke, and Lowell. Its formal features (though the *Dream Songs* are in a triple movement of a delimited eighteen lines) still show in John Berryman's longest poem.

The rhetorical trope of "Not *X* can do *Y*," with which Sonnet 107 begins, a trope of negation for which litotes would be a subclass, harnesses the energies of negation to the end of affirmation. This sonnet begins with a super-hyperbole of cosmic import, linking the transient emotions of the speaker to apocalypse. Far transcending "Not marble nor the gilded monuments" is "Not mine own fears, nor the prophetic soul / Of the wide world dreaming on things to come." The fears and the soul are joined and repeated in the "sad augurs," with which they are so far continuous. But they are also discontinuous for two related reasons: the speaker is denying his fears, while the augurs are spoken of as sad; his denial of fears is only a trope for asserting his happiness that "Now with the drops of this most balmy time / My love looks fresh." The augurs are sad because they are unsuccessful and are cooperating in their own unsuccess: "And the sad augurs mock their own presage." Actually, this could mean that they are sad because they have survived the failure of their prediction, or else their prediction was dire even if successful, and so they are sad because augury has turned out to be of no use. And a "presage" is somewhat less comprehensive and less certain than a prophecy. The term indicates a vague portent, and therefore already a diminishment, of the "prophetic soul" of the first line.

At every turn, the sonnet is an *amplificatio* of the one that precedes it. So Sonnet 106, in expressing the topos, which goes back to the troubadours, of a beloved whose features are a composite of the best of other beauties, takes those prior poems not only as a source in the past but also as an indication of the future: "So all their praises are but prophecies / Of this our time all you prefiguring." Sonnet 107 then picks up and considerably amplifies what is meant by "prophecies," extending it from the beauties of the beloved to the fate of the entire world, wherein the love directed to those beauties, insofar as it and they are mortal, still transcends that mortality. The fears and the prophetic soul together cannot "the lease of my true love control, / Suppos'd as forfeit to a confin'd doom."

Having said a great deal new, the speaker turns in Sonnet 108 to pretend to disclaim originality—"I must each day say o'er the very same"—in the constant feigning that is part of the play embellishing this deep seriousness. He has nothing new to say but that the very persistence in saying it will overcome its mortality, will "make antiquity for aye his page," setting the ink/writing metaphor of the opening lines ("page" as sheet of manuscript) into ambiguous conjunction with the structure of a court ("page" as servant of a knight).

This is a kind of pause for breath from Sonnet 107, where the discrepancy between love and large-scale, apocalyptic politics, when the poem does not venture to effectuate the Spenserian convergences, is symmetrical with the discrepancy between the generality of the more pointed, though still darkly hinting, prophecies in the vein of Nostradamus or Virgil. These first two lines echo such prophecies and so does the obliquity of this sonnet, with its extreme paucity or effective lack of real clues. The discrepancy in this sonnet between love and apocalypse also qualifies and joins the splitting of persons in the overall sequence, between youth and Dark Lady and between the speaker and the rival poet. As Joel Fineman says of Sonnet 105,

> Speaking of the young man, whom he imagines as a "wondrous scope," and speaking also of the way "all alike my songs and praises be," the poet observes that "one thing expressing, leaves out difference." This omission, specifically the omission of "difference," defines the limits of even the limit case of praise, for it points to that which is, *in principle,* beyond praise, to that which necessarily passes praise because it is beyond, on the one hand, the mimetic resemblance of imitation, and beyond, on the other, the figurative likeness of metaphoric comparison.[10]

The division of the sonnet into three quatrains and a couplet (the "Shakespearean sonnet") is a logical progression both more complex than the Petrarchan sonnet, with its division between octave and sestet, insofar as there are four steps instead of two, and simpler insofar as a couplet sums it up. Here in Sonnet 107, as often, the division is still more complex, because a Petrarchan arrangement overlaps the "Shakespearean"; there is also a division between octave and sestet. The third quatrain and the couplet form a unit that changes to close-range focus the mortality-braving apocalypse of the first eight lines to locate the very appearance of the beloved in the expanded time that has been defined: "Now with the drops of this most balmy time / My love looks fresh." The divisions are firmly marked not only by rhyme but by light rhythmic touches.[11] There is a general narrowing-in; the oracular opening of the sonnet, which carries through the octave and beyond, concludes in the couplet with the pat restatement of what has been said over and over in this sequence: "And thou in this shall find thy monument, / When tyrants' crests and tombs of brass are spent." These lines also leave the Roman background of the sad augurs for a more medieval picture, one still visible in the churches of the day: coats of arms ("crests") and funeral brasses were not used at all in antiquity.

The address is not directly to the beloved. In this sonnet she is addressed in the third person, and a third-person reference, in a context of many second-person addresses, can be taken to trigger the deep shift of persons manipulated constantly by this sequence.[12] This can happen because, by an unusual turn, the poet is equated to, and identified with, the beloved: "Since spite of [Death], I'll live in this poor rhyme"; "And thou in this shalt find thy monument."

The identification of poet with beloved through their initially simple equation here must be taken, the way Fineman takes it, as being deployed through its permutations in the sequence, as one of a whole range of splittings of person in the sonnets generally, and therefore as partaking of, and referring to, those powerful coordinates. As Fineman says,

> for the young man's poet neither the reality nor the ideality of unity serves him as anything but a placeholder or a coefficient with which to multiply and to divide himself by two. . . . The young man sonnets regularly halve and double what are taken to be traditional dual unities, and they do so in order then to place the poet at the intersection of the four terms thus produced, between both the two halves of the four *and* between the division of each half. No doubt this represents a peculiarly double and divided place for the poet to be located, and a peculiarly limited place as well. But this is precisely the point: it is this peculiarity, recognized and felt as such, that individuates the young man's poet and distinguishes him from traditional sonneteering personae. (232, 233)

Shakespeare's stroke of complicating these identifications, a powerful instance of his tendency to double and contrast, as in "The Phoenix and the Turtle," both overbalances desire by providing several vanishing points for it and controls it by providing a non-Platonic scheme for its hierarchies—a move that anti-Petrarchan poems—such as the Eighth Elegy of Donne—will reinforce.[13]

Wyatt, according to Jonathan Crewe, had already begun these powerful modifications of the homogenizations of the troubadour ethic that obtained from Dante through Spenser:

> Yet as the poet of the satires, epigrams, and *Penitential Psalms,* Wyatt does not cease to be crafty in all the senses described above. Indeed, it is in the *Penitential Psalms* that both his political craftiness and peculiar confessional *impenitence* are perceived by Greenblatt. . . . Whether the desire or place of the speaker is accordingly to be located in those disavowed forms of courtly dissimulation and excess, or in the stoic self finally produced in the moment of simulated Horatian self-possession ("Here I am"), remains in doubt: we don't know who or where the speaker is. Again, however, a certain complicity and manipulated exchange between these twin selves, the one who is not and the one who is, must be suspected ("I am not what I am"; "nothing is but what is not," to recall here the language of two of Shakespeare's represented masculine subjects).[14]

Historical certainty in the language of Sonnet 107 is both amplified and undermined by the obliquity of its presentation. "Incertainty" turns out to be a crucial hinge for getting the advantage of the Spenserian Platonic hierarchies while avoiding their convergences. Spenser himself was never a sad augur, nor could he have referred to one. Recent critics have emphasized the contrast between the cruelty of his own administrative activities in Ireland and the otherworldly ideality of *The Faerie Queene.* But Shakespeare manages, even in so succinct a poem, both to gain the Platonic advantage and to bypass its convergences by personalizing the relation between the macropolitical and the erotic personal. He and the beloved are located at this particular intersection of apocalyptic time; both persons are subject to the kinds of readings and influences that such astrologers as John Dee were actually deriving from the moon's eclipses,[15] and living beyond them in the temporal and psychospiritual sense. Unlike *Lear*'s Gloucester, they are not really attentive or wholly subject to "these late eclipses of the moon."

The Faerie Queene, by contrast, offers factorings of allegorical identities that both converge upon Gloriana through the quest of Arthur and split into various figural relations unwound in narratives centering serially on Guyon, the Red Crosse Knight, Artegall, Britomart, and others. The Aristotelian letter to E. K. in Spenser's explanation of the poem leaves all of these somewhat hanging—as the poem itself does. In the large universe of that poem, there is a Platonic contentment that fore-shortens the representation of identities while allowing for a consistent and fine-tuned set of psycho-spiritual abstractions: "O how great won-der would your thoughts devoure, / And infinite desire into your spirit poure!" (2.9.3). These lines join a large number of such effusions in the huge poem. To call the desire infinite, finally, even in this expanding context, keeps it in linear relation to all the ideations the poem evokes. It is not able to carry off, as Blake later can, a relational system for dimensionalizing these figures.[16]

"The prophetic soul / Of the wide world dreaming on things to come" gains its poetic reach from the very obliquity that forbids our identifying the soul here just with the Spenserian Platonic-Plotinian soul or distinguishing it therefrom. It approaches the Spenserian hierar-chy from an angle that includes the scriptural—Shakespeare's phrases could be taken as a characterization of the Book of Revelation—and the Virgilian of the Fourth Eclogue, while the firmly political applica-tion of the terms in the immediately following lines of the sonnet allows us to find in it, as many commentators have, a reference to the *anima mundi* of Giordano Bruno.[17] The directions in which this initial focus opens turns out to play into the desire of the speaker in ways that enlist the very obliquity that would seem in principle to deflect it.[18]

Chaucer, within or nearly within Petrarch's lifetime, had already found his way to a smoothness and comprehensiveness comparable to Spenser's in the vein of courtly love:

> Madame ye ben of alle beaute shryne
> As fer as cercled is the mapamounde,
> For as the cristall glorious ye shyne,
> And lyke ruby ben your chekes rounde.
> Therwith ye ben so mery and so jocounde
> That at a revell whan that I se you daunce,
> It is an oynement unto my wounde,
> Though ye to me ne do no daliaunce.

The tonic reference to the "mapamounde," which can mean both a map of the world and the world itself, coupled with the length of the word (there is no longer word in the stanza), creates at one stroke the

Dantesque and, by anticipation, the Platonic-Spenserian identification on which the speaker can then easily rest as he runs in unstraining measures through the more usual courtly effusions. Given his tradition, there is no sense of the extravagance in which Donne much later indulges when he extends a version of this identification of the ideal woman with the world for the gigantic elaborations of his *Anniversaries*. Not returning to the "mapamounde" as he proceeds through the poem has the effect, along with its leveling pattern, of scaling down her praise, from identifying her with the universe to more ordinary beauties and graces. It is only a touch that Chaucer moves past. But at the same time, all the other praises can be taken to assimilate to it; they are instances of a central principle. In Chaucer's Mozartian fluency, the poem floats among these possibilities and has not given up its own sense of inventive improvisation.

All this is a distillation of a troubadour topos. Chaucer still is far from the self-conscious self-splitting that Shakespeare achieves in the *Sonnets*.[19] This exponentializing of the self, as Fineman implies, leads, as much as Spenser's hierarchies can be said to do, all the way to the psychocosmic dynamics of Blake, the self-extrapolations of Wordsworth, Rimbaud's "je est un autre," Whitman's expansive intrication of "myself" with a future public consciousness, and even Pound's persona-manipulations— still on a troubadour base. Indeed, it is alive in current practice. Refigured persona relations govern the manipulations of the conceptions of the sonnet in such work as Raymond Queneau's *Cent mille milliards de poèmes,* where the simple rhetorical formulas of the sonnet, already close to interchangeable staples in the work of Petrarch, are taken line by line as combinatory modules to a nearly infinite number of poems; or in the "E" of Jacques Roubaud, where poems written in a variously postromantic vein—some of them sonnets and some of them not—are deployed in fictive neutrality on a scheme that corresponds to the 157 moves of an actually recorded game of Go, organizing 361 texts that arbitrarily correspond to the 180 white pieces and the 181 black pieces of the game. And for other work, to choose just a couple among abundant examples, such a manipulation of self vivifies the persona replay of the stock characters of a Western movie mounted by Mac Hammond's *Horse Opera;* or what might be called the "persona-ekphrasis" poem, where Hammond presents himself at the barber shop by the conjunction of his about-to-be-trimmed person with that of a sultan in a seventeenth-century Indian miniature ("An Indian Miniature");[20] or Richard Howard's double refraction of persona objects with photographs of them by Nadar (*Misgivings*). In all these poems, the self, which is resplendent through its very vanishings, as Donne and Shakespeare—and indeed before them, Dante—had begun to find means for expressing, comes into increasingly complex but no less firm assertion.

5

Dante

Trasumanar per verba

1

"Not mine own fears, nor the prophetic soul / Of the wide world dreaming on things to come." Shakespeare's lines sound Dantesque in their normativeness, in their powerful simplicity, in their spiritual orientation, in their measured, even progression, in their forward thrust. In what way are they not Dantesque? To ask this question will allow us to clarify what the particular simplicity and depth of Dante add up to and amount to.

To begin with, these lines are at a slightly higher pitch than the tonic note of the *Divina commedia,* which swells to such oracularity only at certain high moments. The syntax of Dante's earlier *rime,* of the poems in the *Vita nuova* and the *Convivio,* is wrought to a comparable pitch, but by the time of the *Divina commedia,* Dante stays in the calm onward flow of a voice that would be conversational were it not for the tight braiding of his *terza rima.* As T. S. Eliot says of the large poem, "The thought may be obscure, but the word is lucid, or rather translucent."[1] Then, too, these lines of Shakespeare do make Dante's connection between deep human love and theological ultimates, and they do so in a way that goes beyond Petrarch, Sidney, Wyatt, and Spenser—in a way that Dante may be thought of, so to speak, as having empowered for the tradition, though Shakespeare is not likely to have read him. Yet at the same time the connection in Shakespeare's sonnet between love and God, though it rivals Dante's breadth, is quite un-Dantesque. It is too "rhetorical"; and to notice this is to take stock, once again, of the absoluteness of Dante's conviction, the trance- or sleeplike state into which he has projected his poem, which he, with seeming strangeness, characterizes as a "lethargy" ("letargo") in one of the poem's final statements (*Par.* 33.94). That "greater lethargy" is a more permanent, deeper state than the "stupore" produced by a comparable poetic confrontation in the *Convivio* (4.25).[2]

Moreover, Shakespeare's lines are really impossible to locate theologically; they seem to draw on the doctrine of someone like Bruno, but they do not offer coordinates. Dante, on the other hand, always does so, either by explicit ratiocination, by the structure (itself adaptive) of his fourfold allegory, or by deducible concatenations of statement that amount to propositions. Dante, in the modern expositions from Étienne Gilson on, is a philosopher.[3] Shakespeare here advertises a certain obliquity, whereas Dante writes out of a center, the circle of his poem having its center everywhere and its circumference nowhere.

Poetry is both private (internal) and public; by being both intensely, it leaps the difference between the two. Even assuming a rapprochement between poet and reader through the communicative act of writing and then reading the poem, there are always two selves brought to bear on the poem, that of the prior self (about to read or write) and that of the resultant self (having read or written). The resultant self reverberates with recognition of the prior self; in that sense they are one. But the before-and-after do not disappear, nor do they lose—in fact they must, if successful, enlist—all the substructures that the modern idealist philosopher has constructed: of Hegelian phenomenology of mind, Freudian ego reclaiming the forces of the unconscious, Husserlian intentionality, Derridean *différance,* and Lacanian symbolic circularity. All of these may be taken hypothetically together and seen banked in the persona projected by the Dante of the *Divina commedia,* who, by removing himself fictively to the eternal realm of the dead, at a stroke can concentrate on ultimates and slip wholly out of any Heideggerian *Geworfenheit*. The "thrownness" of his "being toward death" has been bypassed by being faced in a way whose radical fictiveness is apparent from the central conception of crossing to "that bourne from which no traveller returns."

There is no Shakespearean splitting of personae in Dante, nothing of the dialectic by which, in the *Sonnets,* the love of Shakespeare for a man and then a woman and then the love of that man for the woman, are set off against one another. Dante's persona, through all his numerous encounters, funds his dialectic in the gradually centering illumination of the pilgrim "I," which is explicitly identified at the very beginning of the *Divina commedia* with humanity at large: "Nel mezzo del cammin di *nostra* vita / *mi* ritrovai" ("In the middle of the road of *our* life / I found *myself*") (1.1–2).[4] In the supreme convergences of the *Paradiso,* "I" and "we" come together in the utterances of the just in the sixth sphere of Jupiter, under the angelic order of Dominations, where saved spirit-lights form a composite Eagle and sing from its beak: "ch'io vidi e anche udi' parlar lo rostro, / e sonar ne la voce e 'io' e 'mio,' / quand' era nel concetto e 'noi' e 'nostro'" ("That I saw and still hear the beak speak / And sound out in its voice 'I' and 'my' / when there was in its conception 'we' and 'our'") (*Par.* 19.10–12).

Dante moves this process to the second, reflexive degree by basing his narrative progress in and on the act of writing/recounting the poem. The self resultant from writing the poem and telling its imagined events looks back and joins the prior self, which began lost in the dark wood, where the reader, too, must begin, retracing those steps and following the hundred cantos to rejoin Dante's resultant self—not only "pure and set up to rise up to the stars" ("puro e disposto a salire a le stelle") as he was/is at the end of the *Purgatorio* (33.135) but also joining an understanding evolved by the end of the *Paradiso* with what "moves and is moved equally," "The love that moves the sun and the other stars" ("l'amor che move il sole e l'altre stelle") (*Par.* 33.145). At the very beginning, there is, as Charles Singleton points out, an elision from an "actual" shore to waters that are no place but in the "lake of the heart": "The whole journey beyond exceeds metaphor. It is irreducible to the kind of allegory in which it had its origin. As this figure of a living man, this whole person soul and body, moves through the doorway to Hell, the poem quits the recognizable and familiar double vision in which it began, to come into single and most singular vision." But, of course, "The poem is distinguishable from Scripture and from reality and from history in its being a fiction."[5]

Such paradoxes are envisaged by the language of the *Paradiso* in describing its own procedures as a human language that analogically gets beyond the human.[6] This is, of course, impossible, but Dante declares it by fiat and then enacts an analogical equivalent for it:

> Nel suo aspetto tal dentro mi fei
> qual si fé Glauco nel gustar de l'erba
> che 'l fé consorto in mar de li altri dèi.
>
> Trasumanar significar *per verba*
> non si poria; però l'essemplo basti
> a cui esperïenza grazia serba.

> In her look I made myself so within
> as Glaucus made himself in tasting the grass
> that made him a consort in the sea with the other gods.
>
> To signify transhumanizing *per verba*
> could not be done—but may the example suffice
> to him for whom grace saves the experience.
>
> (*Par.* 1.67–72)

Here the "inexpressibility trope" of the Middle Ages—that poetry speaks of what it cannot speak and hence declares its own ineffability—is inverted or stood on its head in a radical "expressibility trope";[7] the poet can say what he cannot say; the reach of his poetry is such that it can exceed his grasp, which is the verbal counterpart of a living man declaring that he has by special, but exemplary, condition moved through the realms of the dead in eternity—and been changed thereby, brought round by love with an aid crucially dramatized as coming to reveal itself, to begin the process of education, only when it was all but ended. Beatrice appears only after the poet has been through all the encounters of the *Inferno* and all the transformative removals of sin in the *Purgatorio,* appearing only in Eden, the earthly Paradise, which has the triumphant trappings and image diapason of a realized end, when it is actually a rebeginning. Beatrice is there to conduct him through, but not all the way through, his enlightenment. She replaces Virgil and the temporary assistants, Statius and Sordello—herself to be replaced, finally, by St. Bernard.

There is not exactly an infinite regress, but rather a turn of rhetorical empowering in Dante's comparison of his transformation into conceiving of the (impossible) possibility of using human language, *verba,* to get himself beyond the human. The Latin term *verba* underscores the philosophical force underlying this ideological extension. The paradox is exactly matched, as well as expressed, by the status of "Glaucus and the other gods." Such myths are true with an impermeable undecidability, moving already toward a view of entities like Glaucus—to be developed in the Renaissance by Ficino, Giovanni Pico della Mirandola and others—that such gods are figures or metaphors for spiritual states. But Dante here seems to be moving across both sides of the literal-figurative line—as is validated by the conception of the "contracted" expression of the *Paradiso,* itself final and summary.[8] For Glaucus and other such figures, he has clearly supplemented the view he follows elsewhere, the view of Augustine, for whom the classical gods are not fictions but really demons, like the Siren, Geryon, the Centaurs, Medusa, and others in the *Divina commedia.* Dante reflects the conventional Augustinian view when he dissociates the sphere of Venus in the *Paradiso* from the "ancient error" ("antico errore") of worshipping Venus (*Par.* 8.6). But Glaucus and similar figures, by being presented in a modality more positive than this, bring the full analogy to their poetic workings in wholly affirmative fashion. As Thomas Aquinas says, in a statement that Giovanni Scartazzini brings to bear on this passage, "The faculty of seeing God does not correspond with the created intellect according to its nature but through the light of glory, which has established the intellect in a certain god-formed way."[9]

In the symbolic exchange that Lacan analyzes at the heart of human encounters, the self only gains validation by projecting on the other an idealized Other and thereby, through the very lapses of this process, coming into a power of self symbolically endowed with that which it desires in (though is separated from) the Other. The psychiatrist is the silent mediator of this process. In Dante's dynamic conception, the mediator is Beatrice, desire is simply love, and the Other is Love itself, God, by whom all entities are measured, finally in the objective sequences of the poem (the others are dead), progressively in the subjective development of the poem (the speaker returns to this life empowered by having moved through the realms of the dead).

For Lacan the aim in view must be *jouissance,* the real and symbolic actualization of phallic fulfillment. But the fact that Dante's encounters

99

are with the dead releases them, and himself, from any of the equivoca-
tions that the Lacanian schemes would engender when applied to his
conception. In the *Divina commedia,* the *jouissance* desired is unequivo-
cally love, as it manifests itself more and more fully in the Pilgrim's
ascension to higher and still more enlightened spheres. On each level,
the increase is registered in the eyes of Beatrice and assimilated in the
responding eyes of the Pilgrim, who is imagined as remembering the
whole process and ordering it into the poem. Lacan's terms, however, as
he summarizes them for combinations in his own dialectic, could serve
as a scheme for Dante's *"jouissance,* the Other, the sign, and love."[10]
Dante himself connects love and his own poetic use of signs: "I' mi son
un che, quando / Amor mi spira, noto, e . . . / . . . vo significando" ("I am
one who when / Love breathes in me, takes note, and . . . / . . . goes on
signifying") (*Purg.* 24.52–54).

In speaking of the role of Beatrice, once he is under her guidance,
Dante is direct and proportionate in his distinctions:

> Quel sol che pria d'amor me scaldò 'l petto,
> di bella verità m'avea scoverto,
> provando e riprovando, il dolce aspetto;

> That sun which before had burned my breast with love,
> with beautiful truth had uncovered to me,
> proving and refuting, its beautiful look.

> (*Par.* 3.1–3)

The memory of the troubadour rapture is only a memory. It is paral-
leled in, but superseded by, the acts of theological demonstration that
Beatrice has taken over, they and she thereby gaining in beauty rather
than losing. Even in the *Vita nuova,* there were touches of the opening
into charity through Eros: "quando ella apparia . . . mi giugnea una
fiamma di caritate, la quale mi facea perdonare a chiunque m'avesse
offeso" ("When she appeared . . . there joined me a flame of charity
which made me pardon anyone who had offended me") (10.1). Fleshly
love by implication is approved here and funded into the other relations
to which it contributes—unless it is perverting those other relations. So
Charles Williams extrapolates from the lines about the union of flesh
and spirit in the Last Judgment: "Come la carne glorïosa et santa / fia
rivestita, la nostra persona / più grata fia per esser tutta quanta" ("When
the flesh, glorious and holy, / is put on again, will our person be / more

gratified for being wholly full") (*Par.* 14.43–45).[11] Irma Brandeis, quoting Augustine's *De trinitate,* stresses that *amor* involves both *concupiscentia* and *caritas:* "The entry of souls into the flame of the passageway signifies this fusion of many loves in perfect *caritas* ... [he] unite[s] the two functions of the fire of *caritas* in one bank of flame with successive and related effects: first (in the terrace circle, which is for the Lustful, alone), making every covetous love chaste; and next (in the passageway, which is for all souls upward bound), setting every chaste love blazing in the love of the One."[12] The stiffness and self-preoccupation implied by the erotic focus of troubadour poetry is dimensionalized here by placing the troubadours in a variety of connections and assimilating them to the expressed conception of divine love in a poetry that is, as it were, neutralized in the rose of his Vision.

Dante's initial conception of having his central object of love already dead takes the troubadour ethic beyond even the theorization of Guido Cavalcanti (briefly mentioned in *Inf.* 10.63). Dante thus sublates the "personal" desire, along with the theory of desire, in favor of a love theory that will find its culmination not even in Beatrice's words and allegorical gestures but in those of St. Bernard with a complexity far greater than Cavalcanti's itself masterful formulation of what Peter Dronke calls the sapiential tradition.[13] Yet there are many other views of love in the poem, and the loose relation among them arranges their variety in the primary direction of the *Paradiso*'s draw of love. Again, the encounters allow Dante a range, and a normalizing convergence toward the all-embracing love of God, something that Cavalcanti's systematic approach cannot accommodate.

At the bottom of hell, in the second of the Malebolge (evil pouches) of Fraud, are panders and seducers, covered with human dung (*Inf.* 18.112–36). Far above them in hell is the second circle of incontinently lustful, where the indiscriminately lecherous, such as Semiramis, are startlingly put in the same category with the more devoted and spiritual but adulterous lovers Paolo and Francesca. There is the bald, unclassified lust figured in Dante's dream of the Siren (*Purg.* 19.7–33), not to be identified with the socialized male banter of sexual boasting and ritual sexual insults to women in the sonnets he exchanged with Forese dei Donati, to which Dante need not here refer. Instead, Forese is interposed between the dream of the Siren and the person of Arnaut in the lust-purging fire (cantos 23 and 24).

Forese, it turns out, may perhaps not need to purge the sin of lust at all, or any other but the gluttony of the sphere where Dante meets him, because Forese's wife, the subject of their mutual insults in youth, has been praying him past the other spheres. The gratitude she gains in his expression, and his countervailing excoriation of the immodesty of current Florentine women, invert their old ritual banter to charitable use and make amends for whatever discourtesy he may have shown his wife in the past, about which the poem is also silent. Since Forese is Dante's brother-in-law, he attests to a quiet marital harmony that can be extended, at least by conjectural analogy, to the poet himself. Thus a whole other ideal than the troubadour one comes into view, bounded by the guarded reference to still another member of the family, Piccarda dei Donati, who was forced to break her nun's vows, to become something less than a harmonious wife, by Forese's violent brother Corso, whose violent death is told (24.82–87). Corso's own exact place in hell is uncertain but ominous, and part of his limitation would presumably be an inability to participate in any ideal form of *eros,* lacking the *cor gentil.*

Forese, in castigating the immodesty of Florentine women on the one hand and on the other hand in praising the chastity, piety, fidelity, and love of his wife, is only obliquely referring to "the life we led together," since, once again, this is the sphere of gluttony, not lust. He also picks up echoes of the public lament voiced elsewhere by Brunetto Latini, Guido del Duca, and Cacciaguida. All this, of course, modifies and processualizes the erotic.[14] Troubadours are found throughout the poem, from Bertran de Born in the schismatics section of the *Inferno* (canto 20) to Folquet de Marseilles in the *Paradiso's* sphere of Venus (canto 9). So profoundly successive is Dante's presentation of his narrative progress that it assumes to its ongoing adaptiveness the invented speech of Arnaut Daniel, which is communicated in the form of an imitation so radical that it is cast in Arnaut's language, Provençal. The last line, *"sovehna vos a temps de ma dolor"* ("Remember in time my sorrow") (*Purg.* 26.147), keeps its ongoing syntax in Dante's pattern, as do all the others, and its very sentiment is much more Dantesque than it is Arnaldian.

The troubadours tend to cluster—and allegorically that section of the afterlife situates their deepest concerns—in the *Purgatorio.* But they are not just seen in the single light of lust, either dominant or purified; nor is there a single troubadour in the *Inferno's* sphere of the lustful, except for the indirect mention of Chrétien de Troyes (though Tristan is named there [5.67]). Sordello, for all the violent complications of his adulterous love life—unmentioned by Dante—is making his way through the levels of Purgatory and serving as a supplementary guide. And his most notable paramour, Cunizza da Romano, has already attained forever Venus, the third sphere of Paradise, her generosity of spirit evidently having turned the openness of her many erotic encounters in a charitable direction. So far, Sordello himself has not attained the final terrace, where lust will be purged. The subtlest of the lot, Arnaut, sets their tonic note: they are repenting for excessive *eros.* It would seem, though, that their *eros,* for its very distancing in their poems, would differ from the undistanced love of Paolo and Francesca. These lovers, to be sure, were swept up at the behest of a troubadour-like author, unnamed here and unplaced, though we may identify him as Chrétien. He, in a kind of contradiction or unreconciled discrepancy, does not sound like a candidate for Purgatory, judging from the earlier reference to his poem: "Galeotto fu 'l libro e chi lo scrisse" ("Gallehaut was the book, and he who wrote it") (*Inf.* 5.137).

The love of the troubadours—though, as they witness, love was what dominated them—is enough allied to God's love not to dominate them wholly. Thus Guido Guinizelli, who expressed the tonic note of the troubadour ethic—"Al cor gentil ripara sempre amore" ("To the noble heart love always repairs")—is also brought forward by Dante in the *Purgatorio* to introduce Arnaut as the "miglior fabbro" ("better workman") (26.117). Guinizelli initiates a triad of inductions among himself, Arnaut, and the experiencing Dante.

2

PHILOSOPHY had been a component of Dante's early poetry, and of that of his contemporaries, directed, in the troubadour tradition, at a version of Lacan's subject, at love and *jouissance.* It only gets wholly sublated and redefined in the *Divina commedia* after many testings of thought and style.

Dante saw his common language, a universalized Tuscan, as encouraging such possibilities of extension beyond the erotic subject matter, when the earlier Italian poets, and his earlier self, had not really done so. In the *De vulgari eloquentia,* after listing the characteristics of the dialects and their special properties in very great detail town by town, Dante suddenly shifts to a different ground for the tongue common to all Latium, and he attributes to this tongue the properties of classical (nonvernacular) Latin. Thus can the vernacular transcend itself to appropriate the virtues of its predecessor and opposite. This language turns out to be the language of the would-be Roman citizen, *civis,* the proper instrument for the discrimination of moral virtues, something general and international offering the human sui generis rather than just the local—and certainly not the erotic:

> Nam in quantum simpliciter ut homines agimus, virtutem habemus (ut generaliter illam intelligamus) nam secundum ipsam bonum et malum hominem iudicamus): in quantum ut homines cives agimus, habemus legem, secumdam quam dicitur civis bonus et malus; in quantum ut homines latini agimus, quedam habemus simplicissima signa et morum et habituum et locutionis, quibus latine actiones ponderantur et mensurantur. Que quidem nobilissima sunt earum que Latinorum sunt actiones, hec nullius civitatis Ytalie propria sunt, et in omnibus comunia sunt: inter que nunc potest illud discerni vulgare quod superius venabamur, quod in qualibet redolet civitate, nec cubat in ulla. . . . Itaque adepti quod querebamus, dicimus illustre, cardinale, aulicum et curiale vulgare in Latio, quod omnis latie civitatis est et nullius esse videtur, et quo municipalia vulgaria omnia Latinorum mensurantur et ponderantur et comparantur.

> For insofar as we act as human beings in the simplest sense, we are virtuous (as this term is generally used); for we judge men as good or bad according to this. When we act as men who are citizens, we have the law, according to which a citizen is called good or bad; when we act as men who are Latins, we have certain standards, the simplest [in the categories] of mores, habitual practices, and speech, against which the actions of Latins are weighed and measured. And surely these, the most noble standards against which the actions of Latins are measured, do not belong to any particular Italian cities, and are common to them all; and among these we can now discern that vernacular we have been tracking above, which suffuses its perfume in every city, but has its lair in none. . . . Having thus found what I have been searching for, I declare that the illustrious, cardinal, courtly, and curial vernacular of Latium is that which belongs to all the Latian cities and seems to belong to none, against which all the Latin municipal vernaculars are measured, weighed and compared.[15]

In the *Divina commedia,* Dante assigns these very functions to the purified Tuscan of the *dolce stil nuovo,* and the civic concerns of his interlocutors enter the poem at many points. By addressing an eternal subject that involves constant discriminations about justice, but at the same time by staying resolutely local, Dante manages to combine the international and the local in the encounters of the Pilgrim, transposing the qualities of Latin into the common vernacular. In some final sense, he does so "simpliciter," but all the intermediate steps of the process involve the combination of "Latin" subjects and vernacular events.

Thus Dante participates in the internationalism of the Middle Ages by making the local bear questions of international import, in the light of a love that includes the troubadour *fin amors* but is not confined to it, not even in the figure of his devotion, Beatrice, who does not at all direct her attention to expounding the base of that devotion. That, of course, is exactly what the earlier Dante did, and all his predecessors and contemporaries, notably Cavalcanti.

Quite apart from the bold, complex, somewhat refractory doctrines of Cavalcanti as Bruno Nardi and Dronke have expounded them, there is a dependence in his poetry on a foregrounded, knotty complexity of thought:[16]

> Donna mi priegha
>   perch'io voglio dire
> D'un accidente
>   che sovente
>   é fero
> Ed é si altero
>   che' é chiamato amore
> . . . .
> In quella parte
>   dove sta memor[i]a
> Prende suo stato
>   si formato
>   chome
> Diafan dal lume
>   d'una schuritade
> La qual de Marte
>   viene e fã dimora
> Egli é creato
>   e a sensato
>   nome
> D'alma chostume
>   di chor volontade

A lady asks me
    I speak in season
She asks reason for an affect, wild often
    That is so proud he hath Love for a name
. . . .
Where memory liveth,
    it takes its state
Formed like a diafan from light on shade
Which shadow cometh of Mars and remaineth
Created, having a name sensate,
Custom of the soul,
    will from the heart.
              (Ezra Pound, Canto XXXVI)[17]

Here the verse characteristically orders itself, even in its firmly halting rhythms, on the deductive process of philosophizing, to which the narrative of the lady at the very beginning at once gives way.

Still similar, though smoothed into refined diction and rhythms, are typical poems of Dante, such as "Amor che ne la mente mi ragiona" (*Convivio* 3.1.1–90). The procedure is clear from the first lines of that longish poem:

Amor che ne la mente mi ragiona
de la mia donna disiosamente,
move cose di lei meco sovente
che lo 'intelletto sovr'esse disvia.
Lo suo parlar sì dolcemente sona,
che l'anima ch'ascolta e che lo sente
dice "Oh me lassa! ch'io non son possente
di dir quel ch'odo de la donna mia."

Love that reasons to me in my mind
about my lady desirously
moves matters about her often with me
that the intellect over them loses its way.
Her speech so sweetly sounds,
that the soul which hears and which feels it says
"Alas for me that I have not power
To say that which I hear from my lady."

Here the circuit of narrative doubles back on itself, just as the rhymes and the closed system of the diction do. Boethius's Lady Philosophy, on whom Dante here is drawing, has converged with the figure of a real lady (which must be the case, since "other ladies" are shortly mentioned in the prose commentary). This poem offers a late, purified, easy, abstract version of the standard troubadour posture. Early commentators noted the abstractness; as the "anonimo fiorentino" says, "moral canzoni like this one were not in practice usually set to music for singing [intonare]."[18] This characterization of this canzone as "moral" strikes us as curious; it points to the central abstract or philosophical character not only of its assertions but of its language. And in fact the commentary of the "anonimo" is directed not to the original appearance in the *Convivio* but to the *Purgatorio,* where this canzone *is* sung to Dante, by Casella:

> E io: "Se nuova legge non ti toglie
> memoria o uso a l'amoroso canto
> che mi solea quetar tutte mie voglie,
>> di ciò ti piaccia consolare alquanto
> l'anima mia, che, con la sua persona
> venendo qui, è affannata tanto!"
>> *"Amor che ne la mente mi ragiona"*
> cominciò elli allor sì dolcemente,
> che la dolcezza ancor dentro mi suona.

> And I: "If a new law take not from you
> memory or use of the song of love
> that was wont to calm all my desires
>> with that may it please you to console somewhat
> my soul that, with its person
> coming here, is so much out of breath."
>> *"Love that reasons to me in my mind"*
> he then began and so sweetly
> that the sweetness still within me sounds.
>
> (*Purg.* 2.106–14)

The song need only be adduced for all its abstract coherences to be evoked, which at the same time stand off from the simpler narrative progression here, a fact that may have led the "anonimo fiorentino" to stress the abstractness of the original song. Dante has reembedded it precisely at a point of delay; Casella is waiting in the Ante-Purgatory to begin an upward ascent that Dante himself will begin immediately in the double role he emphasizes of soul, which he shares with Casella, and of "living person" ("persona"), which he does not. The song is cast in a mode of retrospect, of friendly exchange and reminiscence, so affecting that a vain embrace has just been tried. The encounter for Dante also has the aspect of delay, of a lingering and dwelling on the sweetness of his old desire-calming voice echoed in the particular verses of this account, which at the same time refers the whole Cavalcanti-like system to the second degree by quoting it and embedding it in an exchange that must be cut short; Cato abruptly hurries the penitents and the Pilgrim on.

The narrative keeps the verse progression in a constant transition into simplicity and the declarative paratactic adaptiveness that it entails. Ingested and redeployed here are Cavalcanti's abstractions, and the Pilgrim's conjecturing opens out into a gradual expansion of philosophizing, especially in the *Paradiso,* but with no rhythmic trace of Cavalcanti's stress of deductions and none of the particular troubadour intensities thus gathered and transformed. In the *Vita nuova,* Dante set the narrative into simple allegorical sequences, as in the figure of Love, who appears in a vision with the Latin label "Ego Dominus Tuus" ("I am thy Lord"), a strange re-medievalization of the troubadour ethos.

Dante achieved, in the words of Gianfranco Contini, a "gradual freeing of his style from the tight turns of Guittone d'Arezzo. . . . The entire experience of the *stilnovist* is depersonalized, transferred to a universal order."[19] So Dante, in a later context, adduces a poem from the *Vita nuova* where he had begun to have apprehensions of the death of Beatrice:

"Ma dì s'i' veggio qui colui che fore
trasse le nove rime, cominciando
'Donne ch'avete intelletto d'amore.'"
E io a lui: "I' mi son un che, quando
Amor mi spira, noto, e a quel modo
ch'e' ditta dentro vo significando."
"O frate, issa vegg' io'," diss' elli, "il nodo
che 'l Notaro e Guittone e me ritenne
di qua dal dolce stil novo ch'i' odo!
Io veggio ben come le vostre penne
di retro al dittator sen vanno strette,
che de la nostre certo non avvenne."

"But say if I see here him who brought
out the new rhymes, beginning
'Ladies who have intelligence of love.'"
And I to him, "I am one who when
Love breathes in me, take note, and in the manner
he dictates in me, go on signifying."
"O brother, now I see," he said, "the knot
that held the Notary, Guittone, and me back
to the rear of the sweet new style that I hear!
I see well how it is your pens
go close behind the one who dictates,
which surely did not happen to our own."
(*Purg.* 24.49–60)

In these lines, no opening is given to an undecidedness about the limit
between poetry and philosophy. Cavalcanti exemplifies and creates a
struggle into propositional thought presented as poetry. Already
smoother than Cavalcanti's verse, "Donne ch'avete intelletto d'amore"
subsumes and flattens that process.[20] All these gestures converge through
Dante's enactment. All the features of the poem in the *Convivio* are
evoked by the single-line quotation; and they are dismissed as well as
characterized by Dante's own account of an implied stylistic develop-
ment. The speaker who addresses the Pilgrim here, interestingly, is not
one of his major associates and predecessors, not Cavalcanti or Guinizelli
—who actually conducted a poetic dialogue with Buonagiunta—or
Cino da Pistoia. Instead it is a minor rhymer of the Tuscan school,
Buonagiunta da Lucca, a follower of Guittone d'Arezzo, the man he
names, who is coupled with the leader of the Sicilian school at the court
of Frederick II, Giacomo da Lentini, "the Notary"; this constitutes a
background in which Dante simultaneously displaces and delocalizes his
past.

As previously mentioned, this is the sphere of gluttony; the figures are
speaking from their skin-and-bones shrunk shades, and that fact itself
points and displaces the ethereal quotation of Dante's poem, orienting the
self-justification underlying his self-definition here. Buonagiunta prophe-
cies to the Pilgrim—future to him in 1300, though past to the time of
the writing of the poem two decades later—that a woman "not yet car-
rying the marriage veil" ("non porta ancor benda") will make Lucca
pleasing to Dante ("ti fará piacere la mia città"). But the hospitality

offered and the distress of the exiled Dante are equally, by implication, displaced from the subject of the "Donne ch'avete intelletto d'amore."

The *Divina commedia* is elaborately systematized into an order that gives every line, through the echo-reminding emphasis of the *terza rima,* the balance of point, while at the same time subverting it through the predominance of such a narrative flow.

Dante's transmutation of clausal balances falls into relief if it is compared not only with other poetry, including his own earlier verse, but with the prose of Augustine, who sets up such balances as the mode of his discourse, particularly[21] when recounting a conversion that is radically different in structure from Dante's, albeit similar in theme.

Augustine's style is formed, as he learned and taught in the ripe rhetorical schools of the empire, on a stepped-up version of the Ciceronian model. In that model, nearly every member of one clause is matched by a correspondent member, often the same part of speech, in the next clause:

> Et mirantur haec homines et stupent qui nesciunt ea, et exultant atque extolluntur qui sciunt, et per inpiam superbiam recedentes et deficientes a lumine tuo tanto ante solis defectum futurum praevident et in praesentia suum non vident—non enim religiose quaerunt, unde habeant ingenium, quo ista quaerunt—et invenientes, quia tu fecisti eos, non ipsi dant tibi se, ut serves quod fecisti, et quales se ipsi fecerant occidunt se tibi et trucidant exaltationes suas sicut volatilia et curiositates suas sicut pisces maris, quibus perambulant secretas semitas abyssi, et luxurias suas sicut pecora campi, ut tu, deus, ignis edax, consumas mortuas curas eorum recreans eos immortaliter.

> And at these things men wonder and are astonished that know them not; and they that know them triumph and are extolled; and out of an impious pride turning back from thee, failing thereby of thy light, they foresee an eclipse of the sun so long beforehand but perceive not their own in the present. For they enquire not religiously enough whence they have the intelligence with which they seek these things; and finding that 'tis thou that made them, they give not themselves up unto thee, that thou mayest preserve what thou hast made, nor do they kill in sacrifice unto thee, what they have made themselves to be; nor slay their own exalted imaginations like as "the fowl of the air" and their own curiosities like as "the fish of the sea," in which they "wander over the unknown paths of the abyss"; and their own wantonness like as "the beasts of the field"; that

thou, Lord, who art a consuming fire, mayest burn up those dead cares of theirs, and renew themselves immortally.[22]

The instances of "et" are ribbed through the sentence, hinging across the stronger "atque" at the near midpoint. Across these clause and phrase dividers, just about every member has a balancing member, and usually more than one. Thus, of the first four words, "et" sets a form that picks up throughout; "haec" is balanced by "ea," which corresponds to it in function, reference, and grammatical category, as "homines" is subdivided into "qui nesciunt" and "qui sciunt," a logical distribution that balances "mirantur" and "stupent" against "exultant atque extolluntur." But that is not the end, for the chiastic phrase built around "recedentes et deficientes" (its own members themselves corresponding to each other), by varying the doubled declarative verbs with doubled participles, builds to the phrase-nesting oppositions around "praevident" and "non vident"—an opposition which repeats that between "nesciunt" and "sciunt" but first inverts it chiastically, so that not seeing comes second rather than first. And then the phrase sustains all this distinction making under only one half of the earlier category, since all this is described of those who "nesciunt," who do not know.

The constant nesting and subnesting, balancing and varying, of words, phrases, and clauses continue on through this sentence, and indeed can be found throughout the writing of Augustine. All the rhetorical motions in this paragraph intensify the rhetorically placed terminal adverb, "immortaliter," which balances and overbalances "mortuas" and its associated words in antithesis with it, though almost alone here it is matched by no corresponding part of speech. It is, in fact, the only adverb in the entire paragraph except "religiose." It immediately modifies the participle "recreans," but it can be extended back through the entire clause, including the phrases around the verb "consumas," which is an opposite in logic to "recreans" but both includes it by subordinating it as a participle and subsumes it in a theologizing that refers to a constant theme in the Prophets and here may be seen to echo specific phrases in Psalms and Deuteronomy. Indeed, the quotations from Psalm 8.7–8, as indicated by my quotation marks in the translation, constitute a further rhetorical overlay, thematically and musically coded echoes of a subtext (or supertext; it is Scripture) that Augustine touches base on constantly in hundreds of such embedded citations.

Augustine's procedure of balancing phrases and clauses comes close, in fact, to doubling parallelism, which is the basic component of

Hebrew verse and other parts of the Bible. It also accords with the repetition that can be seen as the basic component of any poetry. For that reason, it has analogies to the *terza rima* that Dante invented for his poem. But the *terza rima* combines a double with a triple recursion, and lays both over an ongoing progress that matches lines, usually balanced within themselves, into sentences that are deliberately given a forward progression. Dante's verse progression resists the rhetorical subdivisioning not only of Ciceronian prose but of such verse as the poems of the troubadours, for example, or the poems of the *Vita nuova* or the *Convivio,* where Dante in fact subjects the poems to an analysis according to their progressing and matching, quasi-Augustinian subdivisions. Poetry, then, is a more usual locus than prose for this rhetoric of semantic doubling and pairing. The troubadours, and Dante's own poems, offer examples of it. But in the *Divina commedia,* such semantic pairing falls by the wayside in favor of the ongoing progress of the narrative, except in such set pieces as the "Vergine madre, figlia del tuo figlio" hymn that begins the last canto of the *Paradiso,* where the poem allows itself to converge on, and rest in, these balanced matches, and where the hymn has the added function of characterizing the singer, St. Bernard, who this far on can blend his strong theologizing into simple hymnody. The balances of "Vergine madre, figlia del tuo figlio" are not matched through the poem but rather are themselves nonce effects serving to indicate the glory of the convergences here.

Dante's general avoidance of such balanced structures is the more remarkable because the sound, through the *terza rima,* not only follows such balance in the clausulae but does so far more than is the case in many rhymed poetries. He avoids the effect many poets seek with rhyme, of counterpointing the rhymes against the sentences in such a way that a new rhyme is made part of an old sentence. There are many counterpointing procedures by which a poet may vary a regular rhyme scheme. Dante never, or almost never, uses them; though every single tercet offers him much opportunity to do so. He buoys the tercets up in their individuality, itself a metrical feat comparable in difficulty to that of using *terza rima* to begin with. Characteristically the simple designation eschews rhetoric and moves in a simple, "low" style that is part of what the *dolce stil nuovo* implies:

> Io fui abate / in San Zeno / a Verona
> sotto lo 'mperio del buon Barbarossa,
> di cui dolente ancor Milan ragiona.

I was St. Zeno's abbot in Verona
under the rule of the good Barbarossa,
of whom Milan still speaks, sorrowing.

(*Purg.* 18.118–20)

The first line falls into three balanced segments of sound, as I have marked them, but into no corresponding segments of sense, nor does the second line, "sotto lo 'mperio del buon Barbarossa," which falls into two segments, breaking on "'mperio." The third line also has two segments, "di cui dolente ancor Milan ragiona." It divides at "dolente / ancor," but again only in sound. The sense simply and serenely proceeds ahead without any rhetorical doubling back or matching. This distinction is important because there is such a full elaboration of the synchronic architecture of the poem, as Erwin Panofsky notes.[23] He compares Dante and Petrarch as to structure, and he makes the only partially valid point that Dante, as a Scholastic, is interested in parts and parts of parts, whereas Petrarch emphasizes the internal music of the line. But this is not a true opposition; Dante, as we know from the *De vulgari eloquentia,* was quite consciously attentive to the internal music of his lines, and that attention led him not only to balance them in "Scholastic" fashion but to counterpoint them with a sense that did not obey such subdivisioning. The lines move forward at the quick of his voice and person through all the reticulations of the *terza rima.* Dante exhibits in the *Vita nuova* a compulsion to break poems, themselves short, into two or three parts as the main component of his prose analysis; this process is abandoned and, as it were, recapitulated and subsumed in the two-three movement of the *terza rima.*

3

THE fourfold senses of allegory seal and further structure the transaction with the reader effectuated by the *terza rima's* elaboration. But the transaction begins to be made at the processive point of an encounter. The poem attains its reach by presenting a progression, which appears markedly if we throw the large poem into relief against the *Vita nuova* and the *Convivio.* Both the earlier texts are comparably ordered, but both lack the adaptively fluid and transformative progressions of the *Divina commedia.*

Almost from the beginning, the forward movement and neutralizing

condensation of the *Divina commedia* hinges on a series of encounters, at
first with animals and very soon with human beings of all sorts. These
encounters are not fully contained by all the condensations of theologi-
cal doctrine, all the currents of idea and feeling, all the compacting of
the fourfold senses, all the journey structure of the poem.[24] Dante's
reach is powerful enough to comprise all that; it forcefully expresses
more than such systematizations in the turns of the linear progression of
the speaker through the events of the poem. This progression centers on
his encounters, which cannot be derived from the conventions that
Dante inherited. Many of these structuring constituents can be found to
some degree in the *Convivio*, but the encounters cannot. The encounters
in the *Vita nuova* undergo too heavy a structuring to move toward the
center of the work. In the *Divina commedia*, however, they move to
the center, heightening and vivifying and varying the ongoing move-
ment. The questions and answers coming from these encounters pre-
ponderate in the whole progression of the poem. They are exchanges
that, in Hans Felten's analysis, are accorded the exercise and delight of
the gradual accession to beatitude.[25]

As for the medieval compounding of senses, Dante's poem is unusu-
ally full, of course, but comparable procedures can be found even in the
small compass of such a poem as "Adam lay ibounden":

> Adam lay ibounden,
> Bounden in a bond;
> Foure thousand winter
> Thowt he not too long.
> And all was for an appil,
> An appil that he took,
> As clerkes finden wreten
> In here book.

> Ne hadde the appil take ben,
> The appil taken ben,
> Ne hadde never our lady
> A ben hevene quen.
> Blissed be the time
> That appil take was!
> Therfore we moun singen
> *"Deo gracias!"*

This song, in its clear celebration of the *felix culpa,* is neatly balanced in an Auerbachian figura, with the typologically twinned events given a stanza each. The poem is focused, complex, and even somewhat indirect; and, in a way comparable to Dante's allegorical practice, it needs simply name the apple in its repetitions for the apple to accrue allegorical associations. The apple is anecdotal, mythical, allegorical, theological, all at once. What the apple, and the statements of the poem, lack is the concreteness of Dante, the graininess of the literal, which is the great uniqueness of the *Divina commedia* as against any other medieval poems I have seen—and very likely any at all. In his reach, Dante offers an extraordinarily extensive range of concrete observations and constructions, often spilling over into that which serve to frame the encounters. The concretions may be said to rise from the intentional focus of describing the encounters.[26]

The encounters that release the *Divina commedia* from the enclosedness of such poems and open it up for its ongoing expansions are with people we never meet in the world, thus providing the seal of fiction to the representation: the poet encounters complete persons who lack an unpredictable future. They are complete because they are dead, and they are endowed by the poet with just what the dead lack, a communicative power to engage in a kind of dialogue, subject to the typifying (and allegorized) constraints that are dictated by the particular division of the realm of the dead that they inhabit. The pilgrim-poet's progressive and serial relation to them, if it were coordinated with the theology of the poem, would have to be reckoned entirely a purgatory, since in his future he does not conceive himself as either confined to hell or ready for immediate entrance to heaven. Yet to account the whole poem a purgatory would amount to a contradiction that in fact the very provisionality of the poem and its vagueness on this point allow it to avoid.

On one much explored tangent, the reference of the soul's exit from Egypt into Israel, the cue of Dante himself is wholly adhered to, and the significations of the fourfold allegory are applied to the poem. But on another tangent, there is the whole symbolic pack of preexistent relations, ideas, and actions that get deployed, separated, and interwoven in the poem.

The displacement of the Pilgrim from the center of attention, while keeping him in the dialogic situation of receiving instruction from interlocutors on a long succession, actually has the effect of strengthening and integrating his realization and of putting the auditor of the poem in a comparable position of displacement. The *terza rima* and the elaborate structures of figuration and system keep asserting their presence against, rather than with, the randomness of the encounters. The relative processiveness of the poem, and its flexibility with respect to its own fourfold scheme, can be seen—to take one example involving many various persons—in Dante's indirect confrontation with rulers in the Valley of the Princes (*Purg.* 7.82–136).

In allegorical congruence with the indolence and preoccupation of the princes here enumerated in the Valley of the Ante-Purgatory, Dante does not even speak to the many figures gathered before them but simply listens to Sordello identifying them. That poet has been with Dante and Virgil for the fairly long period of two cantos, and this is the end of a sequence that has begun with Sordello's proudly not speaking at all (6.62–64). Sordello becomes willing to speak only because Virgil identifies himself as sharing Mantuan citizenship, not till much later revealing his own identity as the preeminent Latin poet. All the qualities of the princes, as Dante encounters their presences, can be taken as subsumed under, and fleshed out with, the particularities of Dante's encounter with Sordello, which is not so much allegorized as ideologically extended.

The run about the negligent princes follows Dante's blanket diatribe against Italy (6.76–151), which the presence of these sorrowful, briefly described rulers, as they turn to the joy of communal singing, supersedes and redefines. Even before Sordello appears, Dante has encountered a host of secondary officials (6.13–24), who are less collected in bearing than the princes, as well as of lower earthly standing. Dante, until he breaks into his diatribe, stands nearly silent between Sordello and Virgil, since what they have in common, poetry, does not come into the discussion here. What dominates, compressed into processive anecdote, is the civic probity that Dante had declared to be a proper subject for an international vernacular poetry in the passage from the *De vulgari eloquentia* quoted above. Sordello is an appropriate guide at this point, not just as an Italian troubadour but because he accompanied Charles I of Anjou on his invasion of Italy. There is no special reason to have so great a throng, however, nor is Dante learning more allegorically from a large number than he could have from a small. Allegory here yields to the mental encounter with the tangle of politics and dynastic alliance as it gets gradually resolved in Purgatory.

Here all the definitions of the *De monarchia* are abrogated in favor of a delineation of rulers by simple spiritual style. Taken in the context of Dante's persistent and elaborate theologizing in this poem and in his political writing, this presentation must figure as a foreshortening, a foreshortening dense with the complex of large-scale alliances of the late thirteenth century. In order we are given Rudolph von Hapsburg, whose emperorship (and Dante calls him *imperador*) was not recognized by Ottocar II of Bohemia, who lost his life fighting Rudolph in dispute of that very question. Ottocar was succeeded by Wenceslaus IV, "on whom feed lust and sloth" ("cui lussuria e ozio pasce") (7.102). He is less in life than his father, who has in any case left all that behind in death. Now these rulers stand together in a harmonious throng, along with Philip III the Bold, Charles of Anjou, Peter of Aragon, Henry the Fat of Navarre, Philip IV the Fair, Peter's son Alfonso III, and Henry III "of the simple life" ("de la semplice vita") (7.130), a term of praise that is not only positive; it has a negative limitation on it, too, since Dante at once says he was surpassed by his offspring. Finally another conqueror is brought in, one of lesser import and closer to home for Dante, the Ghibelline leader William Longsword, whose treacherous capture was avenged by his son in a devastation evoked in the last line of the canto.

Dante reads in the faces of Rudolph and Ottocar a neglect and a comfort, both postures contradicting the hostility between them on earth (here unmentioned). He next moves succinctly and disjunctively to a more physical feature, a single stroke of identifying depiction, a more foreshortened version of the concretions noted by Ruskin, a verbal version of what Giotto before him and Masaccio more vigorously afterwards had done in depicting faces. So Philip III is identified by his small nose: he is "Nasetto." The focus shifts once again as the next two rulers are identified respectively as "the benign one" and the one who, sighing, makes a bed for his cheek with his palm. Again, Peter III of Aragon and Charles of Anjou are identified by single strokes of description: the first is "stout-limbed" ("membruto") (7.112); the second has a "masculine nose" ("maschio naso") (7.113).

All these vivid descriptive touches are saliently processive and do not lend themselves to consistent allegorization. As Dante expands on the scene here, he anchors himself on these visualizations, only to leave them behind, simply naming Henry III of England as "the king of the simple life" ("il re de la semplice vita") (7.130) and William VII of Monferrato as looking down and seated physically (but not allegorically) below them (7.133–34). The intermittence of this allegory prevents us from firmly reading his downward look as penitence for "making Monferrato and Canavese weep" ("fa pianger Monferrato e Canavese") (7.136).

These lines mention military operations only as sorrows; they concentrate on nubs of character, and not even on those traits (other than indolence) that might explain the presence of this array of kings. These rulers, having devoted their lives to dynasty, are defined in terms of dynasty, including not only the line from father to son (or sons, in the case of Peter of Aragon) but also from alliance through their wives, and "more than Beatrice and Margaret / Constance boasts still of her husband" ("più che Beatrice e Margherita, / Costanza di marito ancor si vanta") (7.128–29): Constance can be prouder of her husband, Peter, than can the two wives of Charles of Anjou. Not brought to the foreground here is the fact that Constance's father, Manfred, who has not yet got this far in Purgatory, was killed by Charles at the battle of Benevento. Manfred, by contrast, has already spoken of her (*Purg.* 3.143). These foreshortenings stretch the perceptions of the poem into a spiritual definition of politics that the echoes of the biblical prophets in this passage will reinforce.[27]

In another style of confrontation, the principal soul speaks directly to Dante:

> "Io fui abate in San Zeno a Verona
> sotto lo 'mperio del buon Barbarossa,
> di cui dolente ancor Milan ragiona.
>
> E tale ha già l'un piè dentro la fossa,
> che tosto piangerà quel monastero,
> e tristo fia d'avere avuta possa;
>
> perché suo figlio, mal del corpo intero,
> e de la mente peggio, e che mal nacque,
> ha posto in loco di suo pastor vero."
>
> Io non so se più disse o s'ei si tacque,
> tant' era già di là da noi trascorso;
> ma questo intesi, e ritener mi piacque.
>
> E quei che m'era ad ogne uopo soccorso
> disse: "Volgiti qua: vedine due
> venir dando a l'accidïa di morso."
>
> Di retro a tutti dicean: "Prima fue
> morta la gente a cui il mar s'aperse,
> che vedesse Iordan le rede sue.
>
> E quella che l'affanno non sofferse

fino a la fine col figlio d'Anchise,
sé stessa a vita sanza gloria offerse."

"I was St. Zeno's abbot in Verona
under the rule of the good Barbarossa,
of whom Milan still speaks, sorrowing.
    And there is a man with one foot in the grave,
who soon will weep over that monastery,
lamenting that he once had power there,
    because his son, ill in his whole body
and worse in his mind, and who was ill born,
he has put in place of its true shepherd."
    I know not if he said more or was silent—
he had already run so far ahead of us;
but this I heard and was pleased to remember it.
    And he who was my help in every need
said: "Turn around: see out of those, two men
coming who are giving sloth the mock."
    At the tail of all they were saying: "First
were dead the race for whom the sea opened up
before the Jordan saw its heirs.
    And the race that did not suffer stress
until the end with the son of Anchises
offered themselves to life without glory."
                    (*Purg.* 18.118–38)

We are told nothing about this abbot of St. Zeno; his life cannot bear
on the problem, and he transmits a lesson that Dante already transmit-
ted in the Valley of the Princes, the problem in politics discussed since
Plato, that the son in a dynasty may be a declination from the father—
a question to be raised still again by Charles Martel in the *Paradiso*
(8.95–148). The lesson is given by observing the bad practice in appoint-
ments of Alberto della Scala, who happens to be the father of Dante's
patron Can Grande. The abbot's complaint about being supplanted
through an official appointment is not so different from Pier delle
Vigne's (*Inf.* 13), though his reaction was different enough to save him.
Again, we are not told about that, and Dante merely accompanies him
in the speed of his course. Dante "heard" what he said "and was pleased
to retain it" ("questo intesi, e ritener mi piacque").
    At a point in Dante's sequence of reactions, the abbot presents his

career in terms of his own sequence of reactions to those of others—of Milan as it continues in its sorrow to speak about Barbarossa, of the father who will weep and sadden before his power for having appointed a flagrantly incompetent son, and of the abbot himself, the very continuation of whose complaint is uncertain because his speed in overcoming sloth puts him quickly out of earshot. Directed to turn around (and so to posture himself differently toward the sequence), Dante experiences through Virgil's constantly cueing mediation the report of those set in a contrast between the hope and the death of those of the Exodus who did not make the Holy Land and those who abandoned Aeneas for a comfortable life before he had established himself. When all of these, in their sequence, have gone out of sight, Dante speaks of himself as given over to a wandering sequence of random thought, to such a degree (the limit of sequence) that he shut his eyes and "transformed his thought into dream" ("e 'l pensamento in sogno trasmutai") (18.145).

The encounter itself, again, in all its dimensions, is emphasized here rather than the purgation, and Dante makes no further comment on the exempla they contemplate, the Israelites crossing the Red Sea and the exiles from Troy who accompany Aeneas—two groups, where Dante stands singly. His further reaction—it would be hard to call it either slothful or a response to sloth—is to free associate in a way that leads him to sleep and to the dream about the Siren, which leads him on to another set of encounters.

Beatrice is now fairly close, but there is little in the tonality of this approach that would indicate so, as distinct from the progressions in the *Paradiso*. The confrontational sequence of encounters, which cannot be structured such that the system of the poem contains them, nevertheless provides the key for the ongoing movement of the poet. This movement coordinates details for a tonal unity that brings the direst parts of the *Inferno* into harmony with the most sublime reaches of the *Paradiso*. The single moving eye and mind provides a mentation that is phenomenologically participating at every single point. It never stands back, and all the theological summarizing made by Virgil, Beatrice, St. Bernard, and others is directed at this eye and mind, registered in it, and digested as part of the live, ongoing, predominant movement through the narrative.

At many other points, too, there is no real way to harmonize the system of the poem with the resurgent reactions of an encounter. So, for example, Brunetto Latini's measured, dignified excoriation of Florence, his prediction of glory for Dante if he follows his star, and Dante's account of how grateful he is to Brunetto for teaching him "how a man makes himself eternal" ("come l'uom s'etterna") (*Inf.* 15.85) cannot be related without considerable strain and arbitrariness to the sin of sodomy, for which Brunetto is confined to this particular sphere. And the conclusion of the canto, in which he seems "of those / who win and not the one who loses" ("parve di costoro / quelli che vince, non colui che perde") (*Inf.* 15.123–24), cannot be other than theologically inappropriate if one matches it seriously to the categories that, in the scheme, dominate the *Inferno.* Yet it is not felt to be inconsistent; the play of the narrator's feeling is made to take over and supersede.

Dante himself builds together the systematizing structure of the poem and the narrator's varied, simple adaptive movement of encounters. To put the system and the encounters into an opposition would approach the summary of Bakhtin, who speaks of Dante's poem as trying to "synchronize diachrony."[28] "Each image is full of historical potential," Bakhtin specifies, "and therefore strains with the whole of its being toward participation." This characterization, however, if pressed, would almost take back what it has given and overhistoricize the speaking poet. It would push the figures that he encounters back over the line into this world, as though the conversations were taking place before their deaths. But the poet is an elusive figure here, only partially subsumable into his functions of pilgrim and writer. And if poet includes philosopher, in Ernst Curtius's view, he distinctly predominates over the philosopher he includes. The wisdom offered by the poem supersedes any of the contributory doctrines, however complex, that come up in it. They too, indeed, have the status of encounters, and the frame of the poem recedes before its ongoing motion, the ongoing projection of a voice whose strange and special contours we apprehend as we listen to it. The prior definitions of the medieval poet cannot account for this process because Dante transforms them. He is no longer the public performer who runs through many medieval traditions, as Dronke shows us,[29] nor the rhetorician whose various turns Paul Zumthor and others have well delineated,[30] nor simply the master of ideational figurations and configurations depicted by Erich Auerbach and Curtius. As Giuseppe Giacalone aptly writes of the souls in the poem, "The very consistency of the souls has thus two structurations, one 'substantial' that is given by the soul's dimension of eternity, and the other 'accidental' and historical, which is conditioned by its human, temporal earthly dimension."[31] This is true preeminently of the poet as well, who both reverses and recombines those two dimensions into the single, ongoing, forward movement of a constantly recapitulative and "silently" building poem.

The movement temporally through the poem, then, is processive rather than just systematic. The processive is fed back to the systematic to comprehend it. Backing up the progressions through the poems are many passages of humble observation about psychological processes, with only a sub-Scholastic basis.[32] And the processive gives the key to Dante's invention, which is to transpose the possibility of the systematic, already available both in philosophy and in poetry to the generation before his, into an instrument for dynamizing the internality of the self beyond the structurings of the troubadours and the earlier *stilnovisti.*

The need for the guide—the Pilgrim is never without one—can be seen to come from the need to transpose the process into system. The process permits the presentation of the sequenced history of a person, which is then at once transposed into the systematization that it "comes to." To call the result of this process "subjectivity" is in a sense tautologous. If it be so called, it is a newly structured subjectivity, by definition at a dialectical remove from the vestiges of complicated posturing toward Guelph and Ghibelline in politics, and also transcendent over the system that at the same time enables it. The progressive, as evinced by the poem, is what allows it to be systematic, and the balance between the two is maintained at every point. Typically the systematic is retrospective to the processive, and the processive is needed to bring a person to the point of the systematic, both the Dante who moves through the poem and the reader who follows his movement. The person of the Pilgrim, who goes through series of actions and reactions till he is "pure and set up to rise up to the stars" ("puro e disposto a salire a le stelle") in the last line of the *Purgatorio,* has disappeared by the last line of the *Paradiso* into "the love that moves the sun and the other stars" ("l'amor che move il sole e l'altre stelle"). The movement temporally through the poem, then, is processive rather than just systematic.

The love that Beatrice radiates here once the poet meets her in the *Purgatorio* has completely digested even its sublimated erotic form into the courtesy of charitable interchange that at the same time is markedly fueled by memories of what impelled the *Vita nuova.* Desire is retained while being transcended, and once again the prior death of the beloved guide rules out any Platonic limitation on their interchange.

The passage where Dante meets Beatrice, and where for the only moment in the poem his own name is brought forward and the fact commented on, is notable for its bravura of expanded allegorical senses. These narrated events frame, though loosely, the immediate responses of the poet, and for all the allegory, even here the dramatic contours of the encounter govern the narrative line at this intense and culminating point.

As Dante says in the *Convivio*, speaking of the soul and love and quoting Boethius, "ogni subito movimento di cose non avviene sanza alcuno discorrimento d'animo" ("no sudden movement in things comes about without some change of spirit") (2.10). The encounter with Beatrice, a large turning point, encompasses many sudden movements:

> Quando il settentrïon del primo cielo,
> che né occaso mai seppe né orto
> né d'altra nebbia che di colpa velo,
>
> e che faceva lì ciascuno accorto
> di suo dover, come 'l più basso face
> qual temon gira per venire a porto,
>
> fermo s'affisse: la gente verace,
> venuta prima tra 'l grifone ed esso,
> al carro volse sé come a sua pace;
>
> e un di loro, quasi da ciel messo,
> *"Veni, sponsa, de Libano"* cantando
> gridò tre volte, e tutti li altri appresso.
> . . . .
>
> così dentro una nuvola di fiori
> che da le mani angeliche saliva
> e ricadeva in giù dentro e di fori,
>
> sovra candido vel cinta d'uliva
> donna m'apparve, sotto verde manto
> vestita di color di fiamma viva.
>
> E lo spirito mio, che già cotanto
> tempo era stato ch'a la sua presenza
> non era di stupor, tremando, affranto,
>
> sanza de li occhi aver più conoscenza,
> per occulta virtù che da lei mosse,
> d'antico amor sentì la gran potenza.

Tosto che ne la vista mi percosse
l'alta virtù che già m'avea trafitto
prima ch'io fuor di püerizia fosse,
    volsimi a la sinistra col respitto
col quale il fantolin corre a la mamma
quando ha paura o quando elli è afflitto,
    per dicere a Virgilio: "Men che dramma
di sangue m'è rimaso che non tremi:
conosco i segni de l'antica fiamma."
    Ma Virgilio n'avea lasciati scemi
di sé, Virgilio dolcissimo patre,
Virgilio a cui per mia salute die'mi;
    né quantunque perdeo l'antica matre,
valse a le guance nette di rugiada
che, lagrimando, non tornasser atre.
    "Dante, perché Virgilio se ne vada,
non pianger anco, non piangere ancora;
ché pianger ti conven per altra spada."
    Quasi ammiraglio che in poppa e in prora
viene a veder la gente che ministra
per li altri legni, e a ben far l'incora;
    in su la sponda del carro sinistra,
quando mi volsi al suon del nome mio,
che di necessità qui si registra,
    vidi la donna che pria m'appario
velata sotto l'angelica festa,
drizzar li occhi ver' me di qua dal rio.

When the seven-star candelabra of the first heaven,
which a setting never knew, nor a rising
nor other fogging than the veil of sin,
    and which made everyone aware
of what his duty was, just as the lower star makes
the one who turns the helm come into port,
    stopped firmly, the people of the truth
who first came between the griffin and it
turned toward the chariot as toward their peace,
    and one of them, as if sent down from Heaven,

sang *"Veni, sponsa, de Libano,"*
three times, and all the others did so after him.
. . . .
    Just so, inside of a cloud of flowers
that were cast up from the angelic hands,
and then fell back again within and without,
    over a shining veil, crowned with olive,
a woman appeared to me under a green mantle
clothed in the color of living flame,
    and my spirit that already so long
a time had passed that in her presence
I had not been, trembling, struck with awe,
    without having more knowledge from my eyes,
through a hidden power that moved from her,
I felt the great power of old love.
    As soon as in my sight there struck me
the high power that had already pierced me
before I was out of my boyhood,
    I turned to the left with the trust
with which an infant runs to his mother
when he is afraid or when he is afflicted,
    to say to Virgil: "Less than a dram
of blood is left in me that does not tremble:
I recognize the signs of the old flame."
    But Virgil had left us bereft
of himself, Virgil, sweetest father,
Virgil to whom I gave myself for my salvation;
    nor did all that our ancient mother lost
avail to keep my cheeks, cleansed with dew,
from turning dark with tears.
    "Dante, because Virgil goes away,
do not keep weeping, do not keep weeping,
since weeping befits you for another sword."
    Like an admiral who from stern to prow
comes to see the people who are handling
the other ships and encourages them to do well;
    on the left side of the chariot
when I turned around at the sound of my name—

which of necessity is listed here,
    I saw the lady who first appeared to me
veiled beneath the angelic festival,
    direct her eyes to me on this side of the stream.

                    (*Purg.* 30.1–66)

Before this moment, the allegorical entities have progressively crowded in elaborate connection and with elaborate fourfold senses. Indeed, exhaustive allegorizing commentary has been brought to bear on each of the rich integers of this passage and what precedes it: the position of the heavens, the heavens themselves, the chariot with all its passengers, and its accompanying train: the four beasts, the seven candlesticks, the streamers, the Griffin, the twenty-four elders, the colors, and the scriptural quotations. The Church Triumphant in all its history has been unveiled, with Beatrice's central position presumptively like that of Christ, and the convergences of presentation override and enlist the theological concentrations here.[33] Yet from the beginning the relation of all these figures to the present Dante is somewhat oblique. The tradition of a religious allegorizing for the "spouse come from Lebanon" of the Song of Songs, which for Dante ran from Origen through St. Bernard, is just obliquely touched on. Here the reference is set in what seems like the exuberance of randomness, with quotations from Revelation (15), from an unidentified bit of ecclesiastical Latin, from Matthew as applied to Christ, and from the *Aeneid*. Moreover, the "spouse come from Lebanon" cannot be at once Beatrice and the Church, though Beatrice cannot be deflected from the reference, any more than she can be excluded from the beginning of the statement associated in Scripture with Mary, "Blessed art thou who comest (in the name of the Lord)." But with the increase of allegorical complexity, and even equivocation, there is, if anything, a countervailing increase in the directness of the syntax, the simplicity in the ring of the language.

    In this profusion of crisscrossing associations, it would really be impossible without strain to insist on consistent structural connections to doctrine. Nor can the veils (the veil that is absent in line 3, the transparent veil of line 31, and the "veiled" as a past participle ["velata"] of line 66) be set into an allegorical order. In the third reference, the poet cannot be referring to her second veil, since she is "veiled beneath the angelic festival" ("velata sotto l'angelica festa").[34] This elaborate fullness

is still not full-blown in its fourfold allegorical significance. So earlier
(16.72 ff.) there is no particular reason why the doctrine of free will
should be offered at this particular point. Such an exclusive focusing on
theology and structure would ultimately mute the poignancy of the
double association to both the long-present Virgil and the just-present
Beatrice, combined in the poignancy of recall, as the further quotation
from the *Aeneid* reminds Dante of his dead love by referring to it in the
very words of Dido about Aeneas: "agnosco veteris vestigia flammae" ("I
recognize the traces of the ancient flame") (*Aeneid* 4.23). With this
phrase, Dido connects her new love for Aeneas to her old love for her
husband, Sichaeus. It would be perverse to look for strict correspon-
dences in old and new for Dante; his old flame is the same as his new,
though the new has been transformed, which allows him to quote his
guide directly before her rather than to muse and to anguish like Dido.
But he is struck by the phrase enough to give it twice: "d'antico amor
sentì la gran potenza" ("I felt the great power of old love") (39); and
more literally of Virgil's lines, "Conosco i segni de l'antica fiamma" ("I
recognize the signs of the old flame") (48). The looseness of the appli-
cation from Virgil redirects us to the primacy of the encounter with
Beatrice, to the stabs of recognition that he does not at all coordinate
into definition.

His reaction of trembling and stupefaction are familiar from the *Vita
nuova*, where they were recounted over and over, but statically. Here the
same feelings are being enlisted in the tremendous ongoing process of
spiritual expansion. Now, almost at once, Beatrice wants him "hence-
forth to divest yourself of fear and shame" ("Da tema e da vergogna /
voglio che tu omai ti disviluppo") (33.31–32). This far along in the
Commedia, the process has been experienced so extensively that, to
Dante's initial dismay, Virgil himself can now disappear. The old standard
response of trembling fear in the presence of Beatrice fixed the earlier
narrator of the *Vita nuova* in the inspection of his own inner state. Now
that state has been dynamized and projected outward; and he has no
such opportunity for self-inspection, since he moves along, evenly but
definitely, along the time line that the lines of the poem are measuring.
So he must react at once, and he is to move forward, to all the revela-
tions and love capacitations of the *Paradiso.* The progression is delin-
eated in a characteristically matter-of-fact low-pitched summary; it is so
sudden as to be atemporal: "È Bëatrice quella che si scorge / di bene in

meglio, sì subitamente / che l'atto suo per tempo non si sporge" ("And Beatrice is she who conducts me / from good to better, so suddenly / that her act is not extended in time") (*Par.* 10.37–39).

The prose of the *Vita nuova,* by contrast, even when it achieves lovely effects, feeds them back into the static self-preoccupation. There is much weeping and constant chatter among the choruses of ladies who accompany the action and react to it: "Allora queste donne cominciaro a parlare tra loro; e sì come talora vedemo cadere l'acqua mischiata di bella neve, così mi parea udire le loro parole uscire mischiate di sospiri" ("Then those ladies began to speak among themselves; and just as we sometimes see water falling mixed with beautiful snow, so I seemed to hear their words issuing mixed with sighs") (18.25). This is beautiful, a foretaste of the visual precisions and splendors of the *Commedia.* But it is going nowhere, nor is it referred to another order.

At a rosy dawn in a cloudy rain of flowers, Beatrice appears to him in white, red, and green—and he is stupefied. When he begins to come out of it, he is like a hurt child running to mamma—a statement that comes between the two reminiscences of Dido. He tells Virgil that every dram of his blood trembles. And at that point, he notices that Virgil has vanished for both of— *"us":* "Ma Virgilio n'avea lasciati scemi / di sè." The elided syllable, "n'" for "ne," constitutes his first linkage to Beatrice here. "All that our ancient mother lost"—that is, all of the earthly Paradise that remains of Eden, where he now stands—cannot prevent him from wetting with dark tears his dew-cleansed cheeks. Beatrice tells him not to cry because there will be another occasion for that. At once she is compared to an admiral encouraging his officers—somewhat curiously, even if we allow a reminiscence of the "terrible as an army with banners" applied to the Beloved in the Song of Songs. And then Dante perceives her once again.

All this sequence gives the nub of a sort of psychodrama of reaction. This first, climactic appearance of Beatrice, nearly two thirds of the way through the poem, is, if anything, less allegorized than other encounters, while at the same time it reverberates more with the interactions that give the quick of responsive development to the poet. This constant flexible adjustment of fine-tuned dramatic reactions continues into the *Paradiso* and through all the theological instruction she there transmits to him, the changes there often registering as an increase in the brightness of her eyes—but without the closed eye and heart symbology of the *Vita nuova.*

4

In the *Inferno,* ordeals are "homeopathic" and without cure. They are centered on the body of the subject. In the *Purgatorio,* they are allopathic, multiply centered on both body and psyche, and mysteriously curative. That is, where the *effect* of punishment is immediately apparent in the *Inferno,* in the *Purgatorio,* the purgation's *operation* is immediately apparent, but its effect is only ultimately and invisibly carried through by the disappearance of the subject from that sphere, something impossible in the *Inferno,* where he is enclosed forever where he is. In the *Paradiso,* there are no such interactions, only fulfillment and a simultaneous copresence in many places: in the sphere, in the *primum mobile,* in the Mystic Rose, and in the ineffable anagogic center-circumference location of the whole *Paradiso.* This situation heavily modifies, in addition to other qualifications, the application of the fourfold allegory; and its relation to Dante's progress, again, is not especially spelled out or systematized. In the *Inferno,* he simply reacts. In the *Purgatorio,* he is mysteriously purged, his forehead rush-wiped of the seven *P*s on it, and his psyche subjected without reactive comment, though with much doctrinal instruction, till he is described simply as "puro e disposto a salire a le stelle." In the *Paradiso,* however, he is subjected to even more instruction and put through some reactions, but at the very end, his desire and his will are simply subject to God: "l'amor che move il sole e l'altre stelle."

The Pilgrim himself cannot quite be measured in this way; his reactions are as random and spaced as the encounters are constant and structured in varied relation to the overarching system for all their differentiation. Singleton has expounded the elements of conversion that govern the Pilgrim,[35] and Freccero, following Pierre Courcelle and others,[36] has stressed the likenesses of Dante's poem to Augustine's *Confessions.* But the *Divina commedia* projects itself forward and away from the self-centeredness of that work, for all the Augustinian echoes of language and recourse to Augustinian doctrine that such commentators stress. The preoccupation of the *Confessions* with its own experience, by contrast, and its own relation to God throws into relief the dialectical dimensionality of both Dante and, indeed, God, in the *Divina commedia.* The *Confessions* are recursive, expansive, and prayerful as they move the events of the life exponentially toward the praise of God. Where Augustine dwells strongly on himself and his past, we hear about

Dante's past when some ancestor or relative or friend comes onstage, always in conjunction with his interactions with the vast cast of characters who come forward serially in the poem's central narrative progress.

5

THE *terza rima* itself offers at once a closure that at times, if a sentence, is confined to three lines—a version of epigrammatic summary comparable to that of the couplet, and a calmly managed openness, since the center of the three lines must always be connected back or ahead. Dante tends to reinforce the summary ring of his sentences by making them normally coincide with the closures of *terza rima,* rather than, in the more modern style, counterpointing the rhyme endings against the sentence endings.[37] The evenness of this process is reinforced by the tendency, already noted, toward end-stopped lines as the tonic progression of the ongoing rhythm, while the frequent "conversational" recourse to caesurae varies it according to the careful management of the two or three constituents of each hendecasyllable as Dante discusses them in the *De vulgari eloquentia.*[38] There, indeed, Dante discusses caesurae and particularly praises the break after the fifth syllable, which he illustrates with his own line "Donne ch'avete / intelletto d'amore" (quoting there also the line "Amor che ne la mente mi ragiona"). He also says that the hendecasyllable "seems to be the most splendid of all meters because of its duration and because of its capacity for accommodating opinions, constructions, and a range of diction" ("Quorum omnium endecasillabum videtur esse superbius, tam temporis occupatione quam capacitate sententie, constructionis et vocabularum") (2.5.3). And he attends as well to the sound qualities of individual words, which he characterizes as "combed," ("pexa") "smooth" ("lubrica"), hairy ("yrsuta"), and the like.

Take these lines, for example, where the first has a single break, the next three have two lighter breaks per line, and the fifth again has a single break. The lines are end-stopped down to line 11, which inverts that pattern with an enjambment, dropped in the end-stopped line 12, but capped in the polyphonic line 13, where the caesura, coming after the ninth syllable at the highly marked beginning of a quotation, then enjambs very heavily by making its last word a conjunction leading tightly into the next line: "E dentro a l'un senti' cominciar: 'Quando'":[39]

130

Ne la corte del cielo, ond' io rivegno,
si trovan molte gioie care e belle
tanto che non si posson trar del regno;
   e 'l canto di quei lumi era di quelle;
chi non s'impenna sì che là sù voli,
dal muto aspetti quindi le novelle.
   Poi, sì cantando, quelli ardenti soli
su fuor girati intorno a noi tre volte,
comme stelle vicine a' fermi poli,
   donne mi parver, non da ballo sciolte,
ma che s'arrestin tacite, ascoltando
fin che le nove note hanno ricolte.
   E dentro a l'un senti' cominciar: "Quando
lo raggio de la grazia onde s'accende
verace amore e che poi cresce amando,
   multiplicato in te tanto resplende,
che ti conduce su per quella scala
u' sanza risalir nessun discende;
   qual ti negasse il vin de la sua fiala
per la tua sete, in libertà non fora
se non com' acqua ch'al mar non si cala."

In the court of heaven, from which I come
are found many jewels dear and beautiful,
so many that they cannot be taken from the kingdom;
   and the song of those lights was of those jewels;
he who does not take wing to fly up there,
from the mute may await news about it.
   Then, thus singing, those ardent suns
turned round about us three times
like stars neighboring on fixed poles,
   and seemed to me women, not loosed from the dance,
but who stopped suddenly silent, listening
until they had gathered the new notes.
   And within one I heard beginning: "When
the ray of grace, from which is kindled
true love, and then grows in loving,
   multiplied in you so much, shines
that it leads you up by that stair where

without climbing back no one goes down.
Whoever would deny you wine from his flask
for your thirst would no more be in liberty
than water would that does not flow to the sea."

(*Par.* 10.70–90).

In such a varied regularity of modulation, the *terza rima* is felt as a force, then, for both closure and opening, for an idealized conversation that makes points succinctly in ways that Dante's guides remind him are always subject to the time constraints of the analogy between the "real" time that is elapsing and the measured amount of talk—itself, of course, varied—that may be allotted to an encounter. The terms he uses, too, are from the common language, freighted lightly but definitely with theological implication. The word "corte" here cannot be divested from the whole theory of the *De monarchia,* where in heaven there is no longer any need to distinguish between religious and secular authority, a condition bearing on the term "regno." The word "posson" is at once colloquial and vested with the force of the Thomistic *posse.* As it happens, Thomas Aquinas is about to speak. The poem has long established that references to stars imply the whole Ptolemaic cosmology, and in that context references to singing and dancing refer at once to the common activities of Italian society and to the music of the spheres.

The recourse to metaphor and other figures is comparably light, while even more intricated, through the central conception of the poem. Souls who are jewels who are lights who are suns who are stars who are dancing ladies—these attempts to find figures for the lights, which are brighter than the sun in the sphere of the sun, are already grounded in the conception of the poem and of this section of it. Thus there is no sense of extravagance in these successions of images when they are immediately referrable to the poem's theological overview, gradually revealed but controlling. Soon, again without strain, they can be called a "wreath" ("serto," 102) and each a "wax candle" ("cero," 115). The narrative assertions move ahead in a proportionateness that the rhymes of the *terza rima* underscore; they come in a timed, even sequence, and richly ornament, with the suspension of time in this eternity as an envisioned analogy—a suspension just mentioned in this canto of Beatrice ("whose act is not extended in time"; "che l'atto suo per tempo non si sporge," 10.39). And so at the same time the Pilgrim can be intent on both Beatrice and God as he has just said, "e sì tutto 'l mio amore in lui si mise, / che Bëatrice eclissò ne l'oblio" ("And so entirely my love was placed in him / that Beatrice was eclipsed in forgetfulness") (10.59–60). The term "eclipse" is a metaphor, but it finds a precise correlative in the elaborate astronomical calculations at the beginning of this canto, and throughout. "Forgetfulness" is a simple psychological act with profound theological implications but with none of the allegorical baggage from the river of Lethe encountered in the *Purgatorio* (28.25–33).

The speaker here in this fourth sphere of wisdom, the sun, is Thomas Aquinas (not yet sainted), who expounds little doctrine but mainly exemplifies courtesy and loving charity in the terms of praise with which he introduces the spirits of other theologians in his cortège, some of whom were his intellectual opponents in this life. The analogical echoes of his theological language appear in the slightly Latinate cast of his statements, in the fullness of the sounding, interechoing rhymes with which he begins (Quando / accende / amando / resplende / . . . descende), and in the twist of triple negatives through the last lines quoted.

In the two final lines of the entire poem, the poet wraps up his expressed sense and described perception in the love that he derives wholly from God. These lines hinge on a simile that sets the center-circumference of just fifty lines earlier into the motion of a wheel that circles back on itself, through the desire of the poet: "ma già volgeva il mio disio e 'l *velle*, / sì come rota ch'igualmente è mossa, / l'amor che move il sole e l'altre stelle" ("But already was turning my desire and my will / like a wheel that equally is moved / the Love that moves the sun and the other stars"). This is a dynamic revision of Aristotle's "Unmoved Mover."

It also dynamizes Piccarda's earlier summary: "E 'n la sua voluntade è nostra pace" ("And in his will is our peace") (*Par.* 3.85). Here, in harmony with the absolutely even turning of the wheel, enjambments have fallen away; the three lines are fully end-stopped. They open, however, in the middle for the simile of the second line; the sentence can still expand. And the ordinary desire, turned by a love that attends to the whole universe as well as to the interiority of the Pilgrim, is coupled with a will that is put into Latin (*velle*) to keep up the precision and fullness of theological discourse, and also offer it homage. The term here, whose abstractness is underscored by the Latin, gathers into itself other references throughout to will ("voglia," "voluntade"), permuting the many other conjunctions of "desire" and "will" while by implication subsuming the theological discussions about double wills (*Purg.* 5.61 ff.) and absolute versus relative wills (*Par.* 4, 5).

"Equally" must mean not only "in even motion" but "moves exactly as it is moved," where active and passive disappear. Active and passive do not wholly disappear, however, since these lines are the subject of a sentence whose object is the poet, who is mentioned in the line before them and who describes the turning of his desire and his will toward— the writing of the poem? To say that would overspecify it and close off that side of the allegory, when, in fact, even the circle-point is not closed; rather, it is subject to a lethargy that is also an expansion: "Un punto solo m'è maggior letargo" ("One point to me is a greater lethargy") (94). His desire and his will are turned to God, to love, to the writing of poetry, in a sort of convergence that the progression of the poem keeps open. This convergence is not even retrospectively defined, since the person speaking cannot even be confined to the poem he has just completed. He presents himself as continuing to live, carrying forward silently the actions that will define him, as to some degree he has done in the past, here regathered into a visionary future.

6

Trobar

The Pitches of Desire

THE CONFLATIONS ATTAINED through Dante's reach, if we look to his immediate predecessors rather than to Virgil, are brought to their own intensities by the troubadours, in whose reach of conflations around the presentation of erotic desire we can also hear the echoes of fulfillment. At the pitch attained by troubadour utterance, desire and fulfillment powerfully and strangely interact with one another through all the gestures of an abandonment presenting itself as formal control and of desperation fashioned into attainment.

It cannot be denied that these poems evidence a vast and deep change of sensibility, as Gaston Paris and C. S. Lewis urged. A new, profound valuation of women centers on the love experience in an exaltation whose transports could include the divine, sometimes spectacularly in the figure of a woman, as Charles Williams reads the Beatrice of Dante.[1] At the same time, what the troubadour intensities envisage can also be found, usually at somewhat lower pitch, in various cultures and social strata around the world, as Dronke shows.[2] While arising out of a widespread and possibly universal impulse to the poetic expression of desire, the situations and gestures of this poetry can be traced elaborately to a specific complex of social and cultural coordinates and to a confluence of traditions.³ Desire is indeed expressed here in labyrinthine evolutions, but also a vision of fulfillment. The tonality of these poems has a ring of plenitude that gives the auditor the cue that the verse does not echo a sorrowing Virgilian air. Still less could we match it to what just a description of some of its prevalent coordinates would seem to indicate, Virgil's description to Dante of the mood of the souls in Limbo: "Semo perduti, e sol di tanto offesi / che sanza speme vivemo in disio" ("We are lost, and only hurt by so much / That without hope we live in desire") (*Inf.* 4.41–42).

The troubadour convention offers a speaker, usually of noble temperament, who sings publicly of what is "normally" private.⁴ Unlike much modern love poetry since the Renaissance, troubadour verse is not conceived of as just an address to another person conventionally overheard—the second of T. S. Eliot's three voices of poetry, "the poet addressing an audience, large or small."⁵ Here, in fact, the third voice is present, too, "the voice of the poet when he attempts to create a dramatic character speaking in verse." Such a persona is present in any poem but comes forward more dramatically and markedly in troubadour verse when the poet conforms to the type "troubadour." First when he actually performs it and then always fictively, the poet stands forth under the mantle of "troubadour" to declare his desire and possibly also its fulfillment, whether in real life he be an embattled warrior like Bertran de Born or a powerful count like William IX, a merchant like Folquet de Marseilles or a humble itinerant like Peire Vidal. Nor can we exclude from this poetry (and perhaps not from any) "the voice of the poet talking to himself," a first voice markedly present in a poetry that must take a great deal of deliberate care to fashion. And this poetry is wrought to an elaborate tightness. In this tradition, the sense of delectating and exhibited finish is as true of "easy verse" (*trobar leu*), as it is of "closed verse" (*trobar clus*).⁶

The whole audience is asked to engage in the spectacle of an exhibition of a desire expressed by the poet for a woman, in a statement that as one of its gambits may involve the structural complications of endlessly deferred fulfillment. But it may also survey the joy that it assumes has been sought by physical union with the beloved—whether or not in accord with the gambit that the beloved is married to another.⁷ And the convention of the noble speaker in love is, if anything, reinforced by its antitype, the satirical poem, such as William IX's about an eight-day orgy with two women, "Farai un vers, pos mi sonelh" ("I'll make a verse, then go to sleep"); Marcabru's poem of phallic conquest, "Dirai vos in mon lati" ("I'll tell you in my Latin"); or later, Arnaut Daniel's poem about his lady's imperious and specific desire for sexual fulfillment, "Pois Raimon e'n Trucs Malecs / chapten n' Ayman e sos decs" ("Since Raimon and Truc Malec / Defend Dame Ayma and her orders").[8] Like Dante's bawdy sonnets to Forese, such poems present a speaker defecting from the nobility of *fin amors* in his chase for phallic exploits of a merely physical satisfaction.

The sense of fulfillment just in the state of experiencing the expectant feeling of love is so intense that it can override the force of the seasons, even though the loveliness of spring is a topos of love inducement. So, as Bernart de Ventadorn says:

> tan ai al cor d'amor
>   de joi e de doussor
> per que'l gels me sembla flor
>   e la neus verdura.[9]

> So much I have in my heart of love,
>   So much of joy and of sweetness
> That the ice seems to me a flower
>   And the snow a field of green.
>
>   (29.10–13)

This statement is along the lines of the sort of counter-spring topos in Arnaut's "Can chai la fueilla" ("When the leaf falls"), a counterpart to his more direct spring poem, "Lanc an son passat li giure" ("When the frosts are past"):

> Tot quant es gela,
> mas ieu non puesc frezir,
> qu'Amors novela
> mi fa.l cor reverdir

> Now it's all freezing
> But I can't get cold,
> Since new love
> Makes my heart green.

Desire posits an absence or distance, a displacement from which Lacan has derived a whole dialectic of communicational interaction.[10] His profound formulations point out the integral link between a feeling so fundamental and intense as love and the equally fundamental human self-definition by communication. Love is at the root of language, in Lacan's view, as in Freud's, and language is at the root of love. But desire, if its communicative extrapolations are perceived, is by its very nature caught in deferral, in displacements derived from the substratum of the self's relation to an other whom one sees as perceiving oneself as other, a mutually interactive perception that at the same time solidifies and intensifies that link (to add a further inference to Lacan). Desire and fulfillment are thus linked; and through this linkage, presence and absence are also linked.

One engaging turn that emphasizes the linkage of presence and absence is Jaufre Rudel's *canso* (24) "Amor de lonh" ("Love from afar"), which ruminates on the presence in the speaker's spirit of a love who is absent from him:

> Lanquan li jorn son lonc en may
> M'es belhs dous chans d'auzelhs de lonh,
> E quan mi sui partiz de lay
> Remembra.m d'un amor de lonh:
> Vau de talan embroncx e clis
> Si que chans ni flors d'albesbis
> No.m platz plus que l'yverns gelatz.

> When the days are long in May,
> Sweet bird songs please me from afar,
> And when I go away from there
> I recall a love from afar;
> I go with desire depressed and bowed
> So much that songs nor hawthorn flower
> Please me no more than winter's ice.

Thus the first stanza. As he rises to his climax in the fifth:

> Ja mais d'amor no.m jauziray
> So no.m jau d'est amor de lonh,
> Que gensor ni melhor no.n sai
> Ves nulha part, ni pres ni lonh;

> Never in love will I delight
> If not in this love from afar.
> For none nobler or better do I know
> Anywhere, either near or far.

This poem transposes the May topos by connecting its presence and sense of fulfillment to absence and desire. The terminal refrain "de lonh" creates a further, still more concordant echo coming, like a stab of desire, as a crosscurrent into the regular, fulfilled progressions of the rhymed lines—in which "de lonh" functions with the further emphasis of an identical rhyme.

The intensity of this poetry generally manages to effectuate a fusion of desire and fulfillment by suspending the utterance in an absorption that presents its fulfillments as always shot through with desire, its expression of desire characteristically raised to such a pitch that a sense of fulfillment hovers over it.

As R. Howard Bloch says of Bernart's "En cossirer et en esmai" ("In anguish and in torment"), "The passivity of the poetic personality is the logical outcome of a language suspended by contradiction."[11] The set of exhibited contradictions—all stemming from an ambivalence over whether the lady loves him—could be called the present-oriented form of the space-stretched *amor de lonh*.

Desire reaches the pitch of sensed fulfillment in such poems as Bernart's *canso* 37:

> Can vei la lauzeta mover
> de joi sas alas contral rai,
> que s'oblid e.s laissa chazer
> per la doussor c'al cor li vai,
> ai! tan grans enveya m'en ve
> de cui qu'eu veya jauzion,
> meravilhas ai, car desse
> lo cor de dezirer no.m fon.

> When I see the lark move
> With joy his wings against the ray
> That he forgets and lets himself fall
> For the sweetness that comes to his heart,
> Ah, so great an envy[12] comes to me
> Of him whom I see in delight,

> I marvel that at once
> My heart does not melt from desire.

The psychology attaches itself here to the flight of the lark, which at once accompanies and emblematizes the feeling of the speaker. He presents an absorbing series of intense moments as he focuses successively on the lark moving wings joyously against (rather than with!) the rays of the sun, letting himself go, letting himself fall, being overwhelmed with sweetness; and, in a turn away from the lark, the speaker wonders that his heart does not melt with desire (rather than saying it does so). It is Pound, as so often, who underscored the intensely adaptive and exuberantly integrative psychology of this poem.[13]

Regarding this particular poem, and others, Thomas MacCary stresses the poet's accession to the inaccessibility of the lady and his consequent dissolution into his own feeling of narcissistic self-sufficiency, which shades into masochistic subjection:

> If we say that the super-ego is the introjection of the normal resolution of the Oedipus Complex, then we can say that the ego is the introjection of the normal resolution of [Lacan's] mirror stage. In the erotic of the troubadours we retain the image of the pre-oedipal mother, eclipse the father, and end up with a self that is informed by neither ego nor super-ego. We put it under erasure: the self is suspended, like Bernart's lark, over the abyss of Narcissus' pool, with the mother's eyes at the bottom. It swells with pride, inflates itself, a phallus, but it is unstable, lacks a locus, a corpus. It wants to be pinioned, mortified, crucified.... The woman is simultaneously phallic, non-phallic and anti-phallic.[14]

Permuting MacCary's terms would produce various foci and allow us to use their substructures to gloss much of the range of troubadour-expressed desire, to underscore what the poet is transcending in his evocation of fulfillment. In these psychoanalytic terms, the achieved poem itself must not be left out of the reckoning: its call for nobility and its very formation as an utterance center the ego of the poet around an ego ideal tested by passion, one with many dimensions.[15]

As it evolves, the self-presentation of the role of lover-poet is "public" and circular. This presentation builds its own contradictions, including the dimension of sacred-secular, into the very achieved form. Loss is gain, as in Cercamon's *canso* 19 (13–18):

> Per una joja m'esbaudis
> Fina, qu'anc re non amiey tan;

Quan suy ab lieys si m'esbahis
Qu'ieu no.ill sai dire mon talan,
E quan m'en vauc, vejaire m'es
Que tot perda.l sen e.l saber.

For a fine joy I do rejoice
That I never loved anything so much;
When I'm with her I get so mixed up
I don't know how to speak my desire,
And when I go from her, it seems
That I have lost all sense and ken.

Within the social setting, the poet, whatever his age, casts himself often in the role of a *joven,* somebody formally at the peak of youth who at the same time is suspended anthropologically at an intermediate stage between a newly enlisted and a fully enfranchised and functioning knight.[16] And the lady, the *domna*—often strangely kept in the third person, as MacCary stresses—is referred to by a title, *midons,* which shades her power into a common-gender adaptation of a masculine structure of fealty, *meus dominus* ("my lord"). Deeply ingrained in the very language of this poetry is an expression of the poet's submission to the lady.[17] Yet while the poetry may exhibit subjection, its overall mastery makes it not sound that way. The poet, advertising his utterance in the actual or imagined performance of his poetry before a public, predominates in the poise and completeness of the utterance. The boldness of these turns is still present in the many nuances and gestures of Dante's submission before Beatrice from *Purgatorio* 30 on, where the Pilgrim goes through many gestures of obeisance.

It would not be going too far to say that these social specifics of role, like MacCary's psychological diagrams, are not only presented but also sublated and transmuted in the intensity of the utterance. The utterance is so strong that the roles tend to disappear into the attained delight attendant upon these evocations of delight, even when despair is in view. Confident in the range from absence to presence, the poet can shift from one to the other without jarring abruptness, as does Guiraut de Bornelh in one *canso:*

E d'altra part sui plus despers
Per sobramar
Que naus, can vai torban per mar

Destrecha d'ondas e de vens;
Tan m'abelis lo pensamens.

Otherwise I am in more despair
    For over-love
Than a ship when it goes tossed in the sea
Distressed in waves and in wind;
So much the thought pleases me.

        (46.35–39)

The last line is striking in its total reversion; "over-love" is so powerful it need not explicitly contradict; the whole work of transposition is done by "m'abelis" ("pleases me"), where the buoyant tonality forbids our shading the poem into the delectation of some form of masochism.[18]

Raimbaut d'Aurenga brings the beloved and God together in a way that evokes fidelity, but not the renunciation of fulfillment, preserving as he continues all the gestures of delicate secrecy and maintained courtesy:

Ara.m so del tot conquis,
Si que de pauc me sove,
C'oblidat n'ai guag e ris
E plor e dol e feunia;
E no. i faz semblan trop bel
Ni crei—tant ai manentia—
Que res, mas Dieus, me capdel.

        (42.1–7)

Now I am wholly vanquished,
So that I remember little,
For I have forgotten joy and laughter,
And weeping and grief and sadness;
And I make no pretense too fair
Nor think—so very rich am I—
that anything but God rules me.

    (tr. Dronke, slightly altered)

In one of his poems (48), Guiraut provides a *tenso*, or debate poem, as an alternating dialogue that begins by consulting the lady: "Si.us quer conselh, bel' ami Alamanda" ("If I ask advice of you, fair friend Alamanda"). In another poem, his praise of the beauty and inspiration of the lady includes a technique of retrospective introspection:

Mas a cor afranchar
Que s'as trop enduritz,
No deu om los oblitz
N'ils velhs fachs remembrar?

But to soften a heart
That has got too hard,
Must a man not remember
Forgotten things and old deeds?

(50.51–65)

It may be with such formulations in mind that Dante classifies Guiraut as a poet of "rectitude."[19] In this tradition, an ingrained sense of the wisdom available through devotion to the lady provides a wealth of such psychological inference. Images come up more striking than the references to the joy of a lark or a nightingale, as in Rigaut de Berbezil's comparison of himself to a fallen elephant: "Atressi com l'olifans / Que, quan chai, no.s pot levar" ("As the elephant, / when he falls, can't rise") (62.1–2). Arnaut exhibits his fixed attention to the lady in his statement of firmness under love's ordeal: "Sols sui qui sai lo sovrafan qe.m sortz / Al cor d'amor sofren per sobramar" ("I am alone who knows the over-pain that rises / In my heart suffering from over-love") (69.1–2). His lady is instructed by Courtesy ("l'enseignet Cortesi"). Under her domain, he may suffer, "Pero l'afans m'est deportz, ris e iois, / Car en pensai sui de lieis lecs e glotz" ("But pain is sport, laughter and joy, / Since thinking of her I am greedy and gluttonous") (34–35). In a *tenso*, Lanfranc Cigala, too, locates his singing and thinking "Between my heart and me and my knowing" ("Entre mon cor e me e mon saber"):

—Et eu, seignor, en dirai mo voler,
—Zo dis mos senz,—q'eu crei qe.il failla sia
De las domnas, car si fan pregar tan.
Es es tals us qe can la domna ve
Qui ben la prec, ia mais no.il volra be,
Pois prega tal qu'ela non vi pregan;
Mas eu tengra plus bella cortezia
Si de cellui qi l'ames fos amia.—

—And I, lord, will now speak my will.
—So says my mind.—That I think it the fault
Of the ladies, for they do much to be wooed.
And it's usual when a lady sees one
Who woos her well, she never wishes him well,
Then woos the one she sees not wooing;
But I hold it a finer courtesy
That she be the lover of one who loves her.

(158.17–24)

This sets into the psyche of the lady an alternation whose very musicality has the air of a dance that will finally come to the resolution of union.

Cercamon begins a *canso* by expressing a regret in his own distance from fulfillment:

Quant l'aura doussa s'amarzis
E.l fuelha chai de sul verjan
E l'auzelh chanjan lor latis,
Et ieu de sai sospir e chan
D'Amor que.m te lassat e pres,
Qu'ieu anc no l'agui en poder.

Las! qu'ieu d'Amor non ai conquis
Mas cant lo trebalh e l'afan,

When the sweet air gets bitter
And the leaf falls from its branch
And the birds sing changes on their Latin
And I here sigh and sing
Of the love that ties and grips me,
For I never had it in my power.

Alas that I of love I have only won
So much as the torment and the care.

(19.1–8)

Peire Vidal begins a *canso* (87) with a two-stanza evocation of his nostalgia for Provence. Then he abruptly transposes this longing to praise for his beloved in the two concluding stanzas:

Ab l'alen tir vas me l'aire
Qu'eu sen venir de Proensa
. . . .

Qu'om no pot lo jorn mal traire
Qu'aja di leis sovinensa,
Qu'en leis nais jois e comensa
. . . .

E s'eu sai ren dir ni faire,
Ilh n'aja.l grat, que sciensa
M'a donat e conoissensa,
Per qu'eu sui gais e chantaire.
E tot quan fauc d'avinen
Ai del seu bel cors plazen,
Neis quan de bon cor consire.

With my breath I draw the air
That I feel come from Provence
. . . .

None can treat ill the day
That I have of her remembrance
Where in her joy is born and starts
. . . .

And I can do or say nothing
Not owed to her, who gave me
Knowing and understanding,
By which I can joy and sing.
And all I do graciously, I have
From her fair, charming body,
Even when with good heart I think.

This conclusion links sight and thought through the near-homonymy of *cors* ("body") and *cor* ("heart"). The environment of living and the fixation of love become one in the identifications of this poem, as in its rhetorical shift from Provence to the lady.

Love as a theme expands to embrace war in the songs about the Crusades, which constitute a distinct genre. The Crusades evoke dilemmas about the opposition of love and war, whereas these themes are not separated out by Bertran, who celebrates both love and war, but in different poems. Derived from the poetry about war is the age-old rhetorical staple of the lament for a dead hero, a *planh,* and the tonality of lament easily shades from war to love and back again. The Crusader Raimbaut de Vaqueiras, like others, sets up an opposition between love and war:

> viurai de guarr' a lley de mainedier
> e pos d'amor no'm ve autre cofortz
> partirai m'en, et er sieus totz lo tortz.

> I'll live on war by a mercenary's law,
> And since from love no other comfort comes to me
> I will go away and hers will be all the wrong.
> (106.38–40)

In his *planh* for the death of Louis IX (171), Raimon Gaucelm de Bezers blends that form with the Crusade song. In his *tenso* about going on a Crusade (116), Peirol disputes with a personified Love, who argues against his going away: "Quant Amors trobet partit / mon cor de son pessamen" ("When Love found my heart / Separated from thought of him"). Marcabru invokes religion as the goal in his Crusade song "Pax in nomine Domini":

> S'anz non correm al lavador
> C'ajam la boca ni.ls huoills claus,
> Non i a un d'orguoill tant gras
> C'al morir non trob contrafort.

> If we run not first to the cleansing place,
> Before our mouths and eyes are closed,
> None there will have a pride so fat
> That at death he'll not find the adversary.
> (11.34–37)

The Crusades engage such postures of self-dramatization and recall. Another engagement with the Crusade from the angle of love occupies Marcabru's *vers* "A la fontana del verger" ("At the fountain of the orchard"). Here the speaker meets the daughter of the lord of the castle, whose lover has gone off to the Crusade and refuses the poet's consolation. This poem, blending with other types of song, modifies the convention of the pastourelle, the seduction dialogue of a higher-born poet with a shepherdess encountered in the woods, a convention of which Marcabru's poem "L'autrier jost' una sebissa" ("The other day near a hedge") is an early, if not the earliest, example. "A la fontana del verger," which is also early in the tradition, already revises the convention of the pastourelle by elevating the social status of the girl and by transforming the nature of her discourse: she theologizes about her situation, more or less ignoring the poet, rather than bantering with him:

> E quez entendes mon favelh,
> Tost li fon sos afars camjatz.
>
> Dels huelhs ploret josta la fon
> E del cor sospiret preon.
> "Ihesus, dis elha, reys del mon,
> Per vos mi creys ma grans dolors."
>
> When she would understand my talk
> Quickly her attitude did change.
>
> From her eyes she wept by the fount
> And from her heart sighed heavily.
> "Jesus," she said, "king of the world,
> Through you increases my great woe."
> (14.13–18)

The poet easily invokes the power of God to create joy, but just as a seduction gesture:

> "Que selh qui fai lo bosc fulhar,
> Vos pot donar de joy assatz."
>
> "Who makes the wood break into leaf
> Can give you a lot of joy."
> (34–35)

She immediately says that God will satisfy her in the other world, whereas the knight has not done so in this, and she ends with a stab of psychological inference about her crusader-lover in her canny concluding reply: "mas pauc me tey / Que trop s'es di mi alonhatz" ("But little do I care, / for he has gone too far away from me") (41–42). In the context of a submission to the will of God, she performs an homage to the ineluctable laws of erotic union, paying as little attention finally to the crusader-lover's presumed devotional loyalty as she does to the overtures of the poet.

Hovering lightly over the poem is the lady's access to a wisdom of social awareness. More expansively elsewhere, the lady evidences or has attributed to her the force of a theological wisdom, a tradition going back through Boethius's Lady Philosophy to the early Indo-European goddesses whose force and aura are pulled into the figure of the Virgin Mary. In poetry this sapiential tradition reaches its culmination in Dante's Beatrice. But in these pre-Cavalcanti poems, the theological wisdom of the lady is not an elaborate doctrine but an aura.

For the ease and power of combinations under the aegis of such a conviction, without the bald statement that the poet's sense is derived from his love, consider Arnaut's *canso* "En cest sonet coind'e leri" ("In this song gracious and gay"):

> En cest sonet coind'e leri
> fauc motz e capuig e doli,
> E serant verai e cert
> quan n'aurai passat la lima;
> q'Amors marves plan'e daura
> mon chantar, que de liei mou
> Qui pretz manten e governa.
>
> Tot jorn meillur et esmeri
> car la gensor serv e coli
> del mon, so.us dic en apert.
> Sieus sui del pe tro q'en cima,
> e si tot venta.ill freid'aura,
> l'amors q'inz el cor mi plou
> mi ten chaut on plus iverna.
>
> Mil messas n'aug e'n proferi
> e'n art lum de cera e d'oli
> que Dieus m'en don bon issert
> de lieis on no.m val escrima;
> e quan remir sa crin saura
> e.l cors gai, grailet e nou
> mais l'am que qi.m des Luserna.

Tant l'am de cor e la queri
c'ab trop voler cug la.m toli
s'om ren per ben amar pert.
Qu'el sieus cors sobretracima
lo mieu tot e non s'eisaura;
tant a de ver fait renou
c'obrador n'a e taverna.

No vuoill de Roma l'emperi
ni c'om m'en fassa apostoli,
qu'en lieis non aia revert
per cui m'art lo cors e.m rima;
e si.l maltraich no.m restaura
ab un baisar anz d'annou
mi auci e si enferna.

Ges pel maltraich qu'ieu soferi
de ben amar no.m destoli
si tot me ten en desert,
C'aissi.n fatz los motz en rima.
Pieitz trac aman c'om que laura,
c'anc plus non amet un ou
cel de Moncli n'Audierna.

Ieu sui Arnautz q'amas l'aura,
e chatz la lebre ab lo bou
e nadi contra suberna.

In this song gracious and gay
I set words, plane and buff them
And they'll be true and sure
When I will have passed the file;
For love at once smooths and gilds
My song, which moves from her
who guards and governs worthiness.

Every day I get better and purer,
For I serve and honor the world's
Noblest one and tell you openly.
I am hers from head to toe,

And if the wind blows colder,
The love that rains in my heart
Keeps me warm where most it winters.

A thousand masses I hear and offer
And burn lights of wax and oil
That God give me good success
With her, who serves me as no screen,
And when I behold her golden hair
Her body, gay, slim, and new,
I love her more than if one gave me Luserna.

So much my heart loves her and I seek her
That I think she'll be taken from me
If for loving well anything is lost.
For her heart submerges wholly
My own, and it turns not to air;
So much indeed she draws interest
Like the owner of a tavern.

I would not want the rule of Rome
Or that they make me pope
If I could no more return to her
For whom my heart burns and splits.[20]
And if of the pain she doesn't cure me
With a kiss before the new year
She kills me and damns herself to hell.

For the pain that I suffer
I don't pull myself from loving,
And though I hold me as all in a desert,
For her I make words in rhyme.
Worse I live in love than a laborer
For never did the Lord of Moncli
Love Lady Audierna a jot more.

I am Arnaut who amasses air
And drives the hare out of the wood
And swims against the current.

In Arnaut's poem, even in the unavailability of the lady, love for her is
present as an express motive for the poem in the first stanza: "love at

once smooths and gilds / My song." At the end he names himself: "I am
Arnaut who amasses air." Transparency, music, and the *trobar-clus* heap of
syllables all come through in this line, which describes and exemplifies
them all, combining them with a metaphorical posture, "drive the hare
out of the wood," a clause that in itself has a combinatory richness. In
sequence it speaks of the poet's mastery, as swimming against the cur-
rent does, which can also be taken as a metaphor for *trobar clus*. But it
may also indicate a general deftness, a resourcefulness, and even a hint of
desperation, recalling the tradition that situates the wood as a refuge for
the maddened lover, like Peire Vidal wearing a wolf skin in the woods
or Tristan, who wanders there singing.

The hint of incapacity fuses into the hint of mastery, as in troubadour
poems generally, and in this particular poem, where the poet hints at
once of impossibility and of fulfillment. All this, too, could be to swim
against the current and to amass air, which suggests both the mastery of
organizing the *motz* of this verse, as he says earlier in the poem, and the
desperation of trying to make something out of nothing.

The poem is so unified in its recursive ballade rhymes and its nearly
gnomic concision that one must dwell on its richness to perceive what
a wide net it has thrown over the repertory of conventional responses.
Love is united to religion—but the speaker would rather love than
either have Rome or be an apostle. He may or may not have been cured
with the kiss; if not, his death will be matched by the lady's damnation,
and religion has again been drawn into the picture, as it is notably in the
third stanza, where his thousand masses have been said for the love
(something that would be permissible if the union envisaged were a hal-
lowed one, and there is nothing in this text to suggest that it is not so).
In its range through angles of the love, this poem does not include the
figure, frequent in this convention and in Arnaut's own "nail/uncle" ses-
tina, of a jealous husband/father/interloper who forbids the love. God
is enjoined to bless the success of the love, and that outcome (not stated
as infinitely delayed) would please the poet more than if he were to
receive the boon of getting "Luserna," a legendary submerged city—a
medieval Spanish Atlantis—in the *chansons de geste*. But the next stanza
does speak of pain—and speaks of her heart "submerging" his (*sobre-
tracima*), with the longest word in the entire poem. Is this submerging a
union or not? Would such a union offer the total loss of drowning or a
Utopian pleasure like that of Luserna/Atlantis? Does the usurious inter-
est she exacts like a tavern keeper mean that he is getting an equitable

payment even if he has already paid (with the words of the poem, as well as with his pains)? The poem suspends a resolution of these questions, thus poising itself comprehensively between desire and fulfillment. It does, to be sure, end on a note of dejection-in-rejection, if the lost tale of Audierna and the lord of Moncli is, as it seems to be, a model of rejection. But then the poet speaks of a broadly capable recovery in the three lines of the concluding envoi, asserting the mastery of his identity: "I am Arnaut who amasses air."

This poem could not move broadly over the areas it embraces with such assuredness, connecting public domains and social roles, religion and love, responses and definitions, without having completely digested and integrated them. The offhandedness and near-gnomic curtness of the three matched clauses in the envoi indicate this, as do both its own conjunctions of different domains and its own sharp indication through near-asyndeton of their disjunctions. Amassing air, hunting the hare, and swimming against the current in one sense are three ways of saying the same thing; they hover in and out of metaphor, swimming against the current being the most unequivocally metaphoric. They are summary, descriptive, illustrative of mastery but also of randomness, and finally mysterious in their very clarity, along the lines of Angus Fletcher's characterization of the gnomic: "The gnomic always suggests some problem of expression, as if each gnomic utterance partook of the language-game of questioning the limits of language."[21] But at the same time, it rises to solution, all the more insofar as the near-gnomic has been brought into the service of summary when it does not just summarize but introduces a whole new dimension of the poem.

There is a link that the lady at once evokes and serves as a stand-in for between the power of the mistress and the power of song. She is empowering, but he has his own power. As Bernart expresses it in his *canso:*

> Non es meravelha s'eu chan
> melhs de nul autre chantador,
> que plus me tra.l cors vas amor
> e melhs sui faihz a so coman.
> cor e cors e saber e sen
> e fors' e poder i ai mes;
> si.m tira vas amor lo fres
> que vas autra part no.m aten.

It is no wonder that I sing
Better than any other singer,
For more my heart draws to love,
And I'm better made to her command.
Heart and body and ken and sense
And force and might I have set there;
So the rein draws me to love
That to no other side I strive.

(27.1–8)

These poems are rigorously syllabic in form, with only a set number of syllables to the line. That fact, coupled with their prevailingly monosyllabic progression of words, makes each word sound like a pitch of fulfillment, and words of more than one syllable an amplification thereof. The isochronic emphasis on individual syllables would be further underscored in the musical settings, which tend toward isochronic runs of whole notes, usually one note per syllable.[22] Contemporary references to the poetry often speak of "words" (*motz*) or "words and sounds" (*motz e sons*).[23] And the very term for a strophe, *cobla* ("coupling"), foregrounds the act of compositional joining. This momentary intensity, however, is set against an expectancy, like a fulfillment containing a desire, an expectancy of recurrent terminal echo, namely, the rhyme words that in this tradition appear in such elaborate patterns. But there is a further expectancy and a further fulfillment. The rhyme pattern, having been set in one stanza, is exactly repeated, rhyme for rhyme, in the next stanza: the desire of the ear reaches fulfillment by returning to the dominant of the rhyme again and again, until the poem winds down in a *tornada,* an envoi.

This profound interplay of sound undergoes fundamental variations at the hands of such a master verbal composer as Arnaut, Dante's "best blacksmith" ("miglior fabbro"). Arnaut plays up the syllabic foci of these forms by the sharp ordonnance, nominal emphases, onomatopoeiai, and line-length variations of his bravura piece "Doutz brais e critz" ("Sweet squawks and cries"). Another deep transposition, which is later picked up by Dante, comes in his invention of the sestina, a form that carries out the same interplay while dispensing with rhyme words and waiting till the second stanza before any echoes occur. In the sestina, of course, these echoes are not rhymes; they are recursions of the identical words, one of the six chosen for the terminal position of each line.

Minnesang, by contrast, modulates its music without wholly regularizing the syllable count and without making its rhymes recursive from stanza to stanza.[24] The allowance of extra syllables creates not a music of high troubadour tightness, but rather one of alert, adaptive variation, often in lines of varied length.[25] Take the first stanza of Walther von der Vogelweide's "Under der linden":

> Under der linden
> an der heide,
> dâ unser zweier bette was,
> dâ mugt ir vinden
> schône beide
> gebrochen bluomen unde gras.
> vor dem walde in einem tal,
> tandaradei,
> schône sanc diu nahtegal.[26]

> Under the lime tree
> By the heath
> Where the bed of the pair of us was,
> There could you find
> Both fair,
> Broken flowers and grass.
> Before the wood in the valley,
> Tandaradei,
> Fair sang the nightingale.

The play of accents is so assuredly modulated here that a musical sense of constant variation along the line is created, without any actual extra-metrical syllables. The music is as elaborate as the language is simple, and the two can be said to counterpoint against each other in a way that the later art song still does not equal.

The rollicking rhythm of the following poem by Heinrich von Morungen belies its gloomy message, as does the vividness of its evocation of the beloved:[27]

> Si hât mich verwunt
>   reht aldúrch mîn sêle
> in den vil toetlîchen grunt,
> dô ich ir tet kunt
>   daz ich tobte unde quêle

umbe ir vil güetlichen munt.
den bat ích zeiner stunt
 daz er mich ze dienste ir bevêle
 und daz er mir stêle
von ir éin senftez küssen, sô waer ich iemer gesunt.

Wie wirde ich gehaz
 ir vil rôsevarwen munde,
des ich noch niender vergaz!
doch sô müet mich daz
 daz si mir zeiner stunde
sô mit gewalt vor gesaz.
des bin ich worden laz,
 alsô daz ich vil schiere gesunde
 in der helle grunde
verbrunne, ê ich ir iemer diende, in wisse umbe waz.

So has she wounded me,
straight through my soul
on the full deadly ground
that I let her know
that I rage and lament
over her lovely mouth.
Once I asked of hers,
that she bid it to my service
and that it steal for me
a tender kiss from her, and I be healed forever.

How could I be foe
to her rose-red mouth,
that I may still never forget!
Now I rue much
that she at the time
so strongly forbade me,
for which I am become weary
that there all alive,
on the ground of hell
I'd burn forever rather than serve her, without knowing why.

Part of another poem of Heinrich's shows how a long line can exhibit
a sense of psychological control without penetrating very deeply beneath

the standard postures of *fin amors*—or, what is nearly the same thing, *Minne:*

> Owê, war umbe volg ich tumbem wâne,
>   der mich sô sêre leitet in die nôt?
> ich schiet von ir gar aller vröiden âne,
>   daz sî mir trôst noch helfe nie gebôt.
> ....
>   Als swîgende iegenôte, und ein verholner wân,
> wie dicke ich mich der tôrheit underwinde,
> swanne ich vór ir stân und sprüche ein wunder vinde,
>   und muoz doch von ir ungesprochen gân?

> Alas, shall I follow dumb delusion
> that who leads me so into need?
> I part from her bereft of all joys
> while she consoles me with neither help nor bidding.
> ....
> As silent, zealous, and in recovering doubt
> how thickly I undergo stupidity
> when I stand before her and find countless words
> and must go from her without a word of answer.

These *Minnesänger* characteristically exhibit a keen fluency in rhythmic variation, while the elaborate psychological suspensions of the troubadours have been somewhat diminished. Heinrich's poetic contentment before the inaccessibility of the beloved's rose-red mouth retains the troubadour focus without any of the striving and little of the sense of fulfillment. And while Walther's projection for his persona's joyous recall of her union in spring in the vale where the nightingale sang recalls the intensity of troubadour nostalgia, it does not have the density of its self-definitions. But these art songs are still recognizably in the troubadour register, the profundity of which we measure by *Minnesang's* comparably fluent but simpler formulations.

The intensity of the formulations in troubadour poetry, and in *Minnesang,* can be measured still further if we contrast them to the poems of the *Carmina Burana,* where all or nearly all the troubadour doctrines can be found separately, and sometimes even in a weak solution, as Dronke demonstrates.[28] Still, the presentation mostly lacks the troubadour subtlety (*pace* Dronke) and never rises to its pitch. These often resolutely pagan and usually simply phallic poems trip on in a measure that, if it were slackened, would be just one notch short of doggerel:

> Semel, opto, basia
> michi quod offerat,
> quam sorte de infantia
> Natura venustat.
>
> (60a)[29]

> Once, I wish, kisses
> She would offer me,
> Whom by lot from infancy
> Nature beautifies.

★

> Amor tenet omnia,
> mutat cordis intima,
> querit Amor devia.
> Amor melle dulcior,
> felle fit amarior.
>
> (87)

> Love holds all things,
> Changes the inner heart,
> Love seeks the byways.
> Love, sweeter than honey,
> Becomes bitterer than gall.

★

> Gratus super omnia
>   ludus est puelle,
> et eius praecordia
>   omni carent felle;
> sunt, que prastat, basia
>   dulciore melle.
>
> (88)

> Welcome above all things
>   is playing with a girl,

and her heart's regions
    are free of any gall.
Kisses when she offers them
    are sweeter than honey.

★

ergo fac, benigna Phyllis,
    ut iucunder in tranquillis,
dum os ori iungitur   et pectora mamillis.

(156)

So make it, kind Phyllis,
That I be joyed in calmness,
    while mouth is joined to mouth and chest to breasts.

Here the tripping measure, the straightforwardly paratactic syntax, and the instant rhymes all operate in a lightness of expression far from the troubadour verbal polyphonies. And the notions are correspondingly simple.

The persona enunciated by the troubadour, along with the recursive contradictions, expands in one direction into Dante's ordering of transcendences in the *Divina commedia* and into the levelings of Petrarch and the elaborate Platonization of the sapiential tradition at the hands of Spenser. Another direction moves into the suppleness of sonnets, which reach one culmination in those of Shakespeare, another in the robust gloom of Michelangelo's. The tradition never disappears. It can be traced in the Romantics, on into the work of Yeats and Rilke, surfacing again for exact rescoring and citation in Pound's flash-anglings and imbrications of the troubadour pitches of desire.

7

The Transcendence of Hellenistic Norms

The Reach of Catullus

FROM SAPPHO THROUGH PROPERTIUS, or from Virgil and Ovid to the *Pervigilium Veneris,* Eros provided not only a subject but the beginning of a focusing principle for poetry, a powerful center that quickly accommodated such norms as the pastoral but also, as Catullus saliently exhibits, the possibilities for manipulated transcendence—as well as for the subordinated permutations that Eros undergoes in the *De rerum natura,* the *Aeneid,* and the *Metamorphoses.*

Catullus exhibits a skill that is most obviously akin to the Hellenistic tradition, in which he was imbued; his poetry, as he describes the "book" ("libellum") in the first line of his poem 1 is "lepidum," elegant in the Hellenistic way. But he reaches beyond that elegance; the other adjective, the obvious one and as fully justified for him as for Dante and Pound, both of whom described themselves strategically with the same word, was "novum" ("new"). "Cui dono lepidum novum libellum?" ("To whom shall I give this elegant new little book?"), he asks, and though in the poem this rhetorical turn simply introduces Cornelius Nepos, it also hints at the outset that he is reaching far enough to require a new audience. The erotic component and the invective component, to begin with, had not been combined in poetry perhaps since Archilochus, and in some of the poems to Lesbia, Catullus crosses the erotic with the invective in ways more complicated than can be paralleled in any predecessor—or perhaps any successor before Donne—even though the depth psychology of our time finds connections between the anxiety surrounding love and the psychosexual anxiety that is displayed in the utterance of invective, a principle given epigrammatic expression by Catullus himself: "Odi et amo" ("I hate and love") (poem 85).

For the erotic itself, he incorporates the Hellenistic elegance, with its ability to pose neat ambivalences, but almost none of his poems fits comfortably into the universe of elegant love poetry from Alcaeus and Anacreon through Theocritus and Meleager. Even the most Hellenistic of Catullus's poems, the near-translation of Callimachus's "Lock of Berenice" (poem 66), is importantly qualified in being framed by the poem that precedes, introduces, and to some degree undercuts it. Rather, Catullus goes all the way back to Sappho for his measure and also for an erotic urgency quite foreign to the Hellenistic poets. And further, even in his two poems in sapphics, he heavily modifies her monody by including it polyphonically, though briefly, in a vision of its extreme opposite, the public life of imperial administration and long-range history. Thus public and private, the poles of poetic utterance, are set up as poles of the poetic subject matter.

Hence the force and subtlety of Catullus's poetry cannot be derived from what cannot match it, the various Hellenistic and earlier traditions out of which he organizes his combinatory powers. Even in the case of close translation, in his poem 51, a fairly close rendering of Sappho's poem 31, he realigns her poem through many small alterations and through the big alteration of a final stanza that vastly shifts the subject to broaden and complicate the scale:

> Ille mi par esse deo videtur,
> ille, si fas est, superare divos,
> qui sedens adversus identidem te
>   spectat et audit
> dulce ridentem, misero quod omnis
> eripit sensus mihi: nam simul te,
> Lesbia, adspexi, nihil est super mi
> . . . .
> lingua sed torpet, tenuis sub artus

flamma demanat, sonitu suopte
tintinant aures, gemina teguntur
　lumina nocte.

otium, Catulle, tibi molestum est:
otio exsultas nimiumque gestis:
otium et reges prius et beatas
　perdidit urbes.[1]

That man seems to me to be a god's equal,
That man, if they permit, to surpass the gods,
Who sitting across from you constantly
Is seeing and hearing
You sweetly laughing, I wretched that it snatches
All my senses; for as soon as I'd look
On you, Lesbia, there's nothing left for me,
. . . .
But my tongue goes numb, under my joints a slender
Flame flows down, at their very own sound
My ears ring, the lights of my eyes are covered
By a double night.

Idleness, Catullus, is grievous for you:
You exult in idleness and are too active.
In the past idleness has undone kings
And opulent cities.

Sappho's poem goes in English as follows:

Sappho (31L-P)

To me he's more than human that man who
sits by you eye to eye and
hears your voice its sweet-
ness his

and your laughter full of desire. But this
makes my heart rush within
for when I see you my
voice can't

but my tongue snaps silent a thin sudden
fever floods my skin

my eyes see blank my
ears buzz

a cold sweat covers me over trembling
seizes me whole I am
more than grass-green I seem
near dead.

But it must be endured, since even a poor . . .

(tr. Elizabeth Storz)

Catullus's intertextual evocation of Sappho is remarkable not only because he has translated and modified her but also because this and poem 11 are the earliest poems we have in Latin to use the Sapphic stanza. In this innovative act, Catullus has at the same time skewed the perspective, effectuating a powerful displacement when the speaker, who is the third person in the triangle, is a man instead of a woman, with the "I" displaced in what "si fas est" marks, which Micaela Janan calls a "moment of vertigo." The identification with Sappho is both asserted by the translation and occluded by the shift of persons, picking up energetically at the very point where the speaker comes forward with the self-address of his own name in a tremendous change of subject and focus.

Even if Catullus had merely chosen to render exactly, he could not have captured Sappho's numerous echoes of the prior epic language she has transposed. The Latin words and phrases do not trail the hints reverberating from Sappho's own changes.[2] But Sappho also follows the quick of moments in time through a close, nuanced, and rigorous sequence; Catullus abstracts and arrests that flow by the mere placing of the word "simul" in line 6. He throws the spotlight of individuality (through the rich cover-name "Lesbia") by naming his addressee, as Sappho does not, but he distances himself from the scene by using the perfect tense, "adspexi." This turn is the more noteworthy because of the presence of a version of the Lacanian trans-specular "gaze" in these two poems, as Janan points out for the "trapped gaze" of "visens" in poem 11.[3] There are further fairly significant departures from Sappho in the three stanzas that translate her poem.[4] These differences not only add enough to break the run of description in Sappho; they also realign the proportions of the poem, even without the wholly added last stanza. All in all, even before the break of the last stanza, Catullus's poem deals with a different conception and presentation of past, present, and future.

The break is not a complete break, either, because his final address to himself here, "otio exsultas nimiumque gestis," must refer to the love and must be taken to include both the moment of intense jealousy with which the poem opens and the moments of recalled infatuation. The line subsumes them and redefines them as evidences of a single disastrous state, allowing them none of the blessedness that the destroyed cities formerly enjoyed. It would be extravagant to claim that Catullus ends by casting himself metaphorically as a formerly opulent city now destroyed, but he does associate himself with such cities in a final hyperbole that contains rage and regret, while looking outward philosophically at the stretches of historical time. The proverbial ring to these last two lines has been expanded to redirect the historical proverb, the quasi-Herodotean note, so that it can be aligned with the love psychology, which is remembered and recreated from Sappho. The domains of love and long-range history are incommensurate, but they are here made commensurate in the formal expression of a literary persona that associates them. Commensurate and incommensurate define each other across the axes of the two vocatives, "Lesbia" and "Catulle," each placed, with variation, in the second stanza of a two-stanza segment.

The progression of Catullus's caesura-like breaks and enjambments, noted by Walter Ferrari (250), realigns Sappho's skillful breaks in the direction of focused definition, and the first two lines of the poem— more than half of a Sapphic stanza—beginning with a heavy qualification, introduce a tonic note of gradually evolving definition into the poem: thought masters the very passion by which it claims to have been vanquished. And the impossibility of taking "si fas est" ("if the gods permit") either wholly straight or wholly ironically lets a qualification into the poem, one rich enough to prepare it for the giant break of the last stanza.

Interpreting the break from Sappho's account of the effects of love to Catullus's quasi-abjuration of love has exercised many commentators.[5] Just the equation of "amor" and "otium" in itself, the positive and negative poles of a whole life's definition, raises the problem of the deep change of attitude that the poem mounts. "Otium" is pernicious for Catullus, he says as he addresses himself. But "otium" was also pernicious to kings and to cities living in blessedness—so that in the last two lines, the extremely private and the long-range public are set side by side for interdefinition. Some strange civic duty, of which *Romana gravitas* would be only one among many potential examples, is touched on for conclusion, since it must be a duty to see that cities not be ruined if a remedy is forthcoming, and the remedy, the impossible remedy, must be to abjure the very "otium" of which the poem, however, can be taken as an example. If we make its dramatic frame explicit, the speaker has been idling (however miserably) both to observe Lesbia in the company of another and to record it in verse.

In Sappho's poem 31, her beloved must be entering the formality of something like a betrothal, or even a marriage, something with both tender and formal sides; Sappho speaks of what amounts to desire, but a past is not evoked. In Catullus's situation, there is not any social formality of consecration; both past and present are scandalous, and tenderness is by no means present in any stable form. His whole activity is thus more easily classifiable under the city-ruining "otium" of his last stanza.

There is an emotional continuity running through this poem, where the exultations of love and the overwhelming pangs of jealousy are linked to the destructive force of leisure; through poem 11, which is in the same erotic meter, where the complex series of reactions to a dominant woman as the poet leaves for a distant imperial job leads to a devastation compared to a flower cut off by a mere brush with the plow; through poem 63, in which an orgiastic dominant goddess at the extreme end of the world leads a Roman youth to castrate himself into her service, waking up in horror at all he has lost thereafter; and poem 64, in which a woman abandoned by a hero is rescued by an orgiastic god. All of these connect to the unusual explicit mention of adultery-avoidance (61.101–5) and abandonment of homosexual playmates (61.129–43) in the marriage hymn, poem 61. And they all evidence the combinatory force of play through rhetorical registers, beyond the range of Greek epigrammatists (or poets generally), which fuels the savagery and the complexity of Catullus's invective epigrams.

The sapphics of poem 51 transpose the idealized psychology of Sappho into a critique that at the same time incorporates a rhythmic reference to her template of love interaction, as is even more the case with the sapphics of poem 11. But Sappho is writing for an enclosed society. Catullus is applying her enclosures and penetrating perceptions for maximum yield in the riddling brunt of a large, complicated, not wholly traceable society, where the poem that can serve as a bond between friends or a succinct and witty social communication can be elevated to a definer, and by implication also to an instrument of exorcism, for the very sufferings that the capacity of the poet to use his art to further his love has let him in for.

This use of Greek tradition is always nuanced, always complicated, and always combined with Roman elements that have their own already urban sophistication as well as their own quasi-tribal crudeness. So, for example, Catullus's succinct reference in poem 38 to the gestures of Simonides carries through a comparable act of at once incorporating them and distancing the Roman's psychology from the simpler, more idealized Greek's. In the request for a dialogue to console him at a bad time, Catullus asks Cornificius for verses: "Paulum quid libet adlocutio-nis, / Maestius lacrimis Simonideis" ("May it be just a bit of an address, / More doleful than the tears of Simonides")—and a global view of Simonides is caught up in the nascently ironic plaint of fictive conversational interchange. Simonides in fact has here been strategically over-simplified to focus the point, since laments (*threnoi*) are only part of his poetic output.

Throughout Catullus's work, as in his two poems in sapphics, he forces a range of persons into the tight mold of a pointed structure and an unusual range of past, present, and future, combining the summary intensity of a long view with the intimacy of a close look at a moment. In poem 51, he goes from the typification of Lesbia's encounter with lovers to a view of cities and kingdoms ruining through time in the lens of the single word "otium." In poem 11, comradeship is enlisted to end love in a perspective that links the dangerous, expansive, exiling assignments of a young imperial throughout the empire with the fate of a devastated lover. This perspective is again focused by the significant repetition of the single word "ultimus" (significantly broken in its first occurrence across lines 11 and 12 of the stanza's heaviest enjambment); and it verges on phantasmagoria in the reversal of the simile of the flower and the plow, where the plow/furrow and iron/flower metaphors would normally plot on a male/female axis, but Catullus, the "flower" of this simile, is, of course, male, while the "plow," Lesbia, is female. This poem ranges easily through past and future as it allows its play through the present utterance of the poem:

> Furi et Aureli, comites Catulli,
> sive in extremos penetrabit Indos,
> litus ut longe resonante Eoa
>   tunditur unda,

sive in Hyrcanos Arabasve molles,
seu Sagas sagittiferosve Parthos,
sive quae septemgeminus colorat
    aequora Nilus,
sive trans altas gradietur Alpes,
Caesaris visens monimenta magni,
Gallicum Rhenum horribile aequor ulti-
    mosque Britannos,
omnia haec, quaecumque feret voluntas
caelitum, temptare simul parati,
pauca nuntiate meae puellae
    non bona dicta.
cum suis vivat valeatque moechis,
quos simul complexa tenet trecentos,
nullum amans vere, sed identidem omnium
    illa rumpens;
nec meum respectet, ut ante, amorem,
qui illius culpa cecidit velut prati
ultimi flos, praetereunte postquam
    tactus aratro est.

Furius and Aurelius, friends of Catullus,
Whether he will have got through to the farthest Indians
Where the shore is beaten by the Dawn's long-
    Resounding wave;

Or to the Caspians or to the soft Arabians
Or the Persians or the arrow-bearing Parthians
Or the shores that the sevenfold streams of
    The Nile cover;

Whether he will march across the lofty Alps
To see the memorials of great Caesar,
To the Gallic Rhine, the horrible ocean,
    The remotest Britons;

You who together are ready to venture all,
Whatever the will of the gods may bring,
Announce to my girlfriend these few
    Not kindly words:

Let her live and thrive with her adulterers
Whom she holds embraced three hundred together,
Loving none truly but constantly breaking
    The groins of all.

And let her not look, as before, on my love,
Who at her fault has fallen just like a flower of
A meadow's remotest edge after it has been touched
    By the passing plow.

    This poem moves from the extremely public to the extremely private as it goes from the unusual third person of self-reference to the first person, reversing the movement of poem 51. Both poems in their range boldly set the coordinates that Propertius will put into opposition and Horace will arrange into a glossy proportionateness. Catullus, by contrast with Virgil, offers an accomplished but strategically indecisive view of the relation between personality and empire.[6] The subject of poem 11 is also extremely skewed rhetorically, since the introduction obscures the fact that love will be in view at all, let alone that it will be the point of the poem. And the double vocative removes the initial injunction from anything so intimate as the close friendship implied by other poems. The "comites Catulli" are enjoined to think of him as first moving out to the boundaries of empire on an energized leap into the future, which remains still undetermined among the options of the extreme east of India in the first stanza, the nearer east in the second, and the remote Transalpine regions of Gaul, Germany, and Britain in the third.[7] The empire, as Janan urges in her reading, is both absent and present here. In the imaginary map running from due east to northwest, Rome occupies an unmentioned slot between the Nile of line 8 and the Alps of line 9, and there is effectually a return to Rome in the imagined action of the last two stanzas. This Rome, like the "otium" of poem 51, embroils the poet in a subjection that is both public and private. Yet taking up his imperial duties and abandoning "otium" embroils him finally in humiliation, since his career in Rome is dependent on his accepting assignments very far away and abandoning the friends who make it home, together with his mistress, who will not mind crushing him by her infidelities. He here presents a version of the Freudian primal scene, complete with the suggestion of a castration in the last stanza, which will take on its full, cultic dimensions in poem 63.

In the geography that dominates the first half of the poem, it cannot even be said that the movement from hot to cold exactly prefigures the similar movement in the concluding message that is to be delivered to Lesbia, a message that is biting because it is delayed, but then given a full half of the poem in the final three stanzas.[8]

In the pastoral poetry of the Alexandrians, the lover is allegorized as poet and shepherd, and he is set into an enclosed, idealized space, a Sicily imagined as still less extensive than the actual island. Later, in Virgil's *Eclogues,* the Roman countryside has a quite specific climactic range.[9] Here the vast, real, varied space of the empire is evoked, pervaded, as it seems to have been already in Catullus's time, from its perfumes to its architecture, by Eastern undertones and overtones.[10] The lover's preoccupation with matters other than love at once concentrates and diffuses the very last line. Indeed, a muted version of the *odi-et-amo* paradox is built into the single word "moechis" ("adulterers"), since the term could or could not imply a violation of the rights to fidelity of Catullus, who himself could or could not be characterized as a "moechus."

The conception of time, too, looks to a future remote enough to allow at least for the transport of the speaker to far places and at the same time proximate in the imminence of the predictive message, all the more so because it is offered as certain. There are alternatives for Catullus the imperial emissary: he does not know which way he will go. But he predicts no such options for the certain-to-be-unfaithful-mistress nor for her new lovers, whose groins are certain to be broken—nor for himself at his remote distance from Rome, sure to be both disabused and heartbroken (the *odi-et-amo* paradox continues). The voice suspends and rhythmically breaks across the phrase "ut ante," which announces her crucial change away from respect for his love: "nec meum respectet, ut ante, amorem." If he has fallen like the last flower in the meadow before the plow, the fact that her fickleness has done the damage is the more emphatically certain, and so is her fault. Indeed, the message is unequivocally one of blame, and also of pathos, as the severance is accomplished by a light blow from the heavy instrument of the plow, "tactus aratro est."

The corresponding overall shift from hyperbole to pathos tips the scales toward the devastation of the lover, though the logical suggestion hovers that he will have been freed as the physical distance has become a psychological one. In fact, the turn of naming himself—and in the

third person, instead of the first person that the initial vocatives implic-
itly mount[11]—already sets up an armature for the self-definition that is
made the subject of the poem. His language joins him to the "comites
Catulli," while his prediction makes him an object of their, and his own,
pity. This poem composes a post-Sapphic symmetry in its balanced stan-
zas—three for empire, three for farewell to love—rather than following
the Sapphic "subtle fire" of erotic preoccupation through the open
stanza patterns.

Here the effects of politics, if not politics itself, perfuse the poem in
a way already more complex than the mode of a Propertian with-
drawal and elegantly touching in extents of space and ranges of time.
Politics thus remains in the charged field of Roman poetry, unassimil-
able and unbanishable, while the doughty patriotism of Ennius has been
left far behind.[12]

Catullus's opening poem, the dedication to the historian Cornelius,
asks us, through a request to this literary friend, that we juxtapose—and
therefore under the litotes of modesty compare—Catullus's "trifles" ("nu-
gae") with the "cartae laboriosae" of Cornelius.

Elegance is the first concern of Catullus's poem 1, but he also touches
on his comprehensiveness with characteristic indirection:

> Cui dono lepidum novum libellum
> arida modo pumice expolitum?
> Corneli, tibi: namque tu solebas
> meas esse aliquid putare nugas
> iam tum, cum ausus es unus Italorum
> omne aevum tribus explicare cartis
> doctis, Iuppiter, et laboriosis.
> quare habe tibi quidquid hoc libelli
> qualecumque; quod, [o] patrona virgo,
> plus uno maneat perenne saeclo.

> To whom shall I give this elegant new little book
> Polished just now with dry pumice?
> Cornelius, to you, for you were wont
> To esteem my trifles somewhat
> Already then when you, alone of Italians,
> Dared to unfold all the ages in three books,

Learned ones, by Jupiter, and well worked over.
For which take whatever there is in this book
Of whatever sort; which, O sponsoring maid,
Will perdure through more than one era.

This subdued contrast with historical writing sets the tone for the widest range of almost any lyric poet up to then, even though it is composed enough so that its general pattern of oppositions reveals a specifically Callimachian bent toward the limited and a refusal of the then dominant Ennean-epic strain.[13] Callimachus did say "a big book is equal to a big evil" (fragment 359), and the force of his recommendation toward rhetorical containment carries through Propertius's anti-epic posture and Horace's attention to local polish. It may even be taken to provide an impetus toward the justification-by-achievement of Virgil and Ovid in their long poems. But even Propertius and Horace allow politics into their poems, and for Catullus already, who also broaches politics, the element of Ennius or the Roman does not just stand in opposition to the element of Callimachus or the Greek. Catullus is remarkable for allowing a range of tensile reference into a short poem, far more than Callimachus could have imagined or than is to be found in Meleager, a Hellenistic poet who is close to being Catullus's contemporary. In his astonishing success in getting the *multum in parvo* of inclusiveness into a small compass, Catullus stretches his poems so that they can carry off something of what the encyclopedic Cornelius aims for, as he may be taken to imply. Catullus adds to the Hellenistic tradition by managing an equivalent for Ennius while shedding his ponderousness. His longer poems tend to be more conventionally ordered in the choice of subject, but in the Attis poem (63), the emotional, geographical, historical, and religious marginality of the topic applies an equivalent pressure.

This first poem's boldness announces that the poet's reach can effectuate a range by simply touching on a subject and engaging it in the mode of quasi-conversational discourse. It introduces a collection where again and again the pointed, resounding force of the compacted utterance does not have to surrender either variety or complexity. So the term "lepidum" may be taken to imply all that the Hellenistic poet could accomplish, but also to expand it into something "novum." The factor that has led Catullus to address this opening poem to Cornelius is not just his literary connections to this addressee: one of his poet friends, Calvus or another, would seem to have been more germane for that. He says that Cornelius's steady esteem of his "trifles" as "something" ("aliquid") has led him to do so, and at a time when Cornelius had already carried off his very different, historiographic triumph. Catullus's final boast, in fact, hints that he may even surpass his historian friend, whose work takes in "all the ages" ("omne aevum"), while Catullus's own work will itself become part of the ages by lasting for more than an era ("saeclo"). Only as we progress to measure what Catullus has taken in can the quiddity of that "aliquid" be assessed.

It is just this range that Cicero is not likely to have understood, given his expressed Puritanism. His life crossed Catullus's at many points, since they inhabited the same privileged world, and the crosscurrents of mutual ambivalence, more nuanced, it might be imagined, on Catullus's side than on Cicero's, are caught in his epigram of mock praise and self-deprecation, poem 49:

> Disertissime Romuli nepotum,
> quot sunt quotque fuere, Marce Tulli,
> quotque post aliis erunt in annis,
> gratias tibi maximas Catullus
> agit pessimus omnium poeta,
> tanto pessimus omnium poeta,
> quanto tu optimus omnium patronus.

> Most eloquent of Romulus's heirs,
> As many as are and have been, Marcus Tullius,
> And as many as shall be in other years,
> You are offered greatest thanks by Catullus
> Who is the worst poet of them all,
> By so much the worst poet of them all
> As you are the best patron of them all.

As is typical with Catullus, this short poem touches on past, present, and future. Its exact tonality is impossible to establish. And it is so elliptical that only by contextual supposition, and at least two logical sleights (a total reversal for the references to Cicero, a partial reversal for those to himself), can it be deduced to be satirical. This comes clearer if this twist is seen in the light of poem 68, which celebrates a friendship with someone who is Cicero's enemy. A straight reading, however, would make it Catullus's only bad poem, and we do not really need all the dimensions of his relations with Cicero to get on the track of the probable slanted reading(s).[14]

The elegance by which Catullus carries off his comprehensiveness through what begins as a light, but charged, quasi-conversational gesture shows strikingly in poems where he deflects his complexities through an external object, such as a bird (Lesbia's sparrow of poems 2 and 3) or a yacht (poem 4). The yacht poem is ambivalently about an actual yacht or the model or picture of one—and so in any case with an actual one and its history in view, as Frank Copley points out.[15] Catullus makes it heavy with past, present, and future, multirelational in space and time. The *sprezzatura* of the verse carries off that act. "Phasellus ille" ("that little yacht") thrusts the object on us, and at the distance indicated by the pronoun. It then builds upon, up to, and away from that distance. As the very building of the ship is recalled, present and past are mounted to mirror storm versus calm. The "master" ("erus") stands by in the haven of his recollection. It is the ship that has invoked the Dioscuri, the traditional quellers of storms. There are ship epitaphs in the *Palatine Anthology,* but this poem exceeds them in range and deftness. It presents an interplay of the town of Sirmio and Lake Garda and the difficult, intricately charted voyages out and home. All are evoked as memory and relief from stress of voyage. In poem 31, which is addressed to Sirmio, there is a contrast between the "little eye" or "gem" ("ocelle") of Catullus's lake and the "waste sea" ("mari vasto"). At the end, the waves are asked to laugh, and they are, unusually, "Lydian" waves. Indeed, past and present are pulled together in the single word "Lydiae," which refers to a colony of the sixth century B.C. (Herodotus 1.94), taken over by Etruscans in the fourth century and now part of the view that Catullus has by his lake, whose waves are "Lydian" also in the more present, visual sense of being opulently beautiful.

In poem 101, Catullus again evokes past, present, and future in his funeral poem for his brother by locating himself at the point of return from a voyage:

> Multas per gentes et multa per aequora vectus
> advenio has miseras, frater, ad inferias,
> ut te postremo donarem munere mortis
> et mutam nequiquam alloquerer cinerem.
> quandoquidem fortuna mihi tete abstulit ipsum,
> heu miser indigne frater adempte mihi,

nunc tamen interea haec, prisco quae more parentum
    tradita sunt tristi munere ad inferias,
accipe fraterno multum manantia fletu,
    atque in perpetuum, frater, ave atque vale.

Through many peoples brought and through many seas,
    I come, brother, to present these grief offerings,
So that I may give you a final gift in death
    And may speak fruitlessly to your mute ashes.
Since indeed fortune took your person away from me,
    Alas unworthily reft from me, grieving brother,
Now, still, meanwhile these things, for offerings,
    Are handed over, sad gift, in our parents' old way.
Accept them as they flow much with a brother's weeping,
    And forever, brother, hail and farewell.

The past of this poem is remote and inclusive if, as Gian Bagio Conte claims, "multa per aequora vectus" is seen as echoing the *Odyssey*.[16] The very monodic flow of this poem gathers intensity as it cuts off mention of a future for itself as well as for the dead brother, with a look at the past only in the custom of the prior generation ("prisco . . . more parentum").[17] Moreover, the poem is organized dynamically not so much around a eulogy of the brother or general reflections on mortality—the more conventional subjects for epitaph poems—as on the actions, reactions, and expectations of the speaker.[18] It is a poem about the act of grieving and the impact of grieving on the psyche of the speaker. This live presence, as it dominates even the last line of "hail and farewell," becomes an indirect tribute to the brother, including the act of remembering him in the fabric of the speaker's life.

    In another conversational elegy, Catullus sets up his brother's death as a device to frame his translation of Callimachus's "Lock of Berenice" (poem 66). Poem 65 situates that translation as a gift sent to his friend Ortalus to prove he has overcome the separation from poetry brought on by his sorrow over his brother's death. His mind "fluctuates" ("fluctuat"), but he will always sing sad songs over his brother's death, as Philomela does over Itys. The erotic undercurrents of this comparison are picked up and redeployed when, in the final long comparison of this short poem, Catullus declares that he passes on the translation so that Ortalus will not think the friend's words will slip out of his mind—as an apple slips out of the lap of a chaste girl when her mother appears and she blushes at the revelation of her erotic-tinged distractability. Tracing out the correspondences, and also the lack of correspondences, between this vehicle and the tenors of Catullus's literary activity and Catullus's grief could involve a great deal of extrapolative and deductive matching. The terminal metaphor of the girl is cut short, a bold display in which we are not, without overkill, to identify Catullus with the blushing virgin, let alone his interlocutor with her mother. Overriding the possible logical connections in the metaphor, through the assertion of achieved decorum that the poem carries, is the composed grace of presenting it—and bringing it all, but always indirectly, to bear upon "The Lock of Berenice," a Hellenistic court poem in which a lock of a queen's hair is imagined as recounting how it came to be placed in the heavens as a constellation. This pair of poems approaches a frame comparable to the more elaborate one in the single poem 64, where the abandonment of Ariadne by Theseus, depicted on a woven wedding gift, illustrates and contrasts with the happy union of Thetis and Peleus.[19]

Poetry proceeds, in Lotman's analysis, by a skillful mounting of sets of binary oppositions,[20] and Catullus's mastery shows in his ability thus to allow the erotic domain to provide shadings for the domain of lamenting elegy, and both to be taken together as a qualification of, and comment on—which is itself super-Hellenistic—the translation of Callimachus's poem. Thus the levity of such poetry is preserved while at the same time it is situated at the intersection of feelings of great gravity—not itself always separable from levity, especially in love, when a blushing girl's gesture is of the greatest moment and as casual and light as, say, a jaded but fascinating mistress's devotion in playing with a pet sparrow and sorrowing over its death.

All of this play derives from the boldness and suppleness of Catullus's reach, and it is highlighted by comparing his work to that which he has reworked and reached beyond. So, for example, his marriage poems, 61 and 62, are in a genre brought to peerless finish by Theocritus's Idyll 18. But Theocritus's poem, set to the mythological frame of the marriage of Helen and Menelaus, stays wholly within its boundaries, whereas Catullus's poems expand such boundaries, for all their formality and for the similarities of his refrains to Theocritus's. Both his poems, in their differences of meter and progression, still allow touches of his Roman world to expand them from a base with a possible reference to a real marriage of one Roman to another. And while Catullus's poem 61 touches curiously on the threat of adultery, Theocritus entirely leaves aside that threat to the marriage of Helen and Menelaus—which is, of course, built into the myth—except for an oblique reference to the bridegroom's possible fatigue (Theocritus 18.9–14). We cannot know how close poem 66 is to the largely lost "Lock of Berenice" of Callimachus, but the introductory poem, 65, both expands it and undercuts it by giving it the character of an exercise and by juxtaposing its gracile qualifications to the earnestness of mourning and the sociabilities and disruptions of literary careers.

In the instance of this last area of discourse, Catullus notably allows his play through the gestures of literary commentary. In poem 22, for example, he sets up three poets: himself, Varus, and a proximate third party, a bad poet ("Suffenus iste"). Here the sense of the bad poems is super-Horatian, since it contrasts with the social behavior of the man: "Homo est venustus et dicax et urbanus" ("The man is charming and eloquent and urbane")[21]—and yet he is a bad poet, an acute social possibility often instanced in the modern era but of a complexity not envisioned even by so urbane a satirist as Pope. Another complexity is introduced in the capping statement of the last line, where Catullus brings in Aesop's fable of the man who wears one wallet in front carrying others' faults and another, unseen, on his back carrying his own. Here, in what can be only partially ironic, Catullus ends with the self-deprecating doubt that he may indeed be writing in ignorance of his own symmetrical faults, both literary and social.[22]

Poem 17 frames itself on a brutal gesture, exemplified in many early societies, of wishing further indignity upon the older, imperceptive husband of a young, unfaithful wife: he is to topple headlong off a bridge into the muck. This poem is in the Priapean measure, appropriate for such an anthropologically rooted gesture; and if that meter was indeed used in Hellenistic times for hymns to Priapus (it is otherwise unexampled), this poem must refer to and incorporate them. There is some displacement of Catullus's own intent, since he sets his indignation, which cannot be more than a somewhat fictive extravagance of moralizing, in the context of Verona's desire to replace a rotten old bridge with a new one. The town, the "Colonia" (the term taking a sidelong look at its recent official status) is the addressee, and the object of his curse is defined as a "municeps" ("townsman"). The expansive play over the compacted gesture of the curse contains elements of the city and its aspiration for civic repair, of erotic acts and attitudes toward them, and

THE REACH OF POETRY

of the religious festival, the Salisubsali, the riot of which the imagined
stoutness of the new bridge will hold up. Past, present, and future are all
there, all expanded on the simple curse.

A comparable range percolates through poem 10, which is set up as
an account of a random conversation among the poet, his friend, and
the latter's demimondaine mistress, a trio that intensifies this poem's
nuances beyond the similar, more digressive *Epistles* and *Satires* of

Varus me meus ad suos amores
visum duxerat e foro otiosum,
scortillum, ut mihi tum repente visum est,
non sane illepidum neque invenustum.
huc ut venimus, incidere nobis
sermones varii, in quibus, quid esset
iam Bithynia, quo modo se haberet,
et quonam mihi profuisset aere.
respondi id quod erat, nihil neque ipsis
nec praetoribus esse nec cohorti,
cur quisquam caput unctius referret,
praesertim quibus esset irrumator
praetor, nec faceret pili cohortem.
"at certe tamen," inquiunt "quod illic
natum dicitur esse, comparasti
ad lecticam homines." ego, ut puellae
unum me facerem beatiorem,
"non" inquam "mihi tam fuit maligne,
ut, provincia quod mala incidisset,
non possem octo homines parare rectos."
at mi nullus erat nec hic neque illic,
fractum qui veteris pedem gravati
in collo sibi collocare posset.
hic illa, ut decuit cinaediorem,
"quaeso," inquit "mihi, mi Catulle, paulum
istos commoda: nam uolo ad Serapim
deferri." "mane," inquii puellae,
"istud quod modo dixeram me habere,
fugit me ratio: meus sodalis—
Cinna est Gaius,—is sibi paravit.

uerum, utrum illius an mei, quid ad me?
utor tam bene quam mihi pararim.
sed tu insulsa male et molesta vivis,
per quam non licet esse neglegentem."

My friend Varus, when he saw me idling there,
Had led me from the Forum to his love,
A little whore, as I saw right away,
Not, indeed, inelegant, not unlovely.
When we arrived there we got into
All sorts of talk, among other things how it is
Now in Bithynia, how the place is making out,
Whether I profited there financially.
I answered how it was: nothing for the praetors
Themselves, and not for their staff either,
As to why anyone would bring back an oilier head—
Especially those whose praetor was
A fucker and valued his staff not a hair.
"But surely, anyway," they say, "you managed
To get what they say are native there,
Some litter-bearers." I, so that to the girl
I could make me out to be one of the luckier,
"No," I say, "It was not so foul for me there,
That however bad the province happened to be,
I couldn't get together eight straight-backed men."
But I had none here or there who on his neck
Could balance the broken leg of an old bedstead.
Then she, as befits a nymphomaniac
Says, "I'd like you, Catullus dear,
To lend them to me for a little. I want them
To carry me to the Temple of Serapis."
"Tomorrow," I told the girl, "When I said just now
I owned them, my senses had left me. My buddy
is Cinna, Gaius. He's the one who got them.
But really, whether his or mine, what's it to me?
I have use of them as if I'd got them myself.
But you live a life so tasteless and pernicious
A man can't let his attention slide at all."

This single incident offers a broadly varied cast of characters: Varus, Catullus himself, the official Memmius, the young prostitute, the cohort, the Bithynians present both in Rome and in the province (as well as falsely on Catullus's staff, and truly on Cinna's). The places the poem touches on are equally varied: the Forum where they stand, the distant Bithynia, and the temple of Serapis of the young prostitute's devotional desire.

Catullus's strategy here, and elsewhere, is to use the situation of engaging an addressee to carry off the sharp statement of a predominant point while allowing details from other domains, thus stretched and twisted by the act of importation, into the ongoing flow. Writing in a tradition of subdramatic interchange recognizable from the Hellenistic tradition and most pointedly exemplified by the *Mimes* of Herondas, Catullus goes beyond them in the way that he has a range of reference and psychological nuance play off one against the other: male friendship around the Forum; male sharing shaded by male rivalry in the company of light women; the pretensions of the latter to carry on political rather than erotic discourse; the complex of relations to the exploitation of the provinces in Asia Minor; the consequent interrelations, both coordinate and subordinate, of the staffs; the tendency, worthy of a portrayal by Flaubert or Zola, for the demimondaine to greedily cadge services from the friends of her paramours; her seemingly unrelated tendency to seek refuge in religion; the popularity of the nonindigenous religions from the East; the use of this for status as well as for refuge; the touchy sense of ego as it can rise to the surface in the remembering speaker when he is confronted; the susceptibility and defenselessness of the demimondaine to the insult that can always come her way—all these countercurrents flow through and across Catullus's poem.

A comparable play, though more intense for its greater personal bearing, dominates poem 37, which begins with a salacious pothouse and its denizens, among whom the expectantly lecherous Lesbia is found sitting:

> Salax taberna vosque contubernales,
> a pilleatis nona fratribus pila,
> solis putatis esse mentulas vobis,
> solis licere, quidquid est puellarum,
> confutuere et putare ceteros hircos?

Salacious pothouse, and you buddies,
Nine pillars from the skull-capped brothers,
Do you think you're the only ones with cocks,
The only ones allowed to fuck any
Of the girls, and think that other men are goats?

The poem stays at this pitch of rage to focus on Lesbia as she hangs out there, ready to take any of them on, including, at the end of the poem, a Spaniard who cleans his teeth with urine:

hanc boni beatique
omnes amatis, et quidem, quod indignum est,
omnes pusilli et semitarii moechi;
tu praeter omnes une de capillatis,
cuniculosae Celtiberiae fili,
Egnati, opaca quem bonum facit barba
et dens Hibera defricatus urina.

Love her, good and fortunate ones,
All of you, and indeed—it's disgusting—
You are all puny adulterers off the streets,
You above all alone among the long-haired,
Son of bunny-cultivating Spain,
Egnatius, whom a dense beard makes good,
And teeth polished with Iberian piss.

More savage and more condensed still is poem 58:

Caeli, Lesbia nostra, Lesbia illa,
illa Lesbia, quam Catullus unam
plus quam se atque suos amavit omnes,
nunc in quadriviis et angiportis
glubit magnanimi Remi nepotes.

Caelius, our Lesbia, that Lesbia,
That Lesbia whom alone Catullus
Loved more than himself and all his own
Now at the crossroads and in alleys
Shags the grandchildren of great-souled Remus.

The extreme angle at which the addressee, Caelius, is portrayed helps to complicate the five lines of this poem, three of which are devoted to a near-litany about the displaced love, centering around the large space given in this short compass for three namings of Lesbia and the repetition of the phrase "Lesbia illa."[23] Yet in its narrow space, the poem can still include a first, second, and third person—Caelius, Catullus, and Lesbia—along with the hordes of the descendants of Remus whom she shags. Here the space of Rome is bisected among points of motion— the four-directioned crossroads ("quadriviis")—and points of withdrawal—the alleys, narrow ones ("angiportis") where obsessive sexual congress takes place with both parties standing upright. The decline of the lustful patrician woman is mirrored in the decline of the descendants of Remus. He was great-souled; they stand there passively to be serviced.

Catullus's Lesbia is a complex departure from the pattern of Freudian *Dirnenliebe,* love of a prostitute, to which Propertius's Cynthia may be said to correspond.[24] In the Freudian "special type of object choice," a man who cannot stand the sexuality of the mother but wishes at the same time to face and embrace it chooses a woman who will be compulsively unfaithful to him. Since he takes the posture of rescuing her from this, he is to some degree identified with his own father, while separated from him because he cannot hold the mother. This tutelary posture characteristically necessitates a woman of a somewhat lower class, to whom the lover can condescend, a guarantee of his unconscious contempt for her because of the very sexuality that attracts him. Thus the Cynthia of Propertius, and others of the type; but Lesbia, as a patrician *matrona,* diverges from the type. And Catullus, in the devastating present, does not show himself as wishing to save her: infidelity has destroyed the preciousness of their love, though he continues to love. In another divergence from the Freudian pattern, there was no such threat in the past: mutual devotion gave an eternal cast to the love ("aeternum foedus") (109.6), and the presence of a third party, in the person of Lesbia's husband, is carefully kept out of the picture, so much so that Catullus can use (doubtless with some play of ambiguity) the term "moechus" ("adulterer") to describe the rivals who have violated his beloved, as though he were her husband. In the past, she respected (and was faithful, the context tells us), to his love: "nec meum respectet, ut ante, amorem" (11. 21). The love persists on his side, whatever she does (poem 75), but the compact between them has vanished in the present of the poems that portray her infidelity, not only with the nameless others of poem 11 but in such images of intense obscenity as those in poem 37, with its urine-mouthed Spaniard, and poem 58, with its lecherous patrician descendants of the "magnanimus" Remus.

Poem 85 summarizes, and goes beyond summary:

> Odi et amo. quare id faciam, fortasse requiris?
> nescio, sed fieri sentio et excrucior.

> I hate and love. Why I should do that you may well ask.
> I do not know but I feel it done and am racked.

The generality of this epigram forbids our confining it just to the present of the poems about infidelity, though it applies most pointedly to them. It is hard to reconcile, except as a general human observation, with the poems of absolute devotion. They indulge in the playfulness and tenderness of the "sparrow" poems, where folkloric identification of bird with penis ("the bird in the nest" of more modern folklore) reinforces the sublimation involved on the part of both poet and pet-owning mistress. In the elegy for the sparrow, their love is shadowed by death in a tenderness that only enlists itself for love. "The journey from which they say no one returns" ("iter . . . unde negant redire quemquem") (3.3) echoes the "night that is an all-time dreamless sleep" ("nox est perpetua una dormienda") of "Vivamus, mea Lesbia, atque amemus" ("Let us live, my Lesbia, and let us love") (poem 5). The sparrow poem combines two types, the lament for a pet and the love declaration.[25] But when adultery commences, the very bed is the witness, as is the body of Flavius and his bed's "fucked-out sides" ("latera ecfutata") (poem 6). Allowing for present, past, and future, as in the desolate poem 11, erotic memory haunts the verse when the speaker of poem 8 trembles on the edge of envisioning that Lesbia will "nibble the lips" of others ("labella mordebis") (8.18), a trailing off climax that causes the speaker to tell himself to "hold out steadfastly": "At tu, Catulle, destinatus obdura."[26]

In poem 28, as elsewhere in his work, the extremity of a deep anthropological convention is evoked to suggest homosexuality as opprobrious subjection. Catullus and his patron Memmius both "get fucked." The metaphor is transposed to a whole system of events surrounding the provincial administration where Memmius was a procurator and Catullus some sort of *cliens*. A final hint of opprobrium resides in the reference by contrasting it to the legendary founders of Rome, "Romuli Remique"; but this turn is itself inverted in poem 29, which opens with and repeats "cinaede Romule" ("pederast Romulus") as a metaphor for

Caesar. By line 13 of this poem, "vestra defutata mentula comesset" ("Your fucked-out cock might eat") provides the nightmare of a total condensation of sexuality, impotence, and dominance.[27]

Catullus's free play of voice exercises a mastery of utterance that controls such psychological extremities as it exhibits them. The speaker's flexibility exhibits itself as empowered to express the turmoils racking him, encapsulating into fixity and also dialectical possibility the final images—as, for example, in poem 58's greedily aggressive Lesbia fondling an upright passive nobleman, an act with its roots, from a Freudian perspective, in the perversion of mother or nurse sexually fondling an infant; or in poem 37's savagery that is tantamount to extreme oral aggression in the Spaniard who cleans his teeth with urine (a habit that informs the invective of the whole of poem 39, which is directed against the same figure). Here the displacement of the genitals to the face is reinforced by the preceding detail, the black beard that "makes him good." In a sentence where he is singled out among adulterers, the combination of hair and the presence of urine mounts an image that hallucinates the genitals, where visual sharpness fixes and blocks the composure of the speaker.

Rather than deploying the strategy of letting the single note of invective control the range of defining associations, the two formal marriage hymns, poems 61 and 62, pass through a celebratory, normative utterance that still gives glimpses of the range they are controlling by admitting touches of what in earlier poets would be impossibly discordant references. In poem 61, there is a glance at old age ("cana anilitas," 154), and at the same time a future noble child ("Torquatus volo parvulus," 210) is envisioned. These poems allow for the contradictions they contain, for the fire of the marriage torch—and of love—in poem 62 to be at once cruelest ("crudelior," 20) and most joyful ("iucundior," 26). The plucked flower loses its appeal on the one hand (38 ff.), but the unwed vine ("vidua vitis") is unfruitful on the other. In poem 61, hilarity is played off against shyness (11, 83–85). These turns are already more complex than the "gather-ye-rosebuds" trope of English Renaissance poetry. In this manner, too, the extremity of grief in poem 65 is allowed to frame and shadow the elegance of literary translation and erotically tinged eulogy in poem 66.

Poem 64, a heavily ornamented poem about embroidery, presents through myth an intersection of love psychologies. The connection between the myths is a decoration: the figure of the abandoned Ariadne watching Theseus sail away is one of those embroidered on a cover ("vestis") for a couch in the middle of the palace of the bridegroom Peleus. The marriage of Peleus and Thetis, itself looking ahead to Achilles (337 ff.), opens into and encloses the abandonment of Ariadne by Theseus and her subsequent hopes for union with her miraculously arriving suitor, Bacchus. His rites are counterpointed against her plaints, as are the joys of Peleus and Thetis. The Fates, whom Catullus has substituted for the conventional Muses (320–81), sing the auspicious predictions about the marriage.[28] At a further extreme in the pattern is Aegeus's mistaken lament for Theseus, which gives an erotic tinge to what the anxious king believes to be the funerary. The complexities of love provide the psychology for Theseus's forgetting to change his sails from black to white (240), so that Aegeus misreads them and in sorrow plunges to his death. The link is touched on through the repetition of the word "immemor" ("forgetful") in line 247, brought forward from line 58, where it characterizes Theseus's departure from Ariadne.[29] The pattern at points also contains and transcends the play of the bittersweet in love—reminiscent of the note struck by Meleager[30]—as in the description of Cupid as "Sancte puer curis hominum qui gaudia misces" ("Holy boy, who mixes delights with cares for men") (95). At the same time, at the base of the poem is the intensity of the Catullan love, which becomes explicit in the description of Ariadne's sudden infatuation with Theseus:

> non prius ex illo flagrantia declinavit
> lumina quam cuncto concepit corpore flammam
> funditus atque imis exarsit tota medullis. (90–92)

> No sooner had she turned from him the blazing lights of her eyes
> Then she conceived a flame with her entire body
> And her whole self burned to the depths in her inmost marrow.

In the self-assertion of its utterance, obscenity evidences at once desperation and dominance. It locates itself at the extreme edge of desire and the permissible. As such—and particularly in ancient rites of which traces have not died out even in our time—it can border on the uncanny or "estranged," Freud's *unheimlich*. In such a light, the self-assertive and the self-destructive transpose each other, and the extreme poetic version of this complex of attitudes in Catullus's work is the Attis poem, poem 63, in which the name of this mythical Near Eastern consort is given to a priest of Cybele. The central rite of the priests, or Galli, is self-castration, imaged, according to one reading of the icon, by the strings of scrota across the chest of the Artemis of Ephesus (which used to be read as multiple breasts). The youth at the center of this narrative poem is a Greek, but he could have been a Roman, as there were Roman Galli; and he is identified with Rome implicitly throughout and explicitly at the end, when Catullus himself prays against this possibility befalling him.

The songlike pitch of Catullus's poems, so divergent from later poetry in his vein, may be heard as an incantation against the uncanny—even in such as poem 5, "Vivamus, mea Lesbia, atque amemus," which invokes love as a stay against mortality. The exuberance of the meter of poem 61 is implicitly forced to an extraordinary emotional symmetry:

> Collis o Heliconii
> cultor Uraniae genus,
> qui rapis teneram ad virum
> virginem, o Hymenaee Hymen,
> o Hymen Hymenaee.

And the galliambics of the Attis poem enlist the onrushing thumps of one of the rarest of measures to narrate baldly the horror underlying the act of uncanny devotion, a devotion recalled in the meter, which seems to have been used for hymns in honor of the goddess.[31] Typically the line ends with a speeded-up rattle of short syllables, almost recalling the rattle of the devotee's tambourine, a rattle the more emphatic for not coming with certain regularity; some long syllables are allowed:

> Super alta vectus Attis celeri rate maria,
> Phrygium ut nemus citato cupide pede tetigit
> adiitque opaca siluis redimita loca deae,
> stimulatus ibi furenti rabie, vagus animis,
> devolsit ili acuto sibi pondera silice,
> itaque ut relicta sensit sibi membra sine viro,
> etiam recente terrae sola sanguine maculans,
> niveis citata cepit manibus leve typanum,
> typanum, tubam Cybelles,[32] tua, mater, initia,
> quatiensque terga tauri teneris cava digitis
> canere haec suis adorta est tremebunda comitibus.
> "agite ite ad alta, Gallae, Cybeles nemora simul,

simul ite, dindymenae dominae vaga pecora,
aliena quae petentes velut exules loca
sectam meam exsecutae duce me mihi comites
rapidum salum tulistis truculentaque pelagi,
et corpus evirastis Veneris nimio odio;
hilarate erae citatis erroribus animum."

(63.1–18)

Having coursed the high seas in a swift boat, Attis
When he has touched the Phrygian grove with desire-sped foot
And reached the dense wood-surrounded precincts of the goddess,
Then driven by raging madness, wandering in mind,
Plucked from himself with sharp flint the weights of his groin;
And so when he perceived his members left without manhood,
Spotting the ground of the earth with blood still fresh,
Hastened she took the light tympanum in her snowy hands,
The tympanum, trumpet of Cybele, mother, your rites,
And shaking the bull's hollow hide with tender fingers,
This she began to sing, trembling among her fellows.
"Come, girly priests, now to Cybele's high groves,
Now, shifting herds of the mistress of Mount Dindymus,
Who, seeking out like exiles alien places,
Following my sect, with me as leader, my train,
Have borne the swift salt and fiercenesses of the sea,
And have unmanned your bodies from excess hate for Venus,
Gladden the spirit of your mistress by your rushed wanderings."

In his first speech (12–26), Attis evokes the present of the grove, at the sharp moment of the poem while he wakens from his self-inflicted amputation. The poet, who exemplifies a deep equipoise between the extremities of hate and love—even in not knowing how they work, as in poem 85—here has Attis himself testify to the disastrous sundering of one from the other. His motive, he as much as says, was identical with that of the other castrated priests, "Who have unmanned your bodies from excess hatred for Venus" ("et corpus evirastis Veneris nimio odio") (17). The disproportionate compensation is to "Gladden the spirit of your mistress by your rushed wanderings" ("hilarate erae citatis erroribus animum" (18). This declaration is accompanied by the loud sound of a tympanum or tambourine, rather than by the Roman trumpet—by a rattling and jingling rather than by a blast, and the contrast of sounds images the whole contrast between the assertive directiveness of a masculine world that has been left behind and the new world of rather perverse preoccupations and cyclic vacillations.

In a second speech, Attis evokes his past as a youth in the activities of his city and his associations with family and friends (50–73):

egone a mea remota haec ferar in nemora domo?
patria, bonis, amicis, genitoribus abero?
abero foro, palaestra, stadio et gyminasiis?

(58–60)

Shall I be borne into these groves far removed from my home,
From fatherland, wealth, friends, and parents shall I be gone,
Shall I be gone from Forum, wrestling ground, racetrack, and gymnasium?

His future is a desolate one, punctuated by the monotony of the round he has bound his life into, reinforced by the bareness of the landscape, dominated by ritual sounds almost as much as by sights, and different from the variety of the city he has left behind.[33] The most prominent figure is Cybele herself, who is brought in with her lions to utter a menacing third speech (77–82). Catullus introduces his own person suddenly at the end to measure the uncanniness and put a distance between himself and such a fate—with a prayer to Cybele (!), as though his own susceptibility to extremities contains this possibility: "Dea magna, dea Cybelle, dea domina Dindymi, / Procul a mea tuus sit furor omnis, era, domo: / Alios age incitatos, alios age rabidos" ("Great goddess, goddess Cybelle, mistress goddess of Mount Dindymus, / May all your madness, mistress, be far from my house: / Drive others to be incited, drive others to be enraged") (91–93). Catullus here takes the leap of putting himself at the end of the narrative poem, and this act of dissociation engages the ambivalence of stating itself in a form that echoes Attis's own prayers. It offers a version of Attis's sequence from impulsion to revulsion and then submission, but it does so in a condensed form, whereby the fixity of a nascent fascination being abjured is figured in the obsessive, not merely formulaic gesture, of the four vocatives in these three lines, which are reminiscent of the obsessive namings in the five lines of the fixated poem 58: "Lesbia nostra, Lesbia illa, / illa Lesbia."

Strikingly in this poem, and notably in general, Catullus has found his reach in turning Hellenistic forms to the personal exploration of extremities, transmuting them into broader and subtler expression. He has made the complexities of the expanding *imperium* reverberate with the desolations of a perceptive, reactive spirit caught in the contradictions, amorous and social, of its demanding ways.

8

The Angling of Poetry to Philosophy

The Nature of Lucretius

1

AS DANTE PEERLESSLY demonstrates, and as Blake does later in a profoundly different way, the kinship of poetry to philosophy, if the poetic means reach far enough, can conjoin poetry's intimations and philosophy's reasoned assertions into a single powerful utterance—well beyond the casual deployment of attitudes in countless other poets, including Goethe, with whom George Santayana too hastily and piously linked Dante and Lucretius as "philosophical poets."[1]

Lucretius worked his way past the imbalance between a somewhat primitive rough-hewn poetic tradition and a highly evolved, sophisticated philosophical one, attaining a reach where the imbalance disappears into the fused urgency of his expression.

Lucretius, in urging and expounding an Epicurean system, does so in ways that depart from those of his master by using poetry, for which Epicurus had expressed disdain.[2] In the process, Lucretius carries off a unique fusion of the somewhat antithetical domains of poetry and philosophy, forcing the poetry to produce a tonal unification of the physi-

cal theory and the ethics of Epicurus along such lines that one would
have to go back to Parmenides for even a partial parallel in poetry.[3] One
could trace the shift in Epicurus's indifferent use of the term στοιχεία,
which can refer equally to moral and to physical constituents (as well as
to letters), whereas the equivalent term(s) in Lucretius are always or
almost always physical.[4] He even compares, and often, the *multa ele-
menta,* the many "elements," of the letters composing his verses to the
mixture of atoms in nature (1.197, 1.822–26, 1.912, 2.686–89, 2.1013).[5]
And the radical nature of his physical thinking should not be forgotten,
according to Michel Serres, who connects that radical thinking to the
theory of the *clinamen:* "Existence, time, sense, and language proceed
together down that inclined plane."[6]

An implied antithesis—one that could be expressed as between po-
etic force and philosophical rigor—surfaces in the very first lines, if we
take Lucretius's poem as a whole:

> Aeneadum genetrix, hominum divumque voluptas,
> alma Venus, caeli subter labentia signa
> quae mare navigerum, quae terras frugiferentis
> concelebras, per te quoniam genus omne animantum
> concipitur visitque exortum lumina solis:
> te, dea, te fugiunt venti, te nubila caeli
> adventumque tuum, tibi suavis daedala tellus
> summittit flores, tibi rident aequora ponti
> placatumque nitet diffuso lumine caelum.
> nam simul ac species patefactast verna diei
> et reserata viget genitabilis aura favoni,
> aeriae primum volucres te, diva, tuumque
> significant initum perculsae corda tua vi.
> inde ferae pecudes persultant pabula laeta
> et rapidos tranant amnis: ita capta lepore
> te sequitur cupide quo quamque inducere pergis.

> Aeneas's sons' mother, joy of men and gods,
> fostering Venus, under the sky's gliding signs,
> you who make teem the ship-carrying sea
> and the fruit-bearing earth, since through you every race of the living
> is conceived and, arisen, sees the light of the sun:
> you, goddess, you do winds flee, you, clouds of the sky,

and your arrival; for you does the wizard earth
put forth sweet flowers, for you waves of the deep smile,
and the sky, pacified, shines with diffused light.
For as soon as the spring face of day opens up
and the unleashed breeze of the fruitful west wind gets strong,
at first the birds of the air show, goddess, you
and your beginning, their hearts struck by your force.
Then do wild herds leap over your joyful pastures
and swim swift streams; so, taken by loveliness, each
follows you in desire wherever you drive to lead.

(De rerum natura, 1.1–16)

"The identification of Natura with Venus," Anne Amory says, "brings the natural world into close relation with *voluptas,* the center of Epicurean ethics."[7] However, the tonality of this *voluptas* is quite different in this passage from the posture of Epicurus himself toward erotic pleasure, toward which he recommends prudence rather than a creative surging.[8] And Lucretius's own views toward love, as expressed in book 4, see it, in an Epicurean manner, as a disturbance, much like the religion from which he would seem to be getting a poetic lift in this invocation. This proem already offers a sort of double contradiction to the overriding argument of the poem, since first the poem maintains that one should get peace by freeing oneself of religion, not by subjecting oneself, as here, to any one god. Second, according to the Epicurean view, the gods have no effect on the world, let alone the intimate and forceful effect of the Venus depicted here. Rather, they sit off by themselves in supreme enjoyment. The phenomena here attributed to the influence of Venus are to be analyzed in the poem as the effects of atomic organization: the winds (1.271–97), the clouds (6.451–534), the creation of life on earth (5.785–836), and the motions of the constellations (5.509–37). To say that these effects, and love, await the atomic analysis that they will get later in the poem does not really diminish the force of the assertions here.[9] In the light of just this passage, Lucretius's tonality toward the gods must be called adaptively responsive and intermittent, even syncretic, whereas Epicurus does not waver in setting the gods calmly into the perspective of his system.

In the passage cited above, the enumeration of the creatures of sky, sea, and earth follows a poetic, but not a philosophical, convention that is exemplified by Alcman (fragment 89) and Sophocles (*Antigone*, second chorus). Sky, sea, and earth are quickly named. Each is given an epithet, thus already condensed into the activity, which is later to be revealed as atomic, that involves them in creative motion: the constellations are gliding in the sky, the sea is bearing ships, the lands of earth are producing fruits. All exhibit the crowding or teeming of the generative force, *concelebras*. Then come the creatures, given a name, "animantum," that jibes only sketchily with Lucretius's later discussions of *anima* and *animus*. Once conceived and come forth ("exortum"), they exercise a faculty that will have a large role in the poem, the faculty of sight ("visitque"). The object of sight is here generalized to the light of the sun ("lumina solis"), which in a few lines will be diffused through the sky and subjected to that feeling of peace, the *pax,* which is Lucretius's version of Epicurus's *ataraxia;* their sky will be *placatum.*

This feeling of pleasure, for Lucretius, always fuses into the poeticized apprehension of the physiological message, whereas for Epicurus, from the accounts we have, pleasure was itself subject to analysis in the subclassification of pleasures and the distinction between pleasure (*hedoné*) and bliss (*eudaimonia*), of which pleasures were constituents. Lucretius never once uses the Latin noun for *ataraxia,* "tranquillitas," as Seneca and others later do. In his work, the adjective "tranquillus" is applied to "pax" to characterize the lives of the gods (2.1093), a peace that a human being may have if correctly freed from the notion that the gods influence human life (6.69, 6.78).[10] Yet at the same time, and paradoxically, Venus endows people with *tranquilla pax* (1.31). Lucretius praises a "tranquil breast" as a possibility for a person in his survey of the physiological correlatives of the emotions (3.393). As an achievement of Epicurus, it is applied not to the conduct of life but to the doctrine, a haven won and secured:

> quique per artem
> fluctibus e tantis vitam tantisque tenebris
> in tam tranquillo et tam clara luce locavit

> who through art
> out of such great floods and such great darknesses
> set life in so tranquil and so clear a light.
>
> (5.10–12)

Life is seen at the opening of the poem as a motion, the way it is here and elsewhere (2.251–56 and passim). Again, in the invocation of the first book, even the motion of the winds and clouds away from the approach of Venus is assimilated to a repeated and varied description of earth, sea, and sky: the sky is the locus of moving winds and diffused light; the earth, cunningly manifold ("daedala"), puts forth sweet flowers; and the waves of the deep ocean laugh. Still again, the birds will move in the sky, carrying the signs ("significant") of her force, just as the constellations ("signa") did in the sky; the wild herds leap over the meadows, which are joyful in their fertility, and they swim the rapid streams. The poem has begun, via the age-old convention of an invocation (here to Venus, not the Muses), not by setting out an argument or an explicit summary, as even the *Iliad* does. Rather it exemplifies its own force, setting up a vantage point from which the sweep of the argument can assimilate to the sweep of the verse.

By the time Lucretius gets to his last book, as he approaches the "shining marks of the final chalk-line" ("supremae praescripta ad candida calcis") (6.92), declaring that his explanations shed enough light to free people from being like children frightened of the dark (6.35–50), he invokes not Venus but rather the traditional Muse of epic poetry, Calliope (6.94). She is characterized as providing for people a quiet that is akin to tranquillity, but for gods a pleasure, the very pleasure that Epicurus states as a goal for humanity: "Calliope, requies hominum divumque voluptas" ("Calliope, respite of men and delight of gods"). By excluding humans here (strangely) from *voluptas*, Lucretius is varying the *hominum divumque voluptas* applied to Venus in the very first line of a poem, which begins first by naming people ("Aeneadum") and then this goddess ("genetrix").

The emphasis of the formal exposition, as the poem very quickly begins, is all but exclusively on the scientific side of Epicurus, whereas in the developing Roman speculation of his contemporaries, it was the ethical side that was considered. On the face of it, indeed, one would expect poetry at this date also to be ethical in emphasis, not scientific. Again, the yield of the poem, its effect as well as its message, is a kind of ethics: to produce peace by contemplating the proper scientific view. This peace is a peculiarly Lucretian one, indistinguishable from the pitch of excitement that the invocation plunges into, through the presentation of the affirmative side of his paradox in simultaneously asserting this goddess and denying the gods. Already the meld of poetry and philosophy has got around the paradox in a contradiction that philosophy by itself could not countenance. Only such a poetic strategy will work, and it has worked here. In fusing poetry and philosophy, Lucretius found a posture profoundly distinct not only from the prose of his master, Epicurus—and all but completely free of the local epic poet Ennius— but also from the earlier masters who couched their philosophy in verse, from the time of Empedocles, whom he does mention, and Parmenides, whom he does not. In a different linkage of poetry and philosophy, Plato skirted the whole problem of philosophy in poetry with all the complexity of his approach to poetry. But Aristotle attempted to address the problem, oversimply, by characterizing Empedocles as having nothing of poetry except meter (*Poetics,* 1447b).

The first word of the *De rerum natura,* "Aeneadum," measures Lucretius's departure from Ennius, who is soon mentioned explicitly (1.114– 26), honored but left aside, for he sang erroneously of the transmigration of souls, even though he was "the first who brought down / from pleasant Helicon a crown with eternal leaves" ("qui primus amoeno / detulit ex Helicone perenni fronde coronam"). It is quite striking, in view of Lucretius's main theme, that a national perspective begins the poem, as though the poet's master were not Epicurus but Ennius. We might well think that the Epicurean view should be presented from an internationalist perspective, and that the beginning with "Aeneadum genetrix" would be a discordant element, or at least a subsidiary one, even though it is soon effectually picked up by the mention of the dedicatee, Memmius, and his possible embroilment in political affairs ("patriai tempore iniquo," 41).

The fiction of the noble lay auditor Memmius undercuts the philosophical schools, setting Lucretius rhetorically into a situation where he must start wholly afresh, whereas in the ideal post-Aristotelian Greece of his master, there was a highly developed variety of schools, and the Garden of Epicurus was one among many professional communities. And actually, if we reconstruct the situation and climate around the philosophical writings of his contemporary Cicero, there were many philosophical professionals and devotees operating in Lucretius's Rome. But Lucretius writes as though they did not exist, going all out in the strategy of underscoring the essentials and ignoring the qualifications of local controversy. Memmius is not only a pupil but, if the usual identification is correct, a powerful political figure. So he is more complex in his posture than the addressees of Epicurus's letters, though both Lucretius and his master—who himself is part of the compound addressee of the *De rerum natura*—are following the ancient convention, found in Egypt with Ptah-Hotep as well as in Greece with such composite poetic personae as "Theognis," of setting up a discourse rhetorically in the form of a communication to a younger learner.

There is a particularly Roman twist to Lucretius's Venus, too, if this invocation is compared to the Homeric "Hymn to Aphrodite"; Venus was interwoven with Roman life in the first century B.C.[11] But we do not again hear of the function celebrated here, and very little directly of Venus, not even in the book devoted to love, book 4. The emphatic presence of Venus at the beginning carries a force that will find its explanation later on in the main exposition of the poem. The invocation sets a tone of urgency for that explanation, in which the *signa* in the sky and the fact that they are gliding and the sky itself will be analyzed as subject to a single structure, a structure only mysteriously connected to Venus—but certainly not for Epicurus, whose gods were causally unconnected to terrestrial life, and who downplayed the force of love being emphasized here.

2

I T is at the point where he is expounding the necessary mixture of various seeds, the "beginnings" and "first bodies" ("corpora prima") on earth as the atomic mixture produces fire, streams, leaves, and mountain-ranging animals (2.588–98), that Lucretius shifts to a figure comparable in many ways to his Venus, the Great Mother. The shift of subject does not obviously entail a tonal shift, since he has stayed at the pitch of metrical excitation for his unfolding of scientific data. Lucretius's *Magna Mater* has none of the perversity, the threatening alienation and desperate rapt absorption, found in the galliambic meter of Catullus's poem 63. Instead, she is initially comprehensive, cutting across domains that philosophers, including Epicurus, keep separate: "quare magna deum mater materque ferarum / et nostri genetrix haec dicta est corporis una" ("Wherefore she alone is called the great mother of the gods / and mother of the beasts and generator of our bodies"). The "wherefore" leaps a large logical space, insufficiently buttressed by the "mountain-ranging kind of beasts" ("montivago generi . . . ferarum") of the previous line. It is Lucretius's declaration of this principle, retaining the allegorical proposition of her linkage to earth (here designated not as "terra" but as "tellus") that introduces the panorama of the chariot of Cybele and her lion procession. "Old Greek poets" ("veteres graium poetae," 2.600) (and of course Catullus, too) have sung this procession, which, Lucretius asserts, signifies that earth "hangs in the space of air" ("aeris in spatio ... pendere") rather than being based on other earth. A symbolic reading of the ritual attributes in the Mother's procession follows: the crown on her head indicates cities defended on the heights. She has the castrated priests (Galli) assigned to her to show that those who have offended her are unworthy to have offspring—a theologizing depersonalization of Catullus's picture of exacerbated sterilization.

Many of the Mother's functions are those of the Venus that Lucretius invoked, and the rationale he gives for her rites would seem further to endorse her. But he rejects all this as unreason, "though it is well and illustriously recounted in parts" ("quae bene et eximie quamvis disposta ferantur") (2.644). The gods really, he says—in one of his clearest endorsements of the Epicurean view of their separation—live separate from humans "in highest peace" ("summa cum pace") (2.647). Still, Lucretius here permits people to call the sea Neptune, grain Ceres, wine Bacchus, and the earth mother of the gods—so long as thereby they do not succumb to *religio.*

This *religio,* a "binding" into religious terror, incapacitates people from receiving the pacifying and liberating lesson of the universal Epicurean atomic flux; "human life is oppressed under heavy religion" ("humana vita oppressa gravi sub religione") (1.62–63). *Religio* is repeatedly excoriated as a blind antithesis, similar only in the strength of its emotional tonality, to the informed clarity he enjoins. Lucretius brings the heavens to earth, as Cicero said of Socrates,[12] by applying Ionian/Epicurean cosmology to human emotions more extensively than had Epicurus—who is a sort of savior, and even a god (5.19), in Lucretius's presentation:

> E tenebris tantis tam clarum extollere lumen
> qui primus potuisti inlustrans commoda vitae,
> te sequor, o Graiae gentis decus, inque tuis nunc
> ficta pedum pono pressis vestigia signis,
> non ita certandi cupidus quam propter amorem
> quod te imitari aveo; quid enim contendat hirundo
> cycnis, aut quidnam tremulis facere artubus haedi
> consimile in sursu possint et fortis equi vis?
> tu pater es, rerum inventor, tu patria nobis
> suppeditas praecepta, tuisque ex, inclute, chartis,
> floriferis ut apes in saltibus omnia libant,

omnia nos itidem depascimur aurea dicta,
aurea, perpetua semper dignissima vita.

You who from so much darkness raised up so clear a light,
who first were able to illumine the comforts of life,
you do I follow, glory of the Greek race, and now in your
marked footsteps do I put the fixed tracks of my feet,
not so much wanting to compete as through love
that I crave to imitate you; how could a swallow
contend with swans, and can kids with trembling joints
race in a way like the strength of a powerful horse?
You are the father, finder of things, you provide
fatherly precepts for us, glorious one, and from your pages,
like bees in flower-bearing meadows, we sip all things.
On all your golden words we feed the same way,
golden words, always most worthy of perpetual life.

(3.1–13)

The suspension here of the second-person pronoun till the third line
includes it hypotactically in the balanced hyperbole of the contrast of
light and darkness. The visual metaphor develops through a visual hint
about footsteps and the contrast of swallow with swan and trembling kid
with powerful horse. All these details frame, illustrate, and carry the dec-
laration of discipleship and eschewed competition. The method contin-
ues in the comparison of disciples to bees and, in the established context,
the repeated comparison of Epicurus's words to gold. So the (internal)
terrors of spirit and the (external) "walls of the universe" ("moenia
mundi") (16) are mastered in a way that makes the human situation, with
the help of the godlike Epicurus, close in temper to the situation of the
gods, which the passage immediately describes.[13]

These walls of the universe are real, though infinitely receding. They
are entirely caught in the movement of the atoms, and in the poetic
afflatus here they yield easily to the metaphorical tinge in the naming
of winds, clouds, showers, hoarfrost, white snow, ether, and broadly
diffused laughing light (17–30).

In the tonality sustained by Lucretius's verse, the "peace of spirit" that
the gods enjoy and that the poem envisions will find a metaphorical
anchorage in the invisibility of the temples of Acheron, along with the
visibility of all things, unimpeded by earth and by the void underfoot.
The poet's consequent reaction, transcending Epicurean pleasure in its

196

complex intensity and poetic excitation, links the combination of per-
ception and reaction to both shrinking (the root meaning of "horror")
and pleasure ("voluptas . . . atque horror") (3.28–29), as P. H. Schrijvers
points out.[14] This complex feeling is a reaction to an entire state of
affairs, "his rebus," when nature lies manifest, covered by the "force" of
Epicurus "from all angles" ("ex omni parte") (3.28–30).

The gods are caught in the tension of the negative, but the tension
persists, so that, in the notable introductory case of Venus, Lucretius can
affirm them where Epicurus could not have consistently done so.
Correspondingly, the impetus toward proof sparks the constructive-
affirmative in this poem so forcibly that it can carry its own energy
toward a concreteness that is quite un-Epicurean, and also quite distinct
from the elegant economy of philosophical presentation in general.[15]

3

BOTH Plato and Aristotle connected their ethical postures to elaborate
political imperatives and analyses, buttressing them with physical and
psychological analyses that are intermittent but not incidental. Less than
half a century later, Epicurus's situation distances him from such social
considerations, and the ethical part of his writing resembles that of the
Stoics in detaching all the ethical speculation from any constructive
assessment of social desiderata. The Roman citizen was not the citizen
of a free Athens. Lucretius, too, belonged to a society that was large,
complex, and so subjected to large forces that he followed both
Epicurus and the Stoics in withdrawing his attention from such prob-
lems. His social descriptions—of the plague, for example—are merely
descriptive. They imitate Thucydides but have no connection to an
overall process of enchained decisions in the society, which he eschews,
as Ennius did not. He reorients Ennius and internationalizes him, but
also effectively privatizes him.

In keeping with the focus of his absorptions, Lucretius does not deal
directly with Plato, Aristotle, or the Stoics, even when their discussions
bear on the questions he addresses. Rather, he confines himself to
Epicurus—and beyond Epicurus, to those who are on a par as prede-
cessors of Plato and Aristotle, the pre-Socratics: Heraclitus (1.635–705),
Anaxagoras (1.830–951), Democritus (3.369–79), and Empedocles
(1.716–34). The *carmina* of Empedocles make him "scarcely human"

("vix humanus") as a hero (1.730), but his doctrines require a qualification that paradoxically removes him from full parity with the mastery of Epicurus. Yet Epicurus wrote no poetry. So for the combination of poetry and correct philosophy, Lucretius can stand alone. He does see himself as an originator: "avia Pieridum perago, loca nullius ante / trita solo" ("I cross out-of-the-way places of the Pierides, / trod by the sole of none before") (1.926). And while a follower in philosophy, he is an originator in poetry: it is the untrod places of the *Pierides* that he crosses.

In the invocation of book 5 (1–50), Lucretius characterizes Epicurus as the strict Epicurean would not characterize other philosophers: he is like a god in outdoing the labors of Hercules; and in surpassing Ceres, who supposedly brought grain to man; and Bacchus, who brought wine: "quo magis his merito nobis deus esse videtur" ("This one the more deservedly seems to us to be a god") (5.19). Epicurus was able "to lay out the whole nature of things in words" ("atque omnem rerum naturam pandere dictis") (5.54)—while Lucretius's task is effectually to raise this pitch and found it in a song ("carmen"), a song that requires a "powerful breast," one that will be "worthy of the majesty of things and these discoveries" ("quae potis est dignum pollenti pectore carmen / condere pro rerum maestate hisque repertis?") (5.1). The complicated near-litotes of this address disclaims this possibility, even as the poet is in the process of executing it, evoking the majesty as he summarizes the theory.

Epicurus's explanations tend to be undetailed, along the lines of the principle he states in the *Letter to Herodotus,* 35: τῆς γὰρ ἀθρόας ἐπιβολῆς πυκνὸν δεόμεθα, τῆς δὲ κατὰ μέρος οὐχ ὁμοίως ("We intensely need a collected apprehension, but not one in detail to the same degree"). Lucretius not only versifies Epicurus but transposes this principle and precisely alters the master's intentional focus by offering expansive concrete detail. Epicurus's explanation of earthquakes, for example, is quite short and undetailed (*Letter to Pythocles,* 105). Lucretius's own account, characteristically, is quite expansive and detailed (6.535–611), as though the direction of verbal attention must go into such detail so that account may deflect fear by evoking it.

4

CHIEF among Lucretius's details are visual ones. He turns to the visual again and again for his major effects, even when there is nothing in his assertion of the moment to recommend his doing so. Epicurus himself is presented as having empowered our eyes: "Primum Graius homo mortalis tollere contra / est oculos ausus primusque obsistere contra" ("First a Greek man dared raise his eyes against it / and was the first to take a stand against it [religion]" (1.66–67).

Lucretius comes across almost as a proto-Husserl in his intentional structurings of visual impressions. So, for example, in his demonstration that nothing comes from, or disappears to, nothing (1.150–215), he dwells far more extensively on the visual than his propositions oblige him to do, beginning with a statement that "it is therefore necessary not for the rays of the sun / nor day's shining arrows to dispel this terror and darkness / but the external look of nature and reason" ("Hunc igitur terrorem animi tenebrasque necessest / non radii solis neque lucida tela diei / discutiant, sed naturae species ratioque") (146–48). Nevertheless, in what follows, much attention is given to the visual beauties sealed into the facts, of the "external look of nature." At the climax of this discussion, he presents in a short space (1.250–65) the passing showers as the bright air sends them headlong into the lap of earth; the shining fruits rising and branches greening on weighed-down trees; glad cities flowering with children; leaf-bearing woods resounding with birds on all sides; herds, tired by their fat, lying down in the glad pastures; shining milk flowing from their distended udders; the young with weak joints sporting through the tender grass, their "new minds struck toward pure milk" ("lacte mero mentis perculsa novellas") (1.261).

A prolonged presentation, fleshed out intermittently with comparable visualization, is given to the complex discussion of *simulacra*, "idols" or "images," as they strike the eyes, even though he says he "will give it out in verses sweet rather than numerous" ("suavidicis potius quam multis versibus edam") (4.180). This presentation runs for more than three hundred lines (4.120–467) and continues in a somewhat briefer discussion of other senses. It includes a detailed explanation of how mirrors work (4.269–327), handling five separate cruces about them in the process.

Lucretius repeatedly portrays in visual terms the doctrines he has evolved abstractly:

> E tenebris autem quae sunt in luce tuemur
> propterea quia, cum propior caliginis aer
> ater init oculos prior et possedit apertos,

insequitur candens confestim lucidus aer
qui quasi purgat eos ac nigras discutit umbras
aeris illius. nam multis partibus hic est
mobilior multisque minutior et mage pollens.
qui simul atque vias oculorum luce replevit
atque patefecit quas ante obsederat aer
(ater), continuo rerum simulacra sequuntur
quae sita sunt in luce, lacessuntque ut videamus.

    Moreover, out of darknesses we see things in light
because when the nearer black air of the murk
first enters and possesses our open eyes,
there instantly follows a bright shining air
that, as it were, purges them and dispels the black shadows
of that air, for the last is in many ways
more mobile, many times more minute, and more powerful.
As soon as it has filled the channels of the eyes with light
and opened up what dark air besieged before,
at once the simulacra of things follow
that lie in light, and excite our eyes so we see.

(4.337–47)

While this passage goes on to give further specifics of the atomic actions that result in the perception of light, in this run Lucretius merely touches on the underlying structure, expanding his attention toward the qualities of dark and of light, at first by using three different words for each in the first five lines ("ater," "caliginis," "nigras"; "candens," "luce," "lucidus"). This leaves out "tenebris," a frequent word of Lucretius's. The invocation of the third book, which begins "e tenebris tantis," has been fleshed out through Lucretius's spirited attention to the visual.

    Eleanor Winsor Leach notes that in still other passages, "The consistency of Lucretius's interest in the perceiver's reception of the visual image appears in . . . his well-known comparison of the invisible seething of atomic motion with the spectacle of a grazing flock on a green hillside (2.317–322) [and also] in the order human agriculture imposed upon the visible landscape (5.1370–1378)."[16] The context of this passage, as often, is ostensibly to testify to the unreliability of sight. While affirming this, as against the reliability of the atomic combinations, Lucretius carries through an identification and an affirmation of the visual richness that a realization of this very unreliability can be taken to anchor more deeply: false inferences sheared away by the theory, viewers are free to take the sights they see, in effect pacified because they are now presented for the qualities they do have:

> nam saepe in colli tondentes pabula laeta
> lanigerae reptant pecudes quo quamque vocantes
> invitant herbae gemmantes rore recenti,
> et satiati agni ludunt blandeque coruscant;
> omnia quae nobis confusa videntur
> et velut in viridi candor consistere colli.

> for often on a hill shearing the glad fodder
> the wool-bearing flocks creep wherever, calling them,
> the grasses invite them, bejewelled with fresh dew,
> and the satiated lambs play and butt pleasantly—
> all things that from a distance we see confusedly,
> and as though a shining whiteness stood on the green hill.

(2.317–22)

Here one uncertainty measures another: as the movement of atoms to any visual sight, so the illusory whiteness to the actual sheep, who themselves seem illusorily compact if measured by the flow of atoms composing them. But the illustration falls away, and the green of the hill and the white of the sheep remain, just as the hill was there for both visions of the sheep. This green, if looked at theoretically, must be subject to Lucretius's atomic theory of color, itself given a long treatment (2.742–841). But the sights, the close sheep and the distant whiteness, remain against the steady background of the green, and the poetic apperception carries its momentary force as well as its position in an argument that by itself does not call for so much presentation. The excess leaves a residue of upwelling accommodation to the explained world here, and generally through the poem. For as Leach says, "Throughout the first book of the poem the number of scientific principles introduced is actually very small in proportion to the space devoted to their clarification through visual evidence" (127).

Turning the tables somewhat on Epicurus, for whom the evidence of the senses is direct and primary,[17] Lucretius makes the very action of invisibles connect, by contradiction, to the visible world, and thus have the action of invisibles prove the visible. So the very fact that we cannot see how the abundance of crops arises from rain (1.250–64) proves that there is something of which the visible is evidence, and this can be dwelt on in the poem for the delight of assuredness spiced by the wonderment of what is immediately inexplicable. And thus we see the effects of the invisible wind (1.271–97), and our senses perceive heat and cold without being able to see them (1.298–304). And although we do not see the effect, we can verify when garments become wet or dry (1.305–10). In the long range, the very disappearance of matter testifies to the invisible persistence of matter, testifies that nothing disappears—and, later, that there is a void in which motion will take place: "in parvas igitur partis dispergitur umor / quas oculi nulla possunt ratione videre" ("Therefore the liquid is dispersed into small particles / which the eyes cannot see by any rationale") (1.309–10). The evidences of this dispersal lie in the world around us:

> quin etiam multis solis redeuntibus annis
> anulus in digito subter tenuatur habendo,
> stilicidi casus lapidem cavat, uncus aratri
> ferreus occulte decrescit vomer in arvis,
> strataque iam vulgi pedibus detrita viarum
> saxea conspicimus; tum portas propter aena
> signa manus dextras ostendunt attenuari
> saepe salutantum tactu praeterque meantum.

> Nay, even in the sun's many returning years
> a ring on the finger beneath grows thin for the wearer,
> the fall of dripping hollows a stone, the curved iron
> ploughshare secretly grows less in the fields,
> and the paved streets of the ways we see worn down,
> stone that they are, by the crowd's feet; and at the gates bronze
> statues show their right hands thinning away
> at the frequent touch of those who salute as they pass by.
>
> (1.311–18)

Here, in the long range of time, the wearing down of ring, ploughshare, stone street, and bronze statue takes on the wonderment of keen and repeated observation through reference to the theory without which they would be simply mysterious. The same is true, in the quick of immediate perception, for the movement of fish through water (1.373–75), which is adduced and described as a proof of the void ("inane"); and for the figures of fire (2.385–86). The easier passage of lightning

THE NATURE OF LUCRETIUS

than of pine-torch fire, and of both than of various liquids, shows
through vivid visibilia the variety of shapes taken by the invisible atoms.
Lucretius asserts that light must accompany color and illustrates the
rainbowing effects on a dove's neck and a peacock's tail. As he says,

> Dicere porro oculos nullam rem cernere posse,
> sed per eos animum ut foribus spectare reclusis,
> difficilest, contra cum sensus ducit eorum;
> sensus enim trahit atque acies detrudit ad ipsas.

> To say, further, that the eyes can discern things
> but that the mind looks through them as with open doors
> is difficult, when their sense leads the other way,
> for the sense drags us and thrusts to the very pupils.
>
> (3.359–63)

This principle of the thrust of sight forward is not easily deducible just
from the atomic system; it is presented rather as a psychological postulate.

In the invocation of book 2, the pause of Epicurean detachment is
presented in terms of a long-range view, which shades from the actual
to the metaphorical:

> suave, mari magno turbantibus aequora ventis,
> e terra magnum alterius spectare laborem;
> non quia vexari quemquamst iucunda voluptas,
> sed quibus ipse malis careas quia cernere suave est.
> suave etiam belli certamina magna tueri
> per campos instructa tua sine parte pericli.
> sed nil dulcius est, bene quam munita tenere
> edita doctrina sapientum templa serena,
> despicere unde queas alios passimque videre
> errare atque viam palantis quaerere vitae.

> It is sweet, when on a great sea winds are stirring up waves,
> to look on from land at the great toil of another,
> not that there is joyful pleasure in anyone's being vexed,
> but because it is sweet to discern from what ills you are free.
> It is sweet to behold the great contentions of war
> drawn up through the plains where you have no part in the danger.
> But nothing is pleasanter than to hold on in the high-built

serene temples of the wise, furnished with doctrine,
to look down where you can see others wandering
this way and that, seeking a way of life.

(2.1–10)

As he shifts from the panoramic literal sights to the metaphorical serene temples of the wise, the view "suave, mari" (itself atomizable according to principles elsewhere) is surpassed by the sweetness of doctrine. The term "voluptas" is picked up from the very first line of the poem, and many other changes are rung on this reverberant but undefined Epicurean term. And in the ongoing recursions of the poem, a later passage (3.830) picks up the sea and battle images here.

Again and again, Lucretius leads easily into images, which are entertained while sleeping as well as in waking: the visual changes in burning wood, as in grasshoppers, calves, and snakes (4.25–65); the color shadows of saffron, russet, and dark purple thrown by theater awnings, along with the variegated sights of the spectacle (4.79–90). In so much shifting, a mirror's changes can be compared to the changes of a storm (4.161–75). Shadows (4.420 ff.), the motion of waters (4.448), and cloud shapes (6.170 ff.) are among the many visual phenomena he calls up to analyze—and such perceptual puzzles as why lightning leaves mud intact and evaporates wine (6.234–35). He explains thirteen optical illusions (4.379–468): a moving ship seems to stand still under the stars; hills seem from the sea to be one island; a spinning boy thinks the world spins; the sun appears to rise just behind near hills; in a small pool, the whole sky and clouds appear to be underground; a horse standing in a stream seems to move upstream; a colonnade seems to narrow to a cone; sailors see the sun rising from the sea; moving clouds at night make the stars seem to move, too; we see double when we press the eyeball; in dreams at night, we seem to see the daytime world. All this superabundance of visual effects cannot be taken just to serve the proofs about atomic motion, even if the Epicurean principle of multiple explanation is adduced. It furthers the immersion of the reader in the vividness, orderliness, and at the same time the variousness, indeed the *voluptas,* of the world taken in by his eyes.

5

WITH the substructure of the world vividly presented through the image-buttressed arguments of the poet, the initiate is the more firmly ready, Lucretius effectually feels, to confront large-scale metaphysical perceptions and ethical imperatives. The relation between a universal physical system and imperatives of ethical behavior belongs to the long tradition of earlier Greek philosophy. For Pythagoras, this system was mathematical, and it led obscurely to the basis for a quasi-religious cult. For Plato, there was also an obscure connection between mathematics and virtue,[18] and Epicurus can be said to follow him, though his atomic system and his psychological ethics, so far as we can tell, have few bridging rationales between them, especially because Epicurus departs from both Plato and Aristotle in his view of being, as well as in his avoidance of politics.[19] This concern is effectually somewhat redirected by Lucretius, who seems to honor Memmius for his political involvement, though, like Epicurus, he nowhere addresses the political questions that preoccupied Plato and Aristotle, not even going so far as to abjure them. For him there is no Garden of Epicurus, no group of friends among whom to exercise the virtues; the address to Memmius begins to create a substitute for that. The impetus to his complicated *ataraxia*—which is usually given the less technical, simple term *pax*—is a realization of the universality of the atomic system, as it was for Epicurus, including the important and quasi-religious corollary of personal death. This act of mind is Socratic in its induction of virtue through knowledge. Lucretius is confident that it will lead the convinced reader into the ethical disposition of which the poem itself is a fair expression. In that sense, too, the poem is honey on the cup and a crucial instrument of induction, rather than the post-Platonic hindrance that Epicurus considered poetry to be.

In the writings we have, it is clear that Epicurus gave considerable attention to the pleasures, to discriminating among them and providing for the conditions in which they could come about. Lucretius's departure from Epicurus's evolution of these distinctions is the more remarkable in that he reproduces Epicurus's physical system in all its intricate complexity.[20] Epicurus says, and it is a principle that can be taken to undergird Lucretius's presentations, that the function of the study of nature (φυσιολογία) is not to achieve a mastery of the physical universe

and not to attain an Aristotelian satisfaction of intellectual curiosity but
rather to allay the distressing apprehensions over meteorological phe-
nomena, over death, and over ignorance of "the definitions of sorrows
and desires" (τοὺς ὅρους τῶν ἀλγηδόνων καὶ τῶν ἐπιθυμιῶν). Other-
wise, Epicurus says, "We would have no need of the study of nature"
(οὐκ ἂν προσεδεόμεθα φυσιολογίας).²¹ Lucretius presents nothing of
this line of qualification. Instead, he wraps pleasure up in the assertions
of the poem—and, we may say, in the spirited communication of the
poem itself, which, however, is so intense that it is hard to reconcile with
a goal of *ataraxia*. Epicurus also links justice and pleasure in an aphorism
that could only have been written after Plato and Aristotle had worked
over this ground: Ὁ δίκαιος ἀταρακτότατος, ὁ δ' ἄδικος πλείστης
ταραχῆς γέμων ("The just man is least disturbed, the unjust teems with
the most disturbance").²² Epicurus distinguishes pleasure at rest from
pleasure in movement for both body and soul.²³ But again, Lucretius
gives us none of this, and justice, a main category for Epicurus as for his
great predecessors, does not come within his ken. Lucretius does not use
the noun "iustitia" at all. He uses the adjective once for a "just" propor-
tion in the thickness of semen (4.1141) and once for a "just case" brought
by an allegorized Nature against humanity for expecting immortality
(3.950). A continuation of this passage produces two of his eight uses of
"ius" ("right") (3.963). Of the other six, three refer to physical laws, one
to social behavior (3.61), and two to the history of law (5.1144, 1147).

Consequently, Epicurus's ethical writings enter the *De rerum natura*
only obliquely. Then the complications of behavior, and also the cues
for behavior, appear in Lucretius's recommendations for attitudes toward
love, death, and religion, but they do not receive a systematization of the
term "voluptas." And the limits in the "scantness of the native tongue"
("patrii sermonis egestas") (3.260) of which Lucretius complains will
not account for these divergences and omissions.²⁴

6

IN the propulsive excitation of Lucretius's dense presentations, his main
subject, the universality of moving atomic structures, is caught up in the
hypnotic overall effect, and doctrine assimilates to evocation and visual-
ization. Lucretius is not a philosophical poet in the same sense that Blake
is. He does not *think* poetically and form systemlike poems out of deep,

verbally based intuitions, as it can be asserted that Parmenides did before him, or even Heraclitus. His own naming of Empedocles as a predecessor is significant in that Empedocles comes closest of the ancient poets (leaving aside the possible analogy of some lost Orphic texts) to the fusion that Lucretius effectuates, where a doctrine transmitted intact, with the sorts of minor qualifications any later member of a school would add, is couched in such a way that it produces a mood as well as an intellectual clarification. Lucretius's own primitive simile for his poetry as "honey on the bitter cup" (4.10–25) approximately describes this fusion, if we can imagine honey and cup and bitter contents all become one. In fact, this disjunct presentation forces him to wrench his own sense of his effect, because, on his own showing, the doctrine is not in itself bitter—just difficult to communicate to a humankind fearing mortality.

In his exposition of the four constituents of the soul—air, wind, heat, and a fourth nameless element (3.258–322)—the stark logical discussion swells effortlessly into a characterization of the effects of these constituents on individual creatures, a portrayal that harmonizes with his keen attention to visual detail: lions are hot and irascible, deer cold and timorous. The nature of oxen, more airy, "is sited between both, deer and savage lions" ("interutrasque sitast, cervos saevosque leones") (3.306). The expression that immediately follows expands rhetorically from the reference to oxen, to include the whole presentation: " So is the race of men" ("sic hominum genus est"). He goes on to specify that humans are subject to a variety of temperaments, mixed (as the oxen are, of more than one element), but entering into diversities of combination—as the oxen are not. So the "sic" echoes and resumes logically the analogy to oxen first but then also the whole presentation of the four elements. It illustrates through its rhetoric the capacity for uncoiling outward that the poem continually activates.

The verse acts as though it must sustain its effort to keep one's attention from lapsing into less desirable states. So he urges, after much exposition, at the beginning of book 6, where his auditor is imagined as being threatened with succumbing to *religio* and thus not coming into a tranquil peace like that of the gods (6.48–83). As he says at the end of that run:

> quam quidem ut a nobis ratio verissima longe
> reiciat, quamquam sunt a me multa profecta,

multa tamen restant et sunt ornanda politis
versibus.

And so that truest reason may drive this far
away from us, though many things have already come forth from me
many still remain and are to be adorned in polished
verses.

(6.80–82)

The Epicureans recommended a technique of leading the soul, a *psychagogia* that involved a rhetorical posture toward the initiate in the community of the garden, and Schrijvers plausibly connects Lucretius to this tradition.[25] Lucretius, lacking such a community, has no such rhetorical steps to depend on, and so he must go the practice one further by having recourse to poetry, which Epicurus abjured. And yet the poetry cannot be reduced just to honey on the cup to get the doctrine across; we must give it and its impetus its full value and see Lucretius as the salesman who is his own best customer. He is so enraptured of the doctrine that enlisting his rapture to expound it creates a communicative Möbius strip in which the doctrine, especially for the modern reader, subserves the poetry, even as the poem is asserting that it is there to subserve the doctrine.

He thus makes a point and allows it to expand to a perception, in a sort of binary shuttle, without yielding to extreme points of tension. It is the pull of the doctrine that integrates the range of poeticized feeling. The poet can return to the doctrine, rise further from an already elevated feeling, and return to doctrine again. He asserts that the poetry is honey on the cup, but modern readers, who could not be convinced by much of the doctrine, remain enraptured by the poetry, which for them is the cup itself. Here, for example, his point is made in the first two lines, but it is amplified in the third (and in the lines that follow, too):

quoniam genus ipsa creavit
humanum atque animal prope certo tempore fudit
omne quod in magnis bacchatur montibu' passim.

since [mother earth] has created the race
of man and has poured out at almost a fixed time
all the animals which riot over the mountains.

He here locates animals, as is traditionally done, on the mountains. And he envisions them as participating in the energetic exuberance that the poem evokes by describing them with a word, "bacchatur," that is not at all called for by his logical argument. These energetic touches pervade the poem and even, it may be said, interfuse into it the sweetness of looking at a great sea in turbulence from a safe vantage point ("suave, mari magno"). The energy continues as he rises here from animals to all things: "omnia migrant, / omnia commutat natura et vertere cogit" ("All things migrate, / nature transmutes all and compels them to change") (5.830). In 5.1000–1005, he is still evoking the savagery of the sea. In 5.1339, elephants ("boves lucae") are envisioned as fighting back.

At times the tonal range takes on an explicit binary opposition, as, first of all, in the repeated distinction between light and dark. Then there is the contrast between honey and the bitter cup of message or the early reference to Mars and Venus (1.31) or the use of Paris and Helen (1.470 ff.) to instantiate and introduce the deduction of both love and war from atoms. Terror itself, or horror, can even be included in the tonal range because it is the function of Epicurean doctrine to dispel it. At the triumph of reason, the "terrors of spirit disperse" ("diffugiunt animi terrores") (3.18). As he describes aging at the end of book 2, the description functions not only for itself but as the last of his preparations for the leap to a direct and prolonged presentation of death in book 3, which begins as though spirited on by the clarity of its evocation of the Greeks. The book about death is followed by a discourse on its traditional binary opposite, love, in book 4. In book 5, which expands to include the mortality of the physical universe, he changes his tone as he passes to the beginning of that universe and then finally to the beginnings of vegetable, animal, and human life. Book 6, too, stays in cosmic perspective at first with an account of large-scale celestial and geological phenomena, returning to humanity with an account of medical phenomena. As though picking up from the other end of his long account of primitivism in book 5 (925–1457), he suddenly takes up the civilization of Athens, putting a legendary peak of human history in the light of a graphic "worst-case" description of the plague at Athens, without any of Thucydides' historical inferences, even though he is following Thucydides. This conclusion is the most extreme of his "worst-case" presentations, as though the force of the poem up to this point will stand behind the readers and allow them to stomach a contemplation of such devastations.[26]

If we take our cue from Cicero's descriptions (*Tusculan Disputations,* book 3), the subject, for Stoics and Epicureans, is *perturbationes,* which for Lucretius are to be removed by a contemplation of the universal atomic system. He does not address directly "the notion [of] the imminence of a great evil . . . such that sorrow is called for."[27] And his complicated evocations of death and anxiety, which go beyond Epicurus,[28] are reoriented, subverted, and pacified by the strength of his evocations, though these are so brief as to seem grace notes of a countervailing peace. The process, indeed, comes to seem a distant foreshadowing of Heidegger's organization around a consciousness of death that explicates a deep "thrownness" (*Geworfenheit*) toward death. Some such analogy, however anachronistic, is necessary to account for the persisting integral effect of a poem that for the modern reader must begin by being analyzed as composed of discordant elements, a largely discarded scientific theory brought forward to palliate a perennial complex "care" (Heidegger's *Sorge*) over human existence.

It is, of course, the poetry that carries the onus of this "rational" redirection. Epicurus gives mere *attention* to the passions, while Lucretius recreates them, with a "worst-case" emphasis on the most threatening. In his poetic effect, evasions fuse into confrontations. The visual serves as a sort of askesis and accommodation. So Lucretius sees his unique poetic function in the invocation in book 4. Beginning by declaring that he treads in realms of poetry trod by none before, and concluding with the apology about honey on the bitter cup, he declares:

> primum quod magnis doceo de rebus et artis
> religionum animum nodis exsolvere pergo,
> deinde quod obscura de re tam lucida pango
> carmina, musaeo contingens cuncta lepore.

> First because I teach of great things and drive on
> to loose the mind from the tight bonds of religion,
> next because I spread forth about an obscure thing
> such lucid songs, touching all with the muses' delight.

> (4.6–9)

"Lepor," a favorite word of Lucretius's (he uses it eleven times) can be rendered "gentleness," "loveliness," and "charm" as well as "delight." "Lepor" stands at the soft end of his tonal range, but that does not prevent him from here combining it with "pergo" ("drive"), which moves

to the harder end, the two thus working together, with "pango" some-
where at the center, taking the terminal words of these three lines. "Life
is given to none for possession, to all for use," Lucretius says ("vitaque
mancipio nulli datur, omnibus usu") (3.971). He goes on to show that
figures such as Tantalus, Tityos, and Sisyphus are all projections in life
itself, evasions of peace. As though in anticipation of the later allegori-
cal readings of myth persisting through the Renaissance and beyond, up
to the successors of Jung,[29] Lucretius reads the figures of myth as finding
their actuality in allegorizing what happens in human life, not in an
afterlife or among the gods. They are projections; "they are all there in
our life" ("in vita sunt omnia nobis") (3.979). As David Konstan says,
"Irrational desire (*cupido*), in the form of avarice and ambition, is nour-
ished by the fear of death. The question naturally arises, how is the fear
of death translated into desire? This question takes us to the heart of the
problem . . . desire undermines the security of the soul . . . the result of
ignorance."[30] So Tantalus stands for the fear of death, Tityos for the tor-
ments of love, Sisyphus for the machinations of political ambition. The
Danaids, with their sieve-water vessels, figure the pursuit of pleasure,
while Cerberus, the Furies, and Tartarus reify fears of punishment in the
afterlife that may really come in this one (3. 978–1023). This principle,
once enunciated, could be extended to other figures in the poem.

As presented, the whole effect of the scientific system is not to manip-
ulate the universe or even just to answer the "Ionian" questions about
physics but to produce *ataraxia*. It is not manipulative; it is a unified field
aimed toward the consolatory. Epicurus does speak of a felicity or bliss,
of "bliss in the knowledge of heavenly phenomena" (τὸ μακάριον ἐν τῆι
περὶ μετεώρων γνώσει).[31] But for Lucretius, that serves only as a begin-
ning. And for Epicurus *ataraxia* is "to be delivered from all these [fears]
and to have a continuous memory of universals and of what is most
important" (ἡ δὲ ἀταραξία τὸ τούτων πάντων ἀπολελύσθαι καὶ συνεχῆ
μνήμην ἔχειν τῶν ὅλων καὶ κυριωτάτων) (D.L., 10.82). As Lucretius
presses further:

> Et quoniam docui, cunctarum exordia rerum
> qualia sint et quam variis distantia formis
> sponte sua volitent aeterno percita motu
> quove modo possint res ex his quaeque creari,
> hasce secundum res animi natura videtur
> atque animae claranda meis iam versibus esse

et metus ille foras praeceps Acheruntis agendus,
funditus humanam qui vitam turbat ab imo
omnia suffundens mortis nigrore neque ullam
esse voluptatem liquidam puramque relinquit.

And since I have taught of what sort the beginnings
of all things are and how, diverse in various forms,
they fly off at their own will, driven by eternal motion,
and in what way from them every thing can be created,
after this, it seems, the nature of the mind
and the soul is to be clarified in my verses,
and that fear of Acheron is to be driven headlong away
which disturbs human life most deeply from the ground up,
suffusing all things with death's blackness, and leaves
not any joy behind flowing and pure.

(3.31–40)

"Liquidus" means pure or limpid as well as flowing. In that first sense, "liquidam" doubles "puram"; in the second sense, it extends it. The senses, and the doubling of senses, flow together, miming in the poetry the very liquidity and purity of the peace threatened by the fear of death. Poetry, backing doctrine, alleviates the fear of death, making the message of atom-bound transience palatable.

Lucretius has carried through an imaginative expression of a cosmic comprehensiveness that makes still more apt for him the praise he bestows on Epicurus:

ergo vivida vis animi pervicit, et extra
processit longe flammantia moenia mundi.

Therefore his mind's vivid force won through and passed far
beyond the flaming walls of the universe.

(1.72–73)

9

The Multiplicities and
Comprehensions of Pindar

1

As GREGORY NAGY has shown,[1] Pindar's poetry—like Greek poetry generally—follows the conventions of Indo-European verse in its rhythms, its mythic subject matter, and its conception of the role of the poet. Yet a comparison with the hymns of the Rig-Veda will throw into relief the singularity of Pindar, as indeed will a comparison with such religious poems as the Psalms or the Hebrew Prophets. Pindar, even more than the Prophets, addresses himself in his *epinikia,* or victory odes, to a particular occasion, the victory of a single winner in one of the established games. And when he brings a myth to bear upon it, he does so with so many qualifications and rhetorical turns of posture that he would be seen to be manipulating a criticism of his own procedure even if he did not also do that as part of the poem. These poems are elevated to a reflective and recursive abstractness not found even in the late, tenth book of the Rig-Veda. The poems thereby become transoccasional for their very occasionality and speculative within their severe adherence to convention.

Pindar's force derives from his constantly adaptive deployment of the many obligatory constituents of his *epinikia* according to what has been called the "program" of such a poem.[2] In Pindar's hands, a poem displays its integrations at the same time that it displays its tensions, linking the victor of the particular occasion to a founding hero and also to the gods while symmetrically placing the poet himself, as a sign of reflexive control, into a comparable connection to the rethought and highlighted religious pieties and ideologies. Pindar is conscious of a long tradition behind him, going back before Homer: "There was indeed a victory song / long ago, and even before the strife of Adrastus and that of Cadmus" (*Nemean* 8.50). That the mention of the celebrant himself has become a stipulated part of the "program" is suggested by Bacchylides' recourse to similar references to his own poeticization, a gesture not found in the poems of Sappho or Alcaeus, Archilochus or Solon, although all of them abound in other types of self-references. But whether or not mentioning one's own poetic act is such a convention in a sense does not matter, because the role that Pindar has mounted stands out in any case as a kind of antithesis to a priestly convention in other cultures, and often in Greece, that the officiant disappears into the office.

When he foregrounds aspects of his poetic and liturgical role, Pindar highlights his control over an ode's multiplicities. This makes his personal intrications in an ode as difficult to decipher as the principle of unified expression to which it is contributing.[3] This personal self-presentation is the more emphatic for its appearing in a song delivered through the medium of choral recitation.[4] There is a constant blending of self-references into other assertions. In *Olympian* 1, the term χάρις ("grace") is applied to both the mood of the victor (18) and the effect of poetic song (30).[5]

Whatever the particular, elusive, and complex force such religious celebrations may have, this poetry shades into the general category of "hymn,"[6] itself a subcategory of "prayer" for a culture in which poetry was characteristically given a public performance, often at religious festivals, into which a successful poem would be incorporated and reperformed.[7] The retention of the religious association of the term "hymnos" is supported by the use of the term to characterize a specific kind of song, one of the seventeen kinds into which Pindar's work was divided by the Alexandrians,[8] while at the same time it remains Pindar's usual word for a poem in general. In such a situation, poetry was incorporated into, and in some ways continuous with, performances of the tragedies, which also took place at religious festivals.[9] And its illocutionary and perlocutionary force must have been aimed at sustaining and furthering the very ideals of integrating personal prowess, both poetic and athletic, into a religious aptness. Implicit prayer is connected to implicit magic, as explicit prayer is to explicit magic.[10]

Just as liturgy is characteristically carried out either by a celebrant whose self disappears in the office or by the sort of chorus we find in the *Partheneion* of Alcman (and in fact probably in the *epinikia* of Pindar), so the event is usually conceived as a perennial one, even if it may have been originated for a particular occasion. In many cultures, an ad hoc liturgy would be a contradiction in terms, as it would be in such earlier Greek compositions as the unoccasionally liturgical Homeric Hymns. But the victory odes are just such ad hoc liturgies. They are linked, initially and permanently, in the actual and then imagined specific occasion for which they were written, a victory in an athletic contest whose origins in, and connections with, religion oblige some reference to it in such a ratiocinative celebration by a wise-man-poet, a *sophos*.[11] As Pindar observes in another kind of poem, where again he steps forward in Alcman's vein—but in a way that Alcman would not have done:

μάντις ὡς τελέσσω
ἱεραπόλος. τίμαι
δὲ βροτοῖσι κεκριμέναι

As a prophet I celebrate,
a priest. Honors
are decided for mortals.

(*Parthenion*, 94a)[12]

The ambiguity of "as"—which could mean either "like" or "in the role of"—excellently covers the contingency of the assertion. The Muse is needed, but Pindar makes a commensurate contribution: μαντεύεο, Μοῦσα, προφατεύσω δ' ἐγω ("Prophesy, Muse, and I shall speak forth") (Fgt. 150).

In this radical occasionality, the victory—such as that of Melissus in the *pancration* of *Isthmian* 4—connects to the splendor of the particular performance, which builds its act of celebration into an implicitly dialogic evocation before an audience initially actual but always imagined.

This initial occasionality is unlike earlier and other poetry. But, as Pindar himself reminds us (O. 9.1–12), poetry has expanded since the time of Archilochus, nearly two centuries before. He links his improvisational adaptations to his skill at pausing before speaking: ἵσταμαι δὴ ποσσὶ κούφοις ἀμπνέων τε πρίν τι φάμεν ("I am standing on nimble feet, taking breath before I speak") (*Nemean* 8.19). Typically the complex of rethinking begins in the incipit of the poem, in the first segment, or priamel, as in *Isthmian* 4:

Ἔστι μοι θεῶν ἕκατι μυρία κέλευθος,
Ὦ Μέλισσ', εὐμαχανίαν γὰρ ἔφανας Ἰσθμίοις,
ὑμετέρας ἀρετὰς ὕμνωι διώκειν.

There is for me, thanks to the gods, a path ten thousand ways,
Melissus, since you have shown a resource in the Isthmian games
for me to pursue your virtues in a hymn.

(*Isthmian* 4.1–3)

In these lines, the victor and the poet stand in a sort of reciprocity, joined through the assertion of the poet as he reaches out to canvass the religious and social implications of the victory, the ground and aim of the celebration. The generations also come into play; Pindar celebrates in the victor's family a resemblance to the gods in continuous glory. Melissus is compared to Heracles, who is both a hero and a god, as well as a sponsor for the victor's city, Thebes, which also happens to be the poet's city as well. Pindar follows the conceived integrations that constitute the much-discussed unity of an individual ode. At the same time, he highlights not just the connections but the substructure on which the connections reside. These may include suffering, as Heracles has suffered in the loss of his eight sons (*Isthmian* 4.61–68), much like the heroic kinsmen of Melissus (34–40).[13]

The act of adaptive identification with the values that are read into the victor's act and circumstances involves the hieratic poet in a questioning and testing. The rhetoric of this remarkable ongoing questioning of himself is thrown forward to an audience that will be collaterally engaged in such questioning if it attends to the poem. This is apparent at the beginning of *Olympian* 1, where the famous metaphors operate not only as a hyperbolic key signature and entry into a symbolic universe but also as a deduction and a testing-by-contrast: "Best is water but gold is a flashing fire / in that it shines out in the night supreme over lordly wealth." This compressed deductive proposition[14] is at once connected to the posture of questioning by the poet, who publicly addresses his intimate self in a connection that is internal and external, while at the same time multiple as it ties into the rest of the ode:

> Best is water but gold is a flashing fire
> in that it shines out in the night supreme over lordly wealth.
> If prizes you wish
> to sing, dear heart,
> look for no hotter
> bright star in the day than the sun through the desert ether,
> and let us declare no finer contest than Olympia
> whence the many-speeched hymn is cast round
> with the counsels of the wise to proclaim.
>
> (O. 1–9)

Having set up the self-superseding principles of his deductive series, the poet is free—and advertises his freedom—to continue a questioning about the relation of the victor and his surrogates to the gods, to the past, to the city, to the founding myth of the Olympian games, as he settles the details of the myth of Pelops. Then he brings up generalities about life, returning to the religious or quasi-religious sets of injunctions that are offered both as a deep expression of tradition and as the achievement of the self-presenting poet. According to his principles, the act of questioning will keep in view, but not lock in, a glimpsed code of codes—in our terms, the possibility of a Foucauldian episteme. The elements are all there for recombination, and always the same, and always kept open.[15]

From the opening of the poem on, a sort of triple pull is effectuated. The entry into a symbolic disposition does seem casual in its gnomic curtness, premetaphoric or submetaphoric. Yet second, it has a super-metaphoric extensibility. And third, both of these rhetorical gestures are inextricably knotted together in double connection to the speaking poet and to the specific victor. The utterance is universal and at the same time radically occasional: προμαθείας δ' ἀπόκεινται ῥοαί ("The streams of forethought lie afar") (Nemean 11.46).[16]

The "hymns"—note the plural form—remain "lords of the lyre," and their lordship is connected to the act of questioning, which is implied by the act of foregrounding the openness of the poet's choice, as at the beginning of *Olympian* 2:

Ἀναξιφόρμιγγες ὕμνοι,
τίνα θεόν, τίν' ἥρωα, τίνα ἄνδρα κελαδήσομεν;

Hymns, lords of the lyre,
what god, what hero, what man shall we sound forth?

Along these lines of querying and testing, *Isthmian* 7 begins by asking at some length which of the many myths that the poet lists offers the greatest delight for Thebes. All this self-probing is public and conceived of as public. The act of public amplification is intimately connected to an act of public questioning, which would seem to go against the grain of liturgical celebration. In this poetry, however, it contributes a fortiori to the act of liturgical celebration, raising the religious into a dialectic that might have subverted it by a secularization instead of by this reconsecration of what could have seemed secular gestures.

2

PINDAR'S accessibility, and his imagined arrival from a city often other than his own, put him on a plane of Panhellenic possibility, holding a neutrality that is sometimes strained by recent political allegiances and events. He carries off his integrations by setting cities into combination. Homer is a Panhellenic poet, and he is easily assimilated to that natural role, since his subjects are ones that unite Greek-speaking peoples. After Homer, however, poets preceding Pindar—even Archilochus, who moved from Paros to Thasos, and Alcman, who migrated from Asia Minor to Sparta—tend to be associated with a single city. Pindar is Panhellenic, but problematically, as in all his other integrations. The locale of the victory and its relation to the victor's home is only a starting point, a sort of wavering compass needle around which Pindar builds the compass of his ode. *Isthmian* 6, to a Corinthian, leads with a quotation from Hesiod, then a reference to the Muses; it offers song from the springs of Dirce at Thebes, before the poet returns to himself and Panhellenic diplomacy. *Isthmian* 8 (478) involves an apology for Thebes, which had been siding with Persia in the recent Persian Wars, and brings in, as though to assert Thebes's age-old Greek connection,

myths associated with Thebes itself. The ode's overlay of myths includes
the founder of Aegina, Aeacus, who is connected—along with his son
Peleus and his grandson Achilles—to the Trojan War and to Asia Minor,
which had recently been Persian territory. In *Pythian* 11, the wanderings
of Orestes are presented as a sort of Panhellenic recuperation.

While the Greater Dionysia had a Panhellenic cast, it was located in
Athens, and the associations of all the tragedies and comedies, already
performed from early in Pindar's career, gravitate around Athens. In that
sense, Aeschylus and Sophocles are as local as Sappho and Alcaeus.
Pindar, however, is a Theban and is commissioned to celebrate a victor,
whether he be from Thebes, Aegina, Syracuse, or Cyrene. This already
for the most part brought two cities into play, Pindar's own and that of
the victor. And these cities might be of very different religious traditions
and social organizations. A third location necessarily comes into play as
well, the locale where the festival took place, Olympia or Delphi,
Nemea or the Isthmus.

In handling this spectrum of obligations and occasional allegiances,
Pindar advises the poet to be like the color-changing octopus. In these
lines, as is so often the case, he appears to be talking to himself:

ὦ τέκνον, ποντίου θηρὸς πετραίου
χρωτὶ μάλιστα νόον
προσφέρων πάσαις πολίεσσιν ὁμίλει

My son, set your mind most of all
like the skin of the rock-sea beast
when you consort with all the cities.

(*Hymn* 43)

The victor in *Olympian* 12, Ergoteles, achieves success by himself becoming Panhellenic: from Sicilian Himera, he has won in the long run of
Olympian, Pythian, and Isthmian games, instead of being confined to
local victories in Cretan Cnossus, from which he was driven by political upheaval (στάσις). The victor in *Olympian* 6 offers a model Panhellenic career, since he is a citizen both of his Arcadian homeland
(Stymphalos) and of Syracuse. He is an Iamid, and Iamus was both seer
and warrior. Thus in his background stands a conjunction that reappears
in the implicit symmetry between this heroic victor and the poet who
celebrates him. Pindar's homeland, Thebes, also enters in, because of the
comparison with the Theban hero Adrastus. *Olympian* 13 includes at the

end (100–116) a Panhellenic list. First Pindar mentions the Corinthian victor's triumphs elsewhere than at Olympia—in the Isthmian games (near his homeland) and in the Nemean and Pythian games, and in a festival at Athens. The poet goes on from myths about the Trojan War, in Asia Minor, to engage the myth of the itinerant Bellerophon, touching on that figure's travels, and thus bringing in Parnassus, Mt. Lykaion, Argos, Arcadia, Pellana, Sicyon, Megara, Eleusis, Marathon, Euboeia, "and over the whole of Greece." *Pythian* 4, which focuses on the North African city of Cyrene, reaches out to recall the foundation of the city in travels across vectors that include the entire Mediterranean.[17]

3

THE sorting out of the games' origination myth about Pelops in *Olympian* 1 is skeined into Pindar's present at many points—the implied complex analogue between Hieron and Pelops, the establishment of the false myth about him through envy,[18] its replacement by the true story in Pindar's celebratory act. The balance maintained here centers and fuels the poem, as against the simpler presentation in *Bacchylides* 5, which was written for the same victory. In Bacchylides' work, generally many of the Pindaric elements of idea and formal poetic sequence are present, but without the poised strenuousness of Pindar's constant reaccommodations—and without his deep look at a dark side built, for him, into the very genealogy, since while Pelops was falsely maligned, his father, Tantalus, was not; Tantalus's fall from virtue was true and permanent.

In Bacchylides' ode, Hieron is directly and simply praised in the first lines, and then the poet moves to praise the majesty of Zeus and Zeus's eagle. Pindar gets to Hieron soon enough, toward the end of his first strophe, but as a foil and appendage to his dazzling incipit. Bacchylides gradually leads on to his main myth, the power of Heracles and that hero's descent to the underworld, where he meets Meleager, who tells Heracles the story of his early death. "It were best for mortals / never to have been born," Heracles responds, "nor to behold the light of the sun" (160–62). But this commonplace is quickly passed over as Meleager recommends to Heracles someone still alive and virginal, his young sister, Deianeira, "unknowing yet of golden / Cypris who charms mortals" (174–75). "White-armed Calliope" is addressed in the very next verse. The most venerable of the Muses is enjoined to utter a hymn to Zeus and Olympia, and the ode goes back to Hieron in a simple blaze of affirmation.

The dark side of Heracles' union with Deianeira, present in the myth from the mere reference to her (and to the etymology of her name, "Man-slayer"), is occluded by Bacchylides' further silence here and by his immediate transition to Calliope. The Muse and Aphrodite are linked by phrasal association and syntactic congruence to the beauty of Deianeira.[19] Here each glorious female figure is matched to a laudatory physical adjective referring to color:

> λίπον χλωραύχενα
> ἐν δώμασι Δαιάνειραν,
> νῆιν ἔτι χρύσεας
> Κύπριδος θελξιμβρότου.
> λευκώλενε Καλλιόπα

> I left bud-green-throated
> Deianeira at home
> unknowing yet of golden
> Cypris, who charms mortals.
> White-armed Calliope—
> (*Bacchylides* 5, 171–75)

In his ode for this victory, Pindar looks both back and forward with his myth; Tantalus remains a puzzling case both for himself and for the openness of his dark connections to the foundation of the games and, always puzzlingly, to the victory:[20] "If the watchers of Olympus honored any mortal man / That one was Tantalus. / But he could not stomach / His great bliss" (54–57). Tantalus ruined his early success by trying to steal the nectar of the gods, thus incurring an everlasting punishment. At the same time, his son Pelops remained favored by Zeus, though not without his own far more benign actual penalty, the ivory shoulder given him by the infatuated Poseidon when he was dipped in a purifying bath. Yet "gold . . . shines out in the night" (3), and this darkness is picked up thematically in Pelops's arrival at Pisa to court Hippodameia, "alone in the darkness" (οἶος ἐν ὄρφναι) (71). Darkness comes up again here in the general fate of a man who refused risks and so "would sit / digesting his nameless old age in darkness vainly" (ἀνώνυμον / γῆρος ἐν σκότωι καθήμενος ἔψοι μάταν) (82–83).

What does all this have to do with Hieron? Pelops's own ancient and legendary victory at Pisa—which saves his life, furthers his dynasty by marriage with Hippodameia, and leads to these very Olympian games—is linked to Hieron. And what Pelops won there was also a chariot race. But Pindar emphasizes the inclusiveness of this access that his contemporaries enjoy by dwelling on contests of strength (presumably including chariot races) and on *foot* races (95–96). Both the indirection of Pindar's opening and its vast inclusiveness set the tone and the syntactic matrix so that we do not make a fully closed system out of these connections. Whereas Bacchylides begins directly with a simple address to Hieron, Pindar comes from a tangent that at the same time can be made to include the universe: "Best is water but gold is a flashing fire."[21] To use Elroy Bundy's terms, the instant hyperbolic intensity of this first line begins and also "caps" a priamel, serving as a "foil" to what is so far so remote in its reference that only the auditors' knowledge about the convention of the person to be praised can associate it to Hieron. It is already, at the beginning, a "climax," and it is the more forcible in that it uses gnomic expressions, which usually come later in an ode, as foils or caps to begin the ode. Moreover, by contrast with the water of the first half of the first line, the gold of the second half constitutes a foil insofar as there is a contrast, and it is also a possible cap insofar as gold has a greater beauty and value than water—which is at the same time already a cap and therefore an initial climax, since it is "best." An incipient dialectic in this priamel is in one sense complete, hence gnomic. But in the ode, again, this passage, as a priamel, must be anticipating, remotely but firmly, the obligatory mention of the victor, Hieron, who in fact comes at the end of this first strophe. In the next main clause—"Look for no hotter / bright star in the day than the sun"—the poet continues the superlative, but by way of a syntax that enlists another, contradictory Pindaric theme, the necessity to observe a sense of limit, which is brought in more directly at the end of the ode. Thus the peerless is connected with a voluntary restriction; striving is melded into renunciation, a connection that dominates the final epode, where the poet enjoins someone addressed in the second person to "peer no further" (μηκέτι πάπταινε πόρσιον) (114). This could be himself, or it could be the auditor; but it applies most directly to Hieron, since he has been addressed throughout, and since the poet has just said "the ultimate crests / for kings." On the other hand, complementarily and compensatorily, and with no reference to limits, Pindar goes on at once to conclude by wishing that he himself might "go on many times to consort

with victors and to be foremost for wisdom [i.e., song] among the
Greeks everywhere" (115–16).

4

EVEN as Pindar refutes the legend that Pelops had died as the victim of
a cannibalistic feast among the gods, he allows the poem to dwell on the
gory details of the feast that he says could not have taken place.[22] So
Pindar, as is his wont, plays both ways against each other for a dialecti-
cal overview. When Nagy modulates Pindar's own modulation of the
cannibalistic dismemberment/divine reincorporation of Pelops in *Olym-
pian* 1,[23] he is effectually saying that the further modulation of these sav-
age survivals into the public, civilized celebration of Olympian song
sublimates and universalizes them in ways that make them enter a new,
reverberant order. Even Homer, however, tends to avoid the darker side
of mythology, going very light in his references to the more atavistic,
chthonic mythology. But Pindar goes further than Homer in his dialec-
tical manipulations.

A pressure results from Pindar's syncopating attention to crests or
offglancings of myth. The posture of questioning, of dramatizing the
search for an appropriate match in myth to the victory and then for an
appropriate angle, allows for an expandability to the myth.[24] Pindar can
go on about a given myth at great length, or he can cut it off abruptly,
since the presentation keeps the myth entangled in a network of as-
sociations, always seemingly tentative, that can be concluded at any point.
The rapid changes in sound and in the syntax can be perceived to
enforce either an abrupt shift or a continuing amplification.

So in *Isthmian* 1, Heracles is brought in briefly (12–13) to character-
ize Thebes, whose victory, buttressed by others, calls its native son the
poet to write an ode. The city itself is characterized still more suc-
cinctly as "the host of Cadmus," linking the present dwellers of the city
to the legendary founders and touching on another myth, the city then
being specified as "the one in which Alcmene bore her dauntless / son,
before whom once shuddered the harsh hounds of Geryon." Heracles is
brought up briefly again, too, in lines 55 and 56, in a run of other myths.
He gets more extended mention in *Pythian* 9.84–87, though character-
istically the references to him in Pindar are succinct, as though his leg-
end itself is so powerful that it might take over the ode. And indeed, it is

hard to see what the "harsh hounds of Geryon" are doing in *Isthmian* 1. The fact that the hound (the plural "hounds" is also a problem) who guards the cattle that Heracles has taken is located beyond the pillars of Hercules does expand the spatial reference of the poem, but with a puzzling obliquity. Still, whatever else they may signify, the "harsh hounds" do serve as a contrast to the religious harmony of Apollo, whose celebration for Ceos and Delos the poet has just said he is deferring.

This beginning set of effusions about Apollo is the longest in the ode, a priamel that takes nine lines, at the strange angle of an apology for not yet having written the paean to that god.[25] To say that the poet passes over the paean to Apollo under pressure of the commitment to celebrate a Theban chariot victor conforms to the convention of the foil, whereby the second caps the first; but Pindar does not really assert that this ode is greater or more important than the deferred one. In fact, he multiplies his foregroundings of choice by saying he "will yoke the endings of both / leading a dance for the unshorn Phoebus / in flood-girt Ceos with the men of the sea / and the brine-cleaving reef / of the Isthmus" (6–10). The shorter references to other myths stand in contrast to this expansion, and the cresting of brief references continues through the ode. After the preterition/mention of Apollo, the first myth applied to this ode is then a mention of Heracles' rough exploit, which may be taken as setting off the mastery of the six Theban victories, lesser analogues to the exploits of the great Theban hero.[26]

At this point, the succinct and recursive offglancings of myth continue throughout. Castor is brought up as a founder of games (21), with no reference to Pollux or to the whole Trojan cycle; and Iolaus is coupled with him in the same role, with no explicit mention of his other role as the charioteer of Heracles (though he is later implicitly included with Heracles as one of the offspring of Amphitryon). In line 30, Iolaus is mentioned again, by his patronymic, "son of Iphicles." He is characterized this time as "from the clan of the race of the sown men"—sown, that is, by Cadmus from the dragon's teeth. There follows on these rapid references a somewhat longer one to the father of the victor, who survived a shipwreck (32–38). And the ode concludes with a long run on a survey of the athletic games and their locales (52–68), the places where this victor has also won a chariot race, offering a present and Panhellenic conspectus to take over from the nubs of myth evocations. The poet says he adds one such site to another (συμβάλλομαι)—"I add besides the shrine of Phylace" (59)—going on to a location in Thessaly to the north in the last of his list of contests, after beginning with Delos, where it is a Theban victor in the Nemean games who is being celebrated. Those games are held in honor of Poseidon, who is linked to the shipwrecked father in midpassage (30–35). The range of myths is itself touched on by the leap from Cadmus to Iolaus and Heracles, and from them to the victor who is being celebrated. The attention to his father is now buttressed by the use of patronymics to identify Heracles, Cadmus, and even Zeus, referred to here as "son of Kronos" (52).

The mastery of Heracles is expanded on in *Nemean* 1 through a prophecy in the mouth of Tiresias, who predicts the hero's many successes (51–73). And again in *Isthmian* 4, Heracles' career is lauded at length from beginning to apotheosis (42–67)—except that the death of his eight sons, presented through its incorporation in a Theban ceremony, brings a dark side to view.[27] *Olympian* 10 offers the myth of Heracles' foundation of the Olympian games by defeating Augeas. Its complications attest to the mentioned difficulty that attends a prowess once attained and attends the restoration of Epizephyrian Locris.

In a given ode, the thought itself, however, remains relatively simple, through persistently mounting antitheses. Its *connections* with the mythic material can remain the more hidden, and so the more emphatic in the assumed force of their mere presentation, with the pressure of omissions and even of the seeming obliquities heightening the emphasis of single myths.

At the same time, the myths are multiplied. Pindar himself not only manages but also foregrounds the notion of the multiplicity of myths, which is needed properly to celebrate a victory and deduce its meanings: ἀρεταὶ δ' αἰεὶ μεγάλαι πολύμυθοι ("Great deeds of prowess are always many-mythed") (*Pythian* 9.76). "Polymuthoi" can mean "many stories," even those clustering around one myth (as around Pelops in *Olympian* 1). Interestingly, up to this point in *Pythian* 9, Pindar has adduced just a single myth to highlight Telesicrates of Cyrene, victor in the full-armor race: Apollo's fructifying union with the nymph Cyrene after the god's dialogue with the centaur Chiron, which produced the hero Aristaeus. But then, as though in obedience to his own principle, and as though filling out the requirement for the splendor of a foil in the ode, he brings in another myth, and then another: first a Theban one that is also Panhellenic, since it concerns the birth of Heracles. From this Theban vantage point, he brings in Aegina and Megara (90–94); and for continued multiple mythologizing, he returns to Cyrene to set the contest for the marriage of the daughter of Antaeus in the light of the fifty daughters of Danaus (105–25)—itself a complicated myth that provides the background for Aeschylus's *Suppliants*.[28] There is a kind of strain put upon the myth here; its aspects may be presented as flashing facets of a known series of events, rather than presumed squarely, as in Homer or even later in the centralizing foci of Greek tragedy.

In *Nemean* 8, Pindar begins with praise of Aphrodite and swells into ranging through the triumphs and hazards of military prowess, including the envy that undid Ajax and also threatens the poet: it is perilous to thread one's way through the multiplicities of tales and reasonings ("logoi") (20–25). ἔστιν δ' ἀφάνεια τύχας καὶ μαρναμένων ("There is an obscurity of failure even for strivers") (*Isthmian* 4.31). But "For the one who knows, even superior wisdom waxes without wiles" (δαέντι δὲ καὶ σοφία μείζων ἄδολος τελέθει) (*Olympian* 7.53). The holding together of the very alternations in *Isthmian* 1 allows him to conclude that poem, after much praise of the victor, with a sudden and superficially incoherent censure of those who hoard wealth and laugh at others. The actual coherence here derives from a deep impression that the speaker is so secure in his sense of limits that his flights of exposition can pass through assumed ideas and connections to some very different facet of his view, going very generally from light to dark, as here, or from dark to light, as in the transition in *Pythian* 1 from the dark of the giant pinned beneath Aetna to the glory of the victor the poet is praising. At all points, Pindar exhibits and tests a sense of limit, much as did Heraclitus.[29]

John Finley remarks that "The whole system, if anything so fluid and iridescent may be called a system, is strangely complete. It includes not only the exterior sphere of character and state of mind also. This symbolic and mythological cast of thought characteristically looks both outward and inward at the same time, or rather, so objectifies the inward that it appears side by side with the outward."[30] One could organize the constituents of this system in many ways, and Finley's survey of odes under the headings of "vicissitude," "harmony," "attainment," and "excellence" exhibits both resonance and comprehensiveness.

A sense of this mastery gets expressed as a confident affirmation:

τὸ δὲ παθεῖν εὖ πρῶτον ἄθλων, εὖ δ' ἀκούειν·
δευτέρα μοῖρ'· ἀμφοτέροισι δ' ἀνὴρ
ὃς ἂν ἐγκύρσηι, καὶ ἕληι, στέφανον ὕψιστον δέδεκται

Having good looks is the first prize, good repute
is the second fate. A man who chances
on both, and holds them, has received the highest bliss.

(*Pythian* 1.98–100)

Pythian 8 begins with an injunction that a personified Peace "holding the highest keys to councils and wars" receive the Aeginetan victor. "How to do and to undergo alike the gentle / you know with a timing that errs not" (6–7). This Peace also controls the violence of giants. The timing of the proper moment, the καιρός, by the start of the first epode becomes the time (χρόνος) through which force governs the overweening, which is represented as the giants who are overcome. It suddenly happens that it is Apollo who effectuates this; he has both overcome them with his bow and welcomed the victor with gracious mind.

The poet now shifts to the victor's home island. Justice and the Graces have fostered Aegina "from the beginning"—so much that he "would not have time to set it all to the lyre, and to a gentle voice" (the word μαλθακός is repeated). And then another incursion appears: "unless satiety comes to bite" (μὴ κόρος ἐλθὼν κνίσηι).[31] Suddenly a host of hitherto unmentioned antithetic possibilities to gentleness and peace, other than violence, come into view, all built into the word κόρος, which means "satiety" or "tedium," as William Slater glosses it here, but the other senses of the word, "greed" and "envy," are not absent.

The poet continues with an account of the family's victories, so signal that they are to be included, proleptically as it were, in the legendary prophecy of Amphiaraus over the Seven Against Thebes. The word introducing the prophecy, which Pindar now quotes at some length (44–55), αἰνίξατο, also means "riddled." Pindar will also praise the son of Amphiaraus, Alcmeon. There follows a prayer to Apollo, in his role as patron of this festival, that he help the poet keep harmony at every step (62–63). Let the gods not grudge the victor, the poet says, whose triumphs he goes on to list—and he turns, in another sudden foil, to the four losers in this wrestling contest, who are fated to slink home unhonored and unconsoled (81–87).

He then concludes, as though he were cutting in on himself to draw together all these notions—of satiety against achievement, peace against violence, and success against failure, as well as a time over which no shadow had yet been allowed to fall. He breaks in the middle of a line to amplify the implications of these references to time, both the passing gnomic mentions of time and the long time implied by the recollected collocation of legendary with present events:

> He, getting the lot of a new boon,
> at the point of great luxury,
> soars for hope
> on manly wings, having
> a care exceeding wealth. In a brief span for mortals
> does delight wax; even thus it falls to the ground
> shaken by adverse doom.
> Of a day! What is one? What not? A dream of a shadow is
> man. But when the Zeus-given gleam comes
> there is a shining light for mortals and a honeyed age.
> Aegina, dear mother, on a free voyage
> conduct this city with Zeus and with ruling Aeacus,
> Peleus and good Telamon and with Achilles.
>
> (88–100)

The line and a half of resuming and overmastering evocation of transience, in its startling and riddled aphorism, "A dream of a shadow is / man," itself breaks into the abrupt one-word characterization of humans, ἐπάμεροι ("of a day").[32] This is qualified first by a succinct mention of a "honeyed age," a pure afterlife on which Pindar elsewhere expands.[33] It is then qualified by a return, as though for control, to a praise of the city, bringing in Zeus again. The city is included in what amounts to a Panhellenic mastery, in the company of a legendary founder and of the heroes who are associated with the Trojan War. Peleus, Telamon, and Aeacus, however, are all fathers, and thus not parallel to Achilles. Moreover, with Pindar's Homer in view, it may not be too much to say that this last word of the poem, and this here semantically isolated hero, can be seen in the light of the entire *Iliad*. A summary of its conflations of loss and glory could be said to equal the comprehensions of theme that this poem has moved through.

The origin of the games in funeral celebration subliminally brings the poet to the threshold of last things, while at the same time, he places his manifest emphasis on the glory of this life. The very situation allows transience and all the attendant troubles of mortality both to interrupt and to be tensely set into the balance/risk/loss of the games—lack of fame, death in battle (*Isthmian* 4.3 ff.), envy, madness (Ajax in *Isthmian* 4.34–40), shipwreck (*Isthmian* 11.34), and famine (*Isthmian* 1.40). The ode triumphs over them by naming them, going farther than Simonides does.

Nagy correctly claims, "Finally, as we have seen from the diction of Pindar, the ritual ordeals of the athletes are ideologically equated, by way of concepts like *aethlos, ponos,* and *kamatos,* to the life-and-death ordeals of heroes in the past."[34] Yet these athletes are not sacrificial figures themselves, and often the figures to whom they are compared in the myths, such as the Pelops and the Tantalus of *Olympian* 1, simultaneously and paradoxically suffer and overcome the ritual sacrifice to which they are inescapably linked. "In other words, the occasion of victory in a mortal's day-to-day lifetime is that singular moment when the dark insubstantiality of an ancestor's shade is translated, through its dreams, into the shining life-force of the victor in full possession of victory, radiant with the brightness of Zeus."[35] As representatives, glorious through prowess, of the tyrant who is glorious through power, and in the process of being celebrated by the poet who is glorious through his utterance, these victors transcend the sacrificial pattern in the act of reclaiming it, just as in his gnomic base the poet declares that the renunciation of a hope for immortality will add glory to the triumph of the moment: μή, φίλα ψυχά, βίον ἀθάνατον σπεῦδε ("Do not, dear soul, strive for immortal life") (*Pythian* 3.61).

5

PINDAR may serve as one model for the oracular. In his poetry, the mythic, the celebration of a ceremonial victory in a religious setting, and the proverbial are melded. This fusing is effected in a way that admits an adaptability of presentation, thus allowing a self-assertion of the speaker in the full range of *Olympian* 2 or the somewhat curtailed range of *Pythian* 7. Yet the conversational and the oracular become difficult to disentangle from one another once they occur in poetry. Whitman and Mayakovsky, for example, are at once more conversational and more oracular in their poetry than are their contemporaries. In Greek tragedy, we find a split between the different languages, meters, postures, and foci of the dialogue segments and the segments of chorus. Aristophanes, for example, allows us to associate the passages of dialogue with the conversational, and to conceive of them as oral rather than written. But the distinction, itself complicated and disproportionate, will not easily solve the matter, because choral poetry, too, certainly derives from what is in many respects, if not in all, a tradition of oral delivery. And to come to our contemporaries, Ginsberg's poetry, which is aimed especially for oral delivery, is at once highly oracular and highly conversational, as is the very different poetry of O'Hara. The easy flow—not only in a satirical poet such as Archilochus but also in highly wrought poets such as Sappho and Ibycus—suggests the conversational, and certainly all these poets are less oracular than Pindar, who nonetheless may be seen to retain an overall syntactic version of the flow of conversation in the "associativeness" of his progression through a poem, as well as in his personal references. The parenthetical mention of his intimate self—"If prizes you wish / to sing, dear heart"—has a conversational ring; but the conversational has been pulled into the oracular matrix of a complicated, recursive metrical pattern.

The triadic structure of the ode repeats an elaborate stanzaic pattern after it has been broken by two others: strophe matches strophe, after it has been followed by antistrophe (also matched), itself followed by epode (matched in a new pattern as well). What is unique in Pindar's highlighting of these patterns is his constant recourse to wide contrasts of line length and colon type from line to line, a variation constant in his work and found nowhere in previous Greek lyric poetry. Alcaeus uses long lines on occasion, his greater Asclepiadean, but he does not vary long lines with short on anything like so wide a swing. Nor do the elaborate, but still somewhat less varied, choruses of Pindar's near-contemporary Aeschylus, for all the high pitch of his poetic afflatus. Comparable variation appears here and there in the little we have of Simonides, but it is by no means so elaborate. It is not till the splendid choruses of Sophocles that we get anything comparable.

In the first nine lines of the strophe to *Olympian* 1, the cola build and vary so as to keep the voice at once suspended, alertly adaptive, and widely recursive.

Ἄριστον μὲν ὕδωρ, ὁ δὲ χρυσὸς αἰθόμενον πῦρ
ἅτε διαπρέπει νυκτὶ μεγάνορος ἔξοχα πλούτου
εἰ δ᾽ ἄεθλα γαρύεν
ἔλδεαι, φίλον ἦτορ,
μηκέτ᾽ ἀελίου σκόπει
ἄλλο θαλπνότερον ἐν ἁμέραι φαεννὸν ἄστρον ἐρήμας δι᾽ αἰθέρος,
μηδ᾽ Ὀλυμπίας ἀγῶνα φέρτερον αὐδάσομεν

ὅθεν ὁ πολύφατος ὕμνος ἀμφιβάλλεται
σοφῶν μητίεσσι κελαδεῖν

Best is water but gold is a flashing fire
In that it shines out in the night supreme over lordly wealth.
If prizes you wish
To sing, dear heart,
Look for no hotter
Bright star in the day than the sun through the desert ether,
And let us declare no finer contest than Olympia
Whence the many-speeched hymn is cast round
With the counsels of the wise to proclaim

This strophe speaks twice of its own sound, and perhaps of its own sound patterning. αὐδάσομεν ("declare") means to sound out, coming from a root indicating sound; and κελαδεῖν ("proclaim") means literally to sing or to hymn as well as to celebrate.[36] The first two long lines, themselves varied, give way to the varied, but still recursive, three short lines, followed by the still longer polyphonic line 6, which is followed by two varied middle-length lines, and then another short line, rounded out by the end of the strophe (lines 10 and 11, not quoted), a middle-length line and a short one. Of these eleven lines, only lines 3 and 5 have the same metrical pattern in Bruno Snell's analysis. But the pherecratic, an Aeolic staple colon, and its longer variant, the glyconic, appear in five of the first seven lines (and, of course, again on the same scheme in the antistrophe, as the pattern of the form dictates). The epode, by contrast, has only one pherecratic in its eight lines, but, as befits the rounding out of the triadic pattern, its lines are more uniformly long.

The alternation of long and short lines involves pitching the syntax to an elevation of expectancy, because the voice is cued as unable to wind down till the resolution of the strophic element. If we compare this effect to the Sapphic stanza's speeding in the first three lines and slowing in the resolving fourth line, its dimensional intricacy falls into relief. Along with the expectancy, however, there is a counterpointed syntactic resolution. The first line could be taken as a complete unit in itself, and the second line, which is again syntactically complete, as an amplification of the first. The next three lines begin what seems like a new assertion: "If prizes you wish / to sing, dear heart / look for [than the sun]"—and the reference to "prizes" makes it sound as though the victory were to be the topic. But as the strophe swells to its longest, median line, it turns out that this assertion, too, supplements the first line by adducing another bright object of peerless excellence, the sun: "Look for no hotter / bright star in the day than the sun through the desert ether."

The first line breaks cleanly into two clauses, and it also mounts the staple Aeolic pattern, first a glyconic and then a pherecratic. But the two dovetail by having the sound pattern break the syntactic pattern: "Best is water" does not complete the glyconic, though it completes its clause. To complete the glyconic, we must go two syllables into the second clause, ὁ δὲ. And the matching of clauses is emphasized by this Greek particle, which announces a syntactic complementarity, here cast into the matched, but slightly asymmetrical, metrical complementarity. Without continuing the correlation of sound to sense, the flow of sound is furthered in the following lines by repetitions and variations of smaller feet grouped into cola, first by the exact match of cretic with iamb in lines 3 and 5, alternated with the pherecratic of line 4, which picks up those of lines 1 and 2; while line 2 introduces the first cretic, paired with a pherecratic, as in lines 6 and 7, which are also begun with cretics; and lines 9, 10 (which adds one bacchius), and 11 end with cretics, there mixed on a varied pattern with iambs, which constitute the whole of line 8. This line refers exactly to its own rhythmic and syntactic compassing: "Whence the many-speeched hymn is cast round."[37] "Counsels" (μητίεσσι) could also be rendered "crafts," and the term gets extended and occasionally personified into a whole universe of mental and verbal activity.[38]

The effect, again unique to Pindar, is of high variation composed into high control, much as in the combination of semantic elements and mythic topoi in the ongoing statements of the odes. And all this integrating richness is further ornamented by Pindar's braiding together of traditional meters, rather than, as traditionally, keeping them separate.[39]

These complex and bold conflations of sound patternings reinforce the complexity and boldness of an utterance that keeps proclaiming that its comprehensions are mastering, if not resolving, its multiplicities and antitheses of situation, as well as its particularity. The religious—the access to the gods, who are always to be evoked and never to be aspired to—stays open at the behest and through the act of the poet, who mounts all the antitheses but integrates his person and his utterance by not resolving them. The religious comes under redefinition by Xenophanes, the self by Solon. And the Heraclitus who is arguably echoed by Pindar[40] performs a profound set of redefinitions of the consciousness in which the similarities and the differences between the god and the self, while factored out, remain distinct. Pindar, without engaging in philosophy, carries through a comparable integration of his self with his act of utterance by circulating it through the gods. In the stresses of this conception, he moves powerfully from myth to victor to self to poetry to sense of life, as at the end of *Olympian* 1:

> The victor round the rest of his life
> has honeyed calm. This is the highest boon that comes
> day by day to all mortals. And I must crown
> that man with a song for horses
> in Aeolic melody.
> I believe there is no
> host who is both more knowing of good things and more sovereign in
> > power,
> which we shall now embellish in the glorious folds of hymns.
> A god turning to this for you
> having this concern, Hieron,
> cares for your endeavors. If he does not soon leave,
> A still sweeter one
>
> With the swift chariot I hope to hail, finding a path mastering words
> by Kronos's son's daylit mount. Indeed for me
> the Muse nurses the strongest dart in might.
> Some are great in one thing, some in another. The supreme crests
> for kings. Peer no further.
> May you tread on high the whole time, and may I so often
> consort with victors, famous in wisdom among Greeks everywhere.

The conversational, it may be said, obtains by way of a private dialogue between two persons. The oracular engages in one way or another some absent supreme figure or figures; it is also public. Here the intimacy of Pindar's address to Hieron is attested to by his daring to put himself on a par with the royal victor; but at the same time, this is transposed into the particularity, Panhellenic but momentary, of a conception of the chief of the gods that moves in and out of this passage, and of the whole poem. The reach of this poet has brought the conversational and the oracular into a conflation at once high-pitched, as is appropriate for the oracular, and splendidly adaptive, as happens in the *sprezzatura* of the most accomplished conversation. His wizardry, implied in δαιδαλλέω ("embellish"), has moved into the very supremacy that he here praises. And again, "The god fashions all things for mortals and breeds grace for the song" (θεὸς ὁ πάντα τεύχων βρότοις / καὶ χάριν ἀοιδᾶι φυτεύει) (Fgt. 141). This particular fusion of the oracular and the conversational attains a new reach, raising the deep question of how Pindar can paradoxically stay completely and emphatically within the mythic and liturgical givens of his Indo-European inheritance while at the same time deeply transmuting them.

10

The Possible Intersections of Cosmology, Religion, and Abstract Thought in the Lyric Fragments of Alcman

MANY TRADITIONS INTERSECT in Homer. These traditions separate out into the lyrics of Pindar and into the cosmological and ontological speculations of Parmenides and Empedocles. This depth of tradition in Greece is already discernible in the work of Alcman, and therefore already discernible in Sparta in the seventh century B.C., especially as it has come into prominence through the fairly recent papyrus discoveries of this poet's work. His poetry is noteworthy, even the small amount we have, for the forceful interpenetration of areas of discourse normally kept distinct or at least arrayed in some other order.

Lyric delicacy—so notable in Sappho that it obscured the rhetorical function of her poems as something like the hymns of a female sodality —is also present in Alcman, some of whose poems were certainly the texts for something like ritual recitation in a comparable community, except that the crucial role of a male poet—even with a female chorus director—indicates a different orientation for the public performances of that sodality, whatever they may have been, and possibly also a different rhetorical function for the poems.[1] If there are problems about defining such functions for the full choral lyric—of which we have a relatively large segment, the *Partheneion* or Maidens' song (fragment 1²)—then this is all the more the case of briefer fragments, and possibly of at least some whole short poems, for which there are no such locating indications.

The elaborate adduction of anthropological parallels to the *Partheneion* by Claude Calame and others still leaves the outlines of the poem hanging; we do not really know whether we are dealing with a cult poem or an effusion surrounding a cultic act, or precisely what the cult is, or how we are to envision the erotic effusions of members of the chorus, or even whether there is one choir or two. But as Charles Segal abundantly demonstrates in sorting out some probabilities among these vexing questions, we are left with a brilliance of poetic play, especially in lines 45–49 and 60–63, "delicate humor, elegant wit, and delightful playfulness."[3]

We also, as these questions feed back on one another, do not know how to read the stars or the sun in any exact relation to the festival. Nor can we know in this context how a comparison of girls to racehorses feeds back into cultural expectations. Yet we can be reasonably sure that the intrications of separable domains of utterance press beyond, while enlisting, these strictly lyrical delicacies. Take one such passage:

> ἔστι τις σιῶν τίσις.
> ὁ δ᾽ ὄλβιος, ὅστις εὔφρων
> ἀμέραν [δι] απλέκει
> ἄκλαυτος. ἐγὼν δ᾽ ἀείδω
> Ἀγιδῶς τὸ φῶς. ὁρῶ
> ὥτ᾽ ἄλιον, ὅνπερ ἅμιν
> Ἀγιδὼ μαρτύρεται
> φαίνην. ἐμὲ δ᾽ οὔτ᾽ ἐπαινῆν
> οὔτε μωμήσθαι νιν ἁ κλεννὰ χοραγὸς
> οὐδ᾽ ἁμῶς ἐῆι. δοκεῖ γὰρ ἤμεν αὔτα
> ἐκπρεπὴς τὼς ὥπερ αἴ τις
> ἐν βοτοῖς στάσειεν ἵππον
> παγὸν ἀεθλοφόρον καναχάποδα
> τῶν ὑποπετριδίων ὀνείρων.

> There is some recompense of the gods.
> He is blest who of good mind
> weaves through the day

unweeping. But I sing
the light of Agido, I see
her as the sun which for us
Agido invokes
to shine. Neither to praise
nor to blame her does the glorious chorus leader
allow me at all. For she seems to be
outstanding, as though someone
would stand a horse among the grazers,
compact, prize-winning, stamping its hooves,
of the under-wingèd dreams.

(1.36–49)

Here the sequence of sun and racehorse leads one to consider them as conventional superlatives, insofar as they are virtual equivalents. But are they more? We are already, for that matter, in the iconology of Pindar. And indeed, the aphorisms about who may be blest by the gods in a context of collective celebration is quite Pindaric. But we cannot measure the exact force of how deeply the solar cycle is dependent on the beauty of the girl, in the poet's eyes, and how to weigh his own image-making on the one hand, and on the other hand the religious power inherent in the festival being celebrated. Artemis is connected to the moon, not the sun, and yet typically the sun and the moon in post-neolithic systems are intimately connected. The horse, a later but by now traditional addition, has a connection to the system of which the sun is part—for example, in such distantly analogous but not irrelevant rites as the Indian horse-sacrifice (*ashvamedha*).

When, in this act of praising, the poet says he is prevented from either praising or blaming, since both praise and blame are taken for granted as usual functions for poetry,[4] he indulges in a turn that merges what later becomes preterition, litotes, and irony separately. Both praise and blame are present in this poem, since Alcman has begun by blaming those who, like the sons of Hippocoon, aspire too far. "Weaving the day" presents almost a system by itself, all the more in that these words, taken separately, are conventional.

The "under-wingèd dreams" linked to the horses launch the poem into an iconology that is not only Pindaric but even nascently Platonic. If the *Phaedrus* is a creative remanipulation of the Pegasus myth, then so may this strong image be.[5] And Alcman compares not his own poetry

but the chorus leader to the wingèd dream of a horse, keeping this high
level of combinatory perspectives intermittently open through what we
have of the poem:

> ταὶ Πεληάδες γὰρ ἇμιν
> ὀρθρίαι φᾶρος φεροίσαις
> νύκτα δ' ἀμβροσίαν ἅτε σήριον
> ἄστρον ἀυηρομέναι μάχονται
> οὔτε γάρ τι πορφύρας
> τόσσος κόρος ὥστ' ἀμύναι,
> οὔτε ποικίλος δράκων
> παγχρύσιος, οὐδὲ μίτρα
> Λυδία, νεανίδων
> ἰανογ[λ] εφάρων ἄγαλμα.

> These doves at dawn
> as we bear the robe,
> through ambrosial night like Sirius
> the star, rising up, contend.
> Nor is there of purple
> so much surfeit as to defend,
> nor a variegated serpent
> all gold, nor a Lydian
> mitre for young girls,
> of violet eyelids, ornament . . .
>
> (60–69)

The doves[6] may have an erotic tinge, all the more as girls are the focus
and Aphrodite is mentioned at the beginning of the poem. Also the sa-
tiety ("koros") may contain some erotic suggestion. Its basic metaphor
is gustatory. But it, too, seems to have been adapted, unusually for the
prior sense of the word, to offer overtones of Pindaric fulfillment. The
robe itself may well be ritual, as Calame suggests.[7] It has erotic overtones
as well, and it may possibly have cosmological implications. The serpent
certainly does; to mention the serpent and to dwell on it so emphati-
cally opens into a universe of mythological and cosmological implica-
tions, without the specificity of the elaborate deployment of the
Dioscuri, Heracles, and the sons of Hippocoon at the beginning of the
poem.[8]

Indeed, when Alcman says a mortal man cannot "seek to wed

Aphrodite" ([πη]ρήτω γαμῆν Ἀφροδίταν) (line 17), he offers still another manipulation of myth. The usual myths about mortals trying or even succeeding to marry gods (Ixion, Tithonus, Endymion) do not include Aphrodite in the repertory; her failed husband is another god, Hephaestus, and her erotic success is connected to Ares, to war, just as in this poem eros and war—like the later eros and strife of Empedocles—are in close association. To suggest that a battling man might be like one seeking to wed Aphrodite is at once boldly obvious—what more appropriate bride?—and highly original. Even if it cannot be settled exactly what "contend" and "defend" refer to here, they are coherent with the battle that opens the poem.[9]

The purple is royal, the all-gold variegated serpent is legendary, the Lydian mitre is lustrously precise in its anthropological reference to the time when it was worn (and when presumably girls would be in the chorus), the time between initiation and marriage.[10] The violet eyelids are a striking erotic synecdoche, and the ambrosial night offers a rich, if conventional context. Each of these images, taken by itself, is impressive. Their combination is dazzling for its implications of ranging attribution.

Fragment 89 (Page)—which is either a fragment or an entire poem—so clear if taken as a lyric poem, may open toward the cosmological and the mythic in ways we can only begin to conjecture:

εὕδουσι δ᾽ ὀρέων κορυφαί τε καὶ φάραγγες,
πρώονές τε καὶ χαράδραι.
φῦλά τ᾽ ἑρπέτ᾽ ὅσα τρέφει μέλαινα γαῖα
θῆρές τ᾽ ὀρεσκώιοι καὶ γένος μελισσᾶν
καὶ κνώδαλ᾽ ἐν βένθεσσι πορφυρέας ἁλός
εὕδουσι δ᾽ οἰωνῶν φῦλα τανυπτερύγων.

There sleep peaks and ravines of mountains,
headlands and gullies,
creeping tribes, all those black earth nourishes,
mountain beasts and the clan of bees,
and monsters in the depths of the purple sea.
There sleep the tribes of birds that stretch out their wings.

This poem retains its force even in the face of our radical inability to orient a reading of it that would locate it in a seventh-century Spartan context. The horizon fails to fuse, far more than with Homer or Hesiod. Nor can we even confidently locate its distances and proximities of semantic field. We could read it as an entire poem, but there is no evidence to its being other than a fragment. It was transmitted in the context of an entry under "knôdalon" ("sea monster") in the Homeric lexicon of Apollonius the Sophist, a figure who lived a good seven hundred years after Alcman. So Apollonius may not have known, and certainly does not transmit, the evidence by which we could approach it hermeneutically.

The possibly cosmological incorporation of the sea with Thetis into the framework of fragment 5 would license our reading this poem as including speculation about their connection. So it is not clear in the "sleep of nature" poem whether the enumeration of creatures of underground, mountain, sea, and lower and upper air is meant to be especially inclusive, the way Apollonius takes it, quoting the lines to locate the *knôdalon* firmly in the sea, whereas in Homer's single use the word had been more general. Is there a stretched significance to the verb "heudousi" ("they sleep"), repeated in the first and last lines, when it is applied first globally to rugged features of landscape and then to varieties of animals? Is there any significance to the exclusion of people and domestic animals or other land animals from the list?[11] We cannot even know they have been excluded, having no evidence that the lost text would not have continued to list them (assuming the lines to be a fragment).

Yet Martin Heidegger's approach to Johann von Goethe's adaptation of this poem, "Über allen Gipfeln ist Ruh," permits us to read Alcman's "sleep" intensively, the way he has read Goethe's "ist"—the word that Goethe used to translate "sleep," or at least to substitute for it.[12] And the act of speaking encoded into poetry legitimizes our finding an access to some feeling of nature that inheres in the words and rhythms but cannot be fully defined beyond our locating it with reference to various topoi, most of which come later and so are themselves not firmly inclusive of Alcman's lines. We need not connect the words to religion, to the rapture inherent in naming sleep, for the poem to express that rapture.

As we have it, the poem moves in assured and varied logaoedic rhythms, matching its first two words of the first line, εὕδουσι δ᾽ ὀρέων, to the first two words of the last, εὕδουσι δ᾽ οἰωνῶν. Before the poem moves into its enumeration of the fauna on the mountains, it offers a somewhat different description of the mountains themselves, the jagged terrain that particularly in Laconia was felt to be an especially appropriate site for temples.[13] The heavily formulaic diction of the poem here, at what for us is the outset, avails itself of the reduplicative formulas found especially in the parallelism of biblical and other religious poetry, though not especially in Greece. Is it significant here that Alcman's traditional birthplace is in the Near East, in Sardis?[14] To dwell on the beginning:

εὕδουσι δ' ὀρέων κορυφαί τε καὶ φάραγγες,
πρώονές τε καὶ χαράδραι.

There sleep peaks and ravines of mountains,
headlands and gullies.

Peaks match headlands, ravines match gullies. The *charadrai,* the gullies, imply torrents of water swirling or having swirled through them. The black earth and the purple sea are more generic in nomenclature, as though the poet were focusing on a long view as he gets into the poem, picking up the generic term "mountain" for the beasts of the fourth line, a generalizing of the particular features of mountains with which he had begun. To glory in these skilled variations through varied wisdom is surely to lay claim to the very act of naming that Apollonius records.

We cannot even know whether fragment 89 has the religious reference that Alcman's poems do sometimes have. And indeed, at this early date, there is the possibility in this poem, and elsewhere in Alcman, of the very philosophical reference that Heidegger makes much of in the pre-Socratics. But even Alcman's so-called cosmogonic fragment, fragment 5 (Page), only discovered in 1957, offers a puzzle for interpretation, though it is simply taken as cosmogonic by a late Aristotelian commentator, and with qualifications by G. S. Kirk and his associates.[15] Glenn Most, on the other hand, sees complications in a flatly cosmogonic reading.[16] He finally moves it to another category entirely, seeing it to be predominantly allegorical and from a book of *partheneia,* which, he claims, argues against its being exclusively cosmogonic, as does the absence of any testimony in this direction from antiquity. In many passages in scholia, Most shows, *physis* implies allegory. Peleus (metamorphosis) and Thetis (*tithemi,* "place") figure in the passage as foundational; they are easily assimilable to allegory. Yet Kirk and his coauthors exhibit the unwarranted assumption—which Heidegger would never have made, and surely not about pre-Socratic verses—that cosmogony and allegory are mutually exclusive, whereas Most shows a tradition of using allegory and myth for a "physiology" that he makes, however, too explicit for what we have of the poem.

So there may indeed be a concealed cosmogony incorporated into the poetry of this fragment. Here is the "fragment" itself, deeply embedded in commentary:

ὡς γὰρ ἤρξατο ἡ ὕλη κατασκευα[σθῆναι
ἐγένετο πόρος τις οἱονεὶ ἀρχή λ[έγει
οὖν ὁ Ἀλκμὰν τὴν ὕλην πάν [των τετα-
ραγμένην καὶ ἀπόητον εἶτα [γενέ-
σθαι τινά φησιν τὸν κατασκευά [ζονταω
πάντα εἶτα γενέσθαι [πό]ρον τοῦ [δὲ πό-
ρου παρελθόντος ἐπακολουθῆ[σαι] τέ-
κμωρ. και ἔστιν ὁ μεν πόρος οἷον ἀρχή, τὸ δὲ τέ-
κμωρ οἱονεί τέλος, τῆς Θέτιδος γενο-
μένης ἀρχὴ καὶ τέ[λ]ο[ς ταῦτ]α πάντων ἐ-
γένε[τ]ο, καὶ τὰ μὲν πάντα [ὁμο]ίαν ἔχει
τὴν φύσιν τῆι τοῦ χαλκοῦ ὕληι, ἡ δὲ
Θέτις τ[ῆι] τοῦ τεχνίτου, ὁ δε πόρος καὶ τὸ τέ-
κμωρ τῆι ἀρχῆι καὶ τῶι τέλει. πρέσγ[υς
δὲ ἀντὶ τοῦ πρεσβύτης. καὶ τρίτος σκότος.
διὰ τὸ μηδέπω μήτε ἥλιον μήτε σε-
λ]ήνην γεγονέναι ἀλλ' ἔτι ἀδιάκριτ[ο]ν εἶναι
τ]ην ὕλην. ἐγένετο οὖν ὑπο . . . . . πό-
ρος καὶ τέκμωρ και σκό[τος   ] [ἁμάρ
τε καὶ σελάνα καὶ τρίτον σκότος. τας
μαρμαρυγας . . . (7–27)

For when matter began to be arranged there was born a kind of way [poros] as it were a beginning. So Alcman says that the matter of all things was disturbed and unmade; then someone [masculine] came into being who was arranging everything, then a way [poros] came into being, and when the way [poros] had passed by, a limit [tekmor] followed. And the way [poros] is like a beginning, whereas the limit [tekmor] is like an end. When Thetis was born, these became beginning and end of all things, and all things have a similar nature to the matter of bronze, Thetis to that of the craftsman, and the way [poros] and the limit [tekmor] to that of the beginning and end. old for old age, and the third is darkness.[skotos] because sun and moon were not yet born and matter was undifferentiated, there came to be the way [poros] and limit [tekmor] and darkness [skotos] Day and moon and the third darkness. The flashing ones. (Kirk et al., somewhat revised and expanded)

We have here, of course, none of the graces of poetry but simply the
bare bones of the summary of what some kind of poem concerned itself
with. Page indicates by printing the words in heavy type, reasonably
because of the archaic and dialect forms in which they appear, that ἀμάρ
τε καὶ σελάνα καὶ τρίτον σκότος. τας μαρμαρυγας . . . ("sun and moon
and the third thing darkness, the flashing ones") may indeed be an exact
quotation from Alcman's verse, as may, because of the archaic, dialect
diction, πρέσγ[υς] δὲ ἀντὶ τοῦ πρεσβύτης ("old for old age"). And yet
even so, the breadth of the terms, leaving aside the quasi-Aristotelian
correlations of the summarizer centuries later, belong already to phi-
losophy, as Kirk and the others are claiming, as well as firmly to the re-
creative mythology; this writer is a colleague of Anaximander and
Empedocles, but also of Hesiod; and for a lyric poet, of course, the
domain of Sappho remains strong. Along the lines of Anaximander and
Empedocles, as M. L. West says, "From the lemmata and commentary it
is possible in part to reconstruct a Laconian cosmogony unlike any other
known."[17] Indeed, perhaps "reconstruct" is too strong a word, and the
very insistence and repetition of the late commentator (which I have
emphasized by indicating the recurrence of the words "poros," "tek-
mor," and "skotos") signal some difficulty at teasing out any firm doc-
trine here, even partially, let alone one that would harmonize with, or
even lead to, an Aristotelian cosmology. The connections made by the
commentator may be straining against something in the poem, as is indi-
cated by the sentence lining up all the constituents as having a "similar
nature" to the predicated interpretations, rather than the identification
of a direct assertion such as "All things have a similar nature to the mat-
ter of bronze, Thetis to that of the craftsman, and the way and the limit
to that of the beginning and end." Here all we have of Alcman's lan-
guage, so far as we know (there may be more of his actual verbiage in
the text, however), are these three terms—which are not easy, even if
they are allowed to be abstractions, to bring into coherence with each
other—and Thetis, plus perhaps the two other phrases cited and perhaps
the word "chalkou" ("bronze"), since that term is a usual one from the
"bronze heaven" of Homer on, and much rarer for cosmological usage
in Hellenistic times and later. "Poros" is quite unusual, especially this
early, in a metaphorical usage, which it must have here, indicating some-
thing like the course of a life or of existence in general. It shares an area
of reference with "day" in "weave the day" of fragment 1, a usage that is
Pindaric but also reminiscent in the use, analogous but probably not

related, of "yom" ("day") in biblical Hebrew, which can mean a single day, a year, or a large epoch. "Poros," interestingly—and perhaps relevantly for the other sense of the word, "passage," "expedient," "means"—usually refers in Homer to a passage over water, not land. Its sense, again almost uniquely in this passage, seems to relate to the same conception that the "way" ("hodos," fragment B 1) of Parmenides does. Nor can it be dissociated from the Indo-European use of "path" in Sanskrit, as with the "Brahman of a Hundred Paths," the *Shatapathabrahmana*.

Still, it takes a powerful process of ratiocination, which even the commentator's adduction of Aristotle cannot wholly cover, to relate "poros" to "tekmor" ("goal" or "end"). In a casual sense, it is easy to think of a path as leading to a goal, but much definition would still be needed to clarify the connection. "Tekmor" is an archaic word, occurring frequently in Homer without the special philosophical force that Alcman seems to have given it, or at least to be taken for having done so by the commentator. His expansion of the term is the more remarkable for being, so far as we can tell, unique to himself; the term appears not at all in the pre-Socratics, who are already, from Anaximander on, using the later, normative term "telos." It would be still more difficult to make both "poros" and "tekmor" connect to "skotos," a "darkness" that has connotations of confusion and gloom. "Skotos" here precedes the differentiation of day from night, a phenomenon that engaged Heraclitus (fragments B 57 and B 100). And Heraclitus, too, has a puzzling "way," a way up and a way down that are the same, which some commentators have associated with astronomical phenomena. Still, we cannot leap here, as a scholiast and others do, to associate Alcman's early "skotos" with a Hesiodic chaos. The real problem, more relevant than teasing out a doctrine where there is no evidence for it, would be to take the evidence we do have and link "skotos" to "poros" and "tekmor." Whatever their network of reference, it is certainly abstract, surely has cosmological implications, and carries the mark of great poetic-philosophical originality.

The systematization of mythology into a pre-Empedoclean order cannot be carried through wholly by converting "Thetis" to the etymology of her name, "establish"; she is distinctly a mythological personage, as "poros" and "tekmor" cannot be. Thetis is minimally a Nereid and the mother of Achilles and maximally a goddess of whom there is evidence of cult worship, though in that frame she is a sea goddess rather than a figure of the heavens—for which we would rather expect Artemis for Alcman's Sparta.[18] Here the commentator gives Thetis the function of a demiurge, an unusual notion, as Most points out. She is the central figure of the summary and may well have been the central figure of the poem—uniquely for all the analogues offered by Marcel Detienne and Jean-Pierre Vernant.[19] In the summary, Thetis shares the demiurge's stage with the "someone [masculine] who was arranging everything." The later, long tradition and poetic convention of her marriage to Peleus might further endorse an interpretation of this lost poem of Alcman's as at least envisaging the sort of marriage or premarriage rite that the *Partheneion* seems to have been.

Allegory tends to develop out of mythology, characteristically with the help of philosophy, which rationalizes mythology as it disentangles itself from mythology, a process that can already be detected in Homer. Just in the leap from the abstract "poros" and "tekmor" to the personified Thetis, these connections have gone much farther here. They would indeed allow us to read abstraction into the "recompense" ["tisis," also "punishment"] of the gods in fragment 1, quoted above, though it is connected to a point in a mythological transgression in Alcman's primary reference. Still, it could here be already on the way to the encompassing abstractness of the term in Anaximander, "a judgment [*dikē*] and recompense [*tisis*] according to the arrangement of time."[20]

In the domain of mythology, as in others, Alcman tends to offer versions that might well be his original reshaping, since they appear nowhere else. In fragment 21, as elsewhere, he is used by the Homeric scholiast as a source of information about myth. So in fragment 61 he is said to tell of "Thunderbolt" (Ἄκμων) as the beginning of the heavens. "I sing beginning from Zeus," says the female speaker of fragment 29, and even in this slight quotation can be seen both a convention—it is the chief of the gods who is mentioned—and an arresting turn, as Zeus is not usually connected to beginnings, of the world or of song. In fragment 67, the Muses are the daughters of Heaven and Earth, Ouranos and Ge, instead of Zeus and Mnemosyne. An intricate connection is made in fragment 64:

> Εὐνομίας [τε] καὶ Πειθῶς ἀδελφὰ
> καὶ Προμαθήας θυγάτηρ.

> Of Good rule and Persuasion the sister,
> of Forethought the daughter.

A fourth term is introduced here in Plutarch's account, and perhaps a fifth: Chance ("tuché"), aligned with Justice. The feminine Promethea appears nowhere else, which leaves us at once free and powerless to construct for her any affiliation to the more famous Prometheus. Persuasion is normally used in a context where one person is speaking to another, while here it would seem to include a speaking to oneself, becoming persuaded as a function of contributing through Forethought to Good Rule, an ideal much discussed later and finding in these lines one of its earliest expressions. Myth, allegory, and abstraction seem to combine such conjunctions, but they can neither be reduced to one another nor separated out. The very impossibility of making such distinctions testifies to Alcman's particular power. So Calame, noticing the unusualness of the combinations and the uniqueness of the feminine Promethea, indicates these potential elements, even though there is no evidence for separating them or giving them his particular values: "This fragment has no genealogical value, but the filiation is a means for Alcman to associate and to organize abstract concepts. This constellation of personifications is inserted very probably in a reflection of the political order." Calame goes on about the history of the term "eunomia," though with no real evidence for singling out abstraction from allegory and myth as the predominant element of Alcman's thinking here, let alone preeminently politics.[21]

And there is still another break into theological generality further along in the *Partheneion:*

> ἀλλὰ τᾶν . . . σιοὶ
> δέξασθε. [σι]ῶν γὰρ ἄνα
> καὶ τέλος.

> But their [praise] may the gods
> receive, for of the gods is accomplishment
> and an end.

The very power of all these connections testifies to the remarkable synthetic capacity of Alcman's poetic act, and it will serve to indicate the possibility of range in any statement of his that we do have. So the term "fate" ("aisa") in fragment 1, whether or not we couple it with "recompense," is puzzling in its application to the myth of Castor and Polydeuces; but it also testifies to a combinatory reach beyond Homer, though seemingly less tied to distinctness than such terms in Hesiod.

"Fate, the eldest of them all" (Αἶσα παντῶν γεραιτάτοι) (13–14) is here coupled, according to the scholiast, with Poros! Way and Fate, as the eldest of all—through the attribution "eldest" but also possibly through their conjunction—cannot be found in a reconstructible Homeric system. And again this happens in a context that has a myth intersect with the reaching beginnings of a system, while firmly in the celebratory ritual context of a *partheneion.*

In the magnetic field of Alcman's poetry, the possibly climactic "birds that stretch out their wings" at the end of fragment 89 cannot be divorced from the use of birds for augury and from other, perhaps ritual connections, as indicated by the appearance of bird heads on pots for more than a millennium before Alcman. Οἶδα δ' ὀρνίχων νόμως παντῶν ("I know the order of all birds"), says another fragment (Page, 40). "The Muse cries as a clear Siren" (ἁ Μῶσα κέκλαγ' ἁ λίγηα Σηρήν) (fragment 30), and a siren often has the attributes of a bird. The effect is far-reaching, but the meaning of Alcman's assertion (fragment 39) that he had composed in his poetry the voice of partridges is finally indecipherable.[22] The reference to the singing of the swan in fragment 1, 100–101, is a metaphor, but it is very possibly something more, an invocation of a myth and perhaps even, as is often the case with Alcman, a rethinking of one, too. So, too, for the doves who figure the maidens of the chorus earlier in this poem.

When, as legend has it, Alcman got too old (or was considered to be too old?) to participate in *partheneia,* he took recourse, seemingly rare for him, to the conventional hexameter, and to the myth of a bird, the halcyon, that nests on calm waters in spring, when for Alcman the spring of life was long behind him. Perhaps he also refers to the myth that the female halcyon carries the male, when he is weak, on her wings:

οὔ μ' ἔτι, παρσενικαὶ μελιγάρυες ἰαρόφωνοι,
γυῖα φέρην δύναται. βάλε δὴ βάλε κηρύλος εἴην,
ὅς τ' ἐπὶ κύματος ἄνθος ἅμ' ἀλκυόνεσσι ποτήται
νηδεὲς ἦτορ ἔχων ἁλιπόφορος ἱαρὸς ὄρνις.

No longer, sweet-singing holy-voiced maidens,
Can my limbs carry me. Might I, might I be as a fowl
Who flies on the flower of the wave like the halcyons,
With a stout heart, bird of sea-purple spring.

(fragment 26)

The ineluctable simplicity of this poem no doubt draws its power from irretrievable complexities.[23]

Alcman is also said to have commented widely on geography. That Hecatean or Herodotean interest is the exclusive concern of ten of his fragments (148–57). But, on the analogy of what we know of his practice, he is unlikely to have addressed geographical thinking without bringing it into connection with other questions. It is clear from fragment 1 that even within the context of what looks like a formal *partheneion,* he expands the Pindar-like praise and the Sappho-like communal celebration by a reformulation of mythic material, by a more than gnomic recourse to preallegorical systematization, and by the beginnings of abstract thinking. With this cue, we cannot dissociate (and so must associate) myth and allegory and abstraction in his sleep fragment; in the fragment about *poros, tekmor, skotos,* and Thetis; in the bird fragments; and elsewhere. In this extensibility, almost unique to his work, we can distinctly glimpse the range evoked by his esemplastic power of the imagination, to invoke a phrase of Coleridge's. Alcman revised and furthered Homer, but not as Archilochus did—by introducing blame along with praise—and not just by the intense lyric focusing of Sappho and Alcaeus. He reaches further, too, but not by a rethinking of theology on contestatory grounds like Xenophanes. If he is reckoned among the pre-Socratics, he carries along the capacity of poetic thinking, and he is able to meld what would have seemed inassociable areas or stages of statement. Perhaps, if we had more of his work, he could be seen clearly to have been working toward an equivalent of the depoeticization and universalization of Heraclitus, in a manner that preserved as well as transmuted much that had gone before.

Coda

Prophecies and Occlusions
Yeats, Rilke, Stevens, Montale, Char, Celan, Ashbery

POETRY, AT THE QUICK of its best expression, always preserves as well as transmits what has gone before, not just the rhetorical postures of tradition but the processes and acts of thinking that they serve and that underlie them. For modern poetry—or poetry since Baudelaire—the range of integrative gestures is very great, but at their best they do not entail contradictions of one poet by another, even when the choices may involve exclusions. So in the evolutions of expression in the immediate past, Valéry and Guillaume Apollinaire need not be set at odds, or Rilke and Trakl, or Montale and Giovanni Pascoli, or Eliot and Williams.

Williams stresses ordinary language and common subjects, the conversational, in most of his poetry. Yet the pitch of some of his work rises to the prophetic and lets an influx of the oracular into the poet's voice. *Paterson* probes the origins of modern American society and draws some oracular conclusions about the disastrous effect on it of technology. In this it shares some subject matter with a more oracular poem: its seeming antithesis, *The Waste Land*. The conversational and the oracular can be set in polar opposition insofar as the conversational envisages a speaker who is addressing one or a few intimate equals, or else it sets up the model of doing so in a poem or speech; while the oracular envisages a speaker who is set up as though on a platform to address a large group that is asked to turn its attention in some way to ultimates. Still, the conversational and the oracular stand not just as poles for poetry but as constituents that can be present in various mixes. Archilochus is more conversational than Pindar, but he has a touch of the oracular in the fragments that have a public subject; the oracular Pindar, as I have tried to show, has in fact some admixture of the conversational in his utterance.

In one of its modes, modern poetry does emphasize the conversational as an ideal and hold itself to a conversational tone, as in most of Williams, and still more in poets such as George Oppen and James Schuyler. The shift from the high-flown Dylan Thomas to the "flat" voice of the "Movement" poets in Britain was a shift, of course, from the oracular to the conversational. Perse stays close to the oracular end of the spectrum, Éluard to the conversational. Yet modern poetry, with an intensity that tends to fuse the conversational and the oracular, spectacularly performs its prophecies through occlusions that it rings changes on, including occlusions of its own mode of utterance. These occlusions in no sense indicate a blindness in the utterance. They harness the indirectness and the difficult comprehensiveness of what they are trying to say by submitting to that indirectness and by compressions, allusions, and sometimes a metalinguistic reference to themselves and to the occlusions necessary to carry off the comprehensions and urgencies of what they have to say. All this, too, comes through under the aegis of the rhetorical principle that such utterances can show signs of their being "dark sayings." Such poems tend to be implicitly deconstructive and strenuously integrative at the same time.

Yeats

YEATS, to begin with, has a notably strong oracular admixture in his utterance, in which he exhibits and deploys occlusions:

The Gyres

The gyres! the gyres! Old Rocky Face, look forth;
Things thought too long can be no longer thought,
For beauty dies of beauty, worth of worth,
And ancient lineaments are blotted out.

Irrational streams of blood are staining earth;
Empedocles has thrown all things about;
Hector is dead and there's a light in Troy;
We that look on but laugh in tragic joy.

What matter though numb nightmare ride on top,
And blood and mire the sensitive body stain?
What matter? Heave no sigh, let no tear drop,
A greater, a more gracious time has gone;
For painted forms or boxes of make-up
In ancient tombs I sighed, but not again;
What matter? Out of cavern comes a voice,
And all it knows is that one word "Rejoice!"

Conduct and work grow coarse, and coarse the soul,
What matter? Those that Rocky Face holds dear,
Lovers of horses and of women, shall,
From marble of a broken sepulchre,
Or dark betwixt the polecat and the owl,
Or any rich, dark nothing disinter
The workman, noble and saint, and all things run
On that unfashionable gyre again.[1]

The gyres are the fourfold interlocking cones that form a grid for Yeats's system of successive dominances in psychic and in millennial history, as these are laid over the phases of the moon. So much we can easily learn from *A Vision*.[2] His system is not so much a religious system; it has no creed, no body of worshippers, and no sacrament but the séance, toward which Yeats's posture is both detached and attached.[3] Rather, it is a technique of spiritual access, of *vision*ing, and the poems related to it are products of processing the mediumistic messages that he and his wife took down. The evolution of his final versions of poems realized through mediumship, it should be noted, involved the same process of considerable revision that the careful Yeats habitually gave his poems. It can be learned from the discussion at the very beginning of *A Vision*, furthermore, that not just his mysterious source stands behind the system but also, as a millennial speculator, the philosopher Empedocles, who evinced a principle of interaction for order (or love) and disorder (or strife), a principle that itself offers a supervening order for the phases of the moon and for all events whatsoever, natural or human.

Why, then, has "Empedocles . . . thrown all things about"? The tone of praise in this poem assimilates this statement to celebration, but it is not easy to reconcile what is being celebrated with system, that of Empedocles or another. System does not throw all things about. It is as though Yeats is simultaneously using his system and waking up from it, turning this late poem into a prophetic transcendence over subprophecy. That, too, is what can be made of the repeated exclamation with which the poem opens, "The gyres! the gyres!" What of them? Are they being deplored, finally being submitted to, addressed in an incapacitated awe, or being transcended? Something of all these can be felt at work here, and no one of these responses can be excluded. They fuse in the gap between the exclamation and the immediately ensuing command, "Old Rocky Face, look forth." Here the prophecy and the occlusion come into utterance inseparably together. "Old Rocky Face" is certainly obscure, but it can be taken as the moon, especially if the "dark" mentioned in the third line from the end means that the poem is aligned with the first phase of the moon, a total dark that is "complete objectivity," according to *A Vision*. In that case, "look forth" would mean "enter one of your phases out of this absolute dark," a command that need not be given because within the system, the moon is bound to do just that.

But we are not wholly within the system, and the events that the poem names will not produce or match specific phases of the moon. The Trojan War is a kind of permanent presence in the poem, itself not just subjected to the phases: "Hector is dead and there's a light in Troy." Hector is not mentioned in *A Vision,* and his role in the Trojan War is not assessed even in chapter 5, which connects the Trojan War and the rest of Greek history in a millennial view leading up to Rome. Hector's death, to be sure, is included at another angle in the transition from the eleventh phase to the twelfth, as summarized in the poem "The Phases of the Moon": "Eleven pass, and then / Athene takes Achilles by the hair, / Hector is in the dust, Nietzsche is born." This summary is clearly atemporal, but there is no mention of the Trojan War at all in the sections of *A Vision* dealing with the eleventh and twelfth phases of the moon—though indeed Nietzsche does figure prominently in the section on the twelfth phase. Hector's death and the light in Troy are not simultaneous events, because Hector dies before Troy goes up in flames—or is that what the light signifies here? Speaking just of light is an odd way to mention fire, but this poem is an act of a praise riding roughshod over every tragic event, and so perhaps the light would include that legendary fire. It cannot refer specifically and exclusively to that fire, however, and to make it do so is to take away the apocalyptic, nearly gnomic tone of the line "Hector is dead and there's a light in Troy." "Irrational streams of blood are staining earth" includes Hector's death, and the whole Trojan War, and any other war, of which the Trojan War is emblematic. But it cannot take on the prophetic function of Zeus's union with Leda, which culminates in "the broken wall, the burning roof and tower" at the end of the sonnet Yeats sets in *A Vision*, "Leda."

"Things thought too long can be no longer thought" is a psychological rule, itself a gnomic and apocalyptic statement, one that can be applied to Hector and to Troy. They have been thought too long and can be no longer thought; but they can be named, included in oracular utterance, deplored and praised in one gnomic stroke. As for beauty, that is the attribute of the fifteenth phase, not the first. The fifteenth phase has "no description except Complete beauty."[4] Yet here, "beauty dies of beauty, worth of worth, / And ancient lineaments are blotted out." This would seem to admit of moving through the phases of the moon, but again not to be confined to them. "Beauty dies of beauty" could be taken, after all, as a kind of characterization just of the fifteenth phase. "Worth" could be assigned to any of the intensely personal famous figures whom *A Vision* names in various phases. "Worth [dies] of worth" could be taken as a result of the principles of the phases—or as an overriding Ecclesiastes-like wisdom not confined to the phases of the moon. Both "worth" and the "ancient lineaments" would seem to connect most closely with the "noble" in the penultimate line. But again, there is no phase of the moon to which "noble" applies exactly, and still less one for "workman." The only connection to Yeats's system here is the "saint" of the twenty-seventh phase, but too close an attention to the system will obscure the typology of ultimate social roles offered in this line, through its keynote of gnomic and apocalyptic summary: "The workman, noble and saint, and all things run / On that unfashionable gyre again." The gyre is now singular, not plural. And it is "unfashionable," an odd characterization that cannot comprise these roles; they are too permanent to be unfashionable—or at least, if "that . . . gyre" be taken as the vortex governing the kind of society Yeats admired, now vanishing, where a sort of feudal order obtained of "workman, noble and saint." Again, such a society corresponds to none of his twenty-eight phases of the moon.

The poem aspires to a domain of perception beyond the beauty, thought, and worth that one might have considered the poet's governing values. It praises, or cannot be taken not to praise, a condition in which "We that look on but laugh in tragic joy," in which the laugh and the joy submerge the tragedy, as in the ensuing poem, "Lapis Lazuli," where "Hamlet and Lear are gay; / Gaiety transfiguring all that dread." Here we are not given Shakespeare's Hamlet or Lear in any sense but some fierce state beyond them where all that can be signified by their collective presence in the plays has been subjected to a process rhythmically evoked in the roughshod metrical role of Yeats's word "transfiguring," an occlusion enforcing a revelation. This is the tragic joy of "The Gyres," declaring an indifference "though numb nightmare ride on top / And blood and mire the sensitive body stain," an echo and wrenching specification of "Irrational streams of blood are staining earth." This line, cumulative of the three that precede it, sounds at first as though the condition is being deplored, as in "The Second Coming": "twenty centuries of stony sleep / Were vexed to nightmare by a rocking cradle." But this nightmare, "numb" though it be, is celebrated in its very devastations, which include an erasure and forgetting of the "painted forms or boxes of make-up / In ancient tombs," over which the speaker enjoins himself to "heave no sigh." Here too, is a gaiety that transfigures dread, and the speaker listens to a single summarizing emotional injunction: "Out of cavern comes a voice, / And all it knows is that one word 'Rejoice!'"

"The Second Coming" has more direct access to a prophetic voice, in keeping with the biblical, apocalyptic theme it employs and transmutes. In a more pronounced occlusion, "The Gyres," while remaining oracular, stays closer to the folk-gnomic, which is akin to the conversational in its recourse to proverb and what amounts to reminiscence. Its minimal rhetoric evokes the tone and burden of an old man deploring the good old days of yore and finding only a tragic joy with which to face them. Upon the ribs of the rhetoric are built the typologies of "workman, noble and saint" and of the Trojan War, which are subsumed into the quasi-cyclic, quasi-apocalyptic macrohistorical sequences of the phases of the moon, skewed from their presentation in *A Vision,* which at the same time stands over them to guarantee the prophetic clarity that their very occlusions guarantee.

In this poem, Yeats uses his system the way he derived it, as a heuristic principle. He does not conform to it; nor does he handle it consistently. The status of the system remains shadowy; it is not a mere instrument, it is not an eschatology, and it is not a macrohistorical interpretation of history. Rather, it is something of all three. Yet at the same time it stands only as a horizon to this poem, and to its own very shapings of language, which cannot be excluded from "work." "Conduct and work grow coarse, and coarse the soul, / What matter?" The final comma instead of a period elides the human activity the more forcefully for a reach into "dark" and "rich, dark nothing," into a coarseness that blends the activity and the soul into itself. The typology "workman, noble and saint" does not stand in the fixity of summary, because the emphasis on "work" in the first line of the last stanza is so inclusive that it broadens "workman" beyond the usual implications of manual labor. Harmonized with "work," the workman becomes one of any kind devoted to any kind of task—as distinct, perhaps, from the "noble" and the "saint," whose exemption from "work" in the mere listing would betoken a higher existence, rather like the situation in Yeats's poem on the death of Major Robert Gregory, whom Yeats saw as a nobleman and something like a saint in his disregard for the "work" side of a wartime airman's devotion to his cause: "Those that I fight I do not hate, / Those that I guard I do not love." In this poem, "An Irish Airman Foresees His Death," the speaker is imagined to speak out of a state that is finally that of the saint, though it would include a transmutation of the nobleman:

> A lonely impulse of delight
> Drove to this tumult in the clouds;
> I balanced all, brought all to mind,
> The years to come seemed waste of breath,
> A waste of breath the years behind
> In balance with this life, this death.

This state resembles that praised in "The Gyres," except that the later poem accommodates the coarseness and the roughness of "dark betwixt the polecat and the owl," letting the emblematic function of the two animals blur from sexuality and wisdom to the simple shift of light from day to night at the dark of the moon. The polecat traditionally indicates rank sexuality, and that signification would turn the tables on the "Lovers of horses and of women," who are "Those that Rocky Face holds dear." The very opposition between these lovers, presumably noble, and the polecat—as well as the lumping together of horses and women, which itself evidences a kind of coarseness—puts these assertions beyond the praise of rough physical sexuality to be found in these late poems. In all its assertions, "The Gyres" carries off a range of final states, fusing them into an overriding mood.

Rilke

Sixth Duino Elegy

Feigenbaum, seit wie lange schon ists mir bedeutend,
wie du die Blüte beinah ganz überschlägst
und hinein in die zeitig entschlossene Frucht,
ungerühmt, drängst dein reines Geheimnis.
Wie der Fontäne Rohr treibt dein gebognes Gezweig
abwärts den Saft und hinan: und er springt aus dem Schlaf,
fast nicht erwachend, ins Glück seiner süssesten Leistung.
Sieh: wie der Gott in den Schwan . . .

                    Wir aber verweilen,
ach, uns rühmt es zu blühn, und ins verspätete Innre
unserer endlichen Frucht gehn wir verraten hinein.
Wenigen steigt so stark der Andrang des Handelns,
dass sie schon anstehn und glühn in der Fülle des Herzens,
wenn die Verführung zum Blühn wie gelinderte Nachtluft
ihnen die Jugend des Munds, ihnen die Lider berührt:
Helden vielleicht und den frühe Hinüberbestimmten,
denen der gärtnernde Tod anders die Adern verbiegt.
Diese stürzen dahin: dem eigenen Lächeln
sind sie voran, wie das Rossegespann in den milden
muldigen Bildern von Karnak dem siegenden König.

Wunderlich nah ist der Held doch den jugendlich Toten. Dauern
ficht ihn nicht an. Sein Aufgang ist Dasein; beständig
nimmt er sich fort und tritt ins veränderte Sternbild
seiner steten Gefahr. Dort fanden ihn wenige. Aber,
das uns finster verschweigt, das plötzlich begeisterte
     Schicksal
singt ihn hinein in den Sturm seiner aufrauschenden Welt.
Hör ich doch keinen wie *ihn*. Auf einmal durchgeht mich
mit der strömenden Luft sein verdunkelter Ton.

Dann, wie verbärg ich mich gern vor der Sehnsucht:
    O wär ich,
wär ich ein Knabe und dürft es noch werden und sässe
in die künftigen Arme gestützt und läse von Simson,
wie seine Mutter erst nichts und dann alles gebar.

War er nicht Held schon in dir, o Mutter, begann nicht
dort schon, in dir, seine herrische Auswahl?
Tausende brauten im Schooss und wollten *er* sein,
aber sieh: er ergriff und liess aus—, wählte und konnte.
Und wenn er Säulen zerstiess, so wars, da er ausbrach
aus der Welt deines Leibs in die engere Welt, wo er weiter
wählte und konnte. O Mütter der Helden, o Ursprung
reissender Ströme! Ihr Schluchten, in die sich
hoch von dem Herzrand, klagend,
schon die Mädchen gestürzt, künftig die Opfer dem Sohn.
Denn hinstürmte der Held durch Aufenthalte der Liebe,
jeder hob ihn hinaus, jeder ihn meinende Herzschlag,
abgewendet schon, stand er am Ende der Lächeln,—anders.[5]

Fig tree, how long now has it been meaningful to me
the way you almost wholly throw over your blossoms
and on into the fruit that the time has resolved
unpraised, you force your pure secret.
Like the fountain's pipe your bent branchwork drives
the sap upwards and on up; and it leaps out of sleep
almost not waking, into the bliss of its sweetest achievement.
Look, like the god in the swan . . .

                                 We, however, linger,
ah, we're extolled to bloom, and into the belated core
of our final fruit we go on betrayed.
In few does the pressure of action rise so strongly
that they already stand up and glow in fullness of heart
when the temptation to bloom like softened night air
touches the youth of their mouth, touches their eyelids:
Heroes, perhaps, and those called early beyond,
for whom the gardener Death has otherwise bent their veins.
These plunge on, and they are ahead

of their own smile, like the horse team in the mild
molded images at Karnak, of the conquering king.

Marvelously close is the hero to the youthful dead. Lasting
doesn't engage him. His rising is Being. Constantly
he takes himself off and strides into the altered constellation
of his steady danger. Few found him there. However,
what silences us darkly, suddenly enraptured fate
sings him into the storm of its uproaring world.
Yes, I hear none like *him*. At once there goes through me
in the streaming air his darkened tone.

Then, how I'd like to hide myself from the longing; would that I
were a boy and it need only come, and I sat
propped on my future arms and read about Samson,
how his mother first bore nothing and then everything.

Was he not already in you a hero, mother, did there already
not begin in you his mastering choice?
Thousands teemed in the womb and wanted to be *he,*
but look, he seized and passed over—chose and could.
And when he shattered columns, it was so, when he broke out
of your belly's world into the narrower world where he further
chose and could. O mothers of heroes, O source
of raging streams! You gorges, into which
high off of the heart-rim, wailing,
already maidens plunged, in future sacrifices to the son.
For when the hero stormed through the sojourns of love
each heartbeat that meant him, each one raised him on,
turned away already, he stood at the end of smiles, other.

There is a prophetic element in Rilke, emphasized by Heidegger, who speaks of his functioning, the way the prophets did, in a "needy time" ("in dürftiger Zeit").[6] The poetry does not sound needy, but it performs its formulations at the edge of need. In its tone, the voice here echoes its questioning affirmations out of a solitude, reaching forward to a self-definition that implies a need. For all that, these "elegies" have a consolatory and a socializing power. They move forward under the aegis of a rumination that, while conversational, grazes the oracular and apocalyptic, touching base often on the depths of association of hexameter or elegiac distich or pentameter, in the meditative mode that is part of the expectation raised by the key of all three meters.

The fig tree of the Sixth Elegy belongs in the ideal Mediterranean landscape and brings with it associations of warmth, harmony in nature, and simple pleasures—none of which are more than an overtone here. This fig tree is a counterpart to the apple trees of Rilke's poem about an apple orchard, "Der Apfelgarten," in which the sense of the apple trees, bearing the fruit patiently through its stages, is made concordant with a human life that wills one thing. The apple trees were in a northern landscape, Borgeby, Sweden. Here the speaker steps out of such locked interpretations, as though needing something more, turning the fig tree round and round, and before long leaving it behind in the train of other associations it has called up. He addresses it at once for a significance that has been lingering in silence: "how long now has it been meaningful to me." That meaning, that *Bedeutung,* is now come up to but not addressed directly.

What is meaningful about the fig tree is that it skips a step in the natural cycle from blossom to fruit: it almost doesn't blossom, and then "without praise" ("ungerühmt") it "forces [its] pure secret." A pure secret is one that is enclosed away from language, the language of significances or the language of praise. But the poet, who uses language, here denigrates it in the act of bringing it to this high expression. And this act of denigration is really an act of modesty, of self-confessed need, of attending to the significance of the fig tree so that it can be brought to whatever expression is possible after all. Faced with this significance, and by contrast with the fig tree, "We, however, linger" ("Wir aber verweilen"). Humankind glories in the blossoms; instead of ripening in a deeper silence, "we're extolled to bloom" ("uns rühmt es zu blühn").

Praise is one of the oldest, if not the oldest, functions of poetry, the praise of the hero—and the hero will be praised in this elegy before very long. But praise is at the same time a pure act of poetry, as is asserted in the seventh of the first group of *Sonnets to Orpheus:* "Rühmen, das ists!" ("Praising, that's it!"), the poem opens, on an answer so firm and summary (of the preceding sonnets, among other things) that it need not explore the statement but instead goes on to specific acts of praise characterizing the emblematic Orpheus at its center.

The fig tree figures in the Old Testament as an instance of fertility in nature. That role carries over into the New Testament, except that Christ twice makes it problematical. In one parable (Luke 13.6–9), he declares that the fig tree bearing no fruit should be cut down. In another action, he curses a fig tree that has not borne fruit, and it withers (Matthew 21.22; Mark 11.20–25). All these perspectives apply to Rilke's fig tree, which is an instance of fertility that becomes problematical under inspection but then is properly understood and set into a metaphorical measure against humanity—who are at first envisaged as somehow marred, like the cursed fig tree of the second New Testament example.

For Rilke's fig tree, "Like the fountain's pipe [its] bent branchwork drives / the sap upwards and on up." "It leaps out of sleep," an action that forces the hand of mystery, since sleep can be understood only as a human activity; what would the wakefulness of a fig tree be? Presumably its bearing fruit, since it is "almost not waking" ("fast nicht erwachend"). This achievement ("Leistung"), simple and subhuman, is seen as super-human: "Sieh: wie der Gott in den Schwan" ("Look, like the god in the swan"). And with this, another set of complex figures has been grazed, along with the much sublated modification of what Zeus and Leda can mean for human beings, who are all the time carrying on the discourse about them. If nothing else, they are figures in discourse who enlist all the allegorical force of their virtual functions for the very reason that they cannot be accorded actual credence.

Fig tree : fructification :: Zeus : insemination. This proportion adver-tises its occlusions, its elisions and condensations. It only begins to serve as a hinge for the many identifications here to note that "the swan" is, as the poem states, a god disguised in a metamorphosis that has itself undergone many mutations of virtuality since Ovid's already modified presentation of it. But in Rilke's language, it comes through as a simple, almost random, associative point, part of the "praise" of the fig tree, which it itself has not yet engaged in ("ungerühmt"). Our "lingering" presumably involves our not having access to these intensities (except in the language that accounts for them and so, as it were, effectuates a self-transcendence). Our deprivation is built into the immediately following "however," the "aber" of "Wir aber verweilen." And the fig tree ex-ample is only one instance of humanity's comparative incapacity in nature. Humans are contrasted to animals as well in the Eighth Elegy:

> Mit allen Augen sieht die Kreatur
> das Offene. Nur unsre Augen sind
> wie umgekehrt und ganz um sie gestellt
> als Fallen.

With all eyes does the creature see
The open. Only our eyes are
as though turned round and set all about them
like traps.

But the feeble human is only a kind of natural ground; set as an ener-
getic possibility is the seemingly more than human one of the hero, on
whose being the Sixth Elegy proceeds to dwell. This elegy now speaks
of the hero in the third person, of humanity in the first-person plural.
It stretches its utterance toward the heroic, away from a sort of declared
dejection and failure. The fig tree, the hero, the plural "we" included in
the speaking voice—these are entities whose distinctions from each
other remain sharply perceived and plumbed in the definitions; and yet
at the same time, the conception of the utterance, its ruminative direc-
tion, moves toward a comprehensive embrace of all these modes of
being, since it is able to include them in its act of saying. The unnamed
but enacted consciousness of the poet reaches into their essence, and its
acts of summary subsume him, so energetically that by line 27 the
speaker has moved out of "we" into "I": "Hör ich doch keinen wie *ihn*.
Auf einmal durchgeht mich / mit der strömenden Luft sein verdunkel-
ter Ton" ("I hear none like *him*. At once there goes through me / in the
streaming air his darkened tone"). We had not known the air was stream-
ing, or that the hero could be a penetrating music. These features must
be taken as a function of the poetry and as a characterization of it, what
a language can do that may express the fig tree and hero and human
incapacity as it moves along.

In such a universe, the hero can, through apperception, resemble the
early dead because "Lasting / doesn't engage him" ("Dauern / ficht ihn
nicht an"). Instead, he is involved in existence ("Dasein"), "the altered
constellation / of his steady danger" ("[das] veränderte Sternbild /
seiner steten Gefahr"). The condition involves both the hero and the early
dead. The latter are described with terms so much consonant with the
traditional image of the hero that it would seem to be the hero who is
being described, not the early dead; they are like the horse team in the
mild images for the victorious king at Karnak. The Egyptian kings were
not mild, even if the reliefs celebrating their victories can be taken so;
but the focus of the comparison is not teams and kings but the smile.
They precede their own smile, the youthful dead! This preternatural
perception, as the reader tries to make sense of it, would seem to
suggest that the youthful dead, in being fated to die, have a fate that

precedes individual instances of ordinary human pleasure. The fate supersedes the smile. But that is not exactly what it says: the expression only has them ahead of their smile, and what precedes the smile could be another smile, the comprehensiveness of sorrow and joy in a montage sequence not wholly out of tune with the montage of mildness in bas reliefs and their severe subject.

The speaker, as the darkened tone of the hero's existence rushes through him, experiences not the wistful and implicitly retrospective sense of inadequacy triggered by the contemplation of the fig tree but rather a longing ("Sehnsucht"). This longing looks to a future-in-the-past, a boy reading about Samson's birth, which can be seen to resemble the fig tree; just as it breaks into glorious fruit after scarcely having blossomed, so Samson's mother "first bore nothing and then everything" ("erst nichts und dann alles gebar"). The direct address to the mother proprioceptively participates in the teeming conception of Samson, and his birth carries certain resemblances to his heroic death while pulling down the pillars of the temple. This thought moves to ejaculations about mothers of heroes and about "source / of raging streams" ("o Ursprung / reissender Ströme!"). Above, the air was "streaming"; now the adjective has become a noun. And in both instances, the metaphor hovers. We cannot either engage or disengage the streaming air from the thought and words of the poet, which they may stand for. Nor can we get closure for "source," which applies either to the mothers or to the sublime natural world that the poem begins by contemplating. The literal reading would work more actively if we carried "Ursprung" forward into "Ihr Schluchten" ("You gorges"). And then, in a curious reminiscence of a sacrifice that has nothing to do with Samson but rather comes from primitive echoes of Aztec and other cultures, maidens are sacrificed to the son, who is a hero. But they are sacrificed not from a natural precipice but from a "heart-rim" ("Herzrand").

What is happening all along in the poem is what Rilke characterizes as "Herzwerk" ("heart-work"), as distinct from the profound closures and exact significative structures of the "sight-work" ("Sicht-werk") of poems like the *Neue Gedichte*. And as he moves past this cue of the ineluctable psychic-spiritual bearing of this and other elegies, he concludes by attributing to the hero what he had earlier attributed to the young dead. The hero's heartbeats are significant, every one; and what they signify is himself: "each heartbeat that meant him" ("jeder ihn meinende Herzschlag"). Through and past them, as he turned away, "he stood at the end of smiles, other" ("stand er am Ende der Lächeln,— anders"). The "other," though, is not just a terminus that suspends "the end of smiles" between two alternative senses, to mean either "the last of smiles" or else the entrance into a state where smiling is no longer relevant. Instead, this last word moves us to something else, the "wooing no more" that begins the Seventh Elegy. And "wooing" could be taken as a characterization of the whole Sixth Elegy, forging into unknown terrain in order to woo out of it a sense of what it means to be precisely there, ahead of its own smile.

The first line of the Sixth Elegy picks up the note of questioning in the Fifth Elegy, which builds an ekphrasis on Picasso's *Les saltimbanques* from a ruminative self-query, heightened in its first line by the italics of the third word as well as by the truncated transition of the second: "Wer aber *sind* sie, sag mir, die Fahrenden, diese ein wenig . . ." ("Who though *are* they, tell me, the travelers, these a little . . ."). The travelers, it turns out, are actually going nowhere: they are on canvas. But the interlocutor who is to "tell me," who is none other than the ruminative speaker speaking to himself in the fiction of addressing another, will go on to provide a depth interpretation of this family of acrobats as they engage deeply in the phenomenology of a spiritual identification through a visual presentation of their performance. They roll up the rug and move on after the performance, but the poet does not carry us that far. He leaves them on the rug, which is given the last word of the poem, isolated in the single word "Teppich."

Being given a line to itself makes the word "Teppich" iconic, a gnomic and incantatory term, like the destiny envisaged in the Ninth Elegy: "Sind wir vielleicht *hier,* um zu sagen: Haus, / Brücke, Brunnen, Tor, Krug, Obstbaum, Fenster,— / höchstens Säule, Turm . . . aber zu *sagen* verstehs" ("We are perhaps *here* in order to say: house / bridge, well, gate, jug, fruit tree, window,— / at most pillar, tower . . . but to *say,* understand that"). The actualization of language into bare nominalization is at once a high point and a stripping away, and we could take it in one direction with Heidegger's lodging the deepest human significance in the history-laden individual words enlisted by the poet, and in another direction with Ludwig Wittgenstein's language games. Yet it does not imply more of a doctrine than the bare act and so cannot fully be attuned to Heidegger. And it is too earnest, too mysterious, too apocalyptic, to be contained in the counters of a Wittgensteinian language game, which it seems to offer at the same time. (Yet this is not, *pace* de Man, anything like a self-contradiction.)[7] The nominalizations, moving forward, can be used for a summary, as in the Tenth Elegy: "Nicht nur / Zeit—, sind Stelle, Siedelung, Lager, Boden, Wohnort" ("not only / season-time—, they are place, settlement, camp, ground, dwelling-place").

In this sense, as it finally surfaces, the single word "Teppich," isolated in its single short line at the conclusion of the Fifth Elegy, is such a nominalization. And in sequence, the "Feigenbaum," which abruptly begins the Sixth, is also such an urgent nominalization, opening without an article in the vocative and shifting into a long line that leaves behind the monometer of "Teppich." That long line, in the context of the *Elegies,* can be read as a hexameter, except that taken by itself it consists too preponderantly of long syllables to be heard as simply dactylic. The opening of the Fifth Elegy, by contrast, quoted above, is triumphantly dactylic, but it is too long for a dactylic hexameter; it has an extra foot. And yet it is no tripping measure, being interrupted rhythmically in its ruminations too often to be taken that way. Finally, the Seventh Elegy begins with an out-and-out dactylic hexameter (and the meter continues in that elegy): "Werbung nicht mehr, nicht Werbung, entwachsene Stimme" ("Wooing no more, not wooing, voice that's outgrown it"). The "outgrowing," the no-more-wooing, has picked up and glossed the "anders" ("other"), the last word of the Sixth Elegy. And the dactylic hexameter picks up that meter from the last line of the Sixth Elegy. Rhythmically, though, that last line is unusually placed because the last lines of the Sixth Elegy had randomly been moving into elegiac couplets. An elegiac couplet requires that the first line must be a hexameter, the second, concluding line a pentameter. The hexameter that ends the Sixth Elegy should thus be followed by a pentameter—except that the lack of regularity undercuts this expectation and only makes the echo a disappointed one. This disappointment is curtailed and overcome by the strong hexameter that follows at the beginning of the Seventh Elegy: "Werbung nicht mehr, nicht Werbung, entwachsene Stimme."

We hear of "the god," but not of Zeus. So generalized, "the god" is a force as well as a presence, even at the removal of a simile, "the god." Rilke's many references to a divine presence are modulated by suggestiveness, as in the gnomic poem "Herr, es ist Zeit. Der Sommer war sehr gross" ("Lord, it is time. Summer was very great"). In the Sixth Elegy, the simile also acts as a sort of deictic; to say "like the god" implies a form of existence, though the form is only called into being by the poem, without even any of the theory that might be provided by Pico della Mirandola or Carl Gustav Jung. And minimally it is a sexual force, the comparison comprising a physical analogy to semen. Elsewhere in the *Elegies,* there are references not only to "angels" but to "orders of angels," and they are not used as similes. They are put into a question, as though their existence is possible. But intense discussions of the theological modality of these angels, by Romano Guardini and others, have not settled their coordinates, nor can they. They are merely named. The poetry purifies itself by not allowing the theological any exact definitions. The theological is the open end of this poetry, the occlusion enabling its prophecy.

It is with the question about angels that Rilke has chosen to begin the *Elegies,* after a prolonged series of revising manipulations regular for other poets but not for him: "Wer, wenn ich schriee, hörte mich aus der Engel / Ordnungen?" ("Who, if I cried, would hear me out of the angels' / orders?"). He assumes at once that they exist and that if one were to embrace him he would suddenly vanish: "und gesetzt selbst, es nähme / einer mich plötzlich ans Herz: ich verginge von seinem / stärk-eren Dasein" ("and even assuming one took / me suddenly to his heart, I would vanish from his / stronger existence"). To speak of the angel is to press human limits; to join with one would annihilate the speaker, who talks much of "Dasein," and for whom the "existence/being" of the angel is simply "stronger." There remains what follows instantly, the contemplation of beauty, which the poem enacts, exemplifies, and discusses all at once; poetry is not just a ground of theory but a ground of coming to terms with one's own existence, not through words but through beauty, for it is an act not of utterance but of contemplation that is involved here: "Denn das Schöne ist nichts / als des Schrecklichen Anfang" ("For the beautiful is nothing / but the beginning of terror"). If it "serenely disdains / to destroy us" ("es gelassen verschmäht / uns zu zerstören"), as the poem goes on, then it is at its peak like the angel, if not the angel itself. It stands at the limit of human power, and the utterance builds in an awareness of a transcendence of something beyond the poetic expression brought to the verge of it.

The poetry reaches to a point not of union with theology but of a theologizing that would make such a complete union impossible. The power of the rumination here is recapitulative, self-assertive, enlightening, and not bothered by its elisions. It stands, by falling, as the lucky stroke referred to in the last lines of the Tenth Elegy: "Und wir, die an

THE REACH OF POETRY

steigendes Glück / denken, empfänden die Rührung, / die uns beinah bestürzt, / wenn ein Glückliches *fällt*" ("And we who of *rising* luck / think, would perceive the arousal, / which almost dismays us / if a lucky thing *falls*").

Stevens

The Plain Sense of Things

After the leaves have fallen, we return
To a plain sense of things. It is as if
We had come to an end of the imagination,
Inanimate in an inert savoir.

It is difficult even to choose the adjective
For this blank cold, this sadness without cause.
The great structure has become a minor house.
No turban walks across the lessened floors.

The greenhouse never so badly needed paint.
The chimney is fifty years old and slants to one side.
A fantastic effort has failed, a repetition
In a repetitiousness of men and flies.

Yet the absence of the imagination had
Itself to be imagined. The great pond,
The plain sense of it, without reflections, leaves,
Mud, water like dirty glass, expressing silence

Of a sort, silence of a rat come out to see,
The great pond and its waste of the lilies, all this
Had to be imagined as an inevitable knowledge,
Required, as a necessity requires.[8]

Metaphor hovers close to actuality here, yet itself helps to randomize the image of something like an actual exurban dwelling by a pond. The turban makes contextual sense as a reference to a man wearing one—and then metaphorically to any surprising event. It is lack of surprise that lessens the floors, as we may infer from the syntactically and semantically matched preceding line: "The great structure has become a minor house." "The great structure," too, hovers in metaphor, because it could refer at once to the house and to perceptions of the house, the great structure of perceptions about it that have so settled into place that they have become a minor house. In that reading, they assimilate the house to metaphor, but in an alternate reading, the minor house assimilates the great structure to actuality, making it a visible and tangible domestic building. This alternation, in which the great structure and the minor house tug each other back and forth from literalness to metaphoricity, illustrates and exemplifies the very process of metaphysical discourse that can be moving at the surface of Stevens's speculation. The literality is reinforced by the next two lines, which, taken by themselves, describe a house in disrepair. But taken in context, they, too, have a metaphorical aura—even in their literalness, as the next four lines emphasize, on the principle that "the absence of the imagination had / Itself to be imagined."

What follows on that is "The great pond, / The plain sense of it." That pond, too, is initially literal, but the appended phrase, the title phrase of the poem, expands the sense, returning it to itself. In "Credences of Summer," Stevens urges: "Trace the gold sun about the whitened sky / Without evasion by a single metaphor." Yet "Description is revelation" ("Description without Place"), and the attempt to thrust clear to reality-matching utterance is one of the more extravagant tropes of utterance, a trope that nevertheless demands to be enlisted. As Fletcher says, "Stevens . . . attaches . . . questions of mind and world to a vision of actually surviving in this world. To this end Stevens uses gnomic abstractions to call forth, to figure forth, to let loose the forces of thought."[9] The approaches of a poetic summation open on many possibilities, of deprivation, as in the poems of aging—such as this one—or of winter; of plenitude, as in many of the poems of *Transport to Summer;* even of danger, in possible combination with deprivation, as in "Poetry Is a Destructive Force": "That's what misery is, / Nothing to have at heart. / It is to have or nothing." So that short poem begins, moving through animal analogues to a gnomic warning: "The lion sleeps in the sun. / Its nose is on its paws. / It can kill a man."

In this poem, language has been foregrounded, too, but lightly: "It is difficult even to choose the adjective / For this blank cold, this sadness without cause." The great pond, in an adjectival phrase, is "without reflections"—and yet it immediately has appended to it "leaves," which it is hard not to identify with the leaves of the beginning of the poem. Also associated with the description-revelation of the pond are "Mud, water like dirty glass," "silence of a rat," and a "waste of the lilies." That the pond, too, is metaphoric, with all these literalities clinging to it, is indicated by the unique repetition of the phrase "The great pond." And in the last lines, "knowledge" marries "necessity" as resignation merges in prophetic discovery, in a coming to terms with "this sadness without cause."

Here Stevens's dominant rumination lets into itself what is its ultimate subject, human existence, on which all his ontological or quasi-ontological coordinates are being drawn. The ontology, minimally but distinctly present in this poem, serves in all of Stevens, finally, as a giant occlusion. The "plain sense of things" has an ontological reference but also has a reference to a point in the course of mortal life. The two senses do not clearly reinforce one another, but they do not clearly not do so, either; that is one occlusion, as is the bearing of the accidental perceptual and narrative details of the poem. The occlusions give it a tinge of the oracular and locate it in the domain of the prophetic, though the conversational tone is dominant in it. It is come at with a certain obliquity, and obliquity has become for Stevens a constant means for joining prophecy and occlusion. The obliquity is a necessary siting of the human condition, given that "We are not / At the center of a diamond," as he says in the poem whose title gives away its Baudelairean preoccupation and derivation, as well as its Mallarmean focus, "Esthétique du Mal." Here not war but aging is the oblique focus. "The Plain Sense of Things" envisages more than the ontology of its title. "Plain sense," a phrase the poem twice picks up, becomes possible "After the leaves have fallen," a seasonal orientation common for the author of *Transport to Summer* and *The Auroras of Autumn*.

The auroras are past, and shrinkage of perception, the "inert savoir," and "blank cold," are not simply attributed to an aging that, on the year's analogy, sets the stage for them. It is a "sadness without cause." The stubborn demands of a house upon the householder become a metaphor not just for transience but for an ineluctable diminishment that can only be met by such a poetic accounting.

"We are not / At the center of a diamond." The glisterings of the elements of life, inspected by the endless and self-advertisingly arbitrary ontological speculations, enter the poem obliquely. Insofar as they are randomized, they escape the very order that the formulations imply. In other poems, they accommodate officers fighting in World War II and Communists in exile and blacks celebrating a funeral and a cemetery in

Havana and Stevens's grandparents and the eighteenth-century vision of a sexuality heightened by artifice and plantations in Ceylon. There are many other exotic foci in his work, brought back into relation by the speculations to which he has them give rise. Stevens has written of "An Idea of Order"—"at Key West." But there is also "An Ordinary Evening in New Haven." In the poem before us, the exotic has shrunk, like everything else. "No turban walks across the lessened floors." Did a turban ever do so, in such an ordinary domestic locale, when it was not lessened? The poem avoids our being able to penetrate its gnomic formulations with an answer to that question. We must entertain the elided possibility of a turban, like "the mules that angels ride," who "come slowly down / The blazing passes from beyond the sun" in "Le Monocle de Mon Oncle."

It may seem an overemphasis even to indicate this prophetic strain in Stevens's voice at this point. However, for the author of "Sunday Morning," whose register has something in common with that of the author of Ecclesiastes, the logically endless ontological speculations are often put at the service of adumbrations about human destinies. In that sense, these clarifications keep pointing at occlusions, as in this poem, where, while it would be easy to exaggerate such an echo, the conception is not far from the "three-score years and ten" of the Psalms, or for that matter of "one generation goeth and another generation cometh" of Ecclesiastes and the vanishing grasshoppers of Nahum. When the overall statement of "The Plain Sense of Things" is pointed at the riddle of human destiny, something of the oracular is bound to enter even a voice so resolutely conversational.

Montale

Piccolo testamento

Questo che a notte balugina
nella calotta del mio pensiero,
traccia madreperlacea di lumaca
o smeriglio di vetro calpestato,
non è lume di chiesa o d'officina
che alimenti
chierico rosso, o nero.
Solo quest'iride posso

lasciarti a testimonianza
d'una fede che fu combattuta,
d'una speranza che bruciò piú lenta
di un duro ceppo nel focolare.
Conservane la cipria nello specchietto
quando spenta ogni lampada
la sardana si farà infernale
e un ombroso Lucifero scenderà su una prora
del Tamigi, del Hudson, della Senna
scuotendo l'ali di bitume semi-
mozze dalla fatica, a dirti: è l'ora.
Non è un'eredità, un portafortuna
che può reggere all'urto dei monsoni
sul fil di ragno della memoria,
ma una storia non dura che nella cenere
e persistenza è solo l'estinzione.
Giusto era il segno: chi l'ha ravvisato
non può fallire nel ritrovarti.
Ognuno riconosce i suoi: l'orgoglio
non era fuga, l'umiltà non era
vile, il tenue bagliore strofinato
laggiú non era quello di un fiammifero.[10]

Little Testament

This that at night flickers
in the hood of my thought,
mother-of-pearl trace of a snail
or glass-grit trampled,
is not a light of factory or church
that is fed
by a red priest or a black.
Only this rainbow can I
leave you for testimony
of a faith that was fought for,
of a hope that burned slower
than a tough trunk on the grate.
Save this face powder in your mirror-compact
when every torch is quenched,

PROPHECIES AND OCCLUSIONS

the sardana becomes infernal,
and a shadowy Lucifer descends on a prow
on the Thames, the Hudson, the Seine,
shaking wings of pitch, half-
stumps from the burden of telling you: It's time.
It's not a legacy, a charm
that can hold against the crush of the monsoons
on the spiderweb of memory
but a story only survives in ashes
and persistence is just extinction.
Right was the sign. He who recognized it
could not fail to find you again.
Everyone knows his own pride
was not flight, humility was not
craven, that slim ignited dazzle
over there was not that of a match.

This poem uses a title of Villon's and thus faintly suggests a figure urgently caught in the mortality that shadows this poem, as it does the *Testaments* of the harried medieval poet. But it only intermittently adopts the rhetoric of Villon, "I leave *x* to *Y*." The syntax of a will is just grazed; rather, the speaker offers not a testament but a testimony ("testimonianza"), and this testimony is nothing concrete or even easily describable. The enjambments and the free flow of this poem make it less oracular than Villon, but the constant access to strong terms, the theological references (even with their irony), and the urgency of the events narrated draw it toward the oracular. But its very hesitations and its air of sequentiality in progressive assertion keep it in the register of the conversational. It overcomes the finality of a will with the transitory quality, at once trivial and intense, of the perceptions here itemized. The final struck match is a capping occlusion.

The difficulty of description, indeed, is the subject of the poem. "Only this rainbow can I / leave you for testimony" ("Solo quest'iride posso / lasciarti a testimonianza"), and this sole ability of the speaker is itself muted by the enjambment across the lines. What is this rainbow exactly? It is mainly or preponderantly the poem, but not wholly or exactly just that. The rainbow is another name for the lights that are described in the poem with the dazzling specificity of rendering transient perceptions that is one of Montale's great strengths. "This that at night flickers" is a light somewhat like a rainbow. It is also "the hood of my thought," and—in a fusion reminiscent of Stevens—it is therefore either mental, if one takes the hood ("calotta") as the condition behind his thought; or it is physical, if one identifies it with the perceptions on which the thought focuses and beyond which it cannot go—a hood in both senses. Both the "mother-of-pearl trace of a snail" and "glass-grit trampled" have a play of light over them, so they have an irising, which can be included in the reference to the rainbow. Yet in the sentence about the rainbow, we are given further "hoods of thought" that are mental, the residually Christian virtues "faith" and "hope." A metaphor of light defines their process: the hope "burned slower / than a tough trunk on the grate," than the "ceppo," the severed base of a tree trunk used for such durable fires.

Abruptly the addressee, presumably a beloved woman, is enjoined to keep the face powder in her compact, even though a good luck charm ("portafortuna") cannot prevail against what she may face in London, New York, or Paris. Not in Italy, be it noted; the hazards of the traveler are obliquely involved, as well as her separation from the Italian speaker, be she the Italian or the American among Montale's loves. She is asked to carry a small, precious personal object of the sort that is carried in a handbag, much like the ivory mouse carried as a charm by "Dora Markus" in the poem of that title. The mirror and the powder will be a small consolation, like the rainbow offered by the poet, at an apocalyptic time, or an actual time with apocalyptic overtones, a time defined mostly by effects of light—though it is a dance in a fourth city, Barcelona, the sardana, that may concurrently "become infernal." And the last infernal light is also looked at with a revelatory obliquity, "that slim ignited dazzle / over there was not that of a match." The "bagliore" ("dazzle") closes the circuit of "balugina" ("flickers") of the first line; between these lights is a decline, and also an increasing lack of clarity, since the last one can only be defined ominously by its not being a humble domestic light, a match being lit, whereas the first flicker has multiple, exfoliating definitions.

The "shadowy Lucifer" who is "shaking wings of pitch, half- / stumps from the burden of telling you: It's time" looks like the angel of death, a revision of theology on behalf of a powerful metaphor that leaps suddenly into allegory if the scene is visualized, a Goya-like picture of a supernatural creature falling on the prow of a boat on the Thames, Hudson, or Seine. This figure translates the "infernale" attributed to the sardana into a whole possible cosmology, one with political overtones, as one might expect from the author of "Hitlerian Spring," but also religious ones. By this point of the poem, the negations at the beginning have been turned around: "This . . . that flickers / . . . / is not a light of factory or church / that is fed / by a red priest or a black." Nothing so integrated into a five-year plan as a factory, and nothing so institutional as a church is in view. And yet a social process, one monstrous enough to involve also a spiritual process, is envisioned as taking over. Insufficiency is all that can be expected: "It's not a legacy, a charm / that can hold against the crush of the monsoons / on the spiderweb of memory." The human forgetfulness profoundly deplored by Baudelaire is taken for granted: we are as skilled at weaving memory as the spider is at weaving a web. But memory and web are similarly fragile in the violent winds, which are the more metaphoric here for being transferred around the globe. The word "monsoons" skews the very coordinates of east and west, since those storms are found on the Indian Ocean and not over the Thames, the Hudson, and the Seine. On the contrary, however, the sign—of incapacity, of apocalypse—may ring true ("giusto"), but coming to terms with all this stasis and revelation means that those "who recognized it / could not fail to find [it] again." Both pride and humility, usually taken as opposites, are merged and mobilized to recognize what the light seen—is not. It is not ordinary, not that of a match; and so it must be something extraordinary that the poem does not name and cannot, but only evokes.

Char

La Rive violente

Promptes à se joindre, à se réconcilier
 dans la destruction du corps de notre maison,
Immuables sont les tempêtes.

L'une se lève sur mes talons, à peine la nuit dissipée,
Exigeante, sédentaire, sûre d'elle.
L'autre, la fugueuse, roule vers nous des monstres en
 bouillie et les projets des humains.

Avant que ne commençât la veillée des millénaires
Les Pascuans surent que leurs sculpteurs, taillant dans l'île,
Ouvraient devant les morts les portes de la mer.

Nous n'avons plus de morts, plus d'espace;
Nous n'avons plus les mers ni les îles;
Et l'ombre du sablier enterre la nuit.
"Rhabillez-vous. Au suivant." Tel est l'ordre.
Et le suivant, c'est aussi nous.
Révolution qu'un astre modifie,
Avec les mains que nous lui ajoutons.[11]

The Violent Shore

Prompt to link up, to reconcile
       in the destruction of the body of our house,
Immutable are the tempests.

One rises at my heels, night scarcely dissipated,
Exigent, sedentary, sure of itself.
The other, the gusty, rolls toward us some monsters in solution
       and the projects of humans.

Before the vigil of the millennials began,
The Easter Islanders knew that their sculptors, hewing on the island,
Opened before the dead the gates of the sea.

We have no more dead, no more space,
We have no more seas or islands,
And the shadow of the hourglass buries night.
"Get dressed. On to the next one." That is the order.
And the next one is also us.
Revolution that a star modifies,
With the hands we add to it.

This poem comes from a collection in which every separate section
takes the figure of Orion as a point of departure and operates upon that
myth in a combinatory fashion, while distancing its expressions from the
myth.[12] The distancing begins with the title of the collection, *Aromates
chasseurs* ("Spices Hunters"). This title would serve as a model surrealist
phrase, since in no obvious sense are spices hunters or hunters spices.
Myths waft senses the way spices waft odors, however, and in that sense
the myth of a hunter such as Orion could be aromatic. Spices, too, we
learn from Lévi-Strauss, who was much on the horizon during the
writing of these poems, bring with them an elaborate mythological bag-

gage that cannot be dissociated from their utility in cuisine and in medicine. Moreover, Char got the association of mythic figures and spices from the application of these connections to classical myth by Detienne in *Les Jardins d'Adonis: La mythologie des aromates en Grèce*.[13]

Char's title is plural, not singular; there are many Orions. The Boeotian hunter who got drunk and wooed Merope may not be the one who wooed the Dawn, or the one who fought the Scorpion, or the one shot by Artemis and as compensation set as a constellation in the heavens. Coordinating these intellectually would generate the expanding algorithms of structural analysis that Lévi-Strauss provides. Yet Char allows himself much freedom in his combinations. The separate poem in the collection that bears the eponymous title, "Aromates chasseurs," is subtitled "Orion to the Unicorn" ("Orion à la licorne"), an Orion who does not appear exactly in the Greek myth, which knows no unicorns. Bearings are taken throughout on Orion, as on the stars in the sky, which by legend and convention he schematizes. When queried, Char said about his Orion, "There are in our life approaches that are barely noticed, with a touch of the fingers or by great strides. For Orion I contented myself with limiting him in the space where he was found. I put him on my path where you can meet him and follow his drama."[14] Orion is subtle, like an aromatic spice, but he is a hunter, and to follow him one must match in the imagination his great strides. Throughout this collection, where there are references to Hitler and Stalin among others, Char takes the long view of history, which dominates the poem quoted above. His introductory nonpoem in the collection opens by referring to "this century": "This century has decided on the existence of our two immemorial spaces: the first, the intimate space in which our imagination and our feelings play; the second, the circular space, that of the concrete world. The two were inseparable. To subvert the one is to overturn the other."[15] The two spaces are still in view, as is their long-range overturning, in the poem quoted above, where what makes the shore violent is that "We have no more dead, no more space, / We have no more seas or islands." This means that the physical and the imagination have been overturned in their relation; it is a way of giving Heidegger's message about the modern world—which is also that of the Tenth Duino Elegy—that the meaning of the physical world has been rubbed off or overturned. "And the shadow of the hourglass buries night," or dark does in dark, time does in time, a process, that the poem hints, would have begun with the millennials, who were declaring the end of the world at a time in the Middle Ages after the sculptors of the Easter Island statues (which are dated about 800 A.D.). We do not know what their statues mean, but the evocative setting of the large heads on their headland, whatever they mean, can be read as having "Opened before the dead the gates of the sea."

The domain of Orion is the stars of the sky; that symbology is one abiding with Char from Valéry, whom he is usually taken to have supplanted in literary currency. Valéry's young Fate, too, is spread out in the sky in *La Jeune parque*. But in the hieratic figure of Woman, she is passive, as she emblematizes a plenitude; whereas the Orion of Char bristles with activity, leaving a plenitude behind him as he moves toward actions that may bring another plenitude into wary being, or some defection from plenitude that he will be called on to surpass, and we will be called on in his image to do the same.

The surrealist arbitrariness lightens the presentation of this classical model-hunter-turned-into-constellation. The light surrealist filament neutralizes the connections between star and legendary hunter, letting them enter the utterance to capture and restore the union of the imagination and the physical. "The Violent Shore" sounds like a near-oxymoron, turning subsurrealist on inspection. But if we bring the expression to bear on the legend, we find that Orion, pursued around the archipelago—"Escaped from the Archipelago" is the title of the first poem in the collection—tended to encounter violence on his landfalls. The legend remains a subtext concealed in this particular poem. Orion's wanderings through the islands during his legendary lifetime extend, in the poem, to Easter Island, discovered by wanderers who took their bearings by the stars more than a millennium ago—but more than a millennium after the time, itself millennial, of the Orion who is mentioned in Homer.

In the intense shroudings of oracular obscurity, the "we" of the first strophe could be read as "Orion and I," and as "we humans"; and the first reading could be made emblematically equivalent to the second. The complications of "the body of our house," instead of simply "our house," makes the body of the speaker contingently part of the house or standing in a relation to it that merges the external physical world with the mortal body in ways that the elusiveness of the expression both evokes and fails to solve.

The second strophe moves into the first person. In light of the figure of Orion, who is here a vanishing echo, the "tempests" may refer distantly to satyrs, or the Scorpion, who pursued him. A sedentary tempest is another oxymoron, evocative of a spiritual state that is allowed only an alternative dominance in the poem, as it is countered by the other tempest, the gusty one, which "rolls . . . some monsters in solution / and the projects of humans." Are the monsters and the projects in some sense equivalent? That is a combinatory possibility; but it is also possible that the solution ("bouillie") has neutralized the monsters (rather than intensified them) and that the projects of humans are not hampered. The tempests are permanent, but the speaker, a sort of Orion, is moving ahead of them, if not far. They are "at my heels." After the survey of Easter Island, he will revert to the command to move on—something he has been doing, but not on order: "On to the next one." But "the next one is also us," and the last line envisages a revolution modified by a star (one presumably in the constellation of Orion): "With the hands we add to it." Bare hands can modify a revolution—an optimistic assertion that suggests, through a prophetic occlusion, the success of any project, very much including the poems in this series. And the act of adding, in the present tense, can be taken to describe metapoetically the very words of this declaration.

Celan

Von der sinkenden Walstirn
les ich dich ab—
du erkennst mich.

der Himmel
stürzt sich
in die Harpune,

sechsbeinig
hockt unser Stern im Schaum,

langsam
hisst einer, der's sieht,
den Trosthappen: das
balzende Nichts.[16]

From the sinking whale brow
I read you off—
You know me,

The heaven
plunges
into the harpoon,

six-legged
our star squats in the foam,

slowly
one who sees it hoists
the consolation bite, the
pairing nothing.

Celan's pressures on language here, as characteristically, have a spiritual force that enlists a deconstructive survival theology to solder verbal affirmations together. The enormous violence of whaling is here fused with the reactions of someone like a Jonah. The intimate second person, not to be wholly dissociated from God (who is not wholly to be dissociated from the "nothing" of the poem's last word), is read off from the sinking brow of the whale, and a new version of the medieval Book of Nature emerges.

The intimacy, a tremendous one, is reciprocal. The speaker reads off "du"; and "du erkennst mich" ("you know me"). This reciprocity could be taken as a summary of the Book of Jonah, at the beginning of which Jonah tries to evade the mission of prophecy and is recognized by God, who sends him into the belly of the whale, by which Jonah does read God off. It is not clear, however, that any such resolution as Jonah's can be envisioned. In the next strophe, "The heaven / plunges / into the harpoon," the infinite into a single, deadly instrument. In the next, the Holocaust is transmuted still once again; the Star of David is described in terms that suggest an insect. In the foam of the sea, a strange starfish is also suggested—strange because starfish usually have five legs, not six. But the "legged" attribution to the Star of David is also strange; it is usually described as six-pointed. To speak of legs merges the plurality of "unser" with the look of an insect or an echinoderm. But the evocation remains primary of the Star of David, the six-pointed emblem that Jews were forced to wear as a sign of shame, and so metaphorically to squat.

In this emblematic form, the "I" of the first strophe has become a "we," it is "our star."

But the term "our" could include poets, along the lines of the epigraph to the long poem that ends *Die Niemandsrose,* "Und mit dem Buch aus Tarussa." That poem explores the Holocaust and quotes as an epigraph in Russian the statement of Marina Tsvetaeva, "Vsyo poetiy Zhidiy" ("All poets are Jews"). Tsvetaeva was not a victim of the Nazi Holocaust; she was a victim of the Stalin era, and from inner psychic torment; persecuted, she hanged herself. Setting her statement and her figure forward, Celan thereby forbids our confining the persecuted just to his central, penetrating example, the Nazi persecution of the Jews. It must include the other side in the Fascist-Communist standoff of his youth, when he evidenced some sympathy for the great cause of the Spanish Civil War. He himself experienced the oppressions of both sides, since his native Czernowitz was occupied by Russians and by Germans in alternation.

Even that extreme example of human depravity, the Holocaust, then, will not confine his reference. Its specificity and its psychospiritual associability are joined in the compressions of Celan's poetic speech. A specific occasion and a generalized sweep of prophetic utterance often stretch each other in his poems, as in "Tübingen, Jänner," about a visit to the disappointingly silent ex-Nazi Heidegger, and "Du liegst im grossen Gelausche" ("You lie down all ears"), about a visit to Berlin where the loan of a book sharply evoked the Eden Hotel and the river, which were the site of the execution of Rosa Luxemburg and Karl Liebknecht. Derrida and Gadamer have commented on the occasionality of these two poems.[17] While Derrida wants to make much of the specific occasionality of these poems, Gadamer insists that the second can be understood without any reference to the glossed details. His insistence—while refutable, as Haskell Block shows—lodges on his accurate sense that the reference of the poem is too broad to be confined to just one occasion. And Celan's packed utterances do have enormous extensibility. But they are also, as Derrida and Gadamer insist, linked to the temporal and spatial conditions of a given moment, whether the moment be a day, like that of a visit to Berlin, or a whole period, like the Nazi (and Stalin) era.

Indeed, while the Holocaust does not confine the reference of this poem, it urgently centers it and threatens it with a befouled silence. The

Holocaust becomes the giant occasionality of the poem, beyond which it stretches, through which it plumbs. The issue remains not just to reassert the centrality of the Holocaust but to understand how and why the poem governs it, as Winfried Menninghaus insists.[18] The epochal occasionality pulls the poetry away from self-preoccupation, which is its main post-Mallarmean matrix, for all its references to speech and words. The self-questioning reflexivity of that stand contributes to a vibrancy whereby, as Menninghaus specifies, the poems interact with their own silence, saying what they do not say; and so "finally for that reason every boundary between poetry and metapoetry cannot be lifted."[19]

Yet the boundary cannot be maintained fully, either. These poems are put through what, in the title of one that Peter Szondi expounds, is a *stretto*, an *Engführung*, a musical abduction through a strait place.[20] The *Engführung* of the words, curtailed and concentrated with each other, corresponds to the *Engführung* that their prophetic reach performs upon their occluded occasionality. So, in the poem before us, the off-rhyme of "-stirn" and "Stern" ("brow" and "star") wrenches past an identification: the whale and the six-legged star do not really stand in relation. They are parallel as stressed victims, but also as instances in the sea, evoked literally and metaphorically when heaven can enter the harpoon.

Somebody in the third person is operative in the last strophe—"one who sees it"—and the "it" could be the whole apocalyptic event but could also be what it precedes, the "consolation bite." Is this "Happen" ("morsel") the poem itself? Where is the consolation? The colon associates it with a mating dance, for "balzen" means to pair off by going through a mating dance. The mating dance, however, is associated with a large game bird—itself emblematic of the hunting culture—the *Auerhahn* (heath cock or capercailzie). Land has been substituted for sea, a large bird for an incomparably larger sea creature; but on land or on sea, hunting proceeds. There is, however, the "consolation" of mating. But what mates is not the *Auerhahn,* or the whale, or a person, but "nothing."

We are in the domain of the "black milk" of "Todesfuge," though this poem's staccato progression of short lines makes it far less oracular than the orotundities and varied repetitions of the earlier one. Still, the concision here is so strong that it forces an oracular override on the conversational progression. The sexuality glimpsed here in the verbal compressions evinces as well as summarizes the violent and forceful apocalypse of these actions, carrying out in its glancing intensities another fusion at the heart of both Jewish and Christian traditions, the fusion of union with God and sexuality, along with the further fusion of a distinction between self-realization and self-annihilation, apocalypse and death. The poem only comes at these grazingly, but the grazing is so powerful as to compress the language.

The negative theology touched on often in Celan's poems centers on the "nothing" of which Heidegger was the exponent. That exponent defected from the high moral demands of his vision, whose ethical-religious dimension Celan supplies, documenting the failings thereof, including those of Heidegger in "Tübingen, Jänner." Yet Celan is not in any inert way taking over Friedrich Nietzsche's "God is Dead" or Heidegger's reading of Nietzsche's expression.[21] Celan supplies that dimension in the further Heideggerian manner of bringing statements to bear on the questions, statements rooted not just in language but in the history of words out of Grimm's lexicon, in the manner of Heidegger's own reading of such words. The history of a word such as "balzen" ("pair in a large fowl's mating dance") is a palimpsest of human engagements, concretions, strivings, and failures as they work to make sense of the terrifying and illuminating world.

Ashbery

More Pleasant Adventures

The first year was like icing.
Then the cake started to show through.
Which was fine, too, except you forget the direction you're taking.
Suddenly you are interested in some new thing
And can't tell how you got here. Then there is confusion
Even out of happiness, like a smoke—
The words get heavy, some topple over, you break others.
And outlines disappear once again.

Heck, it's anybody's story,
A sentimental journey—"gonna take a sentimental journey,"
And we do, but you wake up under the table of a dream:
You are that dream, and it is the seventh layer of you.
We haven't moved an inch, and everything has changed.
We are somewhere near a tennis court at night.

We get lost in life, but life knows where we are.
We can always be found with our associates.
Haven't you always wanted to curl up like a dog and go to sleep like a dog?

In the rash of partings and dyings (the new twist),
There's also room for breaking out of living.
Whatever happens will be quite ingenious.
No acre but will resume being disputed now,
And paintings are one thing we never seem to run out of.[22]

Tone may not be everything, but tone does a lot of work not only in this poem but also in Ashbery's expansive long poems, such as "A Wave" and *Flow Chart*. The tone permits him to imply a whole muddling but visionary ordinariness that can say "Heck" in the same context where a received version of a view of poetic language—the view effectually shared by Stevens, Rilke, Char, and Celan—is put to these poets' uses: "The words get heavy, some topple over, you break others." Beyond this conversational-colloquial rephrasing of a Mallarmean-normative view of his utterance, the very mixture of discourses of which this arch formulation partakes carries off a large gathering of percepts. This inclusiveness lets it into an expressed overview that has tapped into an oracularity comparable to Pindar's. It becomes large-breathed by fiat, and without tapping into the high afflatus of a Whitman or the radiant stridency of a Mayakovsky. Bourdieu has delineated the "habitus," or vested social implications, of the codings of various groups within a society, groups complexly defined and definable only by tracing the many strands that place them as microgroups.[23] In what amounts to a prophetic sweep, Ashbery performs occlusions on the linguistic structures that form the boundaries of these groups and microgroups, thus erasing the boundaries and uniting the groups—in imagination. This procedure revises the surrealism of earlier work, such as *The Tennis Court Oath*. Instead of mounting revelatory discordances in predication—like Éluard's "La terre est bleue comme une orange"—Ashbery now mounts the discordances of whole areas of discourse.

Here Ashbery also extends and effectively reverses the metalinguistic understanding of language expounded by Raymond Roussel, the subject of his uncompleted doctoral thesis. For Roussel, the metalinguistic activity is arbitrary and, in a sense, negative. A word like "billes" is substituted for one like "pilles," quite different in sense but with just one differential feature of sound, and the substitution calls an expected chain of predications to a halt, thereby releasing the speaker into another chain that has the arbitrariness and suggestiveness of a muted surrealism. In the postsurrealist Ashbery of this poem, such a linguistic atomism is abjured in favor of an assertive overlap of domains of discourse. "Heck" coexists with "partings and dyings." Metalinguistic characterizations of language—"The words get heavy"—melt, like the cake of his introductory sentences, into "the table of a dream" and "a tennis court at night." Each of the assertions takes its place among other items, and their miscellany resists characterization, even as randomness. Just so the shifts in tone do not at all disintegrate into raw incoherence or discordancy but rather establish their own large sphere of a tone in which the separate conversational gestures, for their very discrepancy, open up into an equivalent of the oracular. Hence the poem cannot be assimilated into various jazzy satirical registers. The old lyric topos of life as a journey, recast into something sentimental on the surface, reasserts its force through its combinations, through the layers of the "cake," which at a point get down to "the seventh layer of you." The self and the cosmos enter into an interchange, and the voice of the speaker manages to keep such an assertion at a remove from banality by the connective verve of its associative lightness. The gullible enthusiasm and the incapacity—dramatized as locating the speaker—merge around the phrase "gonna take a sentimental journey." Those words, in fact, are warped through the identification of the speaker with the words quoted and his dissociation from them through quotation, a touch of Ashbery's earlier, occluding and revelatory mixing of persons in discourse as a technique of extension for the poem.

When the journey is simultaneously abjured and embraced in this way, it generates an inspired confusion in which satire and sentiment, melting into each other, produce a further state celebrating both. The cake and the icing are occluded by being both differentiated and subsumed. Something larger is offered than the grim mood of "Life is a handkerchief sandwich" in John Berryman's *Dream Songs*.

The disjunctions are set into gear at once by the mysterious matter-of-factness of the discrepancy between the title and the first sentence. "More Pleasant Adventures" in itself offers a litotes (the adventures are ultimate life experiences in one sense, and thus more than pleasant; and more connected than the random implications of the term "adventures" would allow). This litotes is combined with an irony of self-contradiction (the adventures could be thought of as the opposite of pleasant).

The litotes and the irony levitate through the ambiguity of "more," which could either be an adjective, "additional adventures," or an adverb, "adventures pleasanter than others." And then the poem begins with the matter-of-fact abruptness, the mysterious reversal and simile of the first line—"The first year was like icing"—as icing is added last on a cake, not first. But when "cake started to show through," it is clear that the whole cake in some sense precedes itself—it is the consumption of the cake, not the preparation of the cake, that is in question. In this situation, it is not surprising that the subject "you" "forgot the direction you're taking." The matter-of-fact abruptness proves now to be tonic, an "organizing" principle for the disorganization.

The "you" is radically distractable. Distractability in fact is conceived of as a condition of existence: "Then there is confusion / Even out of happiness, like a smoke." "A smoke" lightly indicates its subordination as just a single item in a broader existence, whereas "smoke" without the article might be taken to cover the field. In the next line, language itself acts on its own to both express and confuse: "The words get heavy, some topple over"; but the words also submit to manipulation at the hands of the subject: "you break others." And confusion would immediately take over if an attempt were made to ascertain of any sequence of words, including the words of the poem, which of the three processes it was exemplifying. Life as a journey happens to Everyman ("it's anybody's story"), but with the fusions, distortions, and mutings, as well as the revelations, attendant on this oracular-conversational reshaping of the classical and normative.

All this does not prevent the dark side of life from showing through; but the dark side also has its visions and compensations, the cake as well as the icing. The occlusions of these details provide a revelatory delight of meaning. Or not; the poet-speaker puts himself in the position of self-realization by not caring. The conversational has been made to yield the oracular, even though part of its occlusion is to abjure any direct access to an oracular tone. Only the subject matter, the ultimate possibility of happiness, brings the oracular into view, more through the play of tones that are part of its occlusion, too, a prophetic part.

This position is a means of caring enormously: "There's also room for breaking out of living. / Whatever happens will be quite ingenious." In its exactness, "ingenious" expands all the more for retaining its colloquial blurring into occlusion. Poetry is the means of breaking out, creating a condition in which every "acre . . . disputed" is superseded. "And paintings are one thing we never seem to run out of." This encouraging conclusion is put forward in the rhetoric of a careful conversational modesty, since it does not mention poems, but there is an implicit comprehensiveness that would include them. "Paintings" can be taken to include poems, either metaphorically or analogously. That is perhaps a small further occlusion. We do not seem to run out of poems, either, and that is crucial to the expansiveness of human existence—to its plain opening of the conversational language of the tribe into the purifications, the visions, of the oracular.

Notes

Introduction

1. Paul Zumthor (*La Lettre et la voix*) finds a "second orality," where a work that has been written down is distributed orally—as distinct from a first orality, where no writing exists, and a mixed orality, where oral transmission is regular in a culture that also has writing (as, e.g., with *Beowulf*). If he is right, then Dante, who was not writing for oral performance, is a very significant exception for poets writing in the vernacular, as Jean de Meun would also be, and some others. Poetry in Latin is another case; Alain de Lille's "Planctus" would not be recited, as a *planh* in the vernacular would be.

Homer, too, combines both "oral" and "written" elements. But all language has an oral base that poetry recursively harnesses by its superadded sound patternings, whereas writing is just a technique, albeit with considerable historical-relational implications, for transmitting language.

2. These are formulated in Cicero, *Orator* 101.

3. As Isidore Okpewho says, "the religious element is frequently superseded by the play interest of the narrator, especially in the fervid context of the open performance" (*The Epic in Africa*, 2).

4. Yuri Lotman, *Analysis of the Poetic Text*.

5. Yuri Lotman, "The Text within the Text," 378. Lotman continues, "The play with meaning that arises in the text, the slippage between the various kinds of structural regularities, endows the text with greater semantic potential than have texts codified by means of a single, separate language. . . . Culture is not a chaotic collocation of texts but a complex, hierarchical functioning system. Every text inevitably appears in at least two perspectives, two types of contexts, opposed on the axis homogeneity-heterogeneity" (378).

6. Erving Goffman, *Forms of Talk,* especially 128–50.

7. For an elaborate demonstration of this element in her work, see Camille Paglia,

"Amherst's Madame de Sade: Emily Dickinson," in *Sexual Personae: Art and Decadence from Nefertiti to Emily Dickinson,* 623–74.

8. For a discussion about images that attempts to move beyond the Aristotelian-propositional analysis of metaphor, see Albert Cook, *Figural Choice in Poetry and Art.* For the dynamics of image perception as it is structured into verse, see Christopher Collins, *The Poetics of the Mind's Eye.*

9. George Lakoff and Mark Johnson, *Metaphors We Live By;* Mark Turner, *Death Is the Mother of Beauty: Mind, Metaphor, Criticism.*

10. Albert Cook, *Myth and Language,* 248–59.

11. G. E. M. Anscombe, trans., Ludwig Wittgenstein, *Zettel,* 155.

12. Dan Sperber, *Rethinking Symbolism,* 60, 85.

13. Reiner Schürmann points this out in "Le Praxis symbolique," *Cahiers internationaux du symbole* 29–30 (1975): 147.

14. Leonard Barkan, *The Gods Made Flesh: Metamorphosis and the Pursuit of Paganism,* 140–63.

15. Heinz Werner, *Die Ursprünge der Metapher.*

16. For further theoretical discussion, see Albert Cook, "Finalities of Utterance and Modalities of Expression," in *Canons and Wisdoms,* 81–100.

17. Pierre Bourdieu, *Language and Symbolic Power; The Political Ontology of Martin Heidegger.* My quotations are from the latter.

Chapter 1

1. Cook, *Canons and Wisdoms.*

2. This, and all translations not otherwise attributed, are my own.

3. At the same time, for such early poets as Alcaeus, Alcman, and Archilochus, so little of the work survives, and its context is so tenuous in the possibility of its reconstructions, that it serves generally to remind us how little hermeneutic purchase is needed to have a sense of the power a poem transmits. We can almost do without a horizon of expectation, though we should remember the caveat of W. R. Johnson about Greek lyric poetry as a whole: "This poetry is all but lost to us . . . essentially inaccessible to us" (W. R. Johnson, *The Idea of Lyric,* 25–26).

4. For some indications as to the elaborate formal use of wine, see Oswyn Murray, ed., *Sympotica: A Symposium on the Symposion.*

5. I am indebted for stress on some of these features to Lowell Bowditch, "Horace and the Gift Economy of Patronage."

6. I am only touching on the large complications and fusions of this highly dialecticized form. For attention to these, see Thomas Rosenmeyer, *The Green Cabinet;* and Charles Segal, *Poetry and Mythmaking in Ancient Pastoral.* The template of the genre is extended as an ideological system in William Empson, *Some Versions of Pastoral.*

7. Denys Thompson, *The Uses of Poetry,* 61.

8. Arthur Quiller-Couch, ed., *The Oxford Book of Ballads,* 140–41.

9. H. M. Chadwick and N. K. Chadwick, *The Growth of Literature,* I.

10. See the large presentation of the implications of Martial's social involvements as

reflected through his poetry in J. P. Sullivan, *Martial: The Unexpected Classic*, especially 78–114 and 211–52.

11. See my discussion of the inadequacy of Claude Lévi-Strauss's and Jakobson's analysis of that poem: "This analysis ends where it should have begun, with the question of why power resides in the implicit analogy between animate and inanimate, then between the cat and the woman. What kind of hieratic interest is invested in a cat? How does the tangential domestication of awe-tinged power in a modern city differ from the sacralization of such animals, often evoked by Baudelaire?" ("Lévi-Strauss: Myth and the Neolithic Revolution," in *Myth and Language*, 32).

12. Stephen Owen, *Traditional Chinese Poetry and Poetics*, 25, 63.

13. Gregory Nagy, *Greek Mythology and Poetics*, viii.

14. Emil Staiger, *Grundbegriffe der Poetik.*

15. As Christopher Ricks further says of this "lovely poem," "it needs to incorporate gratitude to the giver within a larger gratitude to the woman who has given so much larger a gift: herself. . . . The serenity and safety of the poem derive from the tact and secret largeness with which it includes a sense of what the right true end of marriage is. The poem has two sentences only, one beginning 'She bears your gift,' and the other 'She wears the birth'; the parallelism, the internal rhyme, and the words 'bear' and 'birth' all ask us to feel something of a future such as we are usually guided to glimpse in an epithalamium. . . . [T]he birth of physics and of the maritime empires . . . should be felt as indeed births. The poem's climax, they expand to a full sense of the human situation, and of future births as rich" (Christopher Ricks, *The Force of Poetry*, 241).

16. I draw these illustrations, and my information, from Roger S. Keyes, *Surimono from the Chester Beatty Collection.*

17. Robert Creeley, *Gnomic Verses*, 26.

Chapter 2

1. Absolute metaphor, one in which tenor cannot be distinguished from vehicle clearly because both are in some way suspended, has been discussed in modern German theory. See Hans Blumenberg, *Paradigmen zu einer Metaphorologie*, esp. 85–87.

2. Wallace Stevens, "Two or Three Ideas," 209.

3. I owe this point to George Kane.

4. Foucault's own discussion of the modern leans rather too heavily on cases that include extreme elements—of madness (Antonin Artaud) and of deliberate linguistic dissolution (Raymond Roussel) (Michel Foucault, *Les Mots et les choses*, 394–96).

5. The principles of the "rhizoma" are powerfully associative and "poetic" in themselves: "1 and 2. Principles of connection and heterogeneity: any point of a rhizoma can be connected to anything other, and must be. This is very different from the tree or root, which plots a point, fixes an order . . . 3. Principle of multiplicity . . . 4. Principle of a signifying rupture: against the oversignifying breaks separating structures or cutting across a single structure . . . 5 and 6. Principle of cartography and decalcomania: a rhizoma is not amenable to any structural or generative model. It is a stranger to any idea of genetic axis or deep structure." All this is suggestively at once guiding and cautionary for analysis of poetic organizations (Gilles Deleuze and Félix Guattari, *A Thousand Plateaus*).

6. Albert Cook, *Prisms*.

7. Salvatore Quasimodo, "Ed è subito sera," in *Tutte le poesie*, 23.

8. Jacques Derrida, *Signéponge*.

9. Eugenio Montale, "Mottetti," *Le occasioni* (Florence: Mondadori, 1949), 58.

10. A completely different set of particulars in another poem from this series carries through a similar experience:

Motet XVIII

Non recidere, forbice, quel volto,
solo nella memoria che si sfolla,
non far del grande suo viso in ascolto
la mia nebbia di sempre.

Un freddo cala... Duro il colpo svetta.
E l'acacia ferita da sé scrolla
il guscio di cicala
nella prima belletta di Novembre. [60]

Don't cut, scissors, that face
which remains alone in my emptied memory;
don't make her clear, watchful face
into an unending mist.

A chill descends... hard is the cutting blow.
And the wounded mimosa shakes off
the cicada hulls
into the first mud of November.

11. Jean Follain, *Usage du temps* (Paris: Gallimard, 1943).

12. As it happens, there is a block-long Paris street called the allée Verte in the eleventh arrondissement. This, however, would not be quite parallel to rue Verte, since "allée" lexically signifies the presence of trees, whereas "rue" does not.

13. For the elaborate subtleties of principle behind the relationship of free verse to given metric patterns, see Clive Scott, *Reading the Rhythm: The Poetics of French Free Verse 1910–1930*; Jacques Roubaud, *La Viellesse d'Alexandre*.

14. Jules Supervielle, *Gravitations* (Paris: Gallimard, 1932), 11.

15. Richard Wilbur, *New and Collected Poems*, 25.

16. Robert Creeley, *The Company* (Providence, R.I.: Burning Deck, 1988), 30.

17. Aaron Rosen, *Traces* (New York: Sheep Meadow Press, 1991), 29.

18. Federico García Lorca, *Diván del Tamarit, Obras completas* (Buenos Aires: Losada, 1938), 3:162; *Selected Poems of Federico García Lorca* (New York: New Directions, 1955), 163–64.

19. Anna Akhmatova, "He Loved Three Things," in *Sochineniya*, 67.

20. "There are certain delicious sensations whose indefiniteness in no way precludes intensity, and no point is sharper than the Infinite" (Baudelaire, "Le *Confiteor* de l'artiste," *Le Spleen de Paris, Œuvres complètes* [Paris: Gallimard, 1961], 232). As Werner Hamacher points out, "Celan's poem . . . is written on this point of the Infinite as well as with it"

(Hamacher, "The Second of Inversion: Moments of a Figure through Celan's Poetry," 308).

21. Paul Celan, *Die Niemandsrose*, 48–49.

22. The correlations of this poem's phrases with aspects of the concentration camp experience are detailed in Otto Pöggeler, *Die Spur des Wortes*, 327–34.

23. Jacques Derrida, *Schibboleth*, 80.

24. Philippe Lacoue-Labarthe, *Poésie comme expérience*, esp. 47–58, where Lacoue-Labarthe addresses Celan's confrontation of Heidegger in the poem "Todtnauberg."

25. Hans-Georg Gadamer, *Wer bin Ich und wer bist Du? Ein Kommentar zu Paul Celans Gedichtfolge "Atemkristall,"* 35.

Gadamer is here commenting on specific lines of the poem:

> In den Flüssen nördlich der Zukunft
> werf ich das Netz aus, das du
> zögernd beschwerst
> mit von Steinen geschriebenen
> Schatten.
>
> In the floods north of the future
> I throw out the net, that you
> tremblingly weigh down
> with the stone-overwritten
> shadows.

26. Derrida, *Schibboleth*, 94.

27. I owe the posing of this particular question to James Bunn.

28. Francis Ponge, *Pièces*, 125.

29. What Theodor Adorno says of a quotation from Trakl's "Psalm" is apposite here, though in ways he might not have endorsed:

> The lines "Es sind Zimmer, erfüllt von Akkorden und Sonaten" ["There are rooms filled with accords and sonatas"] carry little more with them—still for that reason the childish feeling in the mere naming of a name, they have nevertheless more to do with the false title "Moonlight Sonata" than with composition, and so that is not something accidental. Without the sonatas that his sister played, there would not have been the secluded sounds where the gloom of the poet takes refuge. Even the simplest words in the poem possess something similar, borrowed from communicative speech. . . . Even Trakl's omnipresent copula "is" estranges itself from its conceptual sense in the work of art. It expresses no existential judgment but rather a paled afterimage of such, qualitative to the point of negation; that something "is" more or less carries with it that it is not. Where Brecht or Williams sabotage the poetic in the poem and bring it close to a report on the merely empirical, it becomes nothing like that for such a person. While they polemically mock the exalted lyric tone, the empirical propositions, by their transposition into aesthetic monads, take on something different by their contrast to these. The hostility to song in the tone and the estrangement in the captured facts are two sides of the same content. Transformation contradicts even judgment in the artwork. To judgment are the artworks as analogous as synthesis. Still, in

them they are without judgment, and nobody can attribute to any of them what it judges; none is a so-called assertion [*Aussage*]. (Theodor W. Adorno, *Ästhetische Theorie*, 186–87)

Chapter 3

1. Erving Goffman, *Forms of Talk*, esp. 128–50.

2. M. M. Bakhtin, *The Dialogic Imagination*, 279. For a rich reading of Wordsworth on the principles of Bakhtin, see Don H. Bialostosky, *Wordsworth, Dialogics, and the Practice of Criticism*. Related to this notion is Thomas McFarland's conception of Wordsworth's poetic presentation of "the streaming infrashape," in *William Wordsworth: Intensity and Achievement*, 38–56, and "Problems of Style in the Poetry of Wordsworth and Coleridge," chap. 4 in *Romanticism and the Forms of Ruin*, 216–54.

3. For readings of Rimbaud in a social context, see Edward Ahearn, *Rimbaud;* and Kristin Ross, *The Emergence of Social Space*.

4. James Hutton, *The Greek Anthology in Italy* and *The Greek Anthology in France and in the Latin Writers of the Netherlands*. Hutton is cited and summarized by Geoffrey Hartman, *The Fate of Reading*, 224–33. Hartman subtly applies the notion of point to Valéry, and it could be said that the best definition of Valéry's style, as well as the basis for a distinction between his and Mallarmé's, could well be expressed in terms of point. In an earlier discussion, Hartman specifically develops the notion of point with reference to Wordsworth's abandonment of it: "Wordsworth's subtler mode serves to free the lyric from the tyranny of point" (*Beyond Formalism*, 45). I am here taking Hartman's observations as my locus of departure.

5. In general, see Patricia Ann Meyer Spacks, *Gossip*. Liane Strauss, "The Art of Fame" relates gossip in poetry to notions of Fama in antiquity and the Renaissance. Jan B. Gordon, in a book in progress, of which various studies have appeared, demonstrates that gossip and its conventions are not only a powerful analogue but a kind of central connecting instrument in the novels of writers contemporary with those I am discussing— in Jane Austen, George Eliot, and Thomas Hardy. See Gordon, "Gossip, Diary, Letter, Text: Anne Brontë's Narrative *Tenant* and the Problematic of the Gothic Sequel," *ELH* 54 (1984): 719–45; "Affiliation as (Dis)semination: Gossip and Family in George Eliot's European Novel," *Journal of European Studies* 15 (1985): 155–89. So the removal of gossip from the range of poetry would, on this showing, entail a redistribution of implied literary assignments to genres. Such a redistribution is temporary, since what amounts to gossip does return to poetry before long; Robert Browning's *The Ring and the Book*, among other works, can be seen as a retroduction of gossip to poetic possibility.

6. A. C. Goodson, *Verbal Imagination: Coleridge and the Language of Modern Criticism*, 84.

7. Alan Bewell, *Wordsworth and the Enlightenment*.

8. I quote from Jonathan Wordsworth et al., eds., *The Prelude 1799, 1805, 1850*.

9. They are at lines 21, 30, 47, 60, 79, 81, 87, 107, 127, 137, 145, 150, 201, 228, 238.

10. S. T. Coleridge, *Biographia Literaria*, chap. 17.

11. Walter Jackson Bate, *Coleridge*, 43–51.

12. At a point in the project of *The Recluse*, Wordsworth has spoken of "a roving

School-boy" much like the boy of Winander. This boy, however, does not die to be mourned but converges wholly with the poet: "Since that day forth the place to him— to *me* / (For I who live to register the truth / Was that same young and happy Being) became / As beautiful to thought, as it had been, / When present, to the bodily sense" ("Home at Grasmere," part 1, book 1 of *The Recluse,* in Wordsworth, *Poetical Works,* 5:314).

13. Donald Davie, *Articulate Energy,* 106–15.

14. Paul de Man, "Intentional Structure of the Romantic Image," in *Rhetoric and Romanticism,* 1–17.

15. James Thomson, "Summer," 585–98, *The Seasons,* in *Poetical Works,* 2:82.

16. Such obscure opinions are voiced at various points in Whitman's work, and sometimes in the verse. The floating theoretical basis for his identification with his audience also floats in the poems:

> See, projected through time,
> For me an audience interminable.
>
> With firm and regular step they went, they never stop,
> Successions of men, Americanos, a hundred millions,
> One generation playing its part and passing on,
> Another generation playing its part and passing on in its turn,
> With faces turn'd sideways or backward towards me to listen,
> With eyes retrospective towards me
>
> . . . .
>
> O such themes—equalities! O divine average!
> Warblings under the sun, usher'd as now, or at noon, or setting,
> Strains musical flowing through ages, now reaching hither,
> I take to your reckless and composite chords, add to them, and
>   cheerfully pass them forward.
>
> (Whitman, "Starting from Paumanok," sections 2, 10, in *Leaves of Grass,* 16–17, 21–22)

17. "Crossing Brooklyn Ferry" (1856), 165, l. 115–end.

18. Whitman, *Unpublished Poetry and Prose,* 2:85. The passage is quoted and discussed by Paul Zweig in *Walt Whitman: The Making of the Poet,* 181, 355. Elsewhere in his notebooks (2:66), Whitman uses "Dilation" as a heading, a sort of idiosyncratic, and therefore strongly marked, version of "amplification."

19. Robert D. Faner, *Walt Whitman and Opera.* The exponent of bel canto should be large-lunged, and it is interesting that Montale, a later novice opera singer, should have produced not the Whitmanian open line but a line perpetually pulled back from its own impulse to open out.

20. In his long visionary letter to Paul Demeny of 15 May 1871, Rimbaud declares: "Baudelaire est le premier voyant, roi des poètes, *un vrai Dieu*" ("Baudelaire is the first of seers, king of poets, *a true God*") (Rimbaud, *Œuvres complètes,* 253).

21. Ibid., 249. Letter to Georges Izambard of 13 May 1871. In the poem "Solde" from *Illuminations,* Rimbaud speaks of "les Voix reconstituées" (*Œuvres complètes,* 145).

22. For the difference between Rimbaud and Baudelaire as prose poets, the reflections of Jacques Roubaud are apposite: "In the history of the prose poem, two pos-

sibilities are constantly colliding: either designate as poetry that which otherwise would be prose in poetry, or on the contrary blur the boundaries of verse to make poetry in prose. The prose poem, appearing with Baudelaire as a protective rampart for classic verse, has long belonged to the second category. But the *Illuminations*, before free verse existed as an autonomous verse form, are what could be called a 'poem in prose of free verse'" (*La Vieillesse d'Alexandre*, 135–36).

23. Arthur Rimbaud, "Délires II," *Une Saison en enfer, Œuvres complètes*, 106–8.

24. "Délires II, Alchimie du verbe," *Une Saison en enfer, Rimbaud*, trans. Wallace Fowlie, 193–95 (somewhat revised). This, and other poems here, vary in details from their separate, slightly earlier versions.

25. "Je faisais" is at once more comprehensive and more evasive than the more elaborate version of the separate poem, which casts a contrary-to-fact condition on the simple verb of existence: "Tel, j'eusse été mauvaise enseigne d'auberge."

26. A discussion of Wordsworth and many other poets with respect to the community they are addressing is provided by John W. Erwin in *Lyric Apocalypse*.

Chapter 4

1. Quotations from A. J. Smith, ed., John Donne, *The Complete English Poems*.

2. The images intensify through an action actual or implied, as is characteristic for Donne. As Frank Warnke says, somewhat too exclusively, "Similarity, for Donne, is not a sensually perceptible resemblance of appearance but an intellectually perceptible resemblance of function" (*Versions of Baroque*, 28). For further discussion of these questions, see Cook, "Sound, Sense, and Religion in the Dialogized Context of Donne's Poetry," chap. 5 in *Canons and Wisdoms*.

3. Stephen Greenblatt, *Renaissance Self-fashioning*, along with the work of Joel Fineman, Jonathan Crewe, and others.

4. Such practices are abundantly documented in Foxe's *Book of Martyrs*.

5. "The whole frame of the Poem is a beating out of a piece of gold, but the last clause is as the impression of the stamp, and that is it that makes it currant" (Sermon preached upon the Penitential Psalms, Spring 1626, George Potter and Evelyn Simpson, eds., *The Sermons of John Donne*, 6.1.41). This, interestingly, defines a poem as going into circulation when it is ready. The minting metaphor aptly characterizes the finality built into the poem and exhibited by it.

6. So pervasive were these attributions that foundlings were often left in the Inns, and the name "Temple," after "Middle Temple," often given to them as an assumed last name. I draw these details from George Klawitter, *The Enigmatic Narrator*.

7. Cook, *Canons and Wisdoms*, 81–100.

8. John Kerrigan (*The Sonnets; and A Lover's Complaint*, 313–16) well summarizes the arguments for taking the date as 1603, as does Garrett Mattingly in "The Date of Shakespeare's Sonnet CVII." Kerrigan points out the difficulties of assigning 1595 to this reference, when Elizabeth was beset with troubles. However, Fernand Baldensperger adduces some arresting evidence for the earlier date (*Les Sonnets de Shakespeare*, 164–65): in July 1595, Thomas Cecil wrote his brother Robert, referring to Elizabeth as a moon that had gone through eclipse. In April 1596, he quotes from a sermon of Anthony

Rudd: "The pale-faced moon looks bloody on the earth, / And lean-looked prophets whisper fearful change."

9. The OED attests a number of meanings before 1610 for this word; the ones substantiated with quotations from Shakespeare are: (1) to write as a witness, (2) to write at the conclusion of something, (3) to attest that the writer is the so-named person, (4) to give one's assent or adhesion to, (5) to sign away or yield up, (6) to write one's name as a token of assent, (7) to admit or subject oneself to law or rule, (8) to confess oneself in the wrong, (9) to admit or concede the force, validity, or truth of, (10) to make admission of, (11) to vouch for a person. Most of these uses attested elsewhere in Shakespeare are present in the instance of the word here; the "to me" in "Death to me subscribes" opens the word out for such rich possibilities.

10. Joel Fineman, *Shakespeare's Perjured Eye: The Invention of Poetic Subjectivity in the Sonnets*, 109.

11. Stephen Booth points out that "Only a conjunction ties the couplet to the third quatrain," and that "An emphatic trochee at the beginning of line 9 underscores the unity of the octave" (*An Essay on Shakespeare's Sonnets*, 45, 44).

12. Fineman remains apposite on this question: "Moreover, the sequence as a whole remarks this progress it enacts, remarks it in a thematic way such that these contrasts between the two sub-sequences come to function as dynamic inter-relationships rather than as static oppositions. Because the sonnets to the dark lady explicitly rethink the themes and motifs first presented in the sonnets to the young man, because the two sub-sequences are engaged with each other in this self-consciously thematic way, the progress of the sequence as a whole seems directed from the start. It is as though the sequence were designed to motivate this movement of motifs, as though the sequence were determined to make something consequential of its own sequentiality" (*Shakespeare's Perjured Eye*, 131).

13. Shakespeare's powerful enlistment of pairings goes all the way to the heart of his rhetoric, with his penchant for the figure of "one-through-two," or hendiadys, and with his persistent balancing of doubled terms. For this feature of Shakespeare's style and syntax, see Albert Cook, *Shakespeare's Enactment*, 150–51, and Bertram Joseph, *Acting Shakespeare*. For a general discussion of various kinds of doubling in Shakespeare, including hendiadys, see Frank Kermode, "Cornelius and Voltemand: Doubles in *Hamlet*," chap. 2 in *Forms of Attention*, 33–64.

14. Jonathan Crewe, *Trials of Authorship: Anterior Forms and Poetic Reconstruction from Wyatt to Shakespeare*, 45. As Crewe also says, "This 'original' *Selbstsucht*, of which the 'born' aristocrat is a figure, can be conceived as that which at once knows a self and knows it only as the object of a perpetual, insatiable wishing and seeking ('Such' is also 'quest') to which the only feared and desired end is the paradoxical one of annihilation. This premoral *Selbstsucht* can then be regarded as the constant, inadmissible origin, interior, and undoing of all constructions and putative embodiments that it subsequently inhabits; it can also be regarded, on account of its undoing of itself and everything else, as the paradoxical origin of any possible originality. This *Selbstsucht*, which knows no self except a defective one, wants all selves except mediocre ones, and can be satisfied by none" (78).

15. For astrology in the Renaissance generally, see Wayne Shumaker, *The Occult Sciences in the Renaissance*, 7–55.

16. I am here following the acute deductions of Robert J. Mueller, "'Infinite Desire': Spenser's Arthur and the Representation of Courtly Ambition." As Mueller says, "The wistful confusion of Arthur's utterances signals the extent to which the interlocutors remain unaligned in the poem's allegorical roster. . . . Arthur's experience demonstrates less a failure of his goal than an assumption of attitudes which are defined as unrealizable within the structure of the vision" (748).

17. Baldensperger notes that Bruno was in England from 1593 to 1595. However, Marsilio Ficino, among others, also wrote about the "world-soul." See Shumaker, *The Occult Sciences*, 121–27.

18. Also relevant here are the deductions of Norman Holland: "identity . . . [has at least] three simultaneous meanings, as (1) an agency, (2) a consequence, (3) a representation. . . .

"Identity as representation leads to two possibilities. How do I represent the wholeness of you? How do I represent the wholeness of me? . . . The distinction between the 'inside' and the 'outside' interpreter is also important because in it a theme-and-variations concept of identity poses and preserves the classical psychoanalytic polarity: conscious and unconscious. That is, to someone formulating an identity from outside, like Freud observing the young man or me interpreting Fitzgerald, a given piece of behavior is neither unconscious nor conscious. It is simply behavior" (*The I*, 33, 36).

In the *Sonnets*, Shakespeare has found a way of opening out the simplicities of behavior, without overstructuring them.

19. Still, it should be noted, as I learn from Lee Patterson's qualification of Fineman's claim that Shakespeare's persona-consciousness is completely new (personal communication), that Chaucer alone of several contemporaries introduced the first-person identification in documents still extant at the Public Records Office. See also Patterson, *Chaucer and the Subject of History*.

20. Abdul Hasan Shah, Sultan of Golconda, you
        Are still walking, this fine morning, through
        A late 17th century field of flowers, dressed
        In your tent-like, flowered dressing gown,
        Your beard close-cropped already at dawn
        By the servant who carries your blue sunshade
        Umbrella. You are fat and happy. I remark
        You here, in this museum, among a thousand
        Others because we look alike—are dead
        Ringers for each other. You have plucked
        A flower at your feet and smell the sweetness—
        I always do that when I walk through flowers;
        And, this morning, Chick The Barber cut back
        My black beard, covering my great girth
        With the pitched tent of his flowered barber's cloth.
        Milord, as I take this respite from my rounds
        Of work as sometime teacher and old-time academic pol,
        I am happy to have found you: we are both
        Potentates of minor and provincial states.

               (Mac Hammond, *Mappamundi: New and Selected Poems*, 3)

Chapter 5

1. T. S. Eliot, "Dante," 201.

2. As Charles Williams, says, "Such a stupor produces two results—a sense of reverence and a desire to know more. A noble awe and a noble curiosity come to life" (*The Figure of Beatrice*, 7).

3. Etienne Gilson, *Dante the Philosopher;* Bruno Nardi, "Filosofia e teologia ai tempi di Dante."

4. All quotations are from C. H. Grandgent, ed., C. S. Singleton, rev., Dante Alighieri, *La divina commedia*.

5. Charles S. Singleton, *Dante Studies I: Commedia: Elements of Structure,* 12, 62.

6. "These analogies lay at hand. For Dante they were real, not fictive. Of such a reality the epic poet Virgil, for example, may have been uncertain, and the shadow behind the ivory gate may express his uncertainty: did Aeneas *really* found Rome, is Augustus *really* his descendant, do souls *really* transmigrate in a vast circular order? But Christ, for Dante, really did redeem man. The Bible is really the word of God. The spirit really seeks to know the Good of God. The Church is really a channel of Divine Grace.... Dante need attend to no differences because his poem is based not on metaphor, but on quasi-allegorical or figural analogy ... a theological idea that resembles ... 'the allegory of the theologians'" (Albert Cook, *The Classic Line,* 222–23).

7. In his earlier poetry, Dante touches on the simpler "inexpressibility trope," as in these lines from "Amor che ne la mente mi ragiona": "Però, se le mie rime avran difetto / ch'entreran ne la loda di costei, / di ciò si biasmi il debole intelletto / e 'l parlar nostro, che non ha valore / di ritrar tutto ciò che dice Amore" ("But if my verse would have a defect / when entering into the praise of her, / for that is to blame the weak intellect / and our speech, that does not have the power / of spelling out all that Love says") (*Convivio,* 3.1.14–18).

8. In the letter to Can Grande, the *Paradiso* is called "contractus."

9. "Facultas videndi Deum non competit intellectui creato secundum suam naturam sed per lumen gloriae, quod intellectum in quadam deiformitate constituit" (St. Thomas, *Summa Theologica,* I, 12. 6, cited in Giuseppe Vandelli, ed., *Divina Commedia col Commento Scartazziniano,* 611–12).

10. Jacques Lacan, *Le Séminaire XX: Encore,* 40 and passim. Lacan interestingly here adduces one of Dante's major philosophers, Richard of St. Victor.

11. Charles Williams, *The Figure of Beatrice,* 23 ff.

12. Irma Brandeis, *The Ladder of Vision: A Study of Images in Dante's Comedy,* 191. These fusions of idea are further testimony to Dante's originality as a philosopher. Kenelm Foster points out that "Rhetoric's symbol was the planet Venus" ("The Mind in Love: Dante's Philosophy," 49). Foster stresses Dante's notion of "perfect seeing," "perfetto veder" (*Par* 5.1–6) (52). Further, "insofar as one refers the desired object to one's possession of it, one may be said to find one's ultimate end in a 'using' (*uti* or *usus*).... Dante's very emphatic placing in this text of the *Convivio* [4.22] of *uso* at the *end* of purposeful activity suggests a slightly more subjective approach than St. Thomas' ... connected with the equally strong stress elsewhere in Dante on an *object* of desire that transcends the human subject and the limits of the individual" (54); "stress falls not on

existence, *esse,* but on activity, *operatio"* (55). The activity in which he engages is not at all erotic, but it involves the recall of the erotic.

13. Peter Dronke, *Medieval Latin and the Rise of European Love-Lyric.*

14. Robert Harrison, *The Body of Beatrice.*

15. *De vulgari eloquentia,* 1.16; Robert S. Haller, tr., *The Literary Criticism of Dante Alighieri,* 28.

16. Dronke, *Medieval Latin and the Rise of European Love-Lyric,* 136–55; Bruno Nardi, *Dante e la cultura medievale,* 81–124.

17. I have taken Pound's later version, though his considerably earlier version also highlights the features I am emphasizing.

18. My quotation comes from John Freccero, *Dante: The Poetics of Conversion,* 187.

19. Gianfranco Contini, "Introduction to Dante's *Rime,*" 32.

20. Nardi finds that this poem, which was composed at the time of Dante's closest association with Cavalcanti, incorporates some of Cavalcanti's ideas (*Saggi,* 192–94).

21. The model is a Ciceronian one, even though Augustine (*De doctrina cristiana* 4.17) qualifies and criticizes Cicero's account of low, middle, and high styles (*Orator* 101).

22. Augustine, *Confessions,* trans. William Watts, 5.3.5; revised.

23. Erwin Panofsky, *Gothic Architecture and Scholasticism,* 36–37.

24. C. H. Grandgent is still a succinct expositor of this systematized ordering: "The *Divine Comedy* is not only an Encyclopedia, a Journey, a Vision—it is the Autobiography of a soul" (Grandgent, ed., *La divina commedia di Dante Alighieri,* xxxi). But his close matchings of the progressions of Dante the author-pilgrim with the allegorical structures of his poem, like Singleton's and Freccero's, have an air of arbitrariness about them, for all their ingenuity, whereas the single focus on an allegorical detail or of the entire scheme will often produce full and nearly indisputable readings.

25. "Already from the argument of the *Commedia* on, and already when the simple literal sense is grasped as the depiction of the ascent of a man to bliss, the world of knowing, opening itself more and more in the interplay of questions and answers in the 'science of godly things' according to the traditional representations of 'scienza divina' is the first place accorded, a necessary and constitutive part of the *Commedia"* (Hans Felten, "Zur Frage in der *Divina Commedia,*" 145).

26. John Ruskin commented at length on the sharpness of Dante's articulated observations in *Modern Painters,* 3, chaps. 14, 15. "The first striking character of the scenery is intense definition." Ruskin speaks of Dante's "ultimate and most intense expression of the love of sight" (3:234). Color, for example, which Benedetto Croce also stresses, can be simply named or combined into descriptions, as in the account of the three steps into Purgatory in *Purgatorio* 9 (94–102). The clarity and range of the new poetic access to the concrete allows it to verge into the delicacies noted by Ruskin. Thus the clothes of the angels are "green like leaves that have just been born" ("Verdi come fogliette pur mo nate") (*Purg.* 8.28), and their wings are a green undifferentiated in description and so presumably of a varied complementarity with the green of the clothes.

27. Isaiah 11.5 stands behind line 114, "And righteousness shall be the girdle of his loins, and faithfulness the girdle of his reins." Line 117 echoes Jeremiah 48.11.

28. Bakhtin, *The Dialogic Imagination,* 157.

29. Peter Dronke, *The Medieval Lyric.*

30. Paul Zumthor, *Langue et technique poétiques à l'époque romane.*

31. Giuseppe Giacalone, *Tempo ed eternità nella Divina Commedia,* 9. As he goes on, "Dante's human dynamic finds its first great measure in the Terrestrial Paradise, its most concrete pause, in which Dante's personal history and the history of humanity discover a full humanity between time and eternity"(11); "It is sufficient to recall the two semantic times, the present of eternity, 'I am Buonconte' and the past of 'time' 'I was Caesar,' 'I was Montefeltro'"(31).

32. For example, one could trace such processes in Purgatory 5, in such passages as 5.16–21, in Bonconte di Montefeltro's contrast between the two wills (67 ff.), and in the tonality of the interruption at 130–35.

33. As Singleton says, "It is not Christ who comes. It is Beatrice—Beatrice who comes *as* Christ" (*Commedia,* 52). The two-natured creature often identified—not incorrectly, but oversimply, with Christ—in the procession is the Griffin, but interpreting that figure as Christ or not as Christ leads to extraordinary complication either way. Building on abundant signs of a Roman triumph, after a survey of the evidence, Peter Armour infers that the Griffin is "an image of Rome, . . . more-than-earthly Rome, the ideal agent of God's true arcane will" (*Dante's Griffin and the History of the World,* 72). While Armour substantiates this interpretation with a sharply contextualized reading of the *De monarchia* and much else, the contradiction remains of separating the two-natured Griffin from Christ, even though, for all the conflation of biblical and other sources, "the introduction of a griffin drawing a chariot marks the point at which, having cited these biblical sources, Dante abandons them and begins to employ symbols invented by himself" (3–4).

The general interaction of images at this point is well characterized by Dronke: "The complexity of the visions, and of their later exposition by Beatrice, seems to me to be of the same order as that of the procession which precedes them. . . . It lies in the interplay between inner and outer meaning. What is revealed is in the first place microcosmic: it is aspects of Dante's own consciousness that are crystallised in the apocalyptic images; but when crystallised in this way they also acquire macrocosmic connotations. . . . If the inner and outer force of the images synchronized perfectly, . . . we would have a mechanical operation. . . . The richness of hidden comparisons, as Geoffrey of Vinsauf noted, lies in the fact that they are not like this: they 'fluctuate within and without, here and there, far and near, distant and present'" ("The Phantasmagoria in the Earthly Paradise," 56).

34. There may be a reference to the fact that in the previous canto, Eve is spoken of as *not* veiled (29.27).

35. Charles S. Singleton, *Journey to Beatrice,* 39–57 and passim.

36. John Freccero, *Dante: The Poetics of Conversion,* citing Pierre Courcelle, *Recherches sur les "Confessions" de St. Augustin,* Paris: E. de Boccard, 1950.

37. For his avoidance of that counterpointing, see note 22 above.

38. *De vulgari eloquentia,* 2, chaps. 10–11. See also the discussion in Mario Fubini, *Metrica e poesia,* I, *Dal Duecento al Petrarca,* 35–60. Fubini further points out that on occasion Dante highlights his individual words by an avoidance of elisions that would blend them further into a sentence (35–42).

39. Fubini also discusses Dante's strategy with enjambments, 44–45.

Chapter 6

1. C. S. Lewis, *The Allegory of Love;* Charles Williams, *The Figure of Beatrice.* Emphasis on this special character of *fin amors,* or *amour courtois,* is continued by Henri Davenson (Henri Marrou) in *Les Troubadours,* among others, while one strain of modern discourse stresses the formal or arbitrarily conventional aspects of the poetry: its self-containment by its language, as in Jean-Charles Huchet, *L'Amour discourtois;* its game aspect, "The game of love as 'deep play'" in the words of Laura Kendrick, *The Game of Love: Troubadour Wordplay;* and the assumptions underlying its oral performance, as with Amelia E. Van Vleck, *Memory and Re-creation in Troubadour Lyric.* All these books enrich our understanding of the conventions of troubadour poetry, though they run the danger of inducing the epistemological oversimplification involved in the falsely posed nineteenth-century question as to whether the loves of the poets were "real" or a feigned device, and also in the more modern skeptical version that the intrication of the real and the feigned undercuts the substantiality of the real feeling.

2. Dronke, *Medieval Latin and the Rise of European Love-Lyric.* Dronke's abundant evidence covers a time from the second millennium B.C. in Egypt through the Middle Ages, and a range of medieval verse from Georgia to Iceland. Of course, this expression of desire in verse could be extended through the Renaissance to modern times and to Japan and China. Stephen Owen finds that there are common chords in classical Chinese poetry and in the poetry of the West, from Horace and the troubadours through Neruda, in their ways of addressing desire and connecting it with fulfillment and loss (Owen, *Mi-Lou: Poetry and the Labyrinth of Desire*). Both Dronke and Owen just begin to address the gamut of poetry about love in Arabic, Persian, and Sanskrit. In an epic frame, some attention to love can interact with the heroic imperatives, and it characteristically does so in the *Iliad* and the *Odyssey* and in the medieval Germanic epic. Love heavily qualifies a universalizing view in the *Metamorphoses* of Ovid, and it takes over variously in the *Divina Commedia* and in the work of Blake.

3. René Nelli has done this in *L'Érotique des troubadours.* Nelli allows, but does not overemphasize, the large derivation of troubadour love poetry from the Arabic love poetry preceding it (40–63). He ties in the conventions of goliardic "wandering scholar" love poetry, Carolingian love poetry in epistolary and other forms, liturgical poetry, Spanish May poems, as well as a typology of social roles and popular celebrations.

4. Sarah Kay offers a number of specifications that permute the literary convention with the actual speaker, beginning by taking issue with Zumthor: "if one allows that the representation of subjectivity in language involves a collective dimension, then one can speak of the subject as being 'generalized' rather than 'objectivized' by intertextual reference" (*Subjectivity in Troubadour Poetry,* 6). "Irony [not everywhere present where Kay finds it] . . . suggests how surface meaning can be rendered problematic by the juxtaposition of incompatibles" (20). "One spectacular consequence of reorienting allegory around the subject position is that a rhetorical (and moral) scheme whose original purpose was the assertion of community can become a means of elaborating difference" (52).

5. T. S. Eliot, "The Three Voices of Poetry," in *On Poetry and Poets,* 89–102. Medieval theory offers a counterpart to these (as I am indebted to an anonymous reader for pointing out); see P. B. Salmon, "The 'Three Voices' of Poetry in Medieval Literary Theory."

And indeed the distinction can be traced to Aristotle's account of the "mimesis" of voices in the *Poetics*, 1148a19–29, as expounded by Gerald F. Else, *Aristotle's Poetics: The Argument*, 90–108.

6. The very difficulty of the attempt to elucidate the distinction between these two kinds of verse, as by Ulrich Mölk in *Trobar clus—Trobar leu*, points to the distinction as a secondary one, beneath the primary distinction between troubadour poetry generally and easier folk poetry. These remarkable poems would have to have been built slowly, syllable by syllable, whether the final result be easier or harder in a given case.

7. In one of its postures, this poetry speaks of the lady as deferring union, or even as wholly unattainable. Yet there are numerous clear references to sexual union in the poems of this tradition, as these references are catalogued by Moshé Lazar in *Amour courtois e fin amors*, 120–35.

8. The text of this poem, and others of Arnaut's, is taken from Gianluigi Toja, ed., *Arnaut Daniel: Canzoni*.

9. The texts of all quotations not otherwise attributed are taken from R. T. Hill and T. G. Bergin, *Anthology of the Provençal Troubadours*, vol. 1.

10. Lacan's whole system can be brought to bear on the troubadours, as he himself does in his late work. See Jacques Lacan, *Écrits; Séminaire VII: L'éthique de la psychanalyse*, especially 155–62 and 180–81, which deals explicitly with the troubadours.

11. R. Howard Bloch, *Etymologies and Genealogies*, 124.

12. "Enveya" could also be translated as "desire," along the lines of modern French "envie," as indicated by this gloss in Émil Levy's lexicon. The range of meanings in the word through "envy" and "desire" would be accommodated by the "de" to which it is attached.

13. For Pound's incorporation of Bernart, see Peter Makin, *Provence and Pound*, 34–59.

14. I am drawing on MacCary's challenging study, "When God Became Woman: The Erotic of the Troubadors," a study still in manuscript, which the author has been generous enough to share with me. He continues there, "It is the expression of a love which is insatiable in its own terms, a radical alienation proving that to speak desire, is, in the very nature of both language and desire, the enunciation of an absence; the sense of need that swells within the self can be answered by no other. I think of the Lacanian figures of desire as a Moebius strip where self and other are indistinguishable continuities of each, and male desire as an envelope containing 'the emptiness' of the woman around which the subject speaks himself rather than her." MacCary offers a diagram:

| subject | object (pre-oedipal mother) |
| self | object (oedipal father) |

For the complexities of the potentially phallic mother, he offers another diagram:

the mother has	the mother denies
the phallus	the phallus
the mother affirms	the mother needs/
the phallus	demands/desires
beyond desire	the phallus

15. At the peak of a tradition remote from this one is the similar intensity produced by Sappho in Anne Carson's reading: "We saw Sappho construct this stereoscopic moment in fr. 31 ['That man seems to me equal to a god'] as a three-point circuit of

desire joining herself, her beloved and 'the man who listens closely.' The verbal action of eros in fr. 31 allows our perception to jump or shift from one level of desire to another, from actual to possible, without losing sight of the difference between them. In Sappho's poem the shift of view is momentary, a vertigo and sudden sense of being very close to the core where feelings form" (Carson, *Eros the Bittersweet,* 85).

16. Georges Duby gives the anthropological correlatives of this role: "The 'joven' is a complete man, an adult. He is introduced into the group of warriors; he has received arms; he is knighted. It is a knight. . . . Youth may therefore be defined as the part of existence comprised between knighting and paternity. The presence of such a group at the heart of aristocratic society entails certain mental attitudes, certain representations of collective psychology, certain myths, where are found at once a reflection of literary works and models for them" ("Au XIIe siècle: Les 'jeunes' dans la société aristocratique," cited by Jacques Le Goff, *L'Imaginaire médiévale,* 182–83).

17. This is elaborately expounded and exhaustively documented in Sandra Resnick Alfonsi, *Masculine Submission in Troubadour Lyric.*

18. Martin de Riquer translates "m'abelis" as "aflige," "afflicts," thus missing the strong transpositions (Riquer, *Los trovadores,* 1:484). But with this word, our attention is drawn to the preoccupied transfer of everything here, even despair, into joy when "over-love" is in question. The lexicon is unambiguous on "abelir." That "abelis" means "please" here, as it always or nearly always does, is further substantiated by the possible approach to a formula in the whole sentence "Tan m'abelis lo pensamens," which matches the first line of Folquet's later poem "Tant m'abellis l'amoros pessamens."

19. *De vulgari eloquentia,* 2.9.

20. "Rima" also means "rhymes"; in this equivocation, the verse splits itself on the rack in the very act of carrying through its rhyme.

21. Angus Fletcher, *Colors of the Mind,* 104.

22. In a setting of Bernart's "Can vei la lauzeta mover," for example, the first six syllables of the line get a note apiece, while the two syllables of "mover" get four notes and two notes respectively. In the next line, "de joi sas alas contral rai," seven of the eight syllables get one note, and "con" gets three. See Hendrik van der Werf, *The Chansons of the Troubadors and Trouvères,* 90–95.

23. "Bos motz e gais sons," are referred to, for example, in Bernart's *vida.*

24. See Siegfried Beyschlag, *Altdeutsche Verskunst in Grundzügen,* 52–65, for an analysis of various effects. "Auxiliary syllables often sustain a function of elevation [Erhebung]. . . . A further such stylization is deliberately sought after, an interchange in the weights of stress between metrical stress and speech accent" (60).

25. This feature, I believe, led the contemporary Austrian poet H. V. Artman to assert (too oppositionally) that the metrical inventiveness of the *Minnesänger* surpasses Dante's (personal communication).

26. This text is from Walther von der Vogelweide, *Gedichte,* ed. Carl von Kraus, 63.

27. Texts are from Hugo Moser and Helmut Tervooren, eds., *Des Minnesangs Frühling,* 272–73, 262.

28. Dronke, *Medieval Latin and the Rise of European Love-Lyric,* 300–331.

29. Texts are taken from Otto Schumann, ed., *Carmina Burana.*

Chapter 7

1. Quotations are from R. A. B. Mynors, ed., *C. Valerii Catulli Carmina*.

2. How fully Sappho has drawn on preexisting poetic language for this poem is discussed by Elizabeth C. Storz, "Toward the History of a Lyric Body: Sappho fr. 31, Homer and Elegy."

3. Micaela Janan sees poem 11 and poem 51, in their juxtaposition, as offering a paradigm of Lacanian "knowing" through the contrast of something like a courtly exaltation of the love object in poem 51 and something like degradation in poem 11, together with the deployment of persons beginning with the move to the indirectness of "I" in the translation of Sappho's poem. Such a strenuousness would go far, she urges, to motivate the great leap to the final "otium" stanza that Catullus has added to Sappho's poem (*When the Lamp Is Shattered: Desire and Narrative in Catullus*). It might be said, further, that this structure is sealed by the startling positioning of the self-address in the first line of the "otium" stanza—and also by the sudden transition from the intimate person seen to a macrohistorical perspective. The power of Catullus's communicative dexterity, it may be said, effectually enlists the Lacanian imaginary in the service of the Lacanian symbolic.

4. "Identidem," a word repeated in poem 11, is absent in Sappho (Walter Ferrari, "Il carme 51 di Catullo," 244). The speaker no longer sees either lover or beloved before him, if the perfect of "adspexi" (249) is taken literally, etc. T. P. Wiseman offers his own succinct summary of the differences: "What does he add to Sappho's original? The whole of the second line; *identidem* in line 3, *spectat et* in line 4, *misero* in line 5, *eripit* in line 6, the vocative *Lesbia* in line 7, *suopte* in line 10, *gemina . . . nocte* in lines 11 and 12" (*Catullus and His World: A Reappraisal*, 153).

5. Charles Segal emphasizes the possible connection between *amor* and *otium* in literary tradition and summarizes succinctly the range of discussion that the break of this last stanza has drawn ("*Otium* and *Eros*: Catullus, Sappho, and Euripides' *Hippolytus*," 817n). Still, one expects political effects in a tragedy like the *Hippolytus*, but not in a lyric poem, and even if the tradition of connecting "otium" and "eros" does serve as a bridge here between private and public, the introduction of the public domain is a surprise, both climactic for the poem and anticlimactic for its coherence. In an earlier article, Segal examines Catullus's complex uses of "otium," especially in a literary context but also in a philosophical one, citing Lucretius: "the high valuation of *otium* suggests an Epicurean note" (Segal, "Catullan *Otiosi*: The Lover and the Poet," 28). Here Segal focuses on poem 50, using poem 51 as a foil; but what he says applies to both, though it could be added that the disastrous effects of "otium" in poem 51 would qualify the Epicurean strain of the word.

6. For details of the political in pastoral and its "levels," see Annabel M. Patterson, *Pastoral and Ideology: Virgil to Valéry*.

7. C. J. Fordyce notes that the geography of this poem reflects recent politics. If so, then past, present, and even future are built into the very names (Fordyce, *Catullus: A Commentary*, 164). It is also possible, if Fordyce is right, that there is some shadow of complexity in Catullus's relations with Furius and Aurelius—but not for this poem; their function as messengers and *comites* simplifies them into those converging roles. In poem

46, the band of comrades ("coetus comitum") take "diversae variae viae" ("varied, diverse ways") out to empire.

8. Comparable strategies of combining love and politics are simpler in other poets. Propertius starts out with a stark opposition but then modifies it in his last book. In Tibullus 3, Delia is brought in only at the very end of the poem, which mostly celebrates Messala's trip. Tibullus 7 is entirely given over to the victory of, but ends with a prayer for, progeny.

9. See Eleanor Winsor Leach, *The Rhetoric of Space: Literary and Artistic Representations of Landscape in Republican and Augustan Rome.* Leach sets this tradition, as it culminates in Virgil, into a specific set of visual and psychological practices (197–308, especially 197–260). She speaks of Catullus's "idiosyncratic viewpoint": "Already in Catullus' witty collection we see this principle at work. . . . In Catullus' gallery, however, few settings are explicitly pictured, and the majority of these are located outside Rome" (276). This expresses negatively his sweep of spatial reference, which never lets itself into the Theocritan-Virgilian reverberations.

10. As Jasper Griffin says, "Roman life, and particularly the life of luxury and pleasure, was so strongly Hellenistic in colouring and material that no simple division into 'Greek' and 'Roman' elements is possible" ("Augustan Poetry and the Life of Luxury," 88).

11. Eve Adler sees a dialectic in the strategic mix of first, second, and third persons, even in so small a compass as the "self-division" of poem 85, "Odi et amo." As she says of poem 11, "It is only when we come to poem 11, finally, that we find *Catullus himself* expressing a renunciation of the surrendered aspect of himself to which he otherwise clings so fiercely in the betrayal poems discussed above" (*Catullan Self-revelation,* 150).

12. Meleager makes comparable connections, in a more schematic, less reverberant style, as for example when he sets an elegiac epigram in the internationalist context of his poem 2:

εἰ δὲ Σύρος, τί τό θαῦμα; μίαν, ξένε, πάτριδα κόσμον
ναίομεν, ἕν θνατούς πάντας ἔτικτε Χάος.

If Syrian, what wonder? Friend, we inhabit a single
Fatherland world, Chaos has born all mortals as one.

(Page, 2.5–6)

13. John Petersen Elder, "Catullus I, His Poetic Creed, and Nepos," 143–49.

14. For an acute account of Cicero's functions in Catullus's milieu, see Wiseman, *Catullus and His World,* passim. Cicero's own references to such poetry as Catullus's are slight, but contextualized enough to allow us to score him for incomprehension, even arrogance. In a long discussion of Epicurus and Epicurean principles, he abundantly and admiringly quotes Ennius. Then he breaks away to contrast this conservative paragon to newer poets: "o poetam egregium! quamquam ab his cantoribus Euphorionis contemnitur" ("O distinctive poet! Though he is despised by these singers of Euphorion") (*Tusc.* 3.19.45). Cicero fails to see more than a subjection to the Hellenistic norms of a Euphorion in such work as Catullus's. Similarly, he sneers at these "neoterics" in a letter to Atticus (7.2.1) by composing a spondaized (σπονδειάζοντα) hexameter to describe

his own sea voyage in what he imagines to be a parody of their style. In the *Orator*, in quibbles about spelling and pronunciation, he distances himself from these new poets: "ita non erat ea offensio in versibus quam nunc fugiunt poetae novi" ("So that offense was not in the verses, which now the new poets flee") (161).

15. Frank Copley, "Catullus c.4: The World of the Poem."

16. Gian Biagio Conte, *The Rhetoric of Imitation*, 32–33.

17. This poem is much more focused than Meleager's epigram for Heliodorus, cited by Fordyce (388). And it is also more abundant than most. Catullus's poem retains the simplicity, while expanding the concision, of the conventional epigram.

18. In this connection, see Richmond Lattimore, *Themes in Greek and Latin Epitaphs*.

19. As Conte says about "The Lock of Berenice," "Catullus achieves this ironic 'inconsistency' by using a loftier register, one no longer appropriate to the context because of its associations with historical circumstances and with an epic-tragic pathos no longer in tune with the new aims of poetry" (89). But on the other hand, Catullus retains his range by transforming that ironic-tragic pathos.

20. Lotman, *Analysis of the Poetic Text*.

21. Compare poem 44, in which Sestius is a kindly host, but a bad poet.

22. Since we do not have his work, we cannot assess the possibility that Catullus's friend Calvus had a range comparable to Catullus's own. See Fordyce, 134.

23. For the pervasiveness and signification of repetitions in Catullus, see Janine Évrard-Gillis, *La Récurrence lexicale dans l'œuvre de Catulle: Étude stylistique*.

24. See John P. Sullivan, *Propertius*, 91–101. For a summary of the qualities of Catullus's love for Lesbia, see 84–86.

25. See Fordyce, 92. The achieved fusions of the Hellenistic love epigram offer simpler versions of the same register, as in Meleager's poem 6: δεινὸς Ερως, δεινός ("A terror is love, a terror"). In his poem 4, he speaks of "sweet-teared love" (γλυκύ δάκρυν Ερωτα).

26. Adler says that this poem gives "the direct and comfortless revelation of an experience greater than the poem, which the poem expresses but does not contain or resolve"(12). She well characterizes its range of tensions, even if one dissents from her negative conclusion.

27. The imaginative structure does not change, even if the verbal expression is colloquial (Fordyce, 92). In any case, the oral metaphor is picked up in "devorare," line 22.

28. See Fordyce, 317.

29. See Charles Martin, *Catullus*, 171, for a diagram of the interlocking patterns in this poem.

30. In poem 8, Meleager speaks of love's "bitter laughter" (πικρά γελᾶι) and connects it to myths.

31. One can measure the extremity of Catullus's poem 63 by comparing it to the more conventional, and far more succinct, poem 11 of Meleager, which touches on the same domain: there the poet is an all-night mystery-devotee, a μύστης, of Kypris.

32. Another reading is "typanum tuum, Cybebe"—which dispenses with the trumpet entirely. But the "tubam" reading should be preferred as the *difficilior lectio*, and, of course, for its poetic power. In any case, three good manuscripts, the Oxford, the Paris, and the Vatican, offer "tubam," whereas "tuum" is the correction (or one might say the "poetic" revision) of the nineteenth-century German scholar Karl Lachmann.

33. As Leach says of the Attis poem, "Although the clarity and preciseness in the way the poet matches external and internal experience through symbolism is no more than a slight intensification of a traditional mirroring capacity of landscape familiar in Hellenistic poetry, the design of the poem, with its integration of setting and action, has the lucidity that characterizes Caesar's descriptions of the battle sites of Gaul" (121–22).

Chapter 8

1. George Santayana, *Three Philosophical Poets: Lucretius, Dante, and Goethe.*

2. According to later testimony, Epicurus "piously avoided all of the poetic altogether, as a destructive lure of myths" (ὅς ἄπασαν ὁμοῦ ποιητικὴν ὥσπερ ὀλέθριον μύθων δέλεαρ ἀφοσιούμενος) (fragment 229, Usener). Epicurus himself said that "the wise man alone can rightly discuss music and poetry but will not put poems into activity" (μόνον τε τὸν σοφὸν ὀρθῶς ἂν περί τε μουσικῆς καὶ ποιητικῆς διαλέξεσθαι, ποιήματά τε ἐνεργεῖν οὐκ ἂν ποιῆσαι) (Diogenes Laertius, *Lives of the Philosophers,* 10.121b, hereafter D.L.) My quotations from Epicurus's *Letter to Menoeceus* are from Jean Bollack, *La pensée du plaisir.* And as E. J. Kenney says, Lucretius "was moreover flying in the face of a strong prejudice, if not exactly a fundamental tenet, of the school, which rejected poetry or relegated it at best to an insignificant place in the scheme of things (cf. Cic. *De Fin* 1.71–72)" (Kenney, *Lucretius,* 11). On the other hand, however, some confluence of poetry and philosophy in Roman Epicurean circles of Lucretius's time is exemplified by the case of the Epicurean Philodemus, who was active in Rome and Herculaneum and wrote epigrams and produced among his philosophical works a *Poetics* that states at once the values and the limitations in the use of poetry to convey ideas. See D. Obbink, ed., *Philodemus on Poetry* (I owe this reference to David Armstrong and his ongoing work on Philodemus).

3. For a different emphasis, see the appreciative study by Richard Minadeo, *The Lyre of Science: Form and Meaning in Lucretius.* Basing himself on the discussions of Henri Bergson and Santayana, and devoting his major progressive analysis to Lucretius's presentation of cyclic creation and destruction, Minadeo asserts: "There is no poetry without philosophy in the work, no philosophy without poetry. There is only *naturae species ratioque,* the poetry and the philosophy, unfolding smoothly to their promised end" (21), "*not* as part of the principle of *natura* alone, nor of *naturae ratio* alone, but of the full proposition, the outer form and inner law of nature" (12). One could assent to Minadeo's strategy of effectually bracketing the difficulties of reconciling poetry with philosophy here, so long as his assertions are not taken wholly to abrogate the possibility of attending to these difficulties.

4. As Cyril Bailey discusses in his edition, Lucretius uses a varied terminology to describe his atoms: "figurae," "corpora," "elementa," and "primordia" (*T. Lucreti Cari libri sex,* 2:381–82). Bailey also points out that Lucretius, in fact, uses at least one time (1.81) "elementa" in a nonphysical sense, as first principles—again the στοιχεῖα of Epicurus, as in *Letter to Menoeceus,* D.L., 10.123 (2:73). For elaborations on Epicurus's use of the Aristotelian term στοιχεῖον, see Diskin Clay, *Lucretius and Epicurus.*

5. In 2.1015–17, he compares verses formed of words to indicate sky, sea, earth, rivers, sun, crops, trees, and living creatures with the placement of these actual things. For a

discussion of the inferences that may be drawn from this doubling back of his theory on the constituents of his language, see Mayotte Bollack, *La raison de Lucrèce*, 255–59.

6. Michel Serres, *La Naissance de la physique dans le texte de Lucrèce*, 46. As Serres deduces, "The *clinamen* is thus a differential; and, properly speaking, a fluxion" (10).

7. Anne Amory, "*Obscura de re lucidi carmina*: Scenes and Poetry in *De rerum natura*," 146–47. She reads more force into "honey on the bitter cup" than a skeptic might: "He will touch *cuncta* with poetic grace . . . every detail, perhaps for him every word and letter, will have an aroma from the sweet body of the Muses" (153–54). See also John Petersen Elder, who says, "the poem moves with unembarrassed ease and rapidity from the physical plane to the . . . mental or spiritual, a movement sanctioned if indeed not required by Epicurean physics, since body and mind are both corporeal, coterminous, and cosensitive" ("Lucretius 1.1–49," 91). This produces an "odd dual allegiance" (94).

8. Diogenes Laertius (10.18) quotes Epicurus as saying that a wise man should not fall in love, nor is love sent from the gods.

9. This is the view about the *Magna Mater* that Bailey takes in commenting on 2.571 ff.

10. "Pax" unmodified is used to characterize the gods in 6.69, 3.24, 2.647. It is attributed to animals, too, in 5.868.

11. For telling details, see Pierre Grimal, *Love in Ancient Rome*, 43–44.

12. Cicero, *Disputationes Tusculanae*, 5.4.10.

13. The "walls of the universe" ("moenia mundi") come in at strategic points of Lucretius's presentation. In 5.1212–13, a contemplation of "moenia mundi" wearies the reason and raises the question as to whether the walls themselves will sustain atomic change forever. Epicurus himself is more exclusively mathematical about the edge of the universe, whereas in Lucretius's invocation, he is seen as a hero conquering the "moenia mundi":

> ergo vivida vis animi pervicit, et extra
> processit longe flammantia moenia mundi
> atque omne immensum peragravit mente animoque,
> unde refert nobis victor quid possit oriri,
> quid nequeat, finita potestas denique cuique,
> quanam sit ratione atque alte terminus haerens.

> So the lively force of his mind won through, and he passed
> far beyond the flaming walls of the universe
> and in mind and spirit the unbounded whole,
> whence, a victor, he brought back to us what could arise
> and what not, at last the power to anything is fixed,
> and by what reason, and the deep-set boundary stone. (1.72–77)

14. P. H. Schrijvers, *Horror ac Divina Voluptas: Études sur la poétique et la poésie de Lucrèce*.

15. As Erich Ackermann says, "From his own fear before death and before the mythic underworld, man concludes that the eternity of the gods implies their happiness, a false conclusion from Epicurus's point of view" (Ackermann, *Lukrez und der Mythos*, 125).

16. Leach, *The Rhetoric of Space*, 52.

17. *Letter to Herodotus,* D.L., 10.49–50 and passim. See Jean Bollack, Mayotte Bollack, and Heinz Wismann, *La Lettre d'Epicure,* 97–100.

18. For the connection between mathematics and virtue in Plato, see Joan Kung, "Mathematics and Virtue in Plato's *Timaeus.*" For Plato's expansion into mathematics after his first trip to Sicily, see Gregory Vlastos, *Socrates: Ironist and Moral Philosopher,* 107–31.

19. Ἐκλυτέον ἑαυτοὺς ἐκ τοῦ περὶ τὰ ἐγκύκλια καὶ πολιτικὰ δεσμωτήρια ("Our selves must be delivered from that which has to do with the prison of everyday and political affairs") (*Sententiae Vaticanae,* 58, cited in J. Bollack, *La Pensée du plaisir,* 522). This notion is variously repeated in what we have of Epicurus.

20. For the elaborate detail of these correspondences, see Clay. The argument, especially as it concerns the details of Epicurean physics, attains intricacy, especially when Lucretius deals on questions that intersect with psychology, as Robert D. Brown summarizes his expositions on the senses (*Lucretius on Love and Sex,* 22–44). Nor is he especially syncretic, avoiding, as David Furley shows, explicit or implicit references to the doctrines of the Stoics, who were active in Rome (Furley, "Lucretius and the Stoics"). As Furley says of Lucretius's larger philosophical context, "*De Rerum Natura* is the Atomists' answer to the Aristotelian world-picture" (95).

21. Epicurus, Κύριαι Δόξαι ("Main Opinions") (Maxim 11, cited in J. Bollack, 277).

22. Κύριαι Δόξαι (Maxim 17, cited in J. Bollack, 299).

23. Epicurus's wording is "pleasure at rest . . . and that in motion, both for body and soul" (τὴν καταστηματικὴν . . . τὴν ἐν κινήσει. ὁ δὲ ἀμφότερα ψυχῆς καὶ σώματος) (*Letter to Menoeceus,* D.L., 10.136). As he further specifies in the letter, "Ataraxia and lack of pain are pleasures at rest; but joy and good feeling remain when with enactment in motion" (ἡ μὲν γὰρ ἀταραξία καὶ ἀπονία καταστηματικαί εἰσιν ἡδοναί. ἡ δὲ χαρὰ καὶ ἡ εὐφροσύνη κατὰ κίνησιν ἐνεργείαι βλέπονται).

24. Mayotte Bollack says of Lucretius's attitude toward his language in comparison with Epicurus's that "The difficulty is first of all one of distancing. In one sense, Lucretius turns his back completely on Epicurus when he opts for a resounding literary form of promulgation. Existence can be uncovered by an absence, in a lack (*egestas*). The extent of language is measured by the incommensurable depth of things" (*La Raison de Lucrèce,* 171–72).

25. P. H. Schrijvers, " Éléments psychagogiques dans l'œuvre de Lucrèce."

26. Book 6, 40–41, repeats two lines from book 1 (147–48), as though to buttress by a refrain the strength of *ratio* against the universality of fright.

27. Gisela Striker, "*Ataraxia:* Happiness as Tranquility," 97. She says further, "The conception of happiness that seems to have become popular after the time of Plato and Aristotle . . . seems to come from outside the tradition that began with Plato or Socrates. . . . It is the only conception of *eudaimonia* in Greek ethics that identifies happiness with a state of mind and makes it depend entirely on a person's attitude or beliefs" (97). It may be said that Lucretius, living within the assumption, expands it and feels so free in it that he can even invert it, changing the imperturbable tranquillity of Epicurus into a swelled straining toward the triumph of an intellectual clarity.

28. See Charles Segal, *Lucretius on Death and Anxiety,* and "Boundaries, Worlds, and Analogical Thinking, or How Lucretius Learned to Love Atomism and Still Write Poetry." Segal expounds forcefully the similarities and differences between Epicurus and

Lucretius in their depictions of death, with special emphasis on evocative powers and subliminal implications in Lucretius's presentation. He underscores Lucretius's vivid sense of boundaries of the body and their violation. As he says, "His argument [about the process of dying] is indirect and allusive, perhaps because he is aware that he is dealing with a subject generally avoided by the Master, or perhaps because he realizes that the material takes him into the areas where poetry, with its tendency toward emotional engagement, least comfortably walks the same road as philosophy, with its aim of serene detachment" (*Lucretius on Death and Anxiety*, 26–27).

29. James Hillman especially aptly analyzes this in *The Dream and the Underworld*.

30. David Konstan, *Some Aspects of Epicurean Psychology*, 11.

31. *Letter to Herodotus*, D.L., 10.78.

Chapter 9

1. Gregory Nagy, *Comparative Studies in Greek and Indic Meter*, *Pindar's Homer*, and *Greek Mythology and Poetics*.

2. Wolfgang Schadewaldt lists the name of the victor, the myth, the self-reference of the poet, and the mention of the Muse as formal conventional elements (*Der Aufbau des Pindarischen Epinikion*). An expanded list is given by Erich Thummer, *Pindar: Die isthmischen Gedichte*. More structural in his analysis is Elroy Bundy, *Studia Pindarica, I, II*.

3. Mary Lefkowitz counts three types of self-reference in Pindar: "first of all, the formal professional statements by the poet, like the opening lines of O. 2; then the more subjective, sometimes intensely personal statements which Pindar often seems to make about himself and his art; and, finally, the statements which are clearly made by the chorus speaking about themselves, the choral 'I's'" (*First-Person Fictions: Pindar's Poetic "I,"* 3). She states further that "As we examine N. 9, we discover that every first-person statement serves as an introduction or transition to a new subject or a conclusion to a previous theme" (4).

4. The evidence against Pindar's personal solo delivery of his odes is well presented by Anne Burnett, "Performing Pindar's Odes."

5. Schadewaldt refers to "that most significant representation in Pindar according to which a reciprocity obtains between victory and song; in Greek it is called in brief χάρις" (277).

6. There are about fifty occurrences of this word in Pindar's extant work, as listed in William J. Slater, *Lexicon to Pindar*.

7. Jan M. Bremer, "Greek Hymns." Pindar's deep, many-faceted intrication into the religious beliefs and practices of his time would provide material for extended study, but a hint of this extent can be grasped from the many references to Pindar in Walter Burkert, *Greek Religion*.

8. Nagy, *Pindar's Homer*, 110–11.

9. John Herington, *Poetry into Drama*.

10. Thomas Greene, in a book in progress, expounds the survivals of early magic verse into later poetic practice. As for prayer, Pindar himself is sometimes explicit in his prayer, as in *Olympian* 4.5: κλῦτ', ἐπεὶ εὔχομαι ("Hear me when I pray"). See also the uses at *Olympian* 3.2, *Pythian* 4.293, and *Nemean* 9.54. In Pindar, though, the hint of magic

would only be a sublimated survival from spells of which we have no earlier evidence. As Burkert rightly says, "magic is present only insofar as ritual is consciously placed in the service of some end. . . . Conscious magic is a matter for individuals. . . . In early Greece, where the cult belongs in the communal, public sphere, the importance of magic is correspondingly minimal" (55). At the same time, this distinction between private and public, which does bear on the difference between Sappho and Pindar, raises the question about the public sodality in which Sappho is presumed to have recited her poems or had them recited. Certainly her poem 1, an invocation to Aphrodite to bring a beloved around "even if she is unwilling," is closer to magic than anything in Pindar, and possibly less merely literary than the later fictive spells in Theocritus, which are hard to imagine as actually designed to bring about the magical end.

11. Pindar refers to the poet as *sophos* eight times, in Pythian 3.113, Isthmian 1.45, Paean 18.3, Olympian 1.9, Pythian 9.78, Pythian 10.22, Isthmian 8.47, and Fgt. 35b.

12. Quotations are from Bruno Snell, ed., *Pindari carmina cum fragmentis.*

13. For a recent discussion of the unity-in-multiplicity achieved by Isthmian 4, see Eveline Krummen, *Pyrsos Hymnon: Festliche Gegenwart und mythisch-rituelle Tradition als Voraussetzung einer Pindarinterpretation, 1–98.*

14. "Pindar begins and ends this opening aphorism with the two elements, water and fire, that according to Lévi-Strauss may be taken to sum up and close the 'vast system' of myth. . . . Heraclitus, indeed, also offers us all four of these terms—water in the notion of flux, fire in whatever his doctrine of physical process may mean, 'best' in his social oppositions, and gold in some pointed statements (B 9, B 22, B 90). . . . There is, further, a schematization in Pindar's statement which is logically as well as syntactically analogous to the Heraclitean proportion: Water : best :: gold : fire . . . Fire : all things :: gold : goods. Heraclitus' statement ['All things are exchanged for fire and fire for all things, just as goods are exchanged for gold and gold for goods,' B 90], of course, is a proposition. Pindar's is at once more elaborate, more homely, and more casual" (Cook, *Myth and Language,* 108–11).

15. For the complications of interpreting and coordinating the myths and the assertions of *Olympian* 1, see Krummen, *Pyrsos Hymnon,* 155–216, which summarizes much of the vast prior discussion, including Charles Segal, "God and Man in Pindar's First and Third Olympian Odes."

16. Here forethought (*promatheia*) is triumphantly named and linked to a keen sense of transience that is somewhat reminiscent of the river aphorisms of Heraclitus.

17. See the discussion of this ode in Cook, *Myth and Language,* (116–23), and in Charles Segal, *Pindar's Mythmaking: The Fourth Pythian Ode.*

18. Envy as a problem is a motif in Pindar. Compare the reference in Nemean 8.23 to Ajax and the psychology of envy: κεῖνος καὶ Τελαμῶνος δάψεν υἱὸν φασγάνωι ἀμφικυλίσαις ("That thing [envy] devoured even the son of Telamon, wrapping him round his sword").

19. The shirt of Nessus and the dire end of Heracles, however, are presented by Bacchylides in Dithyramb 15.24–36.

20. Bruno Gentili cogently states that "The Janus-faced character of Pindaric heroes and the contrasting areas of light and shade in their portrayal provide a key for understanding the occasion-oriented attitude of the poet. They are what allow him to remain true to his basic vision of man. Depending on the circumstances he shows the 'beautiful'

to be imitated, or the 'base' to be avoided, in human conduct" (*Poetry and Its Public in Ancient Greece,* 144).

21. As Schadewaldt says, "the unique O. 1, not content with setting a high point at the beginning, piles superlative on superlative" (275).

22. Basil N. Gildersleeve trenchantly underscores the vividness and specificity of the cannibalistic details (*The Olympian and Pythian Odes,* 133–34).

23. *Pindar's Homer,* 116–35.

24. Along these lines, Leonhard Illig says that "the myth, which nearly always intervenes at the middle point of a poem, is conceived by Pindar himself, according to circumstances, as an excursus within the genuine 'program'" (*Zur Form der Pindarischen Erzählung,* 17).

25. If Friedrich Mezger is right that Pindar's opening refers not to a paean at Delos but another *epinikion,* then it would have opened the list of victories now delayed to this point (*Pindars Siegeslieder,* 309).

26. A discussion and systematization of interpretations of this reference to Heracles' exploit is offered in Glenn W. Most, *The Measures of Praise,* 26–34.

27. On the obliquity of this reference, Charles Segal remarks that "The Theban citizens honor Heracles' eight sons with pyres blazing in the night. . . . I call this section a 'myth' in the sense that it is an exemplary description with a narrative core, even though it contains less explicit narrative than either of the preceding paradigms. . . . Perhaps Pindar is deliberately correcting the version of the myth familiar to us from Euripides' *Heracles,* where the berserk hero kills his young children, unnamed and helpless. Pindar, in fact, avoids the explicit statement that Heracles himself killed them, and we cannot be sure exactly what version of the myth he is following" ("Myth, Cult, and Memory in Pindar's Third and Fourth Isthmian Odes," 74).

28. *Pythian* 9.474; *Suppliants,* about 463.

29. *Dithyramb* 61 verges on some notions of Heraclitus:

> Why do you wish it to be wisdom, where just a little
> does one man hold over another man?
> To track out the deliberations of the gods
> is not for a mortal mind, as he was born of a mortal mother.

This renders the small intellectual differences inconsequential and the larger antitheses unresolvable.

30. John H. Finley, Jr., *Pindar and Aeschylus,* 57.

31. In *Pythian* 1.82–83, "satiety blunts hopes."

32. There is a further possible anthropological dimension to this characterization of humanity, if one allows Nagy's reading of the apothegm: "I interpret *skias onar* 'dream of a shade' as a recapitulation of the earlier words of the dead Amphiaraus about his living son. In Homeric usage the word *skia,* 'shade' can designate a dead person. I suggest that the dead person is literally dreaming [a strangely anachronistic and in fact unprecedented inference]—that is, realizing through its dreams—the living person" (*Pindar's Homer,* 195–96).

33. He does this notably in the vision of Persephone presiding over a purified afterlife (Fgt. 133), stressed by Plato in the *Meno* (80b).

34. Nagy, *Pindar's Homer,* 140.

35. Ibid., 195–96.

36. As Most points out, this verb takes as its object gods, heroes, and athletic victors, separately (74). In *Olympian* 2.2, as quoted above, it takes three objects, god, hero, and man.

37. This verb ἀμφιβάλλεται is elusive as well as rich. Slater glosses it as "occupies," while Lewis R. Farnell reads it as the metaphor of the poet casting ideas and sounds round his shoulders (or sounds round ideas?) like a cloak (Farnell, *The Works of Pindar*, 2:5). Gildersleeve, who notes the variety of interpretations, sees it as indicating "a shower of poetic darts" that the poet is casting (130).

38. As Segal says of μητίεσσι as it bears on the long ode, *Pythian* 4, he is discussing (*Pindar's Mythmaking*, 31 and passim), "The choice between the good and bad sides of craft, *metis,* and between a hero of guile and a hero of force, determines not only the nature of poetry, but also the ways in which men communicate with one another and with the gods."

39. See George Thomson, *Greek Lyric Meter,* 70–80, for a discussion of *Olympian* 1. Thomson notes that the Doric dactylo-epitrite, the Aeolic cola I have discussed, and the Paeonic cretic and bacchius all appear in Pindar; and he asserts that they are counter-pointed by "shifts to resolution" and "links," not only to complicate the sound but also to call up the traditional modal associations of these metric groups in Greek culture—sternness for Doric, luxury for Ionic, a celebratory balance for Aeolic, and excitement for Paeonic. As he says of *Olympian* 1, "The principal rhythms employed are Aeolian, Paeonic, trochaic and iambic, with a touch of Dorian and a still lighter touch of Ionian" (77). The varieties within a given colon that occur because substitutions and reversals are admitted, together with Pindar's intricate braiding of meters, allow for several possibilities of alternate analysis. So Thomson finds a bacchius in Ἄριστον, a trochaic shift to pherecratic in line 7, and a shift from iambic to Paeonic in lines 8 and 9 (75).

The analysis of Pindar's Aeolic and dactylo-epitritic meters by Nagy in *Pindar's Homer* (439–64) is so lucidly systematic and complex that its main emphasis on the tradition-ality of their ultimate Indo-European origins might obscure the force of Pindar's own polyphonic line-by-line inventiveness.

40. See notes 14 and 29.

Chapter 10

1. For the rhetoric in its context of convention, see Gentili, *Poetry and Its Public in Ancient Greece,* especially 51–54. On the anthropological situation, see Claude Calame, *Les Chœurs de jeunes filles en Grèce archaïque.* Calame locates the choral groups of young women, whether led by a man or by an older woman, as connected with various fer-tility rites that themselves are brought to bear on the coming of age for nubile young women. Alcman's chorus performs publicly, which differentiates it from Sappho's (rather oblique) group, which has sexualized and further eroticized the beauty-contest aspect. In Sparta the festival is connected with Hera (223, citing Athenaeus 13.609 ff.). In Sparta and throughout Laconia, there are festivals to Artemis Limnatis, Artemis Caryatis, Artemis Orthia, and Artemis Corythalia. Helen is connected to these and to the Dioscuri of fragment 1.

On the complications of these myths, Calame remarks (261–62), "For this reason we can suppose that the Spartan and the Messenian version of the causes of the First Messenian War represent the historicization of two foundation myths attached to the cult of Artemis Limnatis; one through the tale of the rape and suicide of young women participating in the cult would explain the ritual designated for young girls; the other, through the tale of the transvestism and murder of the boys, would have founded the ritual for youth." In this connection, D. L. Page can assert, against the anthropological situation that has been reconstructed for Sappho, that there is no evidence for a cult, a school, and other features of this situation (Page, *Sappho and Alcaeus*). Page also points out that there is no evidence for a chorus in connection with her, and he claims that the epithalamia could be private.

However, in one of the few direct references to Sappho, an epigram in the *Palatine Anthology* (9.89) has her go to the temple of Hera—and as a choregus, though she is there represented as performing a monody, a testimony that will at least blur the distinction begun in Plato *Laws* 764de between choral and monodic poetry in archaic times. See Calame, *Les Chœurs de jeunes filles*, 127.

2. Texts are from D. L. Page, *Poetae Melici Graeci*.

3. Segal, "Sirius and the Pleiades in Alcman's Louvre Parthenion."

4. Alcman, as often, is too fluid here to be confined just to these categories. He passes in and out of them in a large sphere. For the convention of praise before and after Alcman, see Nagy, *Pindar's Homer*.

5. In a slightly different reading, which Nagy follows, the dreams become literally "under the rocks" (ὑποπετριδίων). Thus he insists on not accepting the argument that this word had been metathesized in antiquity from ὑποπτεριδίων, as it appears in two of the manuscripts. For Nagy, taking the "dreams" as "under the rocks" opens on an intricate mythology that crosses the legends about the sun with those of the border between this life and the land of the dead, thus connecting this passage to the White Rock of the *Odyssey* and elsewhere (Nagy, *Greek Mythology and Poetics*, 223–63).

6. In our continuing uncertainties with Alcman, it should be noted that "Pleiades"— "stars," not "birds"—is an important alternate reading of Πεληάδες. So Segal, as cited in note 2 above, takes it, along with many other commentators, though Claude Calame makes a good case for taking it as "doves," along with one ancient scholiast (Calame, *Alcman*, 332).

7. Calame, *Alcman*, 333.

8. For extensions of the serpent myth in Greek culture, see Joseph Fontenrose, *Python*.

9. One possible explanation would be to make fighting a metaphor for the poetic contest that the poets would be holding through their choruses. Such a reading would be strengthened by the Indo-European tradition of poetic contests, and by the Vedic association of war and horse-racing metaphors, both present here, as George Dunkel reads and explains the passage ("Fighting Words").

10. Calame, *Les Chœurs de jeunes filles*, 99.

11. Fragment 106 says, in a context where mortals are distinguished from the gods: εἴπατε μοι τάδε φῦλα βροτήσια ("Tell me these mortal tribes").

12. For a discussion of the principles involved in these conjunctions, see Albert Cook, "Heidegger and the Wisdom of Poetry."

13. See Vincent Scully, *The Earth, the Temple, and the Gods.*

14. Alcman locates his own place of origin as Sardis, fgt. 13d, 16 (Page).

15. G. S. Kirk et al., *The Pre-Socratic Philosophers,* 47–50.

16. Glenn Most, "Alcman's Cosmogonic Fragment (Fgt 5 Page, 81 Calame)."

17. M. L. West, ed., *Hesiod's Theogony,* 13, citing his own earlier studies of Alcman.

18. Thetis, however, has force in the Homeric tradition. See Laura M. Slatkin, *The Power of Thetis.* Slatkin finds in the implications of the *Iliad,* and also in Pindar, a power for Thetis that links her functions to those of Eos, goddess of the dawn, and of Aphrodite.

19. Marcel Detienne and Jean-Pierre Vernant, *Les Ruses de l'intelligence, la métis des grecs,* 134–58.

20. Anaximander, fragment B1, in Hermann Diels and Walter Kranz, eds., *Die Fragmente der Vorsokratiker.* A cosmology cannot really be disentangled from Anaximander's fragment and its commentary, either, even by comparing it with other testimonies, though Kirk et al. have attempted to do so; Simplicius himself, from whom we have the fragment, says Anaximander spoke "with more poetic terms" ("poetikoterois onomasin") (Simplicius, *Commentary on Aristotle's Physics,* 24, 13).

21. Claude Calame, *Alcman,* in the commentary of fragment 105 (500). The stress of response to Alcman's pressure against our own analytic categories appears here, where the careful and accurate Calame is led to attribute a high probability to the presence of political reflections, which, at least directly, are all but totally absent from what we have of Alcman's work.

22. Relevant, here, however, is Nagy's speculation: "As a melodic pattern that is characteristic of distinct speech in distinct habitats, *nomos* serves as the ideal metaphor for conveying the distinctiveness of bird song, as when the voice of Alcman declares that he knows the *nomoi* of all the different kinds of birds in the world (PMG 40). This theme can best be understood in the context of Alcman PMG 39, where the poet names himself as the 'discoverer' of melody and words that put into human language the voices of partridges. In other words [but this is a giant leap!] the song of Alcman is being conceived as a mimesis of bird song, and the varieties of bird song resemble the varieties of *nomoi*" (*Pindar's Homer,* 88).

23. I pass over the richnesses of Alcman's metrical shaping here, but it should be noted not only that the constituents of the metrical patterns had a long history but also that all the musical force comes before the Pythagorean systematization. Lacking the music, the equivalent pattern (Doric?) is irretrievable and hard to correlate fully with the conservative social forms out of which fragment 1, for example, is built. And a large share of the fragments of Alcman occur in a context of citation where the initial focus is metrics.

Coda

1. William Butler Yeats, *Collected Poems,* 291.

2. William Butler Yeats, *A Vision.*

3. George Mills Harper, *The Making of Yeats' 'A Vision': A Study of the Automatic Script.*

4. Yeats, *A Vision,* 97.

5. Rainer Maria Rilke, *Werke*, 1:706–8.

6. Martin Heidegger, "Wozu Dichter in dürftiger Zeit?" *Holzwege*, 248–95.

7. Paul de Man, "Tropes (Rilke)" in *Allegories of Reading*, 20–56. In this sensitive and penetrating essay, de Man wants to allege that Rilke contradicts himself by moving "chiastically" back and forth inconsistently from tenor to vehicle in his enlistment of images, and that this shows an inconsistent overvaluation/undervaluation of poetic language. There is no reason, however, why this could not all be true of Rilke and the poetry could still function as a profound spiritual probe.

8. Wallace Stevens, *Collected Poems*, 502.

9. Angus Fletcher, *Colors of the Mind*, 286.

10. Eugenio Montale, *La bufera e altro*, 97–98.

11. René Char, *Œuvres complètes*, 527.

12. For such "sixth-phase" practices, see the discussion in Cook, "The Large Phases of Myth," *Myth and Language*, 37–66.

13. Paul Veyne, *René Char en ses poèmes*, 466.

14. "Il est dans notre vie des approches qui sont à peine remarquées, avec le toucher des doigts ou à grandes enjambées. Pour Orion je me suis contenté de le déborner de l'espace où il se trouvait. Je l'ai mis sur mon chemin où vous pouvez le rencontrer et suivre son drame" (Char, *Œuvres complètes*, 1261). Among many possible connections for Orion is the identification of the figure with the poet himself, as Paul Veyne stresses, who also traces the echoes of reference in the sequence to large-scale political and social movements (*René Char en ses poèmes*, 466–81). The "great strides" may even make glancing reference to Valéry's "Achille, immobile à grands pas."

15. "Ce siècle a décidé de l'existence de nos deux espaces immémoriaux: le premier, l'espace intime où jouaient notre imagination et nos sentiments; le second, l'espace circulaire, celui du monde concret. Les deux étaient inséparables. Subvertir l'un, c'était bouleverser l'autre."

16. Paul Celan, *Zeitgehöft*, 10.

17. Haskell M. Block, "Interpreting Celan: Szondi, Gadamer, and Others," in Block, ed., *The Poetry of Paul Celan*, 38–43. Block also cites Jean Bollack as pointing out another specific reference in the poem to an execution, the Nazi hanging on meat hooks of the plotters against Hitler in 1944.

18. Winfried Menninghaus, *Paul Celan: Magie der Form*, 54–58, citing Marlies Janz, *Zum Engagement absoluter Poesie*.

19. Ibid., 47.

20. Peter Szondi, "Durch die Enge geführt," in *Celan-Studien*, 47–112.

21. Martin Heidegger, "Nietzsche's Wort 'Gott ist tot,'" in *Holzwege*, 193–247.

22. John Ashbery, *A Wave*, 16.

23. Pierre Bourdieu, *Language and Symbolic Power, Distinction: A Social Critique of the Judgement of Taste,* and *The Political Ontology of Martin Heidegger.* As Bourdieu says about the social siting and power dynamics of all speech, "through the medium of the structure of the linguistic field, conceived as a system of specifically linguistic relations to power based on the unequal distribution of linguistic capital (or, to put it another way, of the chances of assimilating the objectified linguistic resources), the structure of the space of expressive styles reproduces in its own terms the structure of the differences which objectively separate conditions of existence" (*Heidegger,* 57). And, with further

clarification, "The division into classes performed by sociology leads to the common root of the classifiable practices [pratiques] which agents produce and of the classificatory judgements they make of other agents' practices and their own. The habitus is both the generative principle of objectively classifiable judgements and the system of classification (*principium divisionis*) of these practices. It is in the relationship between the two capacities which define the habitus, the capacity to produce classifiable practices and works, and the capacity to differentiate and appreciate these practices and products (taste), that the represented social world, i.e., the space of life-styles, is constituted" (*Distinction*, 169–70).

Works Cited

Ackermann, Erich. *Lukrez und der Mythos*. Wiesbaden: Steiner, 1979.

Adler, Eve. *Catullan Self-revelation*. New York: Arno, 1981.

Adorno, Theodor W. *Ästhetische Theorie*. Vol. 7 of *Gesammelte Schriften*. Frankfurt am Main: Suhrkamp Verlag, 1970.

Ahearn, Edward. *Rimbaud*. Berkeley and Los Angeles: University of California Press, 1983.

Akhmatova, Anna. *Sochineniya*. Munich: Inter-Language Literary Associates, 1965.

Alfonsi, Sandra Resnick. *Masculine Submission in Troubadour Lyric*. New York: Peter Lang, 1986.

Amory, Anne. "*Obscura de re lucidi carmina*: Scenes and Poetry in *De Rerum Natura*." *Yale Classical Studies*, 1969: 143–68.

Armour, Peter. *Dante's Griffin and the History of the World*. Oxford: Clarendon Press, 1989.

Ashbery, John. *A Wave: Poems*. New York: Viking, 1984.

Auerbach, Erich. *Scenes from the Drama of European Literature*. Minneapolis: University of Minnesota Press, 1984.

Augustine. *Confessions*. Translated by William Watts. London: Heinemann, 1912.

Bailey, Cyril, ed. *T. Lucreti Cari Libri Sex*. Oxford: Clarendon Press, 1947.

Bakhtin, M. M. *The Dialogic Imagination*. Edited by Michael Holquist. Translated by Caryl Emerson and Michael Holquist. Austin: University of Texas Press, 1981.

Baldensperger, Fernand. *Les Sonnets de Shakespeare*. Berkeley and Los Angeles: University of California Press, 1943.

Barkan, Leonard. *The Gods Made Flesh: Metamorphosis and the Pursuit of Paganism*. New Haven, Conn.: Yale University Press, 1986.

Bate, Walter Jackson. *Coleridge*. New York: Macmillan, 1968.

Baudelaire, Charles. "Le *Confiteor* de l'artiste." *Le Spleen de Paris. Œuvres complètes*. Paris: Gallimard, 1961.

Bewell, Alan. *Wordsworth and the Enlightenment.* New Haven, Conn.: Yale University Press, 1989.

Beyschlag, Siegfried. *Altdeutsche Verskunst in Grundzügen.* Nürnberg: Hans Carl, 1969.

Bialostosky, Don. H. *Wordsworth, Dialogics, and the Practice of Criticism.* Cambridge: Cambridge University Press, 1992.

Bloch, R. Howard. *Etymologies and Genealogies.* Chicago, Ill.: University of Chicago Press, 1983.

Block, Haskell M. "Interpreting Celan: Szondi, Gadamer, and Others." In *The Poetry of Paul Celan,* edited by Haskell M. Block, 38–43. New York: Peter Lang, 1991.

Blumenberg, Hans. *Paradigmen zu einer Metaphorologie.* Bonn: Bouvier, 1960.

Bollack, Jean. *La Pensée du plaisir.* Paris: Minuit, 1975.

Bollack, Jean, Mayotte Bollack, and Heinz Wismann. *La Lettre d'Epicure.* Paris: Minuit, 1971.

Bollack, Mayotte. *La Raison de Lucrèce.* Paris: Minuit, 1978.

Booth, Stephen. *An Essay on Shakespeare's Sonnets.* New Haven, Conn.: Yale University Press, 1969.

Bourdieu, Pierre. *Distinction: A Social Critique of the Judgement of Taste.* Translated by Richard Nice. Cambridge, Mass.: Harvard University Press, 1984. Originally published Paris: Minuit, 1979.

———. *Language and Symbolic Power.* Edited and Introduction by John B. Thompson. Translated by Gino Raymond and Matthew Adamson. Cambridge, Mass.: Harvard University Press, 1991. Originally published Paris: Fayard, 1982.

———. *The Political Ontology of Martin Heidegger.* Translated by Peter Collier. Stanford, Calif.: Stanford University Press, 1991.

Bowditch, Lowell. "Horace and the Gift Economy of Patronage." Ph.D. diss., Brown University, 1992.

Brandeis, Irma. *The Ladder of Vision: A Study of Images in Dante's Comedy.* London: Chatto and Windus, 1960.

Bremer, Jan M. "Greek Hymns." In *Faith, Hope and Worship,* edited by H. S. Versnel, 193–215. Leiden: Brill, 1981.

Brown, Robert D. *Lucretius on Love and Sex.* Leiden: Brill, 1987.

Bundy, Elroy. *Studia Pindarica, I, II. University of California Publications in Classical Philology* 18 (1962): 1–34; 35–92.

Burkert, Walter. *Greek Religion.* Cambridge, Mass.: Harvard University Press, 1985.

Burnett, Anne. "Performing Pindar's Odes." *Classical Philology* 84 (1989): 283–93.

Calame, Claude. *Alcman.* Rome: Ateneo, 1983.

———. *Les Chœurs de jeunes filles en Grèce archaïque.* Rome: Ateneo, 1977.

Carson, Anne. *Eros the Bittersweet.* Princeton, N.J.: Princeton University Press, 1986.

Catullus. *C. Valerii Catulli Carmina.* Edited by R. A. B. Mynors. Oxford: Clarendon Press, 1958.

Celan, Paul. *Die Niemandsrose.* Frankfurt: Fischer, 1963.

————. *Zeitgehöft.* Frankfurt: Suhrkamp, 1978.

Ceriello, G. R., ed. *I rimatori del dolce stil nuovo.* Milan: Rizzolo, 1950.

Chadwick, H. M., and N. K. Chadwick. *The Growth of Literature, I.* Cambridge: Cambridge University Press, 1932.

Char, René. *Œuvres complètes.* Paris: Pléiade, 1983.

Clay, Diskin. *Lucretius and Epicurus.* Ithaca, N.Y.: Cornell University Press, 1983.

Coleridge, Samuel Taylor. *Biographia Literaria.* Edited by J. Shawcross. London: Oxford University Press, 1958.

Collins, Christopher. *The Poetics of the Mind's Eye.* Philadelphia: University of Pennsylvania Press, 1991.

Conte, Gian Biagio. *The Rhetoric of Imitation.* Translated by Charles Segal. Ithaca, N.Y.: Cornell University Press, 1986.

Contini, Gianfranco. "Introduction to Dante's *Rime.* In *Dante,* edited by John Freccero, 28–38. Englewood Cliffs, N.J.: Prentice-Hall, 1965.

Cook, Albert. *Canons and Wisdoms.* Philadelphia: University of Pennsylvania Press, 1993.

————. *The Classic Line.* Bloomington: Indiana University Press, 1966.

————. *Figural Choice in Poetry and Art.* Hanover, N.H.: University Press of New England, 1985.

————. "Heidegger and the Wisdom of Poetry." *Centennial Review* 34, no.3 (Summer 1990): 49–80.

————. *History/Writing.* Cambridge: Cambridge University Press, 1988.

————. *Myth and Language.* Bloomington: Indiana University Press, 1980.

————. *Prisms.* Bloomington: Indiana University Press, 1967.

————. *Shakespeare's Enactment.* Chicago, Ill.: Swallow Press, 1976.

————. *Soundings: On Shakespeare, Modern Poetry, Plato, and Other Subjects.* Detroit, Mich.: Wayne State University Press, 1991.

————. *Temporalizing Space: The Triumphant Strategies of Piero Della Francesca.* New York and Bern: Peter Lang, 1992.

————. *Thresholds: Studies in the Romantic Experience.* Madison: University of Wisconsin Press, 1985.

Copley, Frank. "Catullus c.4: The World of the Poem." *Transactions of the American Philological Association* 89 (1958): 9–13.

Creeley, Robert. *The Company.* Providence, R.I.: Burning Deck, 1988.

————. *Gnomic Verses.* La Laguna: Zasterle, 1991.

Crewe, Jonathan. *Trials of Authorship: Anterior Forms and Poetic Reconstruction from Wyatt to Shakespeare.* Berkeley and Los Angeles: University of California Press, 1990.

Curtius, Ernst Robert. *European Literature in the Latin Middle Ages.* New York: Harper and Row, 1963.

Daniel, Arnaut. *Canzoni.* Edited by Gianluigi Toja. Florence: Sansoni, 1960.

Dante Alighieri. *Convivio.* Edited by Piero Cudini. Milan: Garzanti, 1980.

Dante Alighieri. *De vulgari eloquentia.* Edited by Sergio Cecchin. Turin: UTET, 1983.

———. *La divina commedia di Dante Alighieri.* Edited by C. H. Grandgent, rev. Charles S. Singleton. Cambridge, Mass.: Harvard University Press, 1972.

Davenson, Henri [Henri Marrou]. *Les troubadours.* Paris: Seuil, 1961.

Davie, Donald. *Articulate Energy.* London: Routledge and Kegan Paul, 1955.

Deleuze, Gilles, and Félix Guattari. *A Thousand Plateaus.* Translated by Brian Massumi. Minneapolis: University of Minnesota Press, 1987. Originally published Paris: Minuit, 1980.

de Man, Paul. *Allegories of Reading.* New Haven, Conn.: Yale University Press, 1979.

———. *Rhetoric and Romanticism.* New York: Columbia University Press, 1984.

Derrida, Jacques. *Qu'est-ce que la poésie?* Berlin: Brinkmann und Bose, 1991.

———. *Schibboleth.* Paris: Galilée, 1986.

———. *Signéponge.* New York: Columbia University Press, 1984.

Detienne, Marcel. *Les Jardins d'Adonis: La Mythologie des aromates en Grèce.* Paris: Gallimard, 1972.

Detienne, Marcel, and Jean-Pierre Vernant. *Les Ruses de l'intelligence, la métis des grecs.* Paris: Flammarion, 1974.

Diels, Hermann, and Walter Kranz, eds. *Die Fragmente der Vorsokratiker.* Berlin: Weidemann, 1960.

Donne, John. *The Complete English Poems.* Edited by A. J. Smith. New York: Penguin, 1973.

———. *The Sermons of John Donne.* Vol. 6. Edited by George Potter and Evelyn Simpson. Berkeley and Los Angeles: University of California Press, 1962.

Dronke, Peter. *Medieval Latin and the Rise of European Love-Lyric.* 2d ed. 2 vols. Oxford: Clarendon Press, 1968.

———. *The Medieval Lyric.* New York: Harper and Row, 1969.

———. "The Phantasmagoria in the Earthly Paradise." Chapter 3 in *Dante and Medieval Latin Traditions.* Cambridge: Cambridge University Press, 1986.

Duby, Georges. "Au XIIᵉ siècle: Les 'jeunes' dans la société aristocratique." *Annales E.S.C.* (1964): 835–96.

Dunkel, George. "Fighting Words." *Journal of Indo-European Studies* 7 (1949): 249–72.

Elder, John Petersen. "Catullus I, His Poetic Creed, and Nepos." *Harvard Studies in Classical Philology* 71 (1966): 143–49.

———. "Lucretius 1.1–49." *Transactions of the American Philological Association* 85 (1954): 88–120.

Eliot, T. S. "Dante." In *Selected Essays.* New York: Harcourt Brace, 1932

———. *On Poetry and Poets.* London: Faber, 1957.

Else, Gerald F. *Aristotle's Poetics: The Argument.* Cambridge, Mass.: Harvard University Press, 1963.

Empson, William. *Some Versions of Pastoral.* 1935. Reprint, London: Chatto & Windus, 1950.

Erwin, John W. *Lyric Apocalypse*. Chico, Calif.: Scholars Press, 1984.

Évrard-Gillis, Janine. *La Récurrence lexicale dans l'œuvre de Catullue: Étude stylistique*. Paris: Les Belles Lettres, 1976.

Faner, Robert D. *Walt Whitman and Opera*. Philadelphia: University of Pennsylvania Press, 1951.

Farnell, Lewis R. *The Works of Pindar*. London: Macmillan, 1930–32.

Felten, Hans. "Zur Frage in der *Divina Commedia*." In *Dante 1985*, edited by Richard Baum and Willi Hirdt, 141–49. Romanica et Comparatistica 4. Tübingen: Stauffenberg, 1985.

Ferrari, Walter. "Il carme 51 di Catullo." In *Catull*, edited by Rolf Heine, 241–61. Darmstadt: Wissenschaftliche Buchhandlung, 1975. Originally published in *Annali della R. Scuola Normale Superiore di Pisa*, Storia e Filosofia, 2d ser., vol. 7, 59–72. Bologna, 1938.

Fineman, Joel. *Shakespeare's Perjured Eye; The Invention of Poetic Subjectivity in the Sonnets*. Berkeley and Los Angeles: University of California Press, 1985.

Finley, John H., Jr. *Pindar and Aeschylus*. Cambridge, Mass.: Harvard University Press, 1955.

Fletcher, Angus. *Colors of the Mind*. Cambridge, Mass.: Harvard University Press, 1991.

Follain, Jean. *Usage du temps*. Paris: Gallimard, 1943.

Fontenrose, Joseph. *Python*. Berkeley and Los Angeles: University of California Press, 1959.

Fordyce, C. J. *Catullus: A Commentary*. Oxford: Clarendon Press, 1961.

Foster, Kenelm. "The Mind in Love: Dante's Philosophy." In *Dante*, edited by John Freccero, 43–60. New York: Prentice-Hall, 1965

Foucault, Michel. *Les Mots et les choses*. Paris: Gallimard, 1966.

Foxe, John. *Acts and Monuments*. Edited by Josiah Pratt. 8 vols. London: George Seely, 1870.

Freccero, John. *Dante: The Poetics of Conversion*. Cambridge, Mass.: Harvard University Press, 1986.

Fubini, Mario. *Metrica e Poesia*. Vol. 1, *Dal Duecento al Petrarca*. Milan: Feltrinelli, 1962.

Furley, David J. "Lucretius and the Stoics." In *Probleme der Lukrezforschung*, edited by Carl Joachim Classen, 75–95. Hildesheim: Olms, 1986. Originally published in *Bulletin of the Institute of Classical Studies* 13 (1966): 13–33.

Gadamer, Hans-Georg. *Wer bin Ich und wer bist Du? Ein Kommentar zu Paul Celans Gedichtfolge "Atemkristall."* Frankfurt: Suhrkamp, 1973.

García Lorca, Federico. *Diván del Tamarit*. Vol. 3 of *Obras completas*. Buenos Aires: Losada, 1938.

———. *Selected Poems of Federico García Lorca*. New York: New Directions, 1955.

Gentili, Bruno. *Poetry and Its Public in Ancient Greece*. Baltimore, Md.: Johns Hopkins University Press, 1988.

Giacalone, Giuseppe. *Tempo ed eternità nella Divina Commedia*. Pescara: Editrice Italica, 1965.

Gildersleeve, Basil N. *Pindar: The Olympian and Pythian Odes*. New York: Harper, 1897.

Gilson, Étienne. *Dante the Philosopher.* London: Sheed and Ward, 1958.

Goffman, Erving. *Forms of Talk*. Philadelphia: University of Pennsylvania Press, 1981.

Goodson, A. C. *Verbal Imagination: Coleridge and the Language of Modern Criticism*. New York: Oxford University Press, 1988.

Gordon, Jan B. "Affiliation as (Dis)semination: Gossip and Family in George Eliot's European Novel." *Journal of European Studies* 15 (1985): 155–89.

———. "Gossip, Diary, Letter, Text: Anne Brontë's Narrative *Tenant* and the Problematic of the Gothic Sequel." *ELH* 54 (1984): 719–45.

Greenblatt, Stephen. *Renaissance Self-fashioning*. Chicago, Ill.: University of Chicago Press, 1980.

Griffin, Jasper. "Augustan Poetry and the Life of Luxury." *Journal of Roman Studies* 66 (1976): 87–105.

Grimal, Pierre. *Love in Ancient Rome*. Norman: University of Oklahoma Press, 1986.

Haller, Robert S., trans. *The Literary Criticism of Dante Alighieri*. Lincoln: University of Nebraska Press, 1973.

Hamacher, Werner. "The Second of Inversion: Moments of a Figure through Celan's Poetry." *Yale French Studies* 69: 276–314.

Hammond, Mac. *Mappamundi: New and Selected Poems*. Binghamton: Belleview Press, 1989.

Harper, George Mills. *The Making of Yeats' "A Vision": A Study of the Automatic Script*. Carbondale: Southern Illinois University Press, 1987.

Harrison, Robert. *The Body of Beatrice*. Baltimore, Md.: Johns Hopkins University Press, 1988.

Hartman, Geoffrey. *Beyond Formalism*. New Haven, Conn.: Yale University Press, 1970.

———. *The Fate of Reading*. Chicago, Ill.: University of Chicago Press, 1975.

Heidegger, Martin. "Nietzsche's Wort 'Gott ist tot.'" In *Holzwege*, 193–247. Frankfurt: Klostermann, 1950.

———. "Wozu Dichter in dürftiger Zeit?" In *Holzwege*, 248–95. Frankfurt: Klostermann, 1950.

Herington, John. *Poetry into Drama*. Berkeley and Los Angeles: University of California Press, 1985.

Hill, R. T., and T. G. Bergin, eds. *Anthology of the Provençal Troubadours*. 2d ed. Vol 1. New Haven, Conn.: Yale University Press, 1973.

Hillman, James. *The Dream and the Underworld*. New York: Harper and Row, 1979.

Holland, Norman. *The I*. New Haven, Conn.: Yale University Press, 1985.

Huchet, Jean-Charles. *L'Amour discourtois*. Toulouse: Privat, 1987.

Hutton, James. *The Greek Anthology in France and in the Latin Writers of the Netherlands*. Ithaca, N.Y.: Cornell University Press, 1946.

———. *The Greek Anthology in Italy*. Ithaca, N.Y.: Cornell University Press, 1935.

Illig, Leonhard. *Zur Form der Pindarischen Erzählung*. Berlin: Junker und Dünnhaupt, 1932.

Jakobson, Roman. "Linguistics and Poetics." In *Style in Language,* edited by Thomas Sebeok, 350–77. Cambridge, Mass.: M.I.T. Press, 1960.

Janan, Micaela. *When the Lamp Is Shattered: Desire and Narrative in Catullus.* Carbondale: Southern Illinois University Press, 1994.

Janz, Marlies. *Zum Engagement absoluter Poesie.* Frankfurt: Suhrkamp, 1976.

Johnson, W. R. *The Idea of Lyric.* Berkeley and Los Angeles: University of California Press, 1982.

Joseph, Bertram. *Acting Shakespeare.* London: Routledge and Kegan Paul, 1966.

Kay, Sarah. *Subjectivity in Troubadour Poetry.* Cambridge: Cambridge University Press, 1990.

Kendrick, Laura. *The Game of Love: Troubadour Wordplay.* Berkeley and Los Angeles: University of California Press, 1988.

Kenney, E. J. *Lucretius.* Oxford: Clarendon Press, 1977.

Kermode, Frank. "Cornelius and Voltemand: Doubles in *Hamlet.*" Chapter 2 in *Forms of Attention.* Chicago, Ill.: University of Chicago Press, 1985.

Keyes, Roger S. *Surimono from the Chester Beatty Collection.* Alexandria, Va.: International Exhibitions Foundation, 1987.

Kirk, G. S., J. E. Raven, and M. Schofield. *The Pre-Socratic Philosophers.* Cambridge: Cambridge University Press, 1983.

Klawitter, George. *The Enigmatic Narrator.* New York: Peter Lang, 1995.

Konstan, David. *Some Aspects of Epicurean Psychology.* Leiden: Brill, 1973.

Krummen, Eveline. *Pyrsos Hymnon: Festliche Gegenwart und mythisch-rituelle Tradition als Voraussetzung einer Pindarinterpretation.* Berlin: de Gruyter, 1990.

Kung, Joan. "Mathematics and Virtue in Plato's *Timaeus.*" In *Plato,* edited by John P. Anton and Anthony Preus, 309–40. Albany: SUNY Press, 1989.

Lacan, Jacques. *Écrits.* Paris: Seuil, 1966.

———. *Séminaire VII: L'éthique de la psychanalyse.* Paris: Seuil, 1986.

———. *Le Séminaire XX: Encore.* Paris: Seuil, 1975.

Lacoue-Labarthe, Philippe. *Poésie comme expérience.* Paris: Galilée, 1986.

Lakoff, George, and Mark Johnson. *Metaphors We Live By.* Chicago, Ill.: University of Chicago Press, 1980.

Lattimore, Richmond. *Themes in Greek and Latin Epitaphs.* Urbana: University of Illinois Press, 1962.

Leach, Eleanor Winsor. *The Rhetoric of Space: Literary and Artistic Representations of Landscape in Republican and Augustan Rome.* Princeton, N.J.: Princeton University Press, 1988.

Lefkowitz, Mary. *First-Person Fictions: Pindar's Poetic "I."* Oxford: Clarendon Press, 1991.

Le Goff, Jacques. *L'Imaginaire médiévale.* Paris: Gallimard, 1985.

Levy, Émil. *Petit dictionnaire provençal-français.* 1909. Reprint, Heidelberg: Carl Winter, 1973.

Lewis, C. S. *The Allegory of Love.* Oxford: Clarendon Press, 1936.

Lotman, Yuri M. *Analysis of the Poetic Text*. Translated by Barton Johnston. Ann Arbor, Mich.: Ardis, 1976.

———. "The Text within the Text." *PMLA* 109, no. 3 (May 1994): 377–84.

Lucretius. *Lucreti De rerum natura*. Edited by Cyril Bailey. Oxford: Clarendon Press, 1922.

MacCary, Thomas. "When God Became Woman: The Erotic of the Troubadours." Manuscript study.

Makin, Peter. *Provence and Pound*. Berkeley and Los Angeles: University of California Press, 1978.

Martin, Charles. *Catullus*. Baltimore, Md.: Johns Hopkins University Press, 1990.

Mattingly, Garrett. "The Date of Shakespeare's Sonnet CVII." *PMLA* 48 (1933): 705–21.

McFarland, Thomas. *Romanticism and the Forms of Ruin*. Princeton, N.J.: Princeton University Press, 1981.

———. *William Wordsworth: Intensity and Achievement*. Oxford: Clarendon Press, 1992.

Menninghaus, Winfried. *Paul Celan: Magie der Form*. Frankfurt: Suhrkamp, 1980.

Mezger, Friedrich. *Pindars Siegeslieder*. Leipzig: Teubner, 1880.

Minadeo, Richard. *The Lyre of Science: Form and Meaning in Lucretius*. Detroit, Mich.: Wayne State University Press, 1969.

Mölk, Ulrich. *Trobar clus—Trobar leu*. Munich: Fink, 1968.

Montale, Eugenio. *La bufera e altro*. Verona: Mondadori, 1957.

Moser, Hugo, and Helmut Tervooren, eds. *Des Minnesangs Frühling*. Stuttgart: S. Hirzel, 1977.

Moshé, Lazar. *Amour courtois e fin amors*. Paris: Klincksieck, 1964.

Most, Glenn. "Alcman's Cosmogonic Fragment (Fgt 5 Page, 81 Calame)." *Classical Quarterly* 37, no. 1 (1987): 1–9.

———. *The Measures of Praise*. Göttingen: Vandenhoeck und Ruprecht, 1985.

Mueller, Robert J. "'Infinite Desire': Spenser's Arthur and the Representation of Courtly Ambition." *ELH* 58 (1991): 747–71.

Murray, Oswyn. *Sympotica: A Symposium on the Symposion*. Oxford: Clarendon Press, 1990.

Nagy, Gregory. *Comparative Studies in Greek and Indic Meter*. Cambridge, Mass.: Harvard University Press, 1974.

———. *Greek Mythology and Poetics*. Ithaca, N.Y.: Cornell University Press, 1990.

———. *Pindar's Homer*. Baltimore, Md.: Johns Hopkins Press, 1990.

Nardi, Bruno. *Dante e la cultura medievale*. 1949. Reprint, Bari: Laterza, 1985.

———. "Filosofia e teologia ai tempi di Dante." Chapter 1 in *Saggi e note di critica Dantesca*. Milan: Riccardo Ricciardi, 1966.

Nelli, René. *L'Érotique des troubadours*. Toulouse: Édouard Privat, 1963.

Nilsson, Martin P. *A History of Greek Religion*. 1925. Reprint, New York: Norton, 1964.

Obbink, D., ed. *Philodemus on Poetry*. Oxford: Oxford University Press, 1994.

Okpewho, Isidore. *The Epic in Africa*. New York: Columbia University Press, 1979.

Owen, Stephen. *Mi-Lou: Poetry and the Labyrinth of Desire.* Cambridge, Mass.: Harvard University Press, 1989.

———. *Traditional Chinese Poetry and Poetics.* Madison: University of Wisconsin Press, 1985.

Page, D. L. *Sappho and Alcaeus.* Oxford: Clarendon Press, 1955.

Page, D. L., ed. *Epigrammata graeca.* Oxford: Clarendon Press, 1975.

———. *Poetae melici graeci.* Oxford: Clarendon Press, 1967.

Paglia, Camille. *Sexual Personae: Art and Decadence from Nefertiti to Emily Dickinson.* New Haven, Conn.: Yale University Press, 1990.

Panofsky, Erwin. *Gothic Architecture and Scholasticism.* 1957. Reprint, New York: New American Library, 1976.

Patterson, Annabel M. *Pastoral and Ideology: Virgil to Valéry.* Berkeley and Los Angeles: University of California Press, 1987.

Patterson, Lee. *Chaucer and the Subject of History.* Madison: University of Wisconsin Press, 1991.

Pindar. *Pindari carmina cum fragmentis.* Edited by Bruno Snell. Leipzig: Teubner, 1964.

Pöggeler, Otto. *Die Spur des Wortes.* Freiburg: Alber, 1986.

Ponge, Francis. *Pièces.* Paris: Gallimard, 1962.

Pound, Ezra. "Canto XXXVI" of *The Cantos.* New York: New Directions, 1986.

Quasimodo, Salvatore. *Tutte le poesie.* Milan: Mondadori, 1960.

Quiller-Couch, Arthur, ed. *The Oxford Book of Ballads.* Oxford: Clarendon Press, 1910.

Ricks, Christopher. *The Force of Poetry.* Oxford: Oxford University Press, 1987.

Rimbaud, Arthur. "Délires II, Alchimie du verbe." In *Une Saison en enfer, Œuvres complètes,* 106–8. Paris: Gallimard, 1972.

———. "Délires II, Alchimie du verbe." In *Rimbaud,* by Wallace Fowlie, 193–95. Chicago, Ill.: University of Chicago Press, 1966.

———. *Œuvres complètes.* Paris: Gallimard, 1972.

Riquer, Martin de. *Los trovadores.* Barcelona: Planeta, 1975.

Rosen, Aaron. *Traces.* Riverdale-on-Hudson, N.Y.: Sheep Meadow Press, 1991.

Rosenmeyer, Thomas. *The Green Cabinet.* Berkeley and Los Angeles: University of California Press, 1969.

Ross, Kristin. *The Emergence of Social Space.* Minneapolis: University of Minnesota Press, 1988.

Roubaud, Jacques. *La Viellesse d'Alexandre.* Paris: Maspero, 1978.

Ruskin, John. *Modern Painters,* vol 3, chaps. 14, 15. New York: John B. Alden, 1885.

Salmon, P. B. "The 'Three Voices' of Poetry in Medieval Literary Theory." *Medium Aevum* 30 (1961): 1–28.

Santayana, George. *Three Philosophical Poets: Lucretius, Dante, and Goethe.* Cambridge, Mass.: Harvard University Press, 1927.

Schadewaldt, Wolfgang. *Der Aufbau des Pindarischen Epinikion.* Halle: Max Niemeyer, 1928.

Schrijvers, P. H. "Éléments psychagogiques dans l'œuvre de Lucrèce." In *Probleme der Lukrezforschung*, edited by Carl Joachim Classen, 375–81. Hildesheim & New York: Olms, 1986.

———. *Horror ac Divina Voluptas: Études sur la poétique et la poésie de Lucrèce*. Amsterdam: Hakkert, 1970.

Schumann, Otto, ed. *Carmina Burana*. Heidelberg: Carl Winter, 1971.

Schürmann, Reiner. "Le Praxis symbolique." *Cahiers internationaux du symbole* 29–30 (1975).

Scott, Clive. *Reading the Rhythm: The Poetics of French Free Verse, 1910–1930*. Oxford: Clarendon Press, 1993.

Scully, Vincent. *The Earth, the Temple, and the Gods*. 1962. Reprint, New York: Praeger, 1969.

Segal, Charles. "Boundaries, Worlds, and Analogical Thinking, or How Lucretius Learned to Love Atomism and Still Write Poetry." In *The Interpretation of Roman Poetry: Empiricism or Hermeneutics?* edited by Karl Galinsky, 137–56. Frankfurt: Peter Lang, 1992.

———. "Catullan *Otiosi*: The Lover and the Poet." *Greece and Rome*, 2d ser., 17, no. 7 (April 1970): 25–31.

———. "God and Man in Pindar's First and Third Olympian Odes." *Harvard Studies in Classical Philology* 68 (1964): 211–67.

———. *Lucretius on Death and Anxiety*. Princeton, N.J.: Princeton University Press, 1990.

———. "Myth, Cult, and Memory in Pindar's Third and Fourth Isthmian Odes." *Ramus* 10 (1981): 69–86.

———. "*Otium* and *Eros*: Catullus, Sappho, and Euripides' *Hippolytus*." *Latomus* 48 (1989): 817–22.

———. *Pindar's Mythmaking: The Fourth Pythian Ode*. Princeton, N.J.: Princeton University Press, 1986.

———. *Poetry and Mythmaking in Ancient Pastoral*. Princeton, N.J.: Princeton University Press, 1981.

———. "Sirius and the Pleiades in Alcman's Louvre Parthenion." *Mnemosyne* 36, nos. 3–4 (1983): 260–75.

Serres, Michel. *La Naissance de la physique dans le texte de Lucrèce*. Paris: Minuit, 1977.

Shakespeare, William. *The Sonnets; and A Lover's Complaint*. Edited by John Kerrigan. New York: Viking, 1986.

Shumaker, Wayne. *The Occult Sciences in the Renaissance*. Berkeley and Los Angeles: University of California Press, 1972.

Singleton, Charles S. *Dante Studies*. Vol. 1, *Commedia: Elements of Structure: Journey to Beatrice*. Cambridge, Mass.: Harvard University Press, 1954.

Slater, William J. *Lexicon to Pindar*. Berlin: de Gruyter, 1969.

Slatkin, Laura M. *The Power of Thetis*. Berkeley and Los Angeles: University of California Press, 1991.

Spacks, Patricia Ann Meyer. *Gossip*. New York: Knopf, 1985.

Sperber, Dan. *Rethinking Symbolism.* Cambridge: Cambridge University Press, 1975.

Staiger, Emil. *Grundbegriffe der Poetik.* Zurich: Atlantis, 1946.

Stevens, Wallace. *Collected Poems.* New York: Knopf, 1957.

———. "Two or Three Ideas." *Opus Posthumous.* London: Faber and Faber, 1957.

Storz, Elizabeth C. "Toward the History of a Lyric Body: Sappho fr. 31, Homer and Elegy." Manuscript study.

Strauss, Liane. "The Art of Fame." Ph.D. diss., Brown University, 1993.

Striker, Gisela. "*Ataraxia:* Happiness as Tranquility." *Monist* 73, no. 1 (January 1990): 97–110.

Sullivan, John P. *Martial: The Unexpected Classic.* Cambridge: Cambridge University Press, 1991.

———. *Propertius.* Cambridge: Cambridge University Press, 1976.

Szondi, Peter. "Durch die Enge geführt." Chapter 3 in *Celan-Studien,* 47–112. Frankfurt: Suhrkamp, 1972.

Thompson, Denys. *The Uses of Poetry.* Cambridge: Cambridge University Press, 1978.

Thomson, George. *Greek Lyric Meter.* Cambridge: Cambridge University Press, 1929.

Thomson, James. *The Seasons.* In *Poetical Works,* vol. 2. London: Pickering, 1847.

Thummer, Erich. *Pindar: Die isthmischen Gedichte.* Heidelberg: Carl Winter, 1968.

Trakl, Georg. *Die Dichtungen.* Edited by W. Schneditz. Salzburg: Otto Müller, 1938.

Turner, Mark. *Death Is the Mother of Beauty: Mind, Metaphor, Criticism.* Chicago, Ill.: University of Chicago Press, 1987.

Usener, Herman. *Epicurea.* Leipzig: Teubner, 1887.

van der Werf, Hendrik. *The Chansons of the Troubadors and Trouvères.* Utrecht: A. Oosthoek, 1972.

Van Vleck, Amelia E. *Memory and Re-creation in Troubadour Lyric.* Berkeley and Los Angeles: University of California Press, 1991.

Vandelli, Giuseppi, ed. *La Divina Commedia col Commento Scartazziniano.* Milan: Hoepli, 1958.

Veyne, Paul. *René Char en ses poèmes.* Paris: Gallimard, 1991.

Vlastos, Gregory. "Elenchus and Mathematics." Chapter 4 in *Socrates: Ironist and Moral Philosopher,* 107–31. Cambridge: Cambridge University Press, 1991.

Vogelweide, Walther von der. *Gedichte.* Edited by Carl von Kraus. Weisbaden: Insel-Verlag, n.d.

Warnke, Frank. *Versions of Baroque.* New Haven, Conn.: Yale University Press, 1972.

Werner, Heinz. *Die Ursprünge der Metapher.* Leipzig: W. Englemann, 1919.

West, M. L., ed. *Hesiod's Theogony.* Oxford: Clarendon Press, 1966.

Whitman, Walt. *Leaves of Grass.* Edited by Sculley Bradley and Harold W. Blodgett. 1965. Reprint, New York: Norton, 1973.

———. *Unpublished Poetry and Prose.* Edited by Emory Holloway. Garden City, N.J.: Doubleday, 1921.

Wilbur, Richard. *New and Collected Poems.* New York: Harcourt, Brace Jovanovich, 1988.

Williams, Charles. *The Figure of Beatrice.* London: Faber, 1943.

Wiseman, T. P. *Catullus and His World: A Reappraisal.* Cambridge: Cambridge University Press, 1985.

Wittgenstein, Ludwig. *Zettel.* Translated by G. E. M. Anscombe. Oxford: Basil Blackwell, 1981.

Wordsworth, Jonathan, M. H. Abrams, and Stephen Gill, eds. *William Wordsworth: The Prelude 1799, 1805, 1850.* New York: Norton, 1979.

Wordsworth, William. "Home at Grasmere." Part 1, book 1 of *The Recluse.* In *Poetical Works,* edited by E. de Selincourt and Helen Darbishire, 5:314. Oxford: Clarendon Press, 1949.

Yeats, William Butler. *Collected Poems.* New York: Macmillan, 1974.

———. *A Vision.* 1938. Reprint, New York: Macmillan, 1961.

Zumthor, Paul. *Langue et technique poétiques à l'époque romane.* Paris: Klincksieck, 1963.

———. *La Lettre et la voix.* Paris: Seuil, 1987.

Zweig, Paul. *Walt Whitman: The Making of the Poet.* New York: Basic Books, 1984.

Index